THE PAPERS OF THE HYMN SOCIETY OF AMERICA

XXVIII

Born To Music

The Ministry of Robert Guy McCutchan

By

HELEN COWLES MCCUTCHAN

THE HYMN SOCIETY OF AMERICA

475 Riverside Drive, New York, N. Y. 10027

BORN TO MUSIC

Robert Guy McCutchan was born September 13, 1877, at Mt. Ayr, Iowa. He himself said, "there was scarcely a moment during the waking hours of the McCutchan family that there was not some tune being sounded about the home. It was a daily custom to sing hymns — at family worship as well as at odd moments. Always the tunes were designated by name; only the Gospel hymns, of which we sang but few, were known by titles or by their first lines. I distinctly remember — although I was not yet four years old at the time — hearing my elder brother say one morning at family worship, 'Let's sing **Avison**'. The word **Avison** intrigued my boyish fancy and when my father told me that tune we had just sung was known by the name of its composer, an interest was born which remains to this day"

Robert was drawn into the Methodist Church when, as a boy in Clarinda, Iowa, the Methodist Church had an organ, while the Presbyterian Church, to which his family belonged, had no musical instrument. So he played the organ or sang in the choir at the Methodist Church. In addition to these useful talents, he possessed the "remarkable and rarely possessed faculty of being able to whistle without using his lips, cheeks, palate or pharynx". He delighted to imitate bird calls as well as to whistle tunes, to the puzzlement and amusement of others not similarly gifted.

Robert's father, Erastus G. McCutchan, possessed a very fine baritone voice and was a musician and conductor of note during his residence in Iowa. He was one of the first supervisors of music in the State, holding this position in both Bedford and Clarinda schools.

In Greenville, Mississippi

With the outbreak of the Spanish American War, many young men of Guy's (as he was then known) acquaintance volunteered for the army. But Guy's lame leg prevented him from being accepted. Sensitive about this, he left Park College and went south to Greenville, Mississippi. Having acquired skill in type-setting and the printer's art back in Iowa, he secured a job with the newspaper, the "Greenville Democrat". Eventually this became the "Delta Democrat-Times" of the famous Hodding Carter. On a return visit to Greenville in the 1940's, Dr. and Mrs. McCutchan enjoyed the hospitality of the Carters, and their continuing friendship.

In those early years, Greenville, a small town on the great river, was in some respects a frontier village with "wild west " flavor. Mr. McCutchan relished telling of two incidents which illustrate this. The editor of his paper inadvertly, or perhaps on purpose, printed a report of the liason between the son of a prominent family and a Negro woman, and her murder. The family thereupon threatened to shoot the editor. The

2

office of the paper was in storefront space facing on the main street, the editor's desk being in front next to the door and window. Guy's desk was at the rear of the room. Now the position of the desks was reversed, Guy being put at the front. And what was more, the editor kept two loaded pistols on top of his desk. Guy's position in the line of fire between window and rear desk was tense to say the least. However, the editor soon decided to return to Texas.

Another bit of excitement occured while Guy was on his way to the office. One day he heard shouts and angry voices, then running feet. Looking up, he saw the school principal racing toward him and a man behind aiming a pistol. Guy jumped into a doorway. Bang ! But the running feet kept on.

But mostly his days in this southern town were enjoyed in the warm friendly atmosphere of fine families and the musical activities of the Presbyterian Church. The following newspaper item speaks for itself.

Christmas 1898 has come and gone. In Greenville Christmas was observed with more decorum than is usual. There was not the usual boisterousness and drunkenness indulged . . .

On Saturday night — Christmas Eve — Christmas trees were enjoyed at the Methodist, Presbyterian and Baptist churches by the little ones and their grownup friends . . .

On Sunday beautiful services were held in all the churches. The praise service in the Presbyterian church on Sunday night was the most brilliant song service perhaps ever enjoyed in a church in Greenville. The quartette by Mrs. C. O. Greenlee, Miss Susie Ireys, R. G. McCutchan and W. H. Negus — "There Were Shepherds:" the soprano solo — "Emmanuel" — by Miss Greenlee, and the duet — "Where He Leads Me," by Miss Susie Ireys and Mr. R. G. McCutchan, were as beautiful and sweet as it is possible to make them, while the chorus was simply grand.

College Education at Simpson

For his college work he attended Park College, Parkville, Mo. 1893-94, then graduated from Simpson College, Mus. Bac., 1904. While at Simpson,

Dr. McCutchan laid the foundation not only for his musicianship but for his executive ability. He was conductor of the Simpson College glee club in 1903 and 1904, arranged the trips, managed the finances, arranged itineraries for Chautauqua work by students, and in fact to a considerable extent was business manager for Dean Barrows and Prof. Emslie, earning his way through college. His name during this time was frequently linked with that of Arthur Middleton, famous baritone (Metropolitan Opera), and L. D. Carpenter, both of whom were widely known in the Middle West . . .

The Simpson Male Quartette, made up of Dr. L. D. Carpenter, first tenor; R. G. McCutchan, second tenor; R. E. Clark, first bass; A. D. Middleton, second bass, and the Apollo Quartette whose members were Gertrude White, Kay M. Spencer, R. G. McCutchan and A. D. Middleton, concertized widely.

In solo singing, Guy used an effective technique. Looking over his audience he would pick out some individual and sing to that person. A love song would be aimed at a young woman, a sad sweet sentimental song would be addressed to a dear older woman.

> And those were the days when clowning was a distinguishing mark of students, and the pranks played by Guy McCutchan and Arthur Middleton have been handed down in tradition . . . McCutchan played the snare drum, and Middleton hammered the bass drum, and the comedy the two put over was the biggest part of the band.

Typical of the fun they made for each other and others is this: At a small town where they were to give a concert, they took their afternoon stroll down the central street. On the sidewalk in front of a store was some sale merchandise among which was an old washing machine with a hand crank. Middleton stepped up to it and turning the crank accompanied this action by humming a hurdy-gurdy air. In a flash McCutchan began to scratch himself, holding out his cap for pennies in true monkey fashion. This funny business and their great guffaws of laughter drew a crowd which thoroughly enjoyed the nonsense.

Such was his enjoyment and skill in clowning, a gift for telling funny stories, and his own contagious hearty belly-laughs as well as real showmanship, that Guy at one time seriously considered making vaudeville a career. Indeed, he was once offered a job with Flo Ziegfield as musical arranger, and was promised — for those days — fabulous rewards. These same abilities proved of great worth in all his work with people, whether directing choruses or leading great audiences in singing.

Marriage

On November 23, 1904, he married Carrie Burns Sharp. She was a wonderful help to him through thirty-seven years. In his positions as head of the music schools at Baker and DePauw universities, and also in his many involvements on commissions, committees and activities of the Methodist Church, their home was continually open to guests, it falling on Carrie to entertain a stream of guests and friends, with teas, lunches, dinners, and receptions. This she did with beautiful grace and efficiency.

She was also active in church work, a real Bible scholar, and a devotee of poetry and the arts. She was something of an artist herself, doing much exquisite china painting, lace making, and embroidery.

Having no children of their own, they adopted a son, Robert John, in February 1914. He brought life and joy, and a host of young friends to enrich their lives.

4

At Baker University, 1904-1910

In 1904 Mr. McCutchan accepted a position at Baker University, Baldwin, Kansas, as a teacher of voice. He then organized the Conservatory of Music of which he became the director. He was brought to the University without salary, with the understanding that his salary and that of his teachers should be paid out of the student fees. "After five years of hard work there was a faculty of six, and by 1910 his Music Department achieved the goal of awarding the degree of Bachelor of Music."

As Director of the Conservatory, Dr. McCutchan built a chorus and choir which concertized widely in the environs of Nebraska, Kansas, Missouri, and Iowa. He initiated a spring three-day music festival to which visitors came from surrounding towns. To house the crowds an enlarged gymnasium was built when the first one burned. He thereupon engaged the Minneapolis Symphony Orchestra to come to Baker for the spring festival. The following year Damrosch brought part of the New York Symphony Orchestra, and to their accompaniment six Baker students sang the Sextette from Lucia, as one of the numbers. (*History of Baker University*, by Homer K. Ebright, 1951).

These ambitious undertakings so in advance of the times in this area, are a mark of the initiative and genius of Mr. McCutchan.

One of his students, Everett K. Foster, wrote in the Baker University News Bulletin, March 1968:

It is of the remarkable series of Music Festivals which Prof. McCutchan launched, and some of the "side lights" of those programs that I reminisce.

Beginning with a modest presentation of Cowan's "Rose Maiden" with students chorus and soloists, with piano accompaniment, each spring Centenary Hall re-echoed with the strains (perhaps "strains" is the proper word) of Costa's "Eli," Haydn's "Creation", Mendelsshon's "St. Paul," Handel's "Messiah," and finally the culmination, an outstanding performance of Mendelsshon's "Elijah", with the New York Symphony Orchestra and four top-notch imported soloists, in Taylor Hall, the successor to fire-destroyed Ripley Gymnasium.

Each year more use was made of outstanding guest soloists, and it was inevitable that sometimes there should be disappointment with one or two of them. It so happened that the year "St. Paul" was given the tenor soloist was just such a disappointment. One of the local humorists thus characterized the performance: "The tenor sang, and the chorus followed with 'Take Him Away'. He sang again and the bass soloist sang 'O God Have Mercy'. The tenor sang a third time and the chorus stood and sang 'Stone Him to Death.'"

It was at this performance also that at the close of the above-mentioned chorus, which ends with extreme suddenness, one of the basses in the chorus, evidently not watching Prof. McCutchan as closely as he should have been, shouted out "Stone . . ." after everyone else was silent. He surely was determined that the martyrdom of Stephen should be complete and he threw an extra rock. In after years the black looks Prof. McCutchan hurled in his direction became delighted chuckles over the incident.

The following conversation took place at a rehearsal of the *Messiah*. The bass soloist was Arthur Middleton, a close friend of Prof. McCutchan.

Middleton — "Look, Mac, you are doing this with piano accompaniment The aria 'The Trumpet Shall Sound' is no good without an orchestra, so we don't do it."

5

McCutchan — "Have you been paid yet?"

Middleton (humbly) — "No."

McCutchan — "Well, then we shall sing 'The Trumpet Shall Sound.' "

A truly remarkable thing occurred when "Elijah" was given. The New York Symphony was delayed in its arrival in Baldwin, and there was only time to rehearse Part I and one chorus from Part II, for the audience was gathering for the scheduled afternoon orchestra concert. So Part II was given that evening without rehearsal, and the only mistake made was when the alto soloist, who of course should have known better, began her aria "O Rest in the Lord" a measure too soon.

Mr. McCutchan enjoyed telling of the time when he was the tenor soloist at a performance of "The Creation" by Haydn. He had just sung the recitative "The Sons of God announced the fourth day, in song divine proclaiming thus his power", when there came a crash of thunder. And all during the ensuing chorus, "The Heavens are telling" a furious thunder storm raged . Could anything have been more spine-tingling !

Europe in 1910

At the end of six years, Dr. McCutchan left Baker University to study music in Germany. While in Berlin, he was honored by being asked to reorganize and take charge of the music in the American Church.

From the **Continental Times** of Berlin, Germany, November 6, 1910 comes the following: "Mr. R. G. McCutchan's Departure — Loss to Berlin-American Community — Mr. and Mrs. McCutchan, much appreciated musical members of the Berlin-American colony, left Berlin last Monday for Paris, where they will remain until December 1, leaving on that date for two or three days in Brussels, sailing from Antwerp on December 3. Mr. McCutchan, who had just been appointed Dean of the School of Music at DePauw University after filling a similar position in Baker University, had expected to spend the entire winter season in enjoyment of Berlin's musical opportunities. His presence was however required at DePauw considerably earlier than expected, and a sudden leave-taking followed.

"The Berlin-American colony is decidedly the loser by Mr. McCutchan's premature departure. Besides being one of its most genial members, Mr. McCutchan had done splendid service as choir master of the American Church, organizing a quartet whose efficiency raised the standard of the musical section of the service to a degree of excellence which probably has not been surpassed, if it has been equalled, in the annals of the church."

6

Dean of the School of Music, DePauw

1911 – 1937

In speaking of the work of Dean McCutchan, Dr. William W. Sweet, the historian, in a history of DePauw University for the centennial celebration in 1937, had this to say:

> With the advent of Dean McCutchan, the DePauw School of Music began to manifest signs of new life. His first task was to reorganize the curriculum, raising the requirements and placing it on a par with the Liberal Arts College.

He writes also of Dr. McCutchan broadening the course of study, increasing the number of teachers, organizing vocal quartets, the orchestra, and the famous DePauw Choir which toured the entire country. And he says:

> As a result of Dean McCutchan's management, during the years from 1911 to 1931, more than $100,000 was added to the receipts and assets of the University through the Music School.

The Worship Chapels which Dean McCutchan planned and ran from 1932 to 1937 were outstanding both as to speakers and music. The following letter to President Wildman from Carman E. Siewart, October 1936, expresses their value:

> This is the fourth year that I have attended Worship Chapels and valued their influence on my own life; but even more important and significant to me is the extraordinary way in which the students have responded to them. Living with the girls as I do, I am frequently surprised at the number who save their Worship Chapel program, quote speakers, and appreciate the music.
>
> I have often thought that had Dean McCutchan never done anything else than planning these services, his life would have been of immeasurable worth in the lives of all at DePauw, for to me the time spent at Worship Chapel is the most satisfying of all the week.

And of these chapels, Amos Thornburg said:

> At other chapel services attendance was required of freshmen. But this one, entirely religious in form and purpose, with attendance voluntary, was the most popular and well-attended assembly. The form, dignity, reverence, and cohesive movement which characterized the service was thrilling to the students and most impressive for all who had a part as participants.

And so they came! Never less than eight hundred to a thousand for a service of twenty minutes.

Widespread Service

While holding responsibilities as Dean of the School of Music, administrator, choir director, counselor, organizer, teacher in summer schools, it was amazing that he could take on still more assignments. But he was music editor of **American Junior Church and Church School Hymnal**

7

(1928), and **Standard Hymns and Gospel Songs** (1929). And with others authored **Better Music in Our Churches** (1925), and **Music in Worship** (1927).

Crowning these earlier works came the **Methodist Hymnal** (1935). This was to replace the **Hymnal** of 1905. The new hymnal was the official hymnal for the Methodist Episcopal Church, the Methodist Episcopal Church, South, and the Methodist Protestant Church. It marked the first time these churches had joined in such an endeavor. The work was en- trusted to the Joint Commission on the Revision of the Hymnal and Psalter appointed in 1924. Representing these three churches, the membership (33) of the Joint Commission was large, and included "men eminent in letters and musicians of unquestioned ability, besides others who are able to judge the value of a hymn from the standpoint of a worshiping congre- gation," as wrote Fitzgerald S. Parker, of the Publishing Society of the Methodist Episcopal Church, South.

This Commission, in December 1931, appointed Dean McCutchan editor-in-chief. He had been serving on the sub-committee on tunes. Also on the editorial committee assisting Dean McCutchan were John W. Lang- dale, Dr. Oscar Thomas Olson, and Prof. Charles C. Washburn.

The editorial committee was faced with the problem of "interpretation of religious experiences of today in terms of present day thought. Hymnals have to be revised about once in every generation. Today we use differ- ent phraseology, have different interests and our music has to change if it is to be effective. The demand has been increasing for new hymns which would express new religious, social, and international conditions and interpret the widening experiences and tasks of the church."

These were Dr. McCutchan's words in the 1930's. And he went on to say, "In the tunes the melodic rather than the rhythmic interest has been sought, and it is hoped that in no case will words and music struggle to convey a different message." Also "in some cases the wording of a hymn was altered a bit as for instance the word 'heathen' was deleted and the line 'Strong men and maidens **meek**' was changed to read 'Strong men and maidens fair.'"

The new hymnal contained 54 of the 6,500 hymns of Charles Wesley, grand old man of Methodism hymnody. His hymn, "O for a thousand tongues to sing," was no longer the first hymn in the book, a place it had occupied in all editions dating from 1779 when John Wesley dedicated a "Collection of Hymns for the Use of the People Called Methodists." The omission of some Wesley hymns in the new hymnal caused anguish to some members of the Commission. At one of the meetings a bishop exclaimed in dramatically shaking, tearful voice, "Brethren, brethren, consider what you are doing to Charles Wesley!" To which Dean McCutchan replied, "Gentlemen, I believe we are saving his reputation."

8

In commenting on the work of the Commission, Fitzgerald Parker, in the **Christian Advocate** of April 1932 said:

> If it is at all in my power, I should like to reassure any fearful saints there may be, of the soundness of doctrine they may count upon in the new hymnal, and of the strictness with which music will be held to true standards of congregational worship. Personal inquiries lead me to believe that some disturbing but unfounded rumors are abroad. With ten bishops on the Commission, there is no need to fear radicalism of any kind.

Speaking of the work of Dean McCutchan, Amos Thornburg said:

> He was trusted and responsible for detail and decision far above the knowledge of most of those who have praised him. There was a time in the finishing of the work that the committee had no more time to meet, and the entire task of finishing the work was for him to achieve. This included both text and tune and other matters where decision and responsibility are usually shared. But the colossal task of finishing the task was left to him, and achieved because of his energy and faith' fulness. The response of the total church in appreciation was monumental.

"As the new hymnal was projected by the Joint Commission" says Jerome Hixson, "Dean McCutchan as its editor, traveled extensively in the South, leading singing groups, lecturing on hymnology, and generally making friends not only for himself but for the Methodist Episcopal Church as it then was. People who sang and laughed with Dean McCutchan, simply could not go on fighting the Civil War. I like to think that when, in 1939, the issue of unification came to the final vote at the Uniting Conference in Kansas City, a share of the credit was due to the backlog of good work done during the years before by Dean McCutchan."

A Hymnal Manual

While working through the years in the field of hymnody, Dean McCutchan was assiduously acquiring and organizing materials about the authors and composers of hymns and tunes. This material was used in **Our Hymnody: A Manual of The Methodist Hymnal** issued in 1937 with a revised edition in 1942. William Reynolds says:

> It was the first significant hymnal handbook produced in America. Here is revealed the years of his careful research, his understanding of the broad field of hymnology, and occasional glimpses of his keen wit and humor. In many respects this was a pioneer venture and those who have since prepared hymnal handbooks have been much in his debt, — to an even greater extent than they have sometimes admitted.

R. A. Schermerhorn, in **The Christian Century,** wrote:

> Human interest stories . . . lighten the pages of the new manual by Professor McCutchan . . . But he has also given us a solid volume of scholarship, with historical notes for every author, composer and melody in the entire *Methodist Hymnal.* Frequently he inserts variant texts of tunes and poems, occasionally from original plates, making the com' pendium a mine of useful information heretofore unavailable except in the larger libraries . . . Also facsimile reproductions make the book of interest to the historical student . . . This volume, though it rests back

upon sources Catholic, Protestant and secular, bears nevertheless the unmistakable earmarks of the denominational spirit.

Since his writings are under consideration, it may be well to continue, here and now, to note those also produced through the retirement years to the time of his illness. His involvement in church, and church-related activities with which they are intertwined, are treated more fully later in this biographical sketch.

Hymns in the Lives of Men (1943) had as its basis a series of lectures given at Southwestern University, Texas, at the invitation of his good friend President J. N. R. Score. In the "**Diapason,** H. D. Bruening said, "It constitutes an appealing miniature course in hymnology for all who sing hymns — at home or in the pew — and especially for clergymen, organists, choir leaders and church workers in general. This remarkable little volume is delightful to read . . ."

That question, "Why Avison?" which he had asked as a child, started a lifetime interest in the names of hymn tunes, and the accumulation of bits and pieces of information relating to it. A card file of hundreds of these names and facts in respect to them grew and grew, finally resulting in some of them being used in the book **Hymn Tune Names: Their Sources and Significance** (1958). The following is quoted from that text:

> Having spent many years in the study of all aspects of hymnology, I have found the matter of tune names to be one of its most intriguing phases. The wide variety of names given to tunes, where they came from, why they were chosen, what significance they have, has offered a challenge which has entailed wide and painstaking research. No other research projects on which I have worked have been so elusive as this. There is almost no literature on the subject. It would be an almost, if not quite, impossible task to list all the sources of information gleaned through the years from scores of hymn and tune books etc. etc. . . . . The work is far from complete but it is a beginning. So I would say as did Cambden: "As for myself, I acknowledge that I cannot satisfy neither them nor myself in all particularities; and well therefore I do like him that said, *He doth not teach well which teacheth all, leaving nothing to subtill wits to sift out!*" And so like him, I do bequeath to more subtile wits the joy of sifting out puzzles raised by the work herein begun.

A series of monographs were the result of papers and addresses given at Northwestern University's church and choral music institutes, from 1934 to 1946. Here are but three of the titles: "The increasing interest in responses, versicles and chants," "The congregation's part in the office of music worship," "The making of a hymnal."

Magazine articles also, flowed from his pen for such periodicals as **Church History, Educational Music Magazine, Adult Teacher, Church School, Religion In Life, Christian Advocate.**

Dictionary and encyclopedia items were requested of him, as: "American Hymns" in the **Dictionary of American History,** also, "The Gospel Song," and "Hymnology," in the **Schaff-Herzog Encyclopaedia of Religious Knowledge.**

In 1953 he was made a member of the American Committee on the Revision of the Julian Dictionary of Hymnology. Here are excerpts from correspondence with respect to his assignment in that forthcoming book: **Dictionary of American Hymnology.**

H. W. Foote to R. G. M. April 13, 1953.

. . . I was requested to ask you to undertake a revision of the section on Methodist hymns and hymn-writers in Julian's article on American Hymnody, and was glad to report that you had already stated your willingness to do so. We hope you will also note entries of individual writers and their hymns which need correction or supplementing, in addition to those you have already sent me.

R. G. M. to H. W. Foote, August 3, 1953.

My specific assignment (Methodist) is proving much more of a task than I had assumed it would be. It involves contributions from the Methodist Episcopal Church from 1784 to 1939; from the Methodist Episcopal Church, South, from 1844-1939; Methodist Protestant Church from 1828 to unification in 1939; Free Methodists from organization to date; Wesleyan Methodists the same. Through much research and voluminous correspondence I have the last two finally straightened out. I was already prepared for the first three. But the Negro branches are proving a real problem. I am making some headway and shall be able to submit some things about them even though what they have done in the past is not specially significant. They are making headway however and should have recognition. At the moment the Colored Methodist Church has a recently formed committee at work on a new book.

R. G. M. to L. Ellinwood, January 11, 1956.

I have submitted to Dr. Foote a list (dating from 1784) of those hymn writers of the following Methodist groups that I consider worthy; (1) Methodist Episcopal, (2) Methodist Episcopal South, (3) Methodist Protestant, (4) Wesleyan Methodist, (5) Free Methodist.

I do not at this time have sufficient information concerning hymn writers of any Negro branches of Methodism.

No significant contribution came from American Methodists until about the middle part of the 19th century. Most of the contributions of Methodist would-be hymn writers, until after 1900, were Gospel Songs.

I have listed eighty some odd hymns which have been published by American Methodists, a goodly number of which have appeared in Julian. I've not taken time to estimate the number of Gospel Songs included but I do not think too many.

I have sent Dr. Foote the biographies of fifty-one or fifty-two writers who should be given consideration. The best known of this list are such men as, Frank Mason North, Earl Marlatt, James L. Milligan, Harry Webb Farrington, William Stidger, Richard Watson Gilder. Of course Fanny Crosby, Charles Gabriel, are perhaps the best known of the Gospel Song writers.

I mentioned earlier in this letter that the Gospel Song certainly should receive sympathetic attention. It is almost the sole musical religious expression known to too many millions of Christians to be tossed aside as a matter of no consequence. I often think with interest of Waldo Selden Pratt's comment to the effect that this proved one of the significant social phenomena in American history and that no reputable historian has given it serious, sympathetic treatment. I should very much like to see something of the kind done in the Dictionary, should it eventually come to print.

A member of the Hymn Society of America, Dean McCutchan served for a number of years as one of those judging hymns submitted for its hymn contests.

Tunes for Hymns and Responses

Some tunes for hymns and responses were written by Dean McCutchan. Seven for hymns and three responses appear in the 1935 **Hymnal.** Those written while he was a member of the Hymnal Commission were submitted under the nom-de-plume John Porter for he said, "It would simply **not do** for it to be known that the editor was their composer." These tunes were "Tiplady," "Masefield," and "All the World."

"Tiplady" was written for Charles Wesley's hymn, "Blest be the dear uniting love," at a time when the Reverend Thomas Tiplady, Superintendent of the Lambeth Mission in London, was a guest in the McCutchan home. The gentleman was in America to attend the Ecumenical Conference in 1931. He admired the tune, so it was named "Tiplady" in his honor.

"Masefield" was so named for John Masefield, since it was composed for his hymn "Sing, Men and Angels Sing." Its last stanza was one of the Dean's favorites:

> After the winter snows
> A wind of healing blows
> And thorns put forth a rose
> And lilies cheer us;
> Life's everlasting spring
> Hath robbed death of his sting;
> Henceforth a cry can bring
> Our Master near us.*

Of his tunes, "All the World" has proved most popular. It was named from the first line of George Herbert's hymn beginning, "Let all the world in every cornor sing," and might very well be called the theme of the Dean's life. The hymn and this tune are included in many hymnals and children's song books. William Reynolds wrote this about using it at the Sixth Baptist Youth World Conference in Beirut, Lebanon: "We closed our last night after seven full days of meetings. We opened every evening session at the Stadium with 3,000 to 4,000 people singing Dean's 'Let all the world in every corner sing,' and I wished for you to hear the crowd from more than fifty nations singing lustily." He and Carlton H. Young have now used the tune in anthem arrangements.

Tunes written earlier are "DePauw," "Oxnam," "Fowler," "Campmeeting." "DePauw" was written in the summer of 1928 at Lake Winona, Indiana, as a setting for Theodore Williams' hymn, "Thou rulest Lord, the

---

*from the Collected Works of John Masefield. Copyright 1929 by John Masefield; Renewed 1957 by John Masefield; Used by permission of the Macmillon Company.

lights on high," and first appeared in **The Standard Hymnal.** "Fowler" was written in response to Carl Fowler Price's request for a tune for the hymn beginning, "My God I thank thee." At the time, Mr. Price and Dr. McCutchan were collaborating on the compilation of **The Standard Hymnal.** "Mr. Price's middle name, Fowler, had been given this distinguished authority on hymns and their tunes after Bishop Charles H. Fowler. Thus the hymn tune bears the name of two churchmen at one and the same time — a great ecclesiastic and an honored layman."

The tune "Oxnam" was written for William P. Merrill's hymn beginning "Rise Up, O men of God," while Mr. McCutchan was dean of the School of Music at DePauw University where G. Bromley Oxnam was president. "The tune was given his name, feeling that President Oxnam exemplified the words of the third and fourth lines of the hymn, 'Give heart and mind and soul and strength to serve the King of King,'" said Dean McCutchan.

"Campmeeting" is a harmonization of an early American melody, and so named because the tune was popular in the old camp-meeting days. "The camp-meeting fostered and further developed the type of folk hymn which had had its beginnings earlier in New England. From the year 1800, the camp-meeting with its social significance and its emphasis on singing had a profound effect; only now are we becoming sincerely appreciative of this," he wrote. It was always his hope that someone would make a thorough and scholarly study of this.

DePauw Centennial

A fitting conclusion to Mr. McCutchan's 26 years as Dean of DePauw's School of Music, was the university's centennial celebration in June 1937. The opening event, an inspiring beginning of the three day affair, was the performance of the "Elijah" under the Dean's direction. Enlarging the University choir were many alumni of the school who had come from all parts of the country for this event and to honor their "Dean." This performance of the Elijah, in itself a triumph of artistry, was in reality a splendid tribute to the Dean himself. It was evidence of the deep hold he has upon the hearts of many hundred former pupils.

At the close of the performance (audience 3,000) Dean McCutchan expressed his deep appreciation of the meaning to him of the return of so many of his former pupils. Then, a former member of the chorus and one of the best known alumni, Frank E. Duddy, Sr., expressed the deep regard the alumni have for Dean McCutchan. As a dramatic closing touch, he remarked, "We cannot endow a chair of music for you, but we do endow a chair," and gestured toward two young men who were bringing to the stage a splendid leather-upholstered chair for the Dean's den. After the program, there were some touching scenes, evidence of this deep esteem.

In Bay View, Michigan

In a history of the famed Summer School of Music at Bay View, Michigan, Clark S. Wheeler wrote:

> Robert G. McCutchan had charge of the Music Department from 1919 to 1926. He also was Assistant Manager of the Assembly. He was the first director to carry the name 'Dean.' He put the Music Department on a high plane which has ever since been the effort of new directors to attain. He gathered around him the best talent possible, and during his regime gave Bay View the greatest musical programs since the dedication of the new auditorium. Perhaps one of the finest features was the DePauw Choir, a group of young college singers trained under Dean Mc-Cutchan and presented on numerous programs. It is to Dean McCutchan that Bay View is indebted for the present traditional Sunday Evening Vesper Concerts. It is he who first presented this type of continuous music for one hour each Sunday evening which has become such a part of the Bay View musical life . . . Famous throughout the Little Traverse Bay Region and the entire resort area of Northern Michigan, these concerts are held at eight o'clock Sunday evening in John Hall Auditorium, seating 2,200 . . . There is no admission charge, but an offering is taken at the entrances."

A Bishop's Tribute

Perhaps the life and service of the subject of this sketch is best summed up in paragraphs quoted from the late Bishop G. Bromley Oxnam's paper, "A very Personal Tribute to Dean Robert Guy McCutchan." The Dean and the Bishop had ministered together for years while the latter was president of DePauw University and then as an episcopal leader of the Methodist Church. The Bishop wrote in part:

"Robert McCutchan was a man who passionately loved human beings. It was easy for him to meet people, he was not awed by titles or wealth. He recognized worth and talent in rich and poor, cultured and uncultured alike. He knew there was more wisdom in the mind and heart of an uneducated and hard-working mother than in many a Ph.D. oral, and more understanding in a coal pit than in some faculty rooms. He seemed to know everybody, and could regale you with stories about them from childhood to the present.

"Nevertheless, he appraised them with uncanny accuracy. He pene-trated sham like an X-ray, and was unafraid to speak the frank and at times critical word. He was a stern disciplinarian but it was the discipline requisite to perfection. He insisted upon his choir meeting the most rigid standards of musicianship. He knew every member of the choir as he knew the members of his own household. He showered his artistic gifts upon them, and brought all the riches of his years of study to the moment. But he demanded all they had.

"And the Dean always bubbled over with rollicking contagious humor. His conversation sparkled with it, and flashed with interesting and illuminat-

14

ing anecdote. He could tell humorous stories as I have never heard them told, but what was more, Dean McCutchan was a wonderful listener. Unlike many story tellers, he was intent when others were telling stories and his laughter was like song itself.

"His vital magnetic personality, his endearing human qualities, his genius for making friends, sparked and added to his success as admin- istrator, teacher, artist, scholar and churchman. These qualities were evi- denced in his success as Dean of the DePauw University School of Music from 1910-1937, and leadership in many fields — choirs, symphonies, great functions of the university and of the church.

"His monumental service to the Church and to scholarship is **The Methodist Hymnal** (1935), **Our Hymnody** (1937), and **Hymn Tune Names** (1957). He was chosen editor to the **Hymnal** by a Commission, wise enough to follow his guidance. Many of his own tunes were chosen by the Commission without knowledge of the fact that John Porter was in fact Robert McCutchan. The tune for 'Let All the World in Every Corner sing: My God and King !' carries the lift and love of this man's faith and the exhilaration of the impact of his personality. He knew the church of the world, he knew and loved the church in the small community, and to lifting its music in worship services he devoted his life and energies during twenty years following retirement."

THE RETIREMENT YEARS

1938 – 1958

Now that the Dean was retired was he really going to recline and relax in that comfortable and handsome chair which was the farewell gift of his choir members and students?

To try it, he and his wife Carrie went to Claremont, California. Here they found a group of congenial friends: President Blaisdell of the Asso- ciated Colleges of Claremont, Dr. Raymond Brooks, Dr. Albert Coe, and Everet Oliver, professor of music, a friend since their Simpson College days.

These friends persuaded the McCutchans to build themselves a home in the unique retirement community called Pilgrim Place. They soon found that members of this community, coming from all over the world, were so actively involved still, that they declared they were "not retired but retreaded". So it was with Dean McCutchan; the upholstered chair was in constant use at a desk where lectures, articles, and a great number of letters were written in response to many requests.

The Hymnal (1935) was being used in ever-greater numbers, but was as yet not well-known to many of the millions of Methodists. In

15

February 1938 when a "Pastor and Layman Conference" was convened in Chicago, the **Christian Century** (February 16, 1938) reported:

> Eminent speakers were scheduled and a program of such quality offered as to bring members beyond expectations. For three days more than 4,000 registered attendants coming from almost every state in the union have taxed the capacity of the "world's largest hotel", the Stevens, on Michigan Avenue. . . . Mention must be made of the carefully planned and effective worship services and particularly of the congregational singing. Dean Robert Guy McCutchan, of DePauw University, was the leader of the singing, and to hear the great crowd of several thousand men in such a hymn as "A Mighty Fortress Is Our God" was an experience to be remembered.

Bishop Oxnam was one of the featured speakers and wrote this:

> The Dean was in charge of the music, I was to deliver the address. I did not know what he was planning to do, but before I was introduced the presiding officer called upon Mr. McCutchan who rose. The Dean announced that the DePauw University Choir was present, that Van Denman Thompson was at the organ, that the audience was to stand and sing "Rise Up, O Men of God". Quietly he said "As you will note in the hymnal, I composed the tune and named it for my dear friend Bishop Oxnam." A few more generous words. He raised his arm in a compelling gesture, a beat, they sang, responding eagerly to his leadership. Such singing! The Dean said, "Turn to the hymn numbered 147." He read the verse:
>
> > "Ask ye what great thing I know
> > That delights and stirs me so?
> > What the high reward I win?
> > Whose the name I glory in?"
>
> He paused a moment, then read the answer:
>
> > "Jesus Christ the crucified."
>
> It was as though he had approached the altar. He said, "You will please remain seated. The choir will sing the questions, together you will answer in song, 'Jesus Christ, the crucified.'" He continued, "Toward the close of the third verse, when I signal you to rise, we will sing together the great affirmation:
>
> > 'This is that great thing I know
> > That delights and stirs me so;
> > Faith in Him Who died to save,
> > Him who triumphed o'er the grave,
> > Jesus Christ, the crucified.'"

And Amos Thornburg wrote:

> What happened at that gathering had its greatest significance for the church, because the new *Hymnal* was opened and interpreted in such a way that every delegate remembered the gathering because of the Song in the lives of people, that had been set ringing by the skillful guidance of the Editor of the Hymnal.

Ministers and laymen returning to churches, theological schools, annual conferences, church music institutes, choir schools, popular assemblies, called on the Dean to help in their leadership. The number of places to which he went is too great to list, taking him to every corner of the country — to places great and small.

This year, too, brought the 200th anniversary of John Wesley's Al' dersgate experience, May 24, 1738, regarded as marking the beginning of Methodism. Again Bishop Oxnam sought the Dean's co-operation in preparing material to be used in churches in celebrating this anniversary. The result was a pamphlet by Mr. McCutchan entitled, **Aldersgate, 1738-1938; A Service in Song,** published by the Methodist Book Concern. With Bishop Oxnam as speaker and Dean as song leader, they observed the historic event in many churches of Iowa and Nebraska.

Soon after starting to serve the church in this way, the Dean's wife Carrie suffered a stroke, making it necessary that he limit his engagements to places near Claremont. He was persuaded to become a member (honorary) of the faculty of the Claremont University College Graduate School He accepted the position without salary on condition that he would admit to his courses only such graduate students as he personally approved. And he was very choosy. This left him free to arrange his own schedule, to accept requests to speak, to direct song services in churches and schools, to write, and to study.

Following Carrie's death in 1941, an active schedule of travel and speaking was resumed. But soon again another period of even more limited activity was forced on him by a coronary occlusion requiring hospitalization. This did not slow down his mind though, and during convalescence he spent much time in the library of the Graduate School. Here he had been given the use of an office workroom where were housed the most valuable items of his considerable collection of rare books.

One of the librarians, Helen Cowles, was fortunate enough to be of some help to him. And so they were married in 1944. Helen was the daughter of missionaries, born and brought up in South Africa. Dean in his characteristic jocular way announced to his friends that he was marrying a Zulu snake-charmer. She being considerably younger than he, and in excellent health, was able to accompany him and help drive the car. In all, they visited every state except Alaska and Hawaii. In 1950 the miles travelled by car and air were 39,500. These travels were to fill engagements, not for pleasure, though there was plenty of that packed in along the way.

The year 1944 saw the completion of **The Book of Worship for Church and Home.** The Dean had been a member of the editorial committee of the Commission on Worship of the Methodist Church which produced this valuable book. His previous study of psalmody, hymnody, and the devotional literature of the Christian church, in connection with his work on **The Hymnal, Our Hymnody,** and the university courses which he offered, had given him the broad comprehensive knowledge fundamental to work on such a book.

It had been his particular joy to help the rural church enlarge its acquaintance with the truly great hymns. Leading the congregation in song, he would begin with familiar old-time favorites, then gradually introduce and familiarize them with other great hymns and their place in the service. He felt deeply that a hymn must be easily singable by the man in the pew, so that he would feel it as his prayer, an expression of his aspiration and of his religion. Its words, its tunes therefore must be appealing and useable, leading to personal, individual participation in the church's worship service. And he particularly emphasized this with ministers and music directors.

An early experience, which he delighted to tell, shows one of the ways in which he did this. Visiting in a backwoods community of Arkansas, a friend took him to one of the many rousing, shouting camp-meetings. Unobtrusively the two men made themselves part of the group, joining in the singing under the direction of the hardworking, arm-swinging, shouting leader. After a number of songs had been belted out, the people were given a chance to suggest favorites to be sung. Mr. McCutchan stood and asked if they could sing "Stand Up for Jesus", and if he might lead the singing. After this, sung lustily as appropriate, he asked that they sing "Softly Now the Light of Day", and to sing it as quietly as the hushed sounds of evening. The response to his authoritative leadership, with its economy of arm-waving, was enthusiastic. He then suggested a child's hymn to be sung by the women in a sweet childlike manner. The results were delightful to everyone. Never before had they enjoyed such direction in singing to express the mood of words and music.

As William J. Reynolds wrote:

He knew the practices and problems of the local churches and was sharply critical of those who wrote about church music from lofty ivory towers, familiar only with the services of metropolitan cathedrals and oblivious and unconcerned about the thousands of smaller churches across the nation where the multitudes worship each week . . . He loved to walk the unfamiliar paths of hymns and tunes and share their wealth with the common man in the pew. He taught the joy of hymn-singing, not in the stilted style of the classroom professor, but as one whose love for hymnic expression was a vital part of abundant Christian living.

Again Dr. Reynolds wrote:

I shall never forget the time that one of America's great choral conductors accompanied one of Dean's hymn singing classes and learned how to play a hymn. About 1952, Dean McCutchan assisted in a state church music leadership school sponsored by Ira C. Prosser, Oklahoma Baptist State Music Secretary. Dean taught hymnology and Noble Cain conducted choral periods. The paths of these two had crossed only once before. After Noble Cain had completed his Master's degree at the University of Chicago, Dean had tried unsuccessfully to persuade him to join the music faculty at DePauw University. While each had kept up with the other's work through the years, they had had no real association since that time. Dean needed an accompanist for his hymn singing in this conference and invited Noble Cain to play the piano. When it was time to sing the first hymn, Dean signaled for the introduction, which Cain provided but much too fast and "showy" to suit Dean's taste. Instead of proceeding with the singing, Dean turned to Noble Cain and, in a manner befitting a music professor kindly chiding an overly zealous freshman pianist, he said, "Now Noble you know better than that. Let's try it once again." Noble smiled sheepishly and started over. Those hymn sessions with Dean McCutchan leading and Noble Cain at the piano were memorable.

And to Helen, Dr. Reynolds wrote:

Here of late Dean has been spending a considerable amount of time in the wilds of Oklahoma, and I have had the opportunity to observe him closely. I don't know whether you are aware of some of these facts or not, but here for your information are some of them. Dean has been going around from town to town instilling into poor Methodists and Baptists a new and hearty enthusiasm in the long neglected music of their churches. He has aroused a tremendous concern over the hymn singing of these churches, to the extent that people are talking about it. Furthermore he has lifted the horizons of church music in the eyes of some of us poor plodding music directors and has challenged us to more effective ministry of music and has shown us ways of doing something about it. This is an unheard of thing for anybody to do, much less a man of his age and experience.

Through Texas and Oklahoma, people were warm and responsive and dear to him. Churches in small towns within easy driving distance of each other would band together to entertain him for a week or so, during which time nightly meetings for song festivals were held. The special purpose was to draw to these gatherings choir members and leaders, ministers and congregations. Pot-luck cooperative dinners and the like accompanied the gatherings, making pleasant sociability. And in between, there were valuable and heart-warming conversations among individuals, establishing those long-lasting personal friendships which it was Dean's great gift to foster and hold.

Some of the places where he enjoyed such happy times were: Oklahoma City, Norman, Lawton, Temple, Hugo, Ada, Paris, Dallas, Fort Worth, Wichita Falls, Houston, Folydada, Georgetown, San Saba, Ennis, Morse, Lockney, Petersburg, Tulia, El Paso.

It was not only in Oklahoma and Texas that he enjoyed bringing hymns into men's lives. All across this country from Texas to New England, from Washington to Florida, from Montana to Arizona to Minnesota, he met with groups, small and informal or in mass meetings. Where he enjoyed the hospitality of homes, he made himself part of the family, at home in the kitchen as well as in the parlor. In the kitchen his hostess often had to let him wash the dishes, where he insisted on "showing her how". The results were so much fun that soon the entire household was in there too. So everywhere along with his gift of music, he carried the warm gift of friendship and laughter, another sound of music in many keys.

Colleges also called on him to share his enthusiasms with students. At Northwestern University, on the invitation of Dr. Beltz, he participated in the summer Church and Choral Music Institutes; a program to " meet the needs for a more extended course in Church Music Studies . . . to prepare church musicians for a larger service in the ministry of music . . . The curriculum and staff have been chosen to give the most thorough preparation in the shortest possible time". This participation was in the years 1938-39, 41-42, 44-45. An extension of this was the National Institute of Church Music, under Dr. Beltz's management. These institutes were held in widely scattered areas, Dean having a part in many of them: Alfred, N. Y., West Palm Beach, Florida, Crete, Neb., Knoxville, Tenn., Washington, D. C., Oklahoma City, to name a few.

Other college assignments were at the University of Montana, The College of Puget Sound, Redlands University, Calif., Purdue University, Duke University, Wesleyan College, Pacific School of Religion's Earl lecturer. Summers from 1943 to 1947 found him at the Pastor's School of Southwestern University, Georgetown, Texas, enjoying his warm friend-ship with President Score and his family and faculty. As has been mentioned, he was a faculty member of the Claremont Colleges Gradute School during the years 1939-54.

The wonderfully warm and happy culmination of his teaching was at the Perkins School of Theology, S.M.U., Dallas. Invited there by his friend Merrimon Cuninggim whom he had known in Claremont, he was visiting professor of church music for a year and a half in 1954-1955. Here on the faculties were many friends of past years, among them President Lee, William W. Sweet, Mrs. Score, Fred Gealy and many more whom he had known during his years of activity in college and church work. Here he was again deep in the heart of Texas as they were deep in his heart.

It was while he was at Perkins that two Methodists appointed to visit and appraise Methodist theological schools throughout the U. S., made their stop there. Dr. Sweet invited them and Dean McCutchan to lunch and a conference one day. It was while they were discussing Southern California, that Dean McCutchan said "Why don't you consider Claremont as a place for the theological school? It has a fine group of colleges with an excellent library, and is rather central to Southern California." Dr. Sweet, who had also taught in Claremont a year, fell in heartily with the suggestion. Perhaps Claremont would have been picked anyway, but at least these men did survey that community, and the results are known: the Southern California School of Theology moved from Los Angeles to Claremont.

In view of all these activities and assignments, it would hardly seem possible that there would be time or energy left for committees, area con-ferences, commissions, conventions and the like. But these were of primary importance in his schedule. They demanded not only his presence but imposed duties which necessitated much time and thought in their preparation. To the Uniting Conference of Methodist Churches in Kansas City he was a delegate-at-large in 1939. Also he was member of the General Conference Commission (Methodist) on Ritual and Orders of Service, the General Con-ference Ecumenical Commission, the Southern California-Arizona Con-ference Committee on Graduate School of Religion, U.S.C., The Seventh Ecumenical Methodist Conference, Springfield, Mass.

Something of what he packed into a few months is indicated in the following letter to Dr. Beltz in 1947:

Dear Oliver:

> Just arrived home this morning at 4 a.m. from Southwestern Pastor's School. Leave Thursday morning early for College of Puget Sound, Tacoma, and to Livingston, Montana, for others. Will not get home until August 18. The next day (19) fly back to Texas for a Town and Country Conference at Southwestern. You can reach me c/o President's Office, College of Puget Sound, Tacoma, Wash., until July; then c/o First Methodist Church, Livingston Montana, until Aug. 12. Then here in Claremont.

> The above to tell you not only where you can reach me but to explain why I cannot get a glossy print for you: the enclosed is the best I can do I doubt if any photograher can do any better ! Sorry.

> Am glad to hear that plans for the October Conference are developing according to your wishes. I'm looking forward to it eagerly. You'll get the best I have. (This was the National Institute of Church Music, Washington, D.C.).

> You will be interested to know that I am one of the committee of several to provide nineteen worship services for the Methodist Ecumenical Conference at Springfield, Mass. While the committee has several members it has turned over to Dr. Score and myself the entire job ! And I've only known of it for some two weeks ! I can see where I'll miss some of the beauty spots around Puget Sound and in the Montana mountains, for Score is frank in saying that I am going to have to do most of the work. Verily, some day I'm going to retire; my retread is growing thin.

Again in planning and preparing these Worship Services for the printer, as in other such publications and his books, the Dean had had valuable experience. The years in his youth when he had worked as a typesetter and printer in Mississippi had given him practical skill of use in subsequent years. Always he made up a dummy, accurately and effectively arranging materials. Also, of course, his thorough study in the ritual. liturgy, and psalmody was evident and relied on by Bishop Oxnam whose right hand he was in planning the services and directing the music in area conferences and campaigns: Iowa and Nebraska 1938, New England and New York 1942, 1944, 1945, 1949.

Of these associations the Bishop said:

> In the Omaha, the Boston and the New York areas he conducted great Festivals of Song and I spoke on "The Faith". We journeyed from town to town together and as I drove I listened to rich and rewarding conversation. And he could tell humorous stories as I have never heard them told . . .

Relaxing between the inspirational meetings they conducted, like boys, they got fun out of inconsequential things. Roaring with laughter over its incongruity, Dean McCutchan used to tell of one such episode. After a strenuous day of meetings in the Omaha area, they had dinner in a small restaurant. The waitress, a pretty Irish girl, came to their table saying, "Evenin' gentlemen, an' what's your orders?" The Bishop replied, "Evenin' Mrs. O'Toole." Good-natured banter followed as she served them. Next morning for breakfast they went to the same place but sat at the counter. As she hurried past balancing a full tray, "Mrs. O'Toole" spied them. Sliding to a stop she said gayly, "Mornin' boys! Why didn't you come back to my table?" Mr. McCutchan looking solemn and impressive replied, "Do you realize who this gentleman is? He is the **Reverend Bishop Oxnam.**" The girl looked stricken, blanched and exclaimed, "My God!" Then Mr. McCutchan added, "Bishop of the Methodist Church." "O hell!" she cried in relief as she hurried away.

The last series of meetings with the Bishop were at Montpelier, Plattsburg, Albany and New York, in 1949. The following are excerpts from letters regarding them:

> (Dean to Helen) The affair at Montpelier last night was a complete and unqualified success. The church was crowded, two good choirs, some fine singing . . . and a bang-up speech by the Bishop. . . . We are having a wonderful time. The Bishop is tired and realizes it. I've talked pretty straight to him and he insists he is beginning to have a little sense about slowing down a bit. He is such a grand fellow. He has been so thoughtful about having rooms ready for us on arrival, that I'm sure we will come through in good shape.

> Tonight (Oct. 21) was one of the high spots of my life. The place (Carnegie Hall) was competely filled, where only standing room is available, was full of people. The stage could accommodate only a few more than 300, so all the choir singers could not find places. And such response — simply tremendous. The choir special number, a hymn-anthem, was beautifully done — even satisfied me completely!! The organist, Tutchings, was excellent. It was a pretty good show.

> (Oxnam to McCutchan, Oct. 31, 1949) I shall treasure through all the years that are mine the recollections of our wonderful trip together. It seemed like old times to me. You know, of course, what your friendship has meant to me and the strange power you possess whereby I seem to do twice as good a job when you're along as I do when I'm alone. I thought you were never better than in the meetings this time. They climaxed as I hoped they would, at Carnegie Hall. That was your presence. Did you ever hear a congregation sing more magnificently? And the choir responded to your genius and did a superb job. All I am trying to say is this, thanks a thousand times. We must do this again.

In May 1955, his term as Visiting Professor, at Perkins School of Theology, Dallas, came to an end. When he said goodbye to his many choice friends there, he had no premonition that he would not see them again. Hospitalization came unexpectedly in October when he underwent emergency surgery. But gradually enough strength was regained so that by June 1956, he attended the DePauw University commencement to receive an honorary **Mus. Doc.** Two close friends of many years, William W. Sweet and Ralph Gwinn were also honored with doctorates. And his son, Bob, a DePauw alumnus, was there to guard his Dad from over-doing. Great joy came to him too at the alumni luncheon where once again he led the singing of some DePauw favorites. Afterwards, he was mobbed, hugged and kissed.

That year the manuscript of **Hymn Tune Names** was completed and sent to the publishers. The galley sheets came to him in January 1957. With all the failing strength his will could muster, and with help from

22

Helen, proof was read and returned to the publishers on February 11. With his characteristic humor and generosity it was dedicated: "To Helen, without whose sympathy, understanding and more or less gentle though persistent prodding, this project might not have been completed". And he enjoyed holding the printed volume in his hands.

"Why Avison?" he had asked as a child. What could have been more appropriate than that this his last publication should give some of the answers to this life-long question about the naming of tunes!

> Let all the world in every corner sing:
>   My God and King!
> The heavens are not too high, His praise may thither fly;
> The earth is not too low, His praises there may grow.
> Let all the world in every corner sing:
>   My God and King!
>
> Let all the world in every corner sing:
>   My God and King!
> The Church with psalms must shout, no door can keep them out;
> But more than all, the heart must bear the longest part.
> Let all the world in every corner sing:
>   My God and King!

The Robert Guy McCutchan
Library of Hymnology

The McCutchan collection of several thousand hymn books and related materials is a by-product of Dean McCutchan's lifetime interest in this field. His was not a systematic acquisition of materials through agents or salesmen, but the result of constant alert watchfulness in his travels throughout the land. Some of his trophies are unique, others are rare. He discovered them in farm barns and woodsheds, at auctions, as discards in trash boxes, in attics, in second-hand bookstores and city side streets. Many were gifts from friends whose family treasures they had been.

As individual items their worth may not be great either in cash or historically, but in a collection as related to others of a period, style or church denomination, they may supply important links in a chain.

The collection includes books of American "Singing Schools", Sunday schools, gospel songs, hymn books of the majority of American religious denominations, Methodist especially, grange and fraternal songs, Civil War songs. It contains also biographies of authors of hymn texts and composers of tunes.

It is not a collection of anthems, choir or organ music, but of music designed for congregational and group participation.

Students of secular as well as religious music and of theology ministers of church music, compilers of hymn books, searchers for quaint American songs and tunes will find in it valuable source material.

Dr. McCutchan gave his collection to Claremont College Graduate School and it is housed in the Honnold Library. Here it is available to faculty and students of the six associated colleges and to others.

Managing People Globally

CHANDOS
ASIAN STUDIES SERIES:
CONTEMPORARY ISSUES AND TRENDS

Series Editor: Professor Chris Rowley,
Centre for Research on Asian Management, Cass Business School,
City University, UK; HEAD Foundation, Singapore
(email: c.rowley@city.ac.uk)

Chandos Publishing is pleased to publish this major Series of books entitled *Asian Studies: Contemporary Issues and Trends*. The Series Editor is Professor Chris Rowley, Director, Centre for Research on Asian Management, City University, UK and Director, Research and Publications, HEAD Foundation, Singapore.

Asia has clearly undergone some major transformations in recent years and books in the Series examine this transformation from a number of perspectives: economic, management, social, political and cultural. We seek authors from a broad range of areas and disciplinary interests: covering, for example, business/management, political science, social science, history, sociology, gender studies, ethnography, economics and international relations, etc.

Importantly, the Series examines both current developments and possible future trends. The Series is aimed at an international market of academics and professionals working in the area. The books have been specially commissioned from leading authors. The objective is to provide the reader with an authoritative view of current thinking.

New authors: we would be delighted to hear from you if you have an idea for a book. We are interested in both shorter, practically orientated publications (45,000+ words) and longer, theoretical monographs (75,000–100,000 words). Our books can be single, joint or multi-author volumes. If you have an idea for a book, please contact the publishers or Professor Chris Rowley, the Series Editor.

Dr Glyn Jones
Chandos Publishing
Email: gjones@chandospublishing.com
www.chandospublishing.com

Professor Chris Rowley
Cass Business School, City University
Email: c.rowley@city.ac.uk
www.cass.city.ac.uk/faculty/c.rowley

Chandos Publishing: Chandos Publishing is an imprint of Woodhead Publishing Limited. The aim of Chandos Publishing is to publish books of the highest possible standard: books that are both intellectually stimulating and innovative.

We are delighted and proud to count our authors from such well known international organisations as the Asian Institute of Technology, Tsinghua University, Kookmin University, Kobe University, Kyoto Sangyo University, London School of Economics, University of Oxford, Michigan State University, Getty Research Library, University of Texas at Austin, University of South Australia, University of Newcastle, Australia, University of Melbourne, ILO, Max-Planck Institute, Duke University and the leading law firm Clifford Chance.

A key feature of Chandos Publishing's activities is the service it offers its authors and customers. Chandos Publishing recognises that its authors are at the core of its publishing ethos, and authors are treated in a friendly, efficient and timely manner. Chandos Publishing's books are marketed on an international basis, via its range of overseas agents and representatives.

Professor Chris Rowley: Dr Rowley, BA, MA (Warwick), DPhil (Nuffield College, Oxford) is Subject Group leader and the inaugural Professor of Human Resource Management at Cass Business School, City University, London, UK, and Director of Research and Publications for the HEAD Foundation, Singapore. He is the founding Director of the multi-disciplinary and internationally networked Centre for Research on Asian Management (http//www.cass.city.ac.uk/cram/index.html) and Editor of the leading journal *Asia Pacific Business Review* (www.tandf.co.uk/journals/titles/13602381.asp). He is well known and highly regarded in the area, with visiting appointments at leading Asian universities and top journal Editorial Boards in the UK, Asia and the US. He has given a range of talks and lectures to universities, companies and organisations internationally with research and consultancy experience with unions, business and government, and his previous employment includes varied work in both the public and private sectors. Professor Rowley researches in a range of areas, including international and comparative human resource management and Asia Pacific management and business. He has been awarded grants from the British Academy, an ESRC AIM International Study Fellowship and gained a 5-year RCUK Fellowship in Asian Business and Management. He acts as a reviewer for many funding bodies, as well as for numerous journals and publishers. Professor Rowley publishes very widely, including in leading US and UK journals, with over 370 articles, books, chapters and other contributions.

Bulk orders: some organisations buy a number of copies of our books. If you are interested in doing this, we would be pleased to discuss a discount. Please email info@chandospublishing.com or telephone +44 (0) 1223 891358.

Managing People Globally: An Asian Perspective

CHRIS ROWLEY
AND
WES HARRY

CP

CHANDOS
PUBLISHING

Oxford Cambridge Philadelphia New Delhi

Chandos Publishing
TBAC Business Centre
Avenue 4
Station Lane
Witney
Oxford OX28 4BN
UK
Tel: +44 (0) 1993 848726
E-mail: info@chandospublishing.com
www.chandospublishing.com

Chandos Publishing is an imprint of Woodhead Publishing Limited

Woodhead Publishing Limited
80 High Street
Sawston
Cambridge CB22 3HJ
UK
Tel: +44 (0) 1223 499140
Fax: +44 (0) 1223 832819
www.woodheadpublishing.com

First published in 2011

ISBN:
978 1 84334 223 6

© C. Rowley and W. Harry, 2011

British Library Cataloguing-in-Publication Data.
A catalogue record for this book is available from the British Library.

Typeset by Domex e-Data Pvt. Ltd.
Printed in the UK and USA.

For Andrea, 'Days are never long enough' – Chris

In memory of Isabella Kennedy McLean – Wes

Contents

List of figures and tables

Figures

Tables

Acknowledgements

Wes Harry wishes to acknowledge the help, advice and guidance of so many Asians in building his understanding of their ways of working and helping non-Asians to have a global instead of a parochial view of managing people. Wes also wishes to thank Glyn Jones for his support in the writing process and to Liz McElwain for her patience in copy-editing the script.

Abbreviations

ACAS	Advisory, Conciliation and Arbitration Service
ACFTU	All China Federation of Trade Unions
AITUC	All India Trade Union Congress
BARS	behaviourally anchored rating scales
BITS	Bureau of Labour and Employment Statistics Integrated Survey
BOS	behavioural observation scales
BPO	business process outsourcing
CAC	Central Arbitration Committee
CBA	collective bargaining agreement
CCP	Chinese Communist Party
COE	collectively owned enterprise
COLA	cost of living allowance
CSR	customer service representative
CUEPACS	Congress of Unions of Employees in the Public and Civil Services (of Malaysia)
DGTU	Director General of Trade Unions
ELM	external labour market
EPZ	export processing zone
ESO	Employees Supply Organisation
E&T	education and training
EU	European Union
FDI	foreign direct investment
FIE	foreign-invested enterprise
FKTU	Korea Federation of Trade Unions
FMCG	fast-moving consumer goods
GCC	Gulf Co-operation Council
GOTEVOT	Government Organization for Technical and Vocational Training
HCN	host country national
HR	human resources
HRM	human resource management
HRP	human resource planning

ILM	internal labour market
IR	industrial relations
ITES	information technology enabled services
JV	joint venture
KCTU	Korean Confederation of Trade Unions
KCTUR	Korean Council of Trade Union Representatives
KEF	Korean Employers Federation
KTUC	Korea Trade Union Congress
LAC	labour arbitration committee
LDAC	Labour Dispute Arbitration Committee
LM	labour market
LMC	Labour-Management Council (of Korea)
MBO	management by objectives
MNC	multi-national corporation
MOET	Ministry of Education and Training
MPL	multi-crew pilot licence
MTUC	Malaysian Trades Union Congress
NGO	non-government organisation
NLAC	National Labour Advisory Council (of Malaysia)
NUBE	National Union of Bank Employees (of Malaysia)
NVQ	National Vocational Qualification
NWPC	National Wage and Productivity Commission
OECD	Organisation for Economic Co-operation and Development
PEST	political, economic, social, technological
PM	performance management
PMA	performance management and assessment
POE	privately owned enterprise
PRC	People's Republic of China
PRP	performance-related pay
R&S	recruitment and selection
SME	small- and medium-sized enterprise
SOE	state-owned enterprise
STP	software technology park
T&D	training and development
TQM	Total Quality Management
TUA	Trade Union Act
UAE	United Arab Emirates
VCGL	Vietnamese General Confederation of Labour
VOTECH	vocational and technical education and training

About the authors

Chris Rowley

Dr Rowley, BA, MA (Warwick), DPhil (Nuffield College, Oxford) is the founding Director of the Centre for Research on Asian Management and inaugural Professor of Human Resource Management at City University, London, UK. He is Editor of the *Asia Pacific Business Review*, Series Editor of the *Working in Asia* and *Asian Studies* book series and Director (Research and Publications) of the HEAD Foundation, Singapore. Professor Rowley has held visiting appointments at leading Asian universities and several journal editorial boards. He has given a range of talks and lectures to universities and companies internationally, with research and consultancy experience with unions, business and government, and his previous employment includes varied work in both the public and private sectors. He conducts research in a range of areas, including international human resource management and Asia Pacific management and business. He publishes widely, including in leading US and UK journals, with over 370 articles, books and chapters and other contributions, and practitioner and knowledge transfer output and engagement.

Wes Harry

Dr Harry is currently Organisation and HRM Adviser to an Asian government ministry. Previous positions include HRM Adviser to Sovereign Wealth Funds in Asia and to the oil sector of a Gulf state, Head of HR of the world's largest Islamic bank based in Saudi Arabia (the only foreigner to have held this post), Head of HR and IT of a major Gulf commercial bank, General Manager – Personnel of a Middle Eastern Airline, and Personnel Manager of an East Asian Airline. He holds a PhD in international human resource management from the Graduate Business School, University of Strathclyde, an MA in Manpower Studies (CNAA) and a BSc Sociology (London). Wes is an

Honorary Visiting Fellow of Cass Business School as well as being a member of the adjunct staff of the University of Bradford School of Management. He supervises doctoral and masters level students, has written chapters and journal articles in academic works on international HRM topics and has worked and travelled in most Asian countries. He has books and journal special editions under way on the subjects of managing sustainably, HRM and human rights, business ethics and managing across cultures.

Introduction: HRM context, development and scope

1.1 Introduction

The management of people remains crucial to all organisations and the achievement of organisational success and is at the heart of many important debates – political, economic and social, as well as managerial and business. The management of people also has impacts from, and on, these macro contextual areas and simultaneously remains an area of management that retains elements of both continuity and flux. In the context of managing people, in this book human resource management (HRM) refers to the function and human resources (HR) refers to the people employed.

Indeed, around the globe the critical nature of the management of people is soon apparent. However, this key aspect of management contains both universal and contingent elements and aspects. On the one hand, there are the universal areas of HRM, such as the need and search for how to efficiently resource the organisation and reward and develop people (see the substantive chapters in this book) consistently, fairly and equitably. On the other hand, these desires are mixed with the contingent areas of HRM, such as the actual practice and operation of policies in those key areas of the function (see the examples in this book). There is also the issue of the degree and level of acceptance of any HRM practice that is formally in operation. It is this tension that forms the key theme running through the book and its content and examples.

This first chapter introduces both the concept of HRM and the philosophy that will guide the reader through the book. This guide includes some of the different perspectives and views on HRM in the West (here taken as the countries of North America and the European Union), its antecedence and evolution as a function of management, and some of the main factors that critically influence HRM's development, variations and practices in Asia (by which we mean the countries mainly in North and South East Asia and, where possible, South Asia). In this manner, it will be apparent that HRM not only retains its ongoing importance and relevance, but also evolves as a subject and area while remaining complex and varied. We have had to use more Western statistics and information than we would have liked to illustrate various aspects of HRM, especially in the tables and figures. These Western illustrations have been necessary because of the paucity of HRM information in some parts of Asia.

It can be argued that some changes in the operating environment and context of HRM have actually made this area of management more important, diffuse and widespread. The operating environment is rapidly changing, particularly in Asia, as some of the countries move from an era of cheap labour and low quality output to one where specialist labour is needed and is in short supply, as the countries and the businesses in Asia move up the business value chain. We should at this point mention that, although we have just referred to 'businesses', the topics we discuss apply in all organisations – to government departments, non-government organisations (NGOs) and to fully commercial employers. In most of Asia, however, it is the commercial sector that competes with international firms, and so is under most pressure to use HR most efficiently and effectively.

The endeavour to use HR efficiently and effectively makes this book relevant especially for managerial and student non-specialists, as well as HRM practitioners, both those in Asia and those who deal with Asia from outside the region. Furthermore, the spreading waves of people management wash over ever broader aspects of business and work. Changes driving these waves include the increase in importance of ideas such as knowledge management, with its assumptions of HR as human capital with value as critical. Then there are notions concerning the competitive advantage that stems from the effective use of HR in a globalised world of fast take-up of other means of competing, such as location, technology, and so on. In some countries, such as the US and UK, the influence of HRM has also spread as a result of the encroachment of laws into what had, traditionally, been a more voluntarist and laissez faire arena.

It terms of this book's stance, content and coverage, several points need to be made. If some specific areas are of particular interest, other specialist books can be consulted for further details. These specific areas include the spheres of recruitment, rewards and managing performance, amongst many others. Similarly, this book is not a prescriptive, 'how to', simple steps or skills guide for 'best' HRM practice per se. Rather, where these practices are noted, this book often goes on to provide a more general overview and feel for the area and the main practices and issues evolving in the West and Asia. As in many aspects of life, the specific HRM issue and problem may result in going in turn to a specialist. While, in some cases, this may well be within HRM itself, the dynamic legal aspects to HRM increasingly require consultation of these sorts of specialist in an era of deepening and broadening juridification and aggressive legality of the work environment.

In discussing HRM in Asia we are trying, in one book, to cover the management practices in organisations throughout the huge area of Asia, including the most populous country in the world – China. The variations in the economies, social expectations and political systems are vast so this book can only draw attention to the main issues and practices; we therefore caution the reader to seek specific country HRM information from elsewhere or publications by the present authors and others. In particular, there is the useful *Working in Asia* series from Routledge (Rowley and Abdul Rahman, 2008; Rowley and Yukongdi, 2009; Rowley and Paik, 2009; Rowley and Troung, 2009; Rowley and Cooke, 2010). Other sources of information on this swiftly changing and dynamic area are listed in Appendix 1 and 2.

We discuss many Western issues and historical developments of HRM in the West because an understanding of HRM in the West is essential in Asia where international organisations operate widely and where Asian organisations may aim to try to emulate Western practices.

1.2 Chapter features and the wider relevance of HRM

1.2.1 Think About/Questions, Overviews and Further Readings

During the course of the following chapters, several issues and questions are regularly raised for readers to think about, reflect on and even note down some responses to, before moving on. We also have a list of questions at the end of each chapter which ask the reader to consider information within the chapter in relation to two case studies which are contained in Appendix 3. These cases describe typical HRM issues which are faced by employers in the region. One case is based on banking and the other on the aviation industry – both sectors are undergoing rapid transformation in Asia. These forms of exercise are to enhance the learning process by, for instance, challenging readers to address issues and bring their own view points, perspectives, experiences and understandings to bear and, in turn, become exposed to alternatives. In this way the complex, contested and dynamic nature of HRM will become apparent, as may some ethnocentricity.

Each of the substantive chapters is provided with its own 'Overview' at the start. The reading of these, and the completion of any tasks within them, allows readers a quick grasp of the whole chapter so they can be treated as 'stand alone' sections. In addition, these Overviews are interactive in allowing readers to undertake some activities themselves. A list of references is provided at the end of each chapter, which will provide readers with a resource to allow them to take their learning and interests further under their own direction. We encourage readers to remain up to date with contemporary developments in HRM by studying relevant professional practitioner and academic journals as well as business focused newspapers and magazines, such as *The Financial Times* and *The Economist,* as noted in Appendix 2.

1.2.2 Wider relevance

The long and enduring relevance of the management of people in popular culture and artefacts is apparent. One of the most explicit ways was in the former Soviet Union and its 'socialist realism' movement in which art depicted certain values, the dignity and importance of work, and so on. The world of literature, films and television further indicate such cultural dimensions. Often these media provide a range of 'lighter' methods of portraying people management, to a greater or lesser extent. These range from books and novels, to television one-off programmes, series and dramas and movie films, some examples of which are noted below (with a fuller list in Appendix 2).

Employment themes in novels and books have a long history. Some historical and contemporary examples follow. Gaskell's (1855) *North and South* novel includes themes of the reciprocal responsibilities of employers and employees. Sinclair's (1906) *The Jungle* is a harrowing account of Chicago's meat-packing industry and its low-skilled and disadvantaged workers. Orwell (1933) in *Down and Out in Paris and London* wrote about restaurant work as a *'plongeur'*. Selby's (1957)

Last Exit to Brooklyn highlights the often brutal nature of early post-war US labour relations. Sheed's (1968) *Office Politics* is about inter-personal conflicts in a publishing house. Lodge (1989) in *Nice Work* compares industrial and academic worlds. Heller's (1989) *Something Happened* is a black comedy of corporate culture and executives in an office. Kemske's (1996) *Human Resources: A Business Novel* is about a HR manager, a 'strange' turnaround specialist and differences in company reorganisation. More contemporary examples include *Death of a Salaryman* (Campbell, 2007), which centres on a salaryman in a television network whose life is disrupted when he is fired on his 40th birthday.

Other books include those about 'real life', such as Hamper's (1986/92) *Rivethead: Tales from the Assembly Line*, which is a fascinating record of working life by an assembly worker in a GM plant. Ehrenreich's (2002) *Nickel and Dimed* is a hard-hitting look at low-wage work in the US. Schlosser's (2001) *Fast Food Nation* is a look at the fast-food industry around the world. Daisey (2002) *Twenty-one Dog Years – Doing Time at Amazon.com* concerns organisational socialisation and culture, utilising the author's experience of being recruited and inducted. Ransom (2001) describes the reality of trade within the developing world, including the working life of Bangladeshi sweatshop workers. Chang (2008) explores the plight of migrant workers and factory life in Dongguan's huge Yue Yuan factory employing 70,000 making Nike and Adidas shoes.

In terms of television documentaries and series, from the UK these include *Bubble Trouble*, with an episode noting Japanese management practices and changes in Japan, the US and UK by Toshiba, Matsushita and Nissan. There was also *Brits Get Rich*, which followed three British entrepreneurs as they open businesses in China. In the US the TV documentary *Behind the Label* explores the sweatshops which produce the goods for prestige brands using indentured and exploited labour. *China Blue* is a documentary on the human costs of producing cheap clothes.

UK comedic examples include *The Office* and its insights into working life in a paper materials company – the role of management, recruitment, training and employee performance appraisals all appear. There have been French and American versions of this series. *Mumbai Calling* focused on a British-Indian accountant sent to India to turn around a newly acquired call centre and who clashes with local management.

Films range from *Modern Times* starring Charlie Chaplin, with its classic view of Tayloristic working life, to *The Man in the White Suit* concerning management-trade union connivance to halt technology, and *I'm All Right Jack* with its satire on post-war UK employee relations. A very early attempt to come to terms with immigration and workplace relations in the UK was in the 1960s film *Flame in the Streets*, which contrasts with *True North* from 2006 concerning the smuggling of illegal Chinese immigrants to the UK.

Other films include those giving a view of the US and its psyche and changes. A common theme covered is the cut-throat nature of American capitalism and business. For example, *Tin Men* is about the rivalry between unscrupulous aluminium-siding salesmen in Baltimore in the early 1960s. *Glengarry Glen Ross* provides a classic US view of work, teams and motivation via a day in the life of real-estate salesmen. *Other People's Money* is a sharp satire on a ruthless asset stripper trying to profit from taking over a family-run firm. *The Pursuit of Happiness* is the story, set in the 1980s, of a penniless salesman trying to land a job on the trading floor of Dean Witter, the stockbroking firm.

Other themes include US economic and business challenges and changes. Some films are concerned with the rise of challenges by groups, countries (such as Japan) and issues, such as *The Devil and Miss Jones* in which a rich boss, sensing union unrest among retail workers, goes back to the shop floor. *Blue Collar* concerns oppressive factory jobs and car workers exploited by their own union. *Norma Rae* is about a US textile worker turning union activist. *All Night Long* is concerned with the frustration of demotion from the company's HQ to night manager at a 24-hour drugstore. *Kentucky Woman* is about discrimination and the role of laws in the US as a woman fights to be accepted as a coal miner. *Disclosure* concerns power politics and sexual harassment in the workplace. *Stand-In* involves an efficiency expert and an accountant sent to assess a failing Hollywood studio. *Bread and Roses* is about non-union immigrant Mexican cleaners in California. *Gung-Ho* uses the backdrop of faltering US economic performance and cross-cultural views on management and workers in a car factory taken over by the Japanese. *Rising Sun* concerns an investigation of a death, showing Japanese etiquette in a conglomerate in the US. *Barbarians at the Gate* is about the power struggles in the takeover bid against American conglomerate Nabisco in the early 1980s. *Antitrust* is set in the cut-throat world of computer software industry and lampoons Bill Gates.

Such areas can be seen in issues in other countries. For example, from Japan, *The Most Beautiful* is about a group of women in a wartime factory producing lenses for Japanese planes. *Congratulatory Speech (Shukuji)* is a satirical film of a salaryman's supreme dedication when asked to give a speech at the wedding of the VP's son. A salaryman's attempt to avoid loss of face after being sacked by hiding his unemployment is covered in *Tokyo Sonata*. From China are the following. *Wu Yong* covers culture and consumerism. *Blind Shaft* is based on work, employment and corruption in the mining industry. *Blind Mountain* is concerned with the abandonment of healthcare and education systems. *Cairo Station* from the 1950s concerns labourers' lives, and achieving unionisation during change in Egypt. *Patent Pending* examines the exploitation of Indian farmers by a US multi-national corporation (MNC). A satire on the effect of Western-style capitalism on Indian life in the 1970s is *Company Limited*.

The rest of this chapter takes the following format. There are sections on what HRM is and its development, some of the rhetoric and reality and tensions in the area, strategy and context. The scope of the book is also outlined.

1.3 What is HRM?

Think About/Question 1.1

What practical areas of business and work is HRM concerned with?

In the most general sense, HRM refers to the management of people in relation to work. Such 'people management' is largely concerned with the more practical aspects of the employment relationship. Nevertheless, HRM is also underpinned by some theory: motivation, for example, is one of the more obvious examples but we must beware of assuming that motivation is constant in all societies – we will return to this issue several times within this book. HRM involves people 'processing', such as staffing requirements and planning, recruitment and selection of employees; 'rewarding' such as establishing pay systems and non-monetary remuneration and performance elements; 'developing', as seen in organising training and setting up performance appraisal systems; and 'relations', such as dealing with rules, grievances and involving employees.

For some commentators, HRM goes further than this. For instance, in somewhat simplistic terms, the central claims of HRM are:

- by matching productivity requirements and the workforce, and raising its quality, organisations can significantly improve performance; and

- People are the key organisational asset, and organisational performance depends upon the quantity and quality of workforce efforts, and hence on their ability and motivation.

The lead in people management within an organisation is often taken by the HRM department, which is charged with the key areas of organising the management of people. A variety of methods are used within these areas, with the exact mix varying and influenced by history, organisational size, sector, location, and so on. Consequently, HRM work is diverse and multi-faceted, requiring a considerable amount of not only specialist knowledge and expertise, but also understanding and tact on the part of practitioners. It is often seen as more of an 'art' than a 'science'. When organisations and HRM practitioners are operating across national and cultural boundaries the level of knowledge, expertise, understanding and tact required when managing people increases exponentially.

1.3.1 Contemporary issues

While the core activities of HRM are relatively easy to identify, at many times fresh HRM issues appear or reappear. These issues may arouse attention for a while and become the subject of debate, then pass and fade quickly. Yet other issues may have more profound and longer term effects.

> Think About/Question 1.2
>
> What issues do you think have become more important in HRM recently?

Fresh issues come to the fore as a result of changes in the economy and society or in the state of knowledge, and so on. These range from changes in labour markets (such as more diverse workforces or demographic changes) to technological developments (such as different processes, skills, means of control, health and safety). They are often reported and commented on in the mass media, such as *The Financial Times* (see Skapinker, 2007; Bolchover, 2009). Some of these environmental and contextual shifts can be monitored, and even to some extent predicted, in a variety of ways. So the context of HRM is vitally important.

1.3.2 Development of HRM

There is, obviously, a long history of the practice of people management. Indeed, writing on the subject dates back to at least the first century, with Columella, a Roman farmer whose *De Rustica* featured one of the earliest tracts on people management. Two or three millennia ago Chinese and Indians wrote manuals on how to manage people effectively. Sun Tzu and *The Art of War* has been revived in the West in the past two decades, but his works and those of the unknown authors of the '36 Strategies' are still in regular use in East Asian management. The Indian *Bhagavad Gita* has been a basis for managing in South Asia even when the Hindu origins of the advice are no longer considered.

Think About/Question 1.3

What earlier forms of people management can you note? Do these forms have any relevance to organisations today?

The more recent incarnation of the management of people, HRM, has in the West guises such as personnel management (PM), 'welfarism' and 'paternalism', which are still prevalent in Asia. While somewhat historical, these forms are not totally exclusive and modern versions and examples can be seen of these, to greater or lesser extents. This history and development of HRM needs to be noted and examined, not least because it, and the goals and values of an organisation's culture, may influence HRM roles. A variety of different terms and schema have been used in this area by various authors. Some of the more common categories are as follows.

1.3.2.1 Welfare tradition

This area developed in the West during the late nineteenth century in particular, and in parts of Asia in the twentieth century. This was associated with the paternalism of larger companies, sometimes extending to creating whole communities and towns forged on the beliefs (often religious) and ideas of their founders. Practical and welfare-based employee services were often provided.

Examples in the UK included Owen's New Lanark experiment early in the industrial revolution, to people and businesses (and products) such as Lever, a soap company which eventually became part of Unilever, at Port Sunlight, and Clarks, shoe manufactures, at Street. Titus Salt, the Yorkshire wool baron and pioneer of 'caring capitalism', built his new mill just outside the polluted town of Bradford in 1848 and over 20 years created Saltaire, a model community for employees. Then there were the Quakers, such as Cadbury at Bourneville and Rowntree, whose village in York had houses around a community hall and who set up a pension fund for employees in 1906, a profit-sharing scheme in 1916 and in 1918 staff shareholding, a revolutionary concept at the time. An example from the US in the same confectionery sector is Hershey, a Mennonite, whose factory town is of the same name. A Dutch example is the chemicals group DSM – its mining past put employees' wellbeing high on its agenda. DSM built houses for workers and funded generous social policies, including medical help and alternative factory work for disabled miners.

Developments such as these in the UK can be seen as being reflected in the founding of the Institute of Welfare Officers in 1913. The concerns of welfare officers ranged from areas such as housing and education to canteens and other amenities at work. Modern versions of paternalism include companies such as the John Lewis Partnership, in which the employees are 'partners' and 'own' the company, with their particular forms of HRM.

In Asia family firms less often evolved into paternalistic companies which looked after workers and their welfare. However, one example in India is that of Jamsetji Tata who, in the nineteenth century, set up India's first steel and textile mills and built a complete city with subsidised housing, free schools and medical facilities for his workers and their families. Tata provided rights for his workers, such as an early example of a maximum eight-hour working day (when the norm was 12), established a provident fund and paid leave in 1920 and maternity benefit in 1928, well before these became common in the West.

The large enterprises in countries such as South Korea, Japan and China (in this book we will use China to mean the People's Republic of China – Hong Kong, Macau and Taiwan will be referred to by those names) are examples of caring for workers and their dependants, but this tradition sometimes grew out of political and social movements rather than paternalism. The level of such provision in these enterprises was very wide, and included company accommodation, ideas of 'cradle-to-grave' employment with them and widespread 'benefits' relating to families, such as assistance with birthdays, parents and even funerals.

1.3.2.2 Administrative tradition

This form of people management was concerned with much of the long-standing work of personnel departments. This included administration in areas such as recruiting, preparing job descriptions, arranging promotion panels, and so on. This personnel tradition, in the West, dates from the early twentieth century. It is linked to the ideas of the Scientific Management movement (championed by Taylor) and Administration movement (encouraged by Fayol).

The administrative tradition is still the basis of much HRM in Asia, especially in South and East Asia. In East Asia, after the Sino-Japanese War and Pacific War of 1937–1945, there was a need to gain and retain employees as a result of the severe labour shortages caused by wartime casualties. This developed into the 'iron rice bowl' of China and 'salaryman' employment environment of Japan and the Korean variant.

1.3.2.3 Negotiating tradition

A strong tradition of negotiating can also be identified in people management. This was the personnel department's involvement in negotiations with workers on both a daily and periodic basis, and individually and collectively. In the UK this aspect of personnel work became especially important from the Second World War onwards. This spread from traditional areas of production and manufacturing to other spheres, such as the public sector.

This form of people management tradition is found in Asian countries such as Korea and Japan. Here strong trade union movements challenge employers on a regular basis as well as during the *shunto* annual pay bargaining sessions.

1.3.2.4 HR development tradition

This tradition of people management is of more recent emergence, from the 1960s and 1970s and especially the 1980s, when it became widespread in the West. The HRM means of managing people has emerged in South East Asia – particularly in Singapore and Hong Kong. This perspective argues that employees need to be seen as a strategic resource of the business. Profitability and success are closely related to the way in which an organisation manages its HR. It propounded that, in the past, management have been too concerned with investments in technology, marketing, and so on, while neglecting the 'human' contribution to a company's strategy. It was argued that PM staff were not employed as reactive 'glorified social workers' or 'rubbing rags' (mediators) between management and employees. Rather, HRM managers were now 'key players' in the business.

In Japan, in the late 1940s, there was a great shortage of labour due to loss of life in the war. HR managers tried hard to find and keep employees and put substantial efforts into training and developing their HR. Major employers offered 'lifetime' employment guarantees to encourage staff to stay and to protect the investment made in HR development.

The crucial point is that there are varied traditions in HRM, and the contexts in which it operates. This influence of the traditions persists to a greater or lesser extent. These traditions also partly help shape the way in which HRM is integrated, or not, into organisations.

1.4 Rhetoric and reality in HRM

When managers are asked 'what is your organisation's greatest asset' they can usually be relied upon to answer in unison: 'our people'. Yet, this platitude is often simply not borne out in reality by anecdotal evidence or research. It is sometimes asserted that HRM has little (or even no) role an organisation and that line managers should do their own HRM. Or, even worse, HRM 'interferes' and actually prevents managers from doing what they want to do, how they want to and when they want to. After all, this line often continues, HRM does not 'add value' to the business (especially not in easily quantifiable and so-called 'hard' terms) in the manner of, perhaps, some other managerial functions. This sort of view is indicated by the decidedly non-politically correct term used previously to describe PM's role – as a 'handmaiden', to serve and service other functions, from which it was 'downstream'. HRM implemented business decisions, it did not help make them, let alone develop strategy. The implication was that HRM was subsequently 'less important' than other functional areas.

In much of Asia the HRM roles are held by non-specialists who will move into other functions at various times in their careers. In Japan a period of service in HRM is part of the career path of most managers. In China senior HRM posts are often held by retired military officers who are thought to know about managing people – and who often have connections (*guanxi*) with influential officials. In Pakistan HRM positions are dominated by ex-military and former trade union officials. Trained and qualified HRM specialists are rare in Asia.

One view stemming from this situation is: why should we bother to study HRM? Sometimes such a view is reinforced as the area is perceived as 'soft' or 'woolly', and not 'hard' or 'clear', without 'real' numbers and lacking single, simple, universal truths, verities and providing answers that only need to be learnt by rote. Answers that could be learned by rote would allow HRM issues to be dealt with successfully from then on, almost on 'automatic pilot', irrespective of the business sector, time or location. This search for such a corpus of 'one best way' practices to manage people is not new. For instance, we need only to think back to the ideas and practices of Frederick Taylor and Henry Ford and the whole Scientific Management movement, whose very label clearly indicates its views on managing, including people management.

Similar ideas became popular in academia, particularly from the 1950s. Asians (and others) observed the success of the US forces in the Second World War and assumed that the expertise in logistics and production techniques, which gave crucial advantage to the US, could be emulated and applied in Asia. There seemed to be a 'best' or only effective way of working, so if this could be discovered and copied it would be successful everywhere. This became part of convergence theory, and this area has become more recently revitalised in the guise of powerful potential role models, such as Japanese management practices and corporations (with ideas of the 'Japanisation' of businesses) in the 1980s, and now, more recently, the area of globalisation. However, this universalistic 'best practice' drive remains unfulfilled, with many caveats and 'ifs', 'buts' and 'maybes' to cloud the issue and any response or prescription in the area of HRM. We will return to this topic later.

Think About/Question 1.4

Why should we bother to study HRM?

Text Box 1.1

Is HRM important or not?

Read relevant reports in *The Financial Times* on this, such as Donkin (2007), Johnson (2008) and Stern (2009).

The position concerning the 'vagueness' of HRM, and so its 'less useful' role, can be countered at several levels. First, numbers do occur in HRM, at macro and external levels, as well as micro and internal levels. These include unemployment, inflation, productivity, labour turnover, labour costs, pay rates, and so on. People cost money and valuable people cost a lot of money. While these figures can be questioned in terms of their construction, collation and collection, this is the case with all 'numbers'. Indeed, some aspects of the above views about the 'robustness' of some areas of management are more difficult to sustain in the aftermath of debacles, such as Enron, WorldCom and others, where it turns out that 'numbers' actually meant very little. We need only to recall Disraeli's famous maxim that there are 'lies, damn lies and statistics' to see this problem.

Second, we only have to look at areas such as those in the case studies in Appendix 3 to see many critical HRM forces in action. This ranges from labour market (LM) issues to skills, and so on. In short, organisational changes here are tightly bounded and constrained by HRM issues.

Third, the style of much management has been changing. Indeed, the hierarchical 'command and control' approaches to managing are seen by many, at least in the West, as less appropriate when compared to the benefits of discretion, self-direction and teamwork in workforces, especially if engaged in high added-value activities. This is linked to areas such as 'responsible autonomy' and empowerment and builds on earlier ideas in Scandinavia, such as at Volvo. These ideas are less common in Asia where, in most organisations, bosses are expected to command and subordinates are expected to obey. However, as jobs in parts of Asia move into more 'knowledge' and 'expert' bases, the retention of 'command and control' becomes less easy to justify. Of course, some types of employment, such as those in extractive processes and mass production, still regularly use this sort of directive managing.

Fourth, it is 'the people' that are the organisation. No organisation can exist without people. People make money, technology and physical assets work; they generate innovation, give a distinctive edge in the marketplace and provide service. How people are resourced, rewarded and developed ensures that organisations have these skills and use them effectively. In particular, one only needs to recall all the debate about 'knowledge management' and the 'knowledge-based economy' to see the relevance of HRM. In the West, companies are coming to depend less on the ownership of physical assets and resources than on their ability to select, pay, train and manage HR. Therefore, the decline in the uniqueness of physical assets may actually give quality HR more outside employment opportunities. Furthermore, people, unlike other resources, can (in theory) walk out at any time they choose, taking their talent, skills and knowledge with them. Asian employment markets have become more competitive and people realise that if they are not at the front of the pack (in terms of education, pay and promotion) others will be ahead of them for all of their work life. Hence, the young Asian with skills, qualifications or networks that are in demand will make the most of these facilities as quickly as possible, and any deferred reward offered – such as 'be patient and stay with us and we will look after you later' – is no longer as attractive as it might have been to earlier generations. The impact of this on HRM practices and ideas in areas such as rewards and development (i.e. long-term investments) are obvious.

Fifth, managing people is not easy. HRM is not a 'science'; rather, it is an 'art'; it involves choices and judgement. Making the right choices in HR and HRM is important for how organisations perform.

Sixth, society and culture differ between continents, countries and even organisations within them. HRM and business has to be sensitive to this (see the examples in the rest of the chapters). As a result, HRM is a challenging, difficult and interesting part of management.

1.5 Tensions in HRM

From the start, it is important to outline the tensions in the field of HRM. These tensions are between the desire for universal answers and the more contingent reality of much practice, which run through all the subsequent areas of HRM and the chapters in this book.

1.5.1 Universal versus contingent perspectives

The universal view of management believes that we can search out and focus on a single approach to dealing with each of the major policies and issues that can be shown (often via a range of proxy variables) to have the 'best' record for practice. For instance, the notion of 'benchmarking' (checking what others do, then emulating the 'best' of them) fits in here. This claims that it is possible both to identify the most effective way to manage, as in HRM, and that these practices are also readily transferable to other organisations and other environments. While not a new issue, ideas such as globalisation have given such universalistic views renewed vigour. It is an attractive prognosis to consultants who are able to sell universalist solutions widely in the belief that standardised solutions to management problems exist.

An alternative view to this is the contingent perspective. This argues that methods and general approaches in management, and especially HRM, vary and are dependent on a range of factors. They are influenced by the specific circumstances and environments of the organisation and its environment. This includes not only size and sector, but also location, with its particular frameworks of institutions and culture. This latter view makes the production of a universalist 'one size fits all' HRM prescriptive prognosis (and HRM books) very difficult, even within one country.

The lack of a simple, universal 'one best way' to manage HR may be somewhat difficult and unpalatable to some of the more naïve management gurus (and managers) who want to peddle or receive 'the answer'. This 'answer' can then be simply regurgitated. Yet, HRM deals not with inanimate objects but with people, who are complex social beings, making management of them messy and not conducive to standard 'answers', but rather a contingent range of perspectives. What may be 'best' at one time may not be 'best' on the next occasion, even in exactly the same context. When the context changes as well we see the chasm of contingency, a kaleidoscope of different possibilities, opening up before us. It is this uncertainty that often infuriates people and leads, in part, to HRM's 'bad press' especially among those who seek simple verities and 'right' answers.

1.5.2 Integration versus independence views

A second tension concerns the area of HRM policies and practices in terms of their integration as a package versus their stand-alone, free-standing, nature. For some commentators, it is not just that HRM practices are standardised and centralised; they argue that there is a need for HRM congruence and complementarity. This 'joined-up', integrated HRM can be in two dimensions: horizontal (with internal fit across the areas of

HRM) and vertical (with external fit between HRM with management of the organisation and broader business strategies and environment). This view is in stark contrast to the almost 'pick and mix' approach to HRM policies and practices found in many organisations. A 'pick and mix' approach is particularly useful and widespread in Asia with the selecting mainly from Western ideas of HRM, but also from well respected regional models, such as those of Japan and Singapore.

1.5.3 Simplicity versus complexity approaches

A further common thread is the tension between the opposing camps in HRM practice. On the one hand there is a common desire for simple, cheap practices that are usable and can be enforced. However, on the other hand, the drive and search to overcome possible limitations and biases in some HRM practices leads to ever more complex, costly methods, but which may in turn be less likely to be carried out. One problem is that such HRM practices may come to be increasingly seen as 'chores' and distracting, imposing extra paperwork, bureaucracy and costs on busy managers and employees. Also, if it seems that the practices were developed for a very different social and political environment then there is greater resistance to their use.

These tensions can be seen in Figure 1.1. These tensions again indicate that there may often be no 'right' answer to HRM questions.

Figure 1.1   **Tensions within HRM**

Universal		Contingent
Integration	Tensions	Independence
Simplicity		Complexity

1.6 A strategic role?

From the 1980s, in particular, came the rise of the term HRM and its replacement of PM in lexicons and jobs. Yet, PM and HRM are often used to refer to same set of issues and activities, and used interchangeably. However, it is worth recognising some suggested differences and how the area of people management is seen to have become more central to management. For some, HRM was simply 'old wine in new bottles'. For others, it was what 'good' PM should have been all along.

> **Think About/Question 1.5**
>
> What, if anything, do you think distinguishes HRM from PM?

For some commentators such distinctions could, and should, however roughly, be made. This can be seen in Table 1.1. We must, however, be aware that many models of HRM have been developed in the West, as can be seen in Figures 1.2 and 1.3. Nevertheless, more recently Asian models have also been developed, especially by Rowley and his colleagues (Rowley et al., 2004; 2007).

Table 1.1   PM and HRM compared

Dimension	PM	HRM
Implementation	Specialists	Line
Stance	Reactive	Proactive
Practices	Ad hoc	Integrated
Time scale	Short term	Long term
Importance to business	Marginal	Key
Level	Operational	Strategic

Figure 1.2   The Harvard framework for HRM

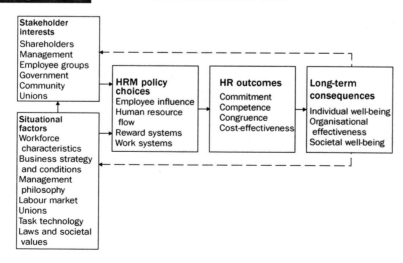

Source: Beer et al. (1984)

Figure 1.3 The HRM cycle

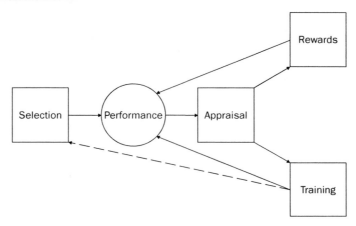

Source: Fombrun et al. (1984)

Thus, a key PM/HRM distinction revolves around the concepts of strategy, integration and implementation. This raises the following set of related questions.

- How strategically do organisations use the HRM function?
- How integrated are HRM policies and decisions with both key business decisions at the strategic level and with each other?
- Do line managers, rather than HR managers, play the major role in developing and implementing HRM?

Some research has gone beyond the proselytising of management gurus and examined the reality of attempts to develop HRM in practice. This has found that there has often been some take-up of HRM-type practices, but such findings are also tempered by the following evidence. First, many HRM experiments were often less than successful, such as Quality Circles (popularised by use in Japanese companies), performance-related pay (we will return to this later), and so on. Second, practices hailed as 'new' had actually often been in use for some time; their newness simply reflected re-labelling. Third, attempts to introduce change rarely occurred in a strategic and planned way, but rather in an incremental or ad hoc fashion. Fourth, there was resistance to change, and this was from not only employees, but also often from managers, who had a preference for previous working practices.

In sum, whilst there is concern to make HRM a key component of senior management decision making, in practice only a few organisations have been successful in strategically integrating HRM with their competitive strategy. Why might this be? Furthermore, why is there such huge variation in what HRM does and how it does it? The context of HRM is clearly important to this.

1.7 The context of HRM

HRM does not exist in a vacuum, but rather operates within constantly changing contexts. Within these contexts, trends and changes in contingent factors exert influence over aspects of people management, while HRM departments and managers vary. These contingent factors include historical influences, social norms, business strategy and competitive positions taken, environment, size of department, type of manager and organisation. In particular, for many in Asia HRM is a Western concept which does not fit very well within non-Western contexts.

1.7.1 Business strategy

One key variable in the practice of HRM is business strategy. Organisations have varied business strategies. We can see these at work in so-called life cycle models (such as Kochan and Barocci, 1985), with their 'start-up', 'growth', 'maturity' and 'decline' phases. Porter (1985) has 'cost reduction', 'quality enhancement' and 'innovation' as strategies. The earlier strategy models of 'defender' and 'prospector' (Miles and Snow, 1978) have been developed into 'internal' and 'market type' employment systems (Delery and Doty, 1996). Another version aligns HRM practices to strategic styles labelled 'products' and 'operations' and 'customers' (Grubman, 1998). Each of these types of strategy has radically different HRM implications.

1.7.2 Environments

Furthermore, the internal and external environments of organisations are critically important to HRM and its role and operation. These can be analysed within a PEST (political, economic, social, technological) category framework. Within this, the labour market (LM) is one of the most important contextual and contingent factors. The type and structure of LMs radically influences HRM. Therefore, it is worth spending some time exploring this factor in further detail.

1.7.2.1 Labour markets

A labour market may be viewed as 'the way work is distributed within a society' (Salamon, 2000:24). LMs can be formed on the basis of geography and skill. Generally, the higher the skill level, the greater the geographic scope of the LM. Unskilled HR are often recruited locally, while more skilled professional, technical and managerial posts can be resourced nationally and even internationally. However, such a neat and clear dichotomy is not always the case. For example, booming Asian economies regularly draw in unskilled but cheap labour from distant lands; these range from Indonesian construction workers in Malaysia to Indian accountants in Dubai.

According to the traditional model, a LM is a place where individuals freely exchange their labour in return for a wage so as to gain the goods they want and need. Such a model assumes that individuals are rational beings who calculate their optimum utility in terms of the hours and rates of pay they receive. Such views of the LM tend to see employees in a fairly neutral way. For example, wages are determined in relation to supply of, and demand for, labour. So, in 'tight' LMs (i.e. economic booms or in the aftermath of war or civil upheaval), when there is a shortage of needed skills or labour, employers have to offer higher wages. In times of 'slack' LMs (i.e. economic downturns or when too many un-needed skills have been produced by the education sector), when there is a surplus of skills and labour, employers can offer lower wages.

According to the human capital school of thought, employees improve their earnings by investing in marketable education and qualifications (i.e. they can increase their human capital) along with training that is general and transferable or in organisational-specific skills. This view assumes that there is a trade-off between skills and wages. Yet, to what extent is this always the case?

Think About/Question 1.6

How do such LM views explain wages not declining in recessions or pay inequalities based on factors such as gender or ethnicity?

The perspectives, described above, are criticised for not taking into account the way in which institutions shape and structure LMs according to the relative power and influence they can exert. Thus, the perspectives ignore the structural organisation of LMs. Some commentators argue that social and political factors structure LMs. Therefore, some employees find themselves in protected spheres and internal LMs (ILMs) whilst others are located in peripheral jobs and sectors and external LMs (ELMs). A typical organisation operating a strong ILM, with its commensurate HR flows, can be seen in Figure 1.4. In parts of Asia labour migration (rural to urban and poor to relatively rich countries) has meant that employers will often not have to raise wages but will change the source of labour in the ELM.

Figure 1.4 Organisational ILM

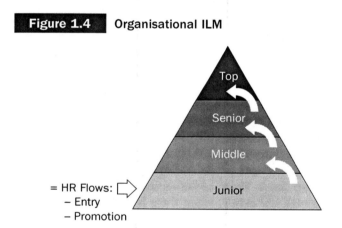

There are some key differences between ILMs and ELMs. Various characteristics of strong ILMs can be seen in Table 1.2.

Table 1.2 Characteristics of ILMs

HRM Area	Characteristics
External recruitment	Confined to junior positions: limited 'ports of entry'
Other vacancies	Filled internally: promotions/transfers
Jobs	Designed/arranged for career progression by experience in lower levels
Tenure	High
Training	Firm-specific (reinforces above)
Rewards	Structures rigid and unresponsive to ELM pressures

It has been argued that organisations distinguish between those employed in primary, ILMs, and those from secondary, ELMs, in the type and style of HRM used. Therefore, LMs affect HRM and how firms manage HR. For instance, those who belong to ELMs were more likely (but not necessarily) to be on precarious temporary work contracts and have inferior conditions and lower pay. In the ILM HR were shielded from the ELM, such as competition from other workers. Traditionally, some large organisations, such as businesses in Japan and Korea and in the public sector in South Asia, developed strong ILMs. These led to the creation in those organisations of HRM practices such as lifetime employment and seniority based rewards.

Think About/Question 1.7

What are the advantages and disadvantages of ILMs?

Organisations developed ILMs for a range of reasons. Some of these can be seen in Table 1.3.

Table 1.3   Advantages and disadvantages of ILMs

Advantages	Disadvantages
✓ Motivation boosted	✕ Lack of responsiveness
✓ Innovation – less job loss fear	✕ Increasingly expensive staff
✓ Costly training investment retained	✕ Recruitment at various times
✓ Inexpensive new workers	✕ Lack of new ideas

1.7.2.2 The flexible firm

Such notions of LMs as 'divided' or 'segmented' have been adapted in the ideas of flexibility and the so-called 'flexible firm' model (Atkinson, 1984). This argued that changes in product markets, technology, and so on, impacted on organisations, which then searched for ways to increase their flexibility in a variety of forms. In terms of HR, this meant reducing so-called 'rigidities' and enhancing seeming 'flexibilities' in the resourcing, use and rewarding of HR in a new, strategic fashion. This can be seen in Figure 1.5, with its main segments of types of employment, each with commensurate implications, issues and questions for the main areas of HRM: employee resourcing, employee rewards, employee development and employee relations.

There are various forms of flexibility resulting from structuring firms in such a manner. These are as follows:

- functional: moving between tasks, blurring of demarcations and multi-skilling;

- numerical: changing workforce size;

Figure 1.5   The flexible firm model

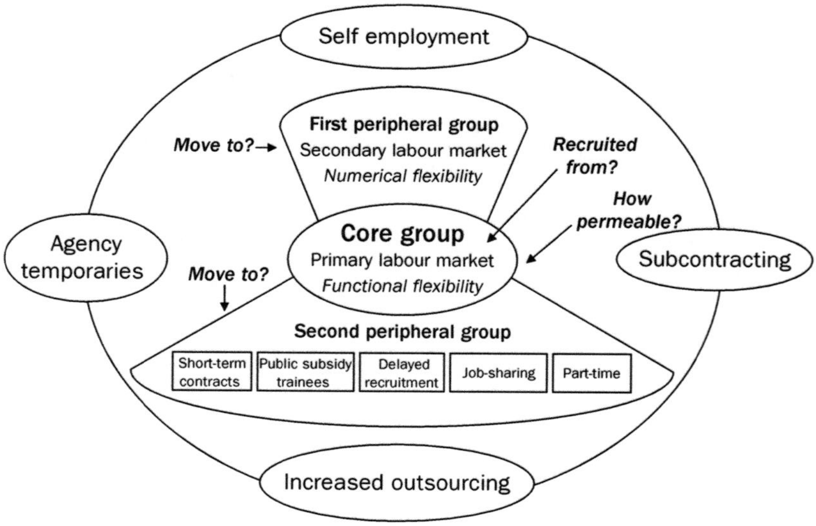

Source: Adapted from Atkinson (1984)

- financial: rewards, such as performance-related pay;
- temporal: adjusting employment over time, both within and between days.

Some, more macro, supportive evidence on the growth of such flexibility is available. Outsourcing to Asia, particularly to India and the Philippines, services such as medical typing or customer contact centres, is one way in which firms have shifted work from the core to the periphery. However, the flexible firm model has been criticised on several grounds.

> **Think About/Question 1.8**
> What might be some of problems with the flexible firm model?

The concept of the flexible firm has been attacked for many reasons. We will quickly note some of these, which include those in Table 1.4.

Some of these points can be seen in the example of information communications and technology services workers. These workers' conditions and importance do not support their commonly located periphery status. Likewise, some service sectors rely on peripheral workers for delivery and customer interface, in contrast to those workers in the core. Other examples may include outdoor entertainment and holiday centres, often reliant on part-timers to match peak demand but who also

Table 1.4 Criticisms of the flexible firm model

Area	Reasons
Empirical base	Manufacturing, yet many changes are in services
Newness	Long history, i.e. part-timers in services, subcontractors in textiles
Strategy	Changes often rather reactive and ad hoc
Contradictions	Practices/outcomes mutually exclusive, e.g. motivation, careers, training
Dichotomy	Some periphery jobs critical to organisations, while some in core are not
Contrast	Not all rigidities are 'bad' nor all flexibilities 'good'

©1341137865OO

come into close customer contact. We can see some of the problems in terms of training provision (we return to this in Chapter 4). Flexibility in terms of numerical 'hire and fire' can weaken not only training (as people may well leave after training or be seen as no longer worth investing in), but also motivation as well as innovation, particularly if new ideas are seen as risky or may lead to job loss. In contrast, the benefits of 'inflexibility' or job security are obvious to most employees.

1.7.3 HRM departments

A further variation is that HRM departments themselves vary greatly in size, structure and role depending on the size, structure and complexity of the organisation, as well as in their history. In larger organisations HRM activity may be supervised by a member of the board of directors or senior management group. The HRM director may have the support of several senior executives, each responsible for specialist functions, for example, training managers. Under this there may be a hierarchy of middle manager-level personnel professionals with clerical/administrative staff at lower levels.

In contrast, in smaller organisations there is much less scope for HRM specialisms and managers become generalists, taking responsibility for a wider range of functions. HRM may not have direct representation at board or senior management level. In the smallest organisations there may be no HRM specialists at all. Here HRM functions may be taken over by administrative staff, general managers or owner-managers.

It is rare for some Asian organisations to have an HRM representative on the board or in senior management as HR are not seen as crucial for success because the concept of human capital is rare. In those Asian countries with apparently 'endless' supplies of HR the role of HRM is not seen as being particularly important.

1.7.4 HRM managers

Another variation is in terms of the nature of HRM managers themselves. Here the classic framework developed by Tyson and Fell (1986) of types of 'people manager' retains its usefulness. This is reproduced in Table 1.5. This clearly indicates that even those managers with the same title, be it PM or HRM, may be radically different in what they do and what is expected.

Table 1.5	Types of HR manager

Type of HR manager	Aspects		
	Discretion	Planning horizons	Roles
'Clerk of the works'	Little	Short term	◆ Services junior line managers ◆ Provides administrative support ◆ Follows routines ◆ Looks for leadership from others
'Contracts manager'	Some, within limits	Medium term	◆ Services and advises middle managers ◆ Provides knowledge of systems and practice ◆ Follows and to some extent modifies systems ◆ Provides leadership within existing structures
'Architect'	High	Long term	◆ Consultant to senior managers ◆ Conceptualises, invents, solves problems ◆ Changes routines and systems as required ◆ Copes rapidly with change ◆ Leads and participates with senior management

Source: Adapted from Tyson and Fell (1986)

More recently, we have had the various ideas around 'Business Partnering' (CIPD, 2007) concerning the future of HRM based on segmentation of the function and its practitioners (see Ulrich, 1997; Ulrich and Brockband, 2001). This prescribes a four-fold HR role as seen in Figure 1.6. This comprises *strategic partner* (aligning HR and business strategy), *administrative expert* (re-engineering organisational processes), *employee champion* (listening and responding to people, displaying its US roots), and *change agent* (managing transformation and change). Some Western businesses state that they have followed the business partner model, albeit in some modified form.

In some parts of Asia most HRM is still very much in the personnel administration tradition with no partnering, employee champion or change agent roles. At best, there is a little of the administrative expert element within the function. Even within international organisations or

Figure 1.6 The business partner model

Strategic

Strategic partner

Change agent

Process ◄——— **Business Partner** ———► People

Administrative experts

Employee champions

Operational

Source: Adapted from Ulrich (1997)

MNCs the HRM function has almost no power due, in part, to this function invariably being the province of the local management while expatriate management dominate in what are seen as crucial functions, such as finance and technical management. In such situations HRM does take on a limited role as employee champion looking after the interests of the host country nationals (local employees and other citizens).

1.7.5 Flexible management for flexible firms

A further factor is that organisational positioning can lead to variation in HRM. First, in terms of organisational variation by competitive position and success, we can develop two models with radically different forms of HRM:

- Short-term, cost-cutting survival approach: here HRM may be downgraded. A 'clerk of works' (administrative support) mode prevails.
- Stronger position and can focus on long-term change: here HRM's position is more robust. HRM may be more likely to adopt an 'architect' mode.

Within this is the impact of the organisation's employment choices on HRM. Again, we can tease out two broad models:

- The 'macho management' type: this may be applied to periphery (secondary) LM jobs.
- A more sophisticated, consultative role: this may be applied to core (primary) LM jobs.

So there is much variability in HRM. There are wide differences between organisations in the way in which HRM activity is organised and delivered. Some of this may be as a result of organisational and employment variations, especially the demographic and educational circumstances of the country. Hence where labour is plentiful, unskilled and cheap (as in China and India) HRM is less important but where labour is in short supply, well educated and expensive (as in Singapore) HRM is treated more seriously.

1.8 Scope

In terms of coverage, the scope of this book includes the following, together with some of the consequent questions raised by these topics. Along with the final, concluding chapter, these form the sequential structure of the rest of the book. These, and the links, can be seen in Figure 1.7. This overview will also allow readers to see immediately what each chapter is about and allow them to make a decision to 'dip in' if, and where, they want to.

Figure 1.7 Overview and integration of HRM

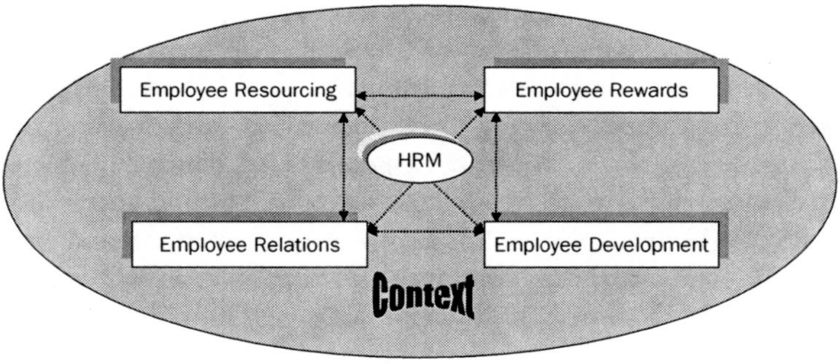

1.8.1 Employee resourcing

This initial phase of HRM starts with the area of HR planning. This is an obvious place to begin as it is concerned with the HR requirements of organisations and how their business strategies can be resourced. This involves forecasting the numbers and types of HR required and available from various sources and taking into account the impacts and developments on these. Next there is recruitment and selection. Given the HR plan, the necessary people need to be attracted and chosen by reliable, valid and cost-efficient methods, which are critical to organisational success.

1.8.2 Employee rewards

This includes the mix and types of reward required to attract, retain and gain the commitment of HR. What reward levels might be based upon is also important. There are numerous types of reward and systems. The issue of 'fairness' remains key in the West, whereas in parts of Asia having a steady source of basic income is crucial to many workers. Some Asian business owners (but not in Japan, South Korea, etc), senior managers and those in powerful positions receive a much higher share of the wealth created than would be considered 'fair' in the West – even in the high paying firms in the USA. The area of 'performance' in rewards has become more important, with greater belief that it has wider relevance across all employment sectors and countries. This view has taken root, despite tricky issues such as criteria and measurement in this type of reward system.

1.8.3 Employee development

There is the perennially important topic of learning and development. The requirement and evaluation of the level and type of training – and if provided 'on-the-job' or 'off-the-job', 'in-house' or 'brought-in' – remain key aspects of this subject. A comparative examination of training shows its provision and underpinning to be very varied, with implications for methods of competition, and so on. Once in place, management needs to try to discover how well HR are now actually working and to provide feedback on performance and indicate future directions and business objectives. This includes employee performance management and appraisal. This is another tricky area with well known problems and biases for management and organisations causing them to be very cautious even within national boundaries, while international and cross-cultural systems are even more challenging in their views of the worth of employee development.

1.8.4 Employee relations

This contentious and contested area forms the final substantive part of the book. The ideas of a 'system' and 'actors' (groups, parties) operating within a context and the frameworks and perspectives of unitarism and pluralism, individualism and collectivism, remain relevant. This also varies cross-nationally. Indeed, the post-1997 political environment, following the election of a New Labour government, has contributed to this in the UK and can be seen in the European Union and many of its directives with a desire for a social dimension to employment relations. In Asia the Financial Crisis, which also started in 1997, caused a re-examination of the power of the cliques of politicians, senior government officials and major employers who had pursued self-interested policies which harmed employees and the general population of many countries. This subject, of employee relations, includes the topic of employee involvement and its numerous practices and the range of benefits it is believed to bring to organisations. Yet, 'involvement' is an elastic concept allowing most people to support it, although its various forms have radically different implications, particularly between Asian and USA–European perspectives.

1.9 Conclusion

The area of people management in its various guises is not new. The topic retains its crucial importance to management; this can be either from a positive (to bring benefits) or negative (to avoid losses) stance. There may be some increasing recognition of the importance of HRM for the competitive success of many organisations. We can still note criticisms of its contribution to organisations. It is argued that HRM should be closely tied to the competitive strategy of the business and internally integrated between its policies. Yet, this co-ordinated strategic stance is often missing, especially in parts of Asia where HRM tends to operate in a more pragmatic and short-term orientation (with a few exceptions) along with ad hoc policies. It is argued that HRM specialists should 'give up' HRM and devolve management of people wholly to line management. Trends and developments in environmental contexts impact on HRM. An important factor is the LM, including flexibility, labour migration and international outsourcing. Yet, how does this impact on any 'strategic' role, especially in a context of organisational decentralisation, for HRM – especially in Asia? We will return to such topics at the end of the book.

All of the above have crucial impacts on ideas of universalism ('best practice') versus contingency in HRM. This is one of the common themes and tensions that run through the rest of the chapters in this book.

End-of-chapter tasks/questions
Based on the bank and airlines case studies in Appendix 3, using and applying information within this chapter

1. How will banks and airlines successfully use the same or different approaches to managing HR?

2. Will there be competitive advantage to using different methods of managing HR between domestic banks and international banks?

3. When an airline says it is 'customer focused' but treats staff badly so that morale is low is there likely to be a different impact on business success in each of the locations in the case study?

4. Discuss the ways in which HRM can make contributions to the business success of the bank in each separate location?

5. Does it make sense for the bank to use the same methods of managing people in each location? If there are to be changes dependent on the location, what methods should be changed and what would be the consequences of these changes?

6. In a rapidly changing aviation industry how can HRM make a contribution to business strategy?

7. What are the main similarities and differences of the ELMs for each airline?

8. What are the main similarities and differences in the ILM in each location in which the bank operates?

9. What are the factors which are important to a bank when it considers outsourcing in each location in which it operates?
10. What functions could an airline outsource? What are the consequences of outsourcing these functions?

References

Atkinson, J. (1984) 'Manpower strategies for the flexible organisation', *Personnel Management*, August: 28–31.

Beer, M., Spector, B., Lawrence, P., Quinn Mils, D. and Walton, R. (1984) *Managing Human Assets*. New York: Free Press.

Bolchover, D. (2009) 'The "war for talent" is first casualty of the crisis', *Financial Times*, 13 April, p.12.

Campbell, F. (2007) *Death of a Salaryman*. London: Chatto & Windus.

CIPD (2007) 'HR Business Partnering Fact Sheet', www.cipd.co.uk.

Delery, J. and Doty, H. (1996) 'Modes of theorizing in strategic HRM: Tests of universalistic, contingency and configurational performance predictions', *Academy of Management Journal*, 39(4): 802–835.

Donkin, R. (2007) 'Why HR people are too big for their boots', *Financial Times*, 20 September, p.11.

Fombrun, C., Tichy, N. and Devanna, M. (1984) *Strategic Human Resource Management*. New York: John Wiley.

Grubman, E.L. (1998) *The Talent Solution*. New York: McGraw-Hill.

Johnson, L. (2008) 'The truth about the HR department', *Financial Times*, 30 January, p.16.

Kochan, T. and Barocci, T. (1985) *Human Resource Management and Industrial Relations*. Boston: Little Brown.

Miles, R. and Snow, C. (1978) *Organizational Strategy, Structure and Process*. New York: McGraw-Hill.

Porter, M. (1985) *Competitive Advantage: Creating and Sustaining Superior Performance*. New York: Free Press.

Rowley, C. and Abdul Rahman, S. (2008) *The Changing Face of Management in South East Asia*. London: Routledge.

Rowley, C. and Cooke, F. (2010) *The Changing Face of Management in China*. London: Routledge.

Rowley, C. and Paik, Y. (2009) *The Changing Face of Korean Management*. London: Routledge.

Rowley, C. and Troung, Q. (2009) *The Changing Face of Vietnamese Management*. London: Routledge.

Rowley, C. and Yukongdi, V. (2009) *The Changing Face of Women Managers in Asia*. London: Routledge.

Rowley, C., Benson, J. and Warner, M. (2004) 'Towards an Asian model of HRM', *International Journal of HRM*, 15(4): 917–33.

Rowley, C., Zhu, Y. and Warner, M. (2007) 'HRM with Asian characteristics', *International Journal of HRM*, 18(5): 745–68.

Salamon, M. (2000) *Industrial Relations Theory and Practice*. London: Financial Times/Prentice Hall.

Skapinker, M. (2007) 'Merit should prevail over racial preference', *Financial Times*, 23 October, p.15.

Stern, S. (2009) 'Resources are scarce and HR must raise its game', *Financial Times*, 17 February, p.12.

Tyson, S. and Fell, A. (1986) *Evaluating the Personnel Function*. London: Hutchinson.

Ulrich, D. (1997) *Human Resource Champions: The Next Agenda for Adding Value and Delivering Results*. Boston, MA: Harvard Business School Press.

Ulrich, D, and Brockband, W. (2001) 'From players to partners: extending the HR playing field', *Human Resource Management*, 40(4): 293–307.

Employee resourcing

2.1 Introduction

We have so far looked at HRM in terms of its common aspects, broad coverage, development and links to strategy and tensions within it. This has given both an overview and framework for the rest of the book. We now shift our focus towards the key initial area in HRM – employee resourcing. How do organisations staff and make operational their business strategies? This concerns the utilisation of HR planning (HRP). A second key aspect of this is employee recruitment and selection. Once strategic and business plans are formulated, how are they 'resourced' with HR? In considering this, we will draw attention to the major differences in resourcing in Asia compared to Western models.

2.2 Overview

HRP is concerned with the acquisition, use, improvement and preservation of an organisation's employees to match its business plans. It attempts to reconcile HR 'demand' (forecast from extrapolating corporate plans) and 'supply' (forecast by working out the availability of HR and calculating likely shortfalls and surpluses). In short, HRP identifies the key characteristics and behaviour of the HR 'stock' and 'sources'. This identification includes the individual's length of service, general statistics on turnover, absenteeism, skills, and so on. Also, part of this HRP involves so-called 'environmental scanning'.

HRP aims to control costs by helping to anticipate, or correct, HR shortages or surpluses before they become unmanageable and expensive – as the maxim goes, to 'employ the right number of people with the right skills at the right time'. In parts of Asia, as a result of the prevalence of low added-value work, the emphasis has been on the 'right number' and 'right time' and the 'right skills' has often been ignored.

In the West, especially between the 1950s and 1980s, HRP was seen to have a crucial role, particularly in large organisations operating in stable operating environments. In the West today, however, even in the largest organisations HRP is sometimes seen as less useful, just as it has been viewed in small firms and in more volatile contexts. In parts of Asia small firms are an important part of the economy and some Asian work environments are volatile, so HRP is less practised – with damaging consequences for the population as well as for the resources of the Asian countries.

The idea of the so-called 'flexible firm' is one response to this volatility. As was outlined in the previous chapter, in this model the business has a stable 'core' of employees who are flexible functionally in terms of jobs and skills. This is surrounded by a 'periphery' of other workers who are flexible numerically in terms of their numbers and which can quickly and easily be expanded or reduced in size to reflect business requirements. This second group are seen to act as the 'shock absorbers' of the business, there to 'soak up' variations in demand, and so on. Another version operates between firms, whereby Asian small- and medium-sized enterprises (SMEs) are often treated as shock absorbers by governments and by larger organisations, although some SMEs have long-term, stable and close relationships with these organisations, as is common in Japan.

The HR resourcing of organisations is sometimes treated in a manner that has been labelled a 'downstream' or 'third-order' activity (by Purcell; see Thornhill et al., 2000: 98–100) – that is, an activity which follows in the wake of the business strategy and which HRM practitioners implement in a somewhat mechanical fashion. In other words, at times HR resourcing is not considered in strategic decisions until late on, or it is considered to be neither that important nor very difficult to achieve. Furthermore, some actions and decisions in the area of employee resourcing may not be internally integrated or 'joined up'. There may well be the management (even political) will to 'do something', but the implications are not always thought through. In parts of Asia, HR resourcing, except for the most senior or influential jobs, is definitely 'third order'.

We consider what might be the problems with this view that HR resourcing is not very important or not very difficult and what are the influences on resourcing an organisation with employees to deliver and fulfil its business strategy? We will explore these issues here and develop models to look more coherently at employee resourcing. We will see that in some rapidly modernising economies of Asia, HR are considered to be so freely available that the potential contribution of HRM is overlooked.

This neglect of the application of systematic HRM techniques is damaging to organisational success because, although HR may be plentiful, they are generally of the wrong type and are often selected on the basis of factors other than capability.

Following this first main section of the chapter we move on to the subsequent substantive part of employee resourcing – that is, recruitment and selection. This topic has been summarised by some as meeting HR requirements by defining vacancies, attracting applicants, assessing candidates and making the final decisions. The area is one of the key activities to achieve important HR and organisational outcomes in some HRM models. We will see that in parts of Asia, HR resourcing is sometimes handled very differently from Western standard methods.

Once the HR plan has been developed, how is it to be implemented? This can be achieved by using a wide variety of quick and simple to long and complex recruitment and selection techniques. Yet, why should organisations invest in sophisticated, but often costly, recruitment and selection? Indeed, there is evidence that some organisations often fail to take this process seriously, while others believe that it is crucial to future success. In parts of Asia some organisations do not take recruitment and selection seriously nor use the processes effectively, as they prefer more non-objective and less systematic methods, as we will see.

While there are many recruitment and selection techniques, much research indicates that most organisations have often relied on the 'classic trio' of methods – application forms, references and interviews. This common use of the trio is despite evidence of problems with these methods in themselves, along with their poor reliability as predictors of job performance. There is also some interesting variability in the use of recruitment and selection methods between businesses across different countries in the West as well as in Asia.

Some of the implications of contemporary developments in employee resourcing in Asia can be seen in reports in the mass media, such as *The Financial Times*. For example, Nakamoto (2006), Lucas (2008) and Whipp (2008) cover some of these in relation to Japan, as does McGregor (2009) in relation to China.

2.3 HRP

HRP is seen as providing organisations with the possibility of reaching the ultimate goal of employing the 'correct' number of people with the requisite skills at the right time. In theory this sounds eminently desirable and achievable and not too difficult, only requiring HRM departments and managers simply to take into account relevant organisational plans and circumstances and then organise the commensurate HR and actions accordingly. We consider later how this might be achieved. We can see HRP issues in the example of China given in Text Box 2.1.

Text Box 2.1

HRP in China

Under the planned economy, China had a centrally established personnel planning system carried out at the government level, not that of the enterprise (Warner, 1992). Conceptually, under central planning the national economic system was run as a large enterprise. The central government set the rules regulating enterprise personnel activities and determined the staffing levels of Chinese enterprises. Each year the government calculated the employment quota and assigned it to SOEs and COEs via local labour bureaux. Production, sales, salary and welfare were all decided by the central government and the enterprises exercised none of the selection, payment or workforce size functions that are standard practice in Western enterprises (Zhu and Warner, 2005). The senior management and personnel departments did not have to worry about the number of employees as this had no financial implications. They implemented solely the quota assigned by the government. As Child (1994) noted, social and political discipline was used as an effective method for controlling the Chinese people. This approach to personnel management often resulted in a mismatch of skills with enterprise needs and meant that enterprises could not use their workforce in order to obtain a strategic or competitive advantage (Child, 1994; Chen, 1995; Warner, 2004). This created low morale for the professionally qualified, and for many years labour mobility remained virtually non-existent (Granick, 1991).

Since the economic reform, the responsibility for utilising the workforce has shifted from a centralised planning authority to forecasting and planning departments within enterprises (Zhu and Dowling, 1994). Enterprises have been asked to be responsible for their employees, including the number and types of employees, and issues of hiring, firing and pay. Enterprises have been given freedom to increase or reduce their workforce. Human resource planning still remains at a fairly low level within enterprises due to the shortage of sufficiently trained personnel and intervention from all levels of governments, although such intervention is now diminishing. Labour is increasingly viewed as a human resource that has strategic and financial implications (Benson and

Zhu, 1999) and labour costs have become a major part of operational costs that enterprises have to take great pains to control. New management strategies emphasising profits and competition have put controlling the workforce at the top of management's agenda and Chinese workers now constantly face the danger of being made redundant in the over-staffed SOEs.

Source: Shen (2007: 31)

2.4 Activities in HRP

Given the above, it can be seen that there are several main activities and stages in HRP. These include the following.

2.4.1 Forecasting demand for HR

HRP is just one element in corporate planning, and cannot be isolated from the organisational planning process as a whole. In order to put into effect the organisational strategic plan, a number of more detailed business plans need to be produced and reconciled with one another. These include, for example, the following:

- marketing plans, outlining which products will be offered and in what quantities;
- operations plans, specifying methods of production, distribution and development; and
- financial plans, detailing how activities will be funded.

HR plans specify the HR needed to execute these business plans. HRM managers need to integrate their HR plans with those of other departments if they are to operate strategically. A demand model is then constructed and data fed in to produce estimates of the required HR levels to accomplish the strategic and business plans.

2.4.2 Forecasting supply of HR

HR supply (from both existing and new sources) needs to be examined, calculated and forecast. This involves the use of a range of data and projections.

The data includes the source of supply (ILMs or ELMs) and skills, profiles, characteristics and behaviour of the required HR and projections of likely influences on this supply. This includes the following, as noted in Table 2.1.

2.4.3 Action and assessment

Following the exercises described above and the collection of relevant information, HR action plans need to be developed and implemented to reconcile HR demand and HR supply and resolve any expected discrepancies in order to produce a close fit of demand and supply. These HR action plans can involve recruitment targets, selection criteria, promotion policies, (re)training, redeployments, redundancies and retirements. An initial HR plan is monitored and evaluated. The achievement of goals is assessed, and changed to meet new conditions

Table 2.1 Data for HRP

External	Demographics	Growing or declining potential future workforce
	Work force characteristics	Skills and age profiles
	Labour market conditions	Recession or boom, skills surplus or shortages
	Location	Levels of labour, skills and competition available
Internal	Business plan	Type of strategy, from consolidation to innovation
	HR 'stock'	Absenteeism, promotion rates, career profiles, skills
	HR 'outflow'	Age profiles, turnover, retirements
	HR 'inflow'	Recruitment

| Figure 2.1 | Model of HRP |

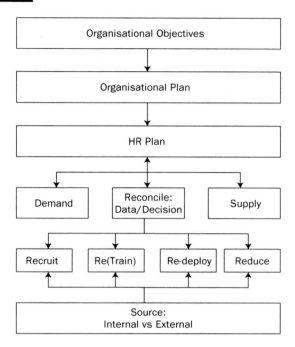

and recover from mismatches. The flow of HRP can be seen in the various versions of traditional models of HRP, as outlined in Figure 2.1.

By such means as the above it is argued that HRP will reduce the costs of the organisation by helping to anticipate and correct HR shortages or surpluses before they become unmanageable and expensive. Furthermore, such plans can provide a better basis for other areas of HRM, such as employee development, in order to make optimum use of HR and to improve employee morale and motivation. By using this planning activity, potential problems and future organisational requirements may be identified and appropriate action taken. However, as with most HRM responsibilities, HRP involves many activities and does not proceed in a linear fashion. Rather, it is an iterative process with feedback to ensure consistency, coherence and integration of the plan.

2.5 Methods and data in HRP

There is a range of possible methods and data that could be utilised in HRP; these are now outlined.

2.5.1 HR databases and analytical software

An initial starting point for HRP is to examine any corporate databases. Here production rates, salaries and financial files can be drawn upon, as well as the main HRM records containing basic facts in a structured format, records of performance appraisals and other reports. These sources can give profiles (such as length of service, skills and qualifications) by section of the existing workforce. A HR information system (HRIS) is most useful in HRP. Larger organisations can use specialist software and sophisticated methods from suppliers such as Oracle and SAP. In contrast, smaller organisations may meet most HRP needs through the use of general purpose analytical tools such as spreadsheets.

In some parts of Asia the use of an HRIS is rare and information technology (IT) applications are concerned with financial data, so the only HR aspect that IT systems will be concerned with is payroll. Personal files of staff are most likely to be held in paper formats, making production of a computerised database laborious.

2.5.2 Work study

One initial question will be: even if 'output' (manufacturing and services) requirements and details of existing HR are fairly certain, exactly how many, and what type of HR are actually needed to resource a business or HR plan? This is where work study can be used to compute standard times and standard work methods for different jobs (this area is returned to in the second part of this chapter). Sales and production forecasts can then be used as a basis for HR demand forecasting. These methods work for the analysis of existing operations and jobs but, obviously, are less useful when new operations and methods of production and services are involved with the uncertainties they bring.

In some organisations in Asia work study tends to be based on historical data rather than the production of standard data. Pieceworking (pay for the number of items produced) is common, with work periods extended to cope with new orders and reduction in working days/weeks if orders drop. In some organisations, particularly those that are government owned, productivity is not considered and numbers of employees are based solely on 'political' and historical factors – topics that will be discussed later.

2.5.3 Modelling techniques

Another critical area of HRP is where business output, and hence HR requirements, are variable over time. Here linear techniques and other statistical models can be used in forecasting and to investigate relationships between variables. These techniques can be used to project future demand based on previous HR levels and sales or relate employment to a variety of factors, such as how technology or market growth will affect employment. A simple example of this is time series analysis, which can be used to look at previous capacity and resourcing and predict future demand and therefore likely HR requirements, all things being equal. Examples here include organisations that face predictable daily business variations and flows (such as those in retailing or banking) or annual production or service demands (such as certain seasonal foods and products, or hotels where staffing will reflect occupancy rates).

Of course, time series modelling is based on beliefs that the future will follow the past. In reality, sudden unforeseen events can make such assumptions redundant, an example being the Hong Kong hotel and restaurant sectors in the wake of SARS with the collapse in demand and hence need for HR. A further example is the post-2008 global financial crisis, which undermined output and growth predictions, and hence HR requirements, in sectors from financial services and aviation to construction and manufacturing.

Asian organisations can analyse daily and weekly data but few, mainly in East Asia, have had the economic stability that aids modelling as their societies and economies are changing so rapidly. In South Asia, India experienced rapid growth, particularly in IT and outsourcing industries, so modelling is often based on data gleaned from other regions.

2.5.4 Key statistics

To assist in HRP various key statistics may be computed by organisations. These statistics are also sometimes used as barometers of the 'health' of the organisation and behavioural aspects of work in areas such as job satisfaction, morale and working conditions. These include the following types of data.

2.5.4.1 Labour turnover

Labour turnover is described by a variety of other terms, including wastage, attrition, 'quits', leaving, drop out, exiting, and so on. This is a key HR statistic, not least as labour turnover can be costly to many organisations. Nevertheless, turnover is not always problematic – for instance, in fast food retailing where the costs of recruitment and training are low. Some HRP outputs, such as those for redundancies, are radically affected by such rates of turnover. For instance, organisations with high rates of turnover face different choices if redundancies are required or training is being considered when compared to those organisations with low rates of turnover.

Importantly for HRP, a variety of reasons for turnover exist, some of which can be foreseen and hence planned for (such as retirements), although others may be less predictable (such as voluntary resignations or dismissals). Critically, labour turnover can be measured to provide an index for comparative reference and some basis for trends. The following shows a common method of calculating turnover.

$$\text{Labour turnover} = \frac{\text{Number of employees leaving in a year}}{\text{Average number employed in a year}} \times 100$$

A simple example of the labour turnover of tellers employed in an Indonesian bank illustrates this. Here the average number employed during the year is 1,000 and the number who left employment during the year was 100. This gives a turnover rate of 10 per cent:

$$\text{Turnover} = \frac{100}{1,000} \times 100 = 10\%$$

Labour turnover, however, is a complex and interactive phenomenon. Therefore, problems for management and organisations can result from reliance on using just simple labour turnover rates.

Think About/Question 2.2

What might be some of the problems with reliance on using just simple labour turnover rates?

These problems are varied. They include those noted in Table 2.2.

| Table 2.2 | Problems with labour turnover rates |

Problem	Characteristic
Confusing	Mixes up leaving and joining
Undifferentiated	Little insight into patterns/sub-stocks (grades, departments, skills, age, etc.) experiencing higher levels
Service	Length of service unclear: 50% turnover rate can be: • Half workforce replaced over the course of a year • 10% of workforce replaced five times each
Location	Unclear where leaving from: all from same job or many different jobs

2.5.4.2 Stability index

Other, more differentiated, data can be generated for use in HRP. These include the development of a stability index, which is used to counter possible distortion of the figures for turnover by short-service leavers. It is calculated as follows:

$$\text{Stability:} \ \frac{\text{Number of staff with more than one year's service}}{\text{Number of staff employed one year ago}} \times 100$$

We can continue to use our earlier example to illustrate this. It will be recalled that the Indonesian bank employed 1,000 tellers, but had a 10 per cent turnover rate. However, the number of tellers with one year's service or more was 950 and the number employed a year ago was 1,000. Hence, the bank actually had a stability index of 95 per cent, calculated as follows:

$$\text{Stability:} \ \frac{950}{1,000} \times 100 = 95\%$$

Taken together, an organisation's turnover and stability index can show if there is a narrower problem with just a few positions, or a wider problem and with many positions. This distinction is important and a critical factor in HRP, as well as HRM practices and decision making.

2.5.4.3 Fringe turnover index

A further statistic that may be used by organisations is a fringe turnover index. This calculates the percentage turnover of short-term workers.

Importantly, this distinguishes those who join and quit quickly from the overall turnover figure. This figure is calculated as follows:

$$\text{Fringe turnover:} \quad \frac{\text{Number of staff joining and leaving within one year}}{\text{Average number of staff during the year}} \times 100$$

Still using our earlier example to illustrate this, we can recall that the Indonesian bank employed 1,000 tellers, but had a 10 per cent turnover rate. However, the number of tellers joining and leaving within the year was 200. Hence, the bank actually had a fringe turnover rate of 20 per cent, calculated as follows:

$$\text{Fringe turnover:} \quad \frac{200}{1,000} \times 100 = 20\%$$

2.5.5 Early patterns of wastage

From the organisational examples given above, we can see that many new recruits leave quickly but once tellers have been with the bank for a year they are much less likely to leave. We will now discuss why this might occur. Statistics can show HRM when people are likely to leave. Research in this area has found 'phases' which form patterns – for example, the 'Three Stage Theory' of wastage. This is composed of the following: first, there is the *induction crisis*, where there is initial shock, false expectations and a lack of identity. This is followed by the *differential transit* phase, when people start to assess the organisation and whether they have place in it; and finally the *settled connection* stage results as 'survivors' become established employees with commitment to their employer.

It should be noted that this theory assumes employee choice. However, as will be seen later, many employees, as is the case in parts of Asia, have little choice in their source of employment, and employers and labour supply agents find a variety of means to prevent employees from leaving.

2.5.6 Absenteeism

Another useful statistic for organisations concerns absenteeism. This can be measured in several ways, which include measuring (a) the percentage of lost working days, (b) days lost per working year, and (c) average length of absence.

Absenteeism is often a serious problem for employers in the West, whereas in parts of Asia few employees, except those with permanent jobs in government service, are entitled to sick pay and great pressure is put on individuals by employers and fellow workers to attend work. However, there is also a tradition in parts of Asia, as a result of poor government services and culture, where family pressure is often applied for people to attend to personal matters (such as disputes with neighbours, family illness or to accompany a close relation who is travelling), which can result in employees being absent for extended periods.

2.6 Impacts on HRP

From the above it seems that HRP should be a most useful tool and resource to aid management and organisations. What then accounts for the common finding that HRP is of limited use in reality? An immediate problem is that organisations do not exist in a vacuum, nor are HR inanimate objects. Rather, variations in organisational size and changes and trends in environments (internal and external) all have influences. At the same time, humans are complex social beings. These factors impact on the assumptions upon which planning is based: unreliable, changeable and tenuous. This can be seen in the following examples of impacts on HRP.

2.6.1 The impact of organisation

HRP techniques can vary in their sophistication and in their use – for instance, between:

- large businesses, which traditionally used sophisticated HRP techniques – examples include international oil companies, public sector groups and commercial banks; and

- smaller and less complex organisations, which used simpler HRP techniques, or even ad hoc judgement – examples include maintenance companies and retail outlets.

Linked to organisation variables impacting on HRP is the operating environment and its level of stability. In the case of parts of Asia, the environment can be dynamic and unpredictable (see Studwell, 2002).

2.6.2 The impact of environment

Changes in the external environment have critical impacts on HRM, as we saw in Chapter 1. To minimise the problems from these external factors, organisations can monitor their environments in various ways, using a range of sources. These include surveys, trade association networks, news media and journals. HRP was valuable to large organisations operating in stable environments.

In this respect, a classic example was Indian retail banking before the 1990s when management and trade unions were able to prevent changes in technology and service standards, so maintaining a stable environment. HRP may be useful in such circumstances. For example, the armed forces, civil service, local government and education change slowly or in predictable ways and therefore place more reliance on HRP. In contrast, for organisations in environments that change more quickly (such as Chinese retail banking post-2000), the value of HRP, especially in its more detailed aspects, is more questionable and difficult.

Volatility in demand is not a problem per se for HRP, because these fluctuations may be somewhat predictable over time, as was noted earlier with the use of time series analysis. However, when customer demand is volatile and unpredictable, greater problems may arise for HRP. This issue of the unreliable nature of demand figures on which HR estimates are based can be difficult to manage.

Another problem is that some of the assumptions on which HRP is based turn out to be wrong. For example, the 1980s debate on the so-called 'demographic time bomb' predicted a shortfall in younger workers caused by falling birth rates and increasing educational participation (i.e. young people staying longer in school and higher education), with commensurate difficulty in finding HR for those sectors that normally recruit young people for their operations. This did not materialise. While this was an issue of concern for many countries again after 2000, it also has a longer lineage, such as in the UK in the late 1980s.

In some parts of Asia the main problem is the rapid increase in the number of young people seeking or soon to be seeking work (see, for example, Harry, 2007). In contrast, there is China's demographic 'time bomb' of an aging population resulting from its one-child policy since the 1970s with India's demographic 'time bomb' of a rapidly growing population of working-age adults. Both countries have a surplus of males in relation to females because of cultural preferences for male children. There is much concern in Japan and South Korea with falling birth rates and consequent declines in typical indigenous labour supplies. Options to address this could be both internal (for example, better utilisation of existing HR such as older adults) and external (for example, use of migrant workers). However, these strategies may face specific Asian cultural constraints, such as restrictive views on gender and ethnicity (see Rowley and Yukongdi, 2009).

However, in many Asian organisations, especially government-owned ones, and in environments where trade unions or political movements are strong, the number and type of staff employed may be based not on the need for a job but on the need to gain favour with influential factions. In most of South Asia a political party, when coming to power, will instruct the civil service or major employers to create jobs for its supporters and resistance to these demands is impossible to contemplate. Yet, the supporters of the previous regime rarely lose their jobs, so the organisation becomes over-staffed. However, few of those appointed are expected to actually work. In a similar way, strong trade unions will fix the numbers to be employed and will resist changes which could make the organisation more effective. For example, well into the 1990s Indian trade unions prevented the introduction of computers into state-owned banks. An extreme example of the impact of outside forces on recruitment is found in Lebanon, where jobs are reserved for members of particular religious groups or sects. Thus, in the Beirut Ports Authority, crane drivers are all of one sect, warehouse staff of another, and so on throughout the port.

2.6.3 A flexible response

Given the above factors, some organisations respond by abandoning detailed HRP in favour of a more flexible response (as we saw in Chapter 1 and the discussion of flexibility and the flexible firm model). Here organisations adopt a strategy of retaining a core labour force in permanent employment whilst having peripheral workers who can be recruited or laid off at short notice. Examples of these have come to light in the post-2008 global financial crisis, such as in the UK with BMW's Mini car factory in Oxford. The core itself can also have some flexibility, such as in the hours, days and weeks worked, and so on. Again, examples of these have appeared as a response to the impacts of the post-2008 financial crisis.

However, whilst pointing out some limitations to HRP, this flexible approach may not totally invalidate the HRP process. The HRP process can still be used to anticipate and prepare for events. It can also involve thinking critically about existing arrangements and performance. Thus, HRP can help to avoid some serious problems.

2.7 HRP in practice

We can see the impacts of failure to use HRP in a range of examples, as shown in the case studies in Appendix 3 and the text boxes below. The issues raised in the case studies provide salutary warnings about the consequences of ad hoc, short-term decisions and impacts on, and from, HR. These can critically undermine organisations and their business strategies.

Text Box 2.2

Globalisation and employment: Unfulfilled promise?

There appears to be a widely recognized view that globalization 'induces' economic growth and its overall gains are larger than its costs. However, the empirical evidence is not clear and is in fact rather thin. A recent review concludes that 'the attempts of a long literature looking at cross-country evidence have failed to provide a convincing answer' on the effect of trade on economic growth. Methodological problems remain unresolved, and the mechanism whereby economic openness is translated into economic growth is yet to be clarified (Hallak and Levinsohn, 2004; see also Winter, 2004). Despite this, the size of these effects is often exaggerated in debates (Freeman, 2003).

Not surprisingly, evidence on the effects of globalization on workers in terms of employment volume, wages, income inequality and poverty is inconclusive and often conflicting (for a recent overview, see Gunter and van der Hoeven, 2004; Rama, 2003a). For example, does globalization create more employment than it destroys? Does job creation exceed job destruction? A positive answer is conceivable if we can safely assume a positive correlation between globalization and economic growth. As mentioned, this assumption is hard to justify. In addition, theoretical models do not help either, as most economic models assume full employment and are only able to predict how the given volume of labour supply will be reallocated to correspond to trade adjustments (see Davidson and Matusz, 2004). Thus, the employment effects of globalization are largely empirical questions and, indeed, empirical evidence varies (Freeman, 2003; Klein, Schuh and Triest, 2003; Rama, 2003a).

The reallocation of employment in the process of economic integration implies changes in wages. While again the evidence is still inconclusive, the repeated finding is that skilled workers (or those with high educational attainments) are more likely to benefit from economic openness, while unskilled and older workers (and the less educated) are less likely to benefit from it (Arbache, Dickerson and Green, 2004; Rama, 2003b). Some other studies indicate that in developing countries the wage effects of openness could be negative in the short term but gradually become positive, presumably through economic growth (Majid, 2004). This study also notes that there is no guarantee that such long-term positive effects will benefit all workers.

To the extent that employment adjustments are associated with different wage outcomes for individual workers, wage/income inequality has attracted much interest and concern. In fact, there appears to be genuine public concern about income inequality, which is reflected in numerous surveys (see Luebker, 2004). Two sets of indicators have been developed to analyze developments in income inequality: global and national Gini coefficients. As for global Gini coefficients, which appear to reflect the idea of a 'global citizen' in a globalized world, both negative and positive developments have been reported depending on data sources and methods of income conversion (see Aisbett, 2005: Table 2). In the case of national Gini coefficients, an increasing wage equality trend is found for many industrialized and developing countries. It is noteworthy here that good news in income inequality often comes from the Asian region (Dollar and Kraay, 2004).

Wages are just one important element of employment conditions, and in the process of globalization, the adjustment of employment tends to involve changes in other aspects of employment conditions as well. For example, a study on the impact of trade reform in Morocco shows that some affected firms increased employment mostly by hiring low-paid temporary workers (Currie and Harrison, 1997). While this implies potential links between trade liberalization and job/employment status, it is plausible that such links can be applied to other aspects of employment conditions such as working time, work organization, work intensity and health and safety (see Vaughan-Whitehead, 2005). By examining this link, we can recognize more explicitly the adjustment costs that individual workers have to bear in the process of economic change.

Source: Lee and Wood (2007: 19–20)

Text Box 2.3

Factors influencing companies' recruitment and selection strategies in Vietnam

An understanding of companies' work environment is vital for analysing their R&S policies and practices. This section discusses in detail the opportunities and challenges that companies have encountered in recruiting and retaining their Vietnamese employees. In particular, the legislation regarding R&S in the state and foreign-invested sectors is discussed and the Vietnamese labour market is examined.

The legislative environment

R&S policies and procedures were introduced only after *Doi Moi*, when the government had loosened control in labour allocation. The 1987 Decision 217/HDBT stipulated that SOEs could either hire workers from locations recommended by the labour offices or request the office to recruit for them according to criteria set by the enterprises. Labour control by residence permit was abandoned; skilled workers could be hired from other locations if they could not be found, or found in sufficient number, in locations where the enterprise was situated. The enterprise could reject any recommended candidate if that person was not qualified or if the recruitment was not needed by the enterprise (Le, 1997; Nguyen and Tran, 1997). Overall, the state sector has displayed satisfaction with the newly found freedom in determining their R&S strategies.

In the foreign-invested sector, the labour legislation relating to R&S is marked by its instability. In the process of developing and defining, the legislation has been continuously changed since 1986, normally to legalise some de facto practices. Three of the most important legislative changes in the recruitment, employment and management of Vietnamese employees working for foreign firms were made in 1998, 1999 and 2002, respectively. These pieces of legislation marked the government's gradual handover of the autonomy in R&S activities to foreign-invested firms.

In 1998, Decree 85/1998/ND-CP1 stipulated that the state's Employees Supply Organisations (ESO) were in charge of the control and management of employees working in foreign-invested companies. ESOs' responsibilities included receiving applications from Vietnamese employees and documents requesting employment from foreign organisations; choosing and supplying Vietnamese employees to foreign organisations; and dealing with administrative formalities related to the management of Vietnamese employees working for foreign organisations. In this case, even though foreign-invested companies had the right to select suitable employees, the recruitment process and recruitment sources were totally dependent on the ESO. In July 1999, the Vietnamese government issued Decree 46/1999/ND-CP2, which allowed foreign-invested firms to directly recruit employees if the ESO were unable to meet the supply requirement within 30 days of the receipt of the requirement. In 2002, the Amendment to the Labour Code allowed MNCs to directly recruit Vietnamese staff without the assistance from ESO, provided that they submit to the labour department in the relevant localities a list of staff hired by them (Article 132). The amendment thus gave MNCs the complete right to recruit and select suitable candidates.

MNCs have been freed from many restrictions imposed on their R&S activities. The role of ESO has changed from managing to administrating and facilitating. However, the legislative environment still affects MNCs' recruitment function in two ways. First, the instability of legislation prevents companies from considering long-term recruitment strategies. Secondly, companies are faced with lots of different kinds of legislation and confusing directives from central, local, formal and informal sources. In practice, enterprises violate some law due to the pressure of business needs, which might be tolerated in some locations, but may be considered unacceptable in other locations, depending on the point of view of local authorities. That is to say, the R&S practices of MNCs in Vietnam need to be flexible and adaptive.

The unbalanced labour market

With a total population of 85.1 million, 89 per cent of which is under and in the working age (GSO, 2008), Vietnam offers an abundant source of labour forces. However, a noticeable aspect of this labour market is the excess of non-skilled and semi-skilled labour co-existing with the shortage of highly skilled labour. On the one hand, one of Vietnam's principal features that attracts foreign investors has been its large and inexpensive labour force. The low-skilled labour force demands a salary as low as USD 50 per month in the foreign-invested sector, which gives companies an opportunity to reduce their labour costs. On the other hand, companies display a demand for skilled labour. It is estimated that in 2005 the size of the labour force who graduated from universities accounted for only 5.28 per cent of the total labour force, although this is the highest figure since 1996 (MOLISA, 2006: 160).

Companies claim that the outputs of the educational system do not meet the required inputs of the companies. The study of management education was not a focus of colleges and universities. Until the early 1990s, management courses, such as business administration, marketing, human resources and others, which are popular in more developed countries, were virtually non-existent in Vietnam. In their surveys in the late 1990s and early 2000s, with leading MNCs in Vietnam, William Mercer repeatedly identified that management and interpersonal skills continue to be a weakness of Vietnamese employees, which is experienced by foreign-invested companies. Recruitment difficulties are acknowledged as one of the main reasons behind the rising and competitive compensation and benefit packages and fast-track promotion for high performers in the foreign-invested sector. Interestingly, while MNCs exhibit a continuous and rising need for talents, SOEs' labour retrenchment means that they require minimum new labour input, with the exception of some newly found and expanding industries such as banking and finance and information technologies.

In foreign-invested companies, high turnover rates of white-collar workers illustrate the seriousness of the retention issue and the importance of recruitment of new skilled staff. Companies typically report average annual turnover rates of 6–8 per cent, but for skilled staff, rates may go up to 25 per cent. As a consequence of the shortage of skills, poaching and job-hopping are popular. Furthermore, in recent years, companies have experienced greater volatility in their operations in Vietnam. The expansion of their businesses might be curbed unexpectedly by changes in government regulations regarding the operation of the industry, forcing the companies to slow down or temporarily cease production – such as the situation that motorbike producers faced in late 2001. The mixture of expansion and restriction makes workforce planning unpredictable and recruitment even more difficult.

A totally different picture has emerged in the state sector. Since *Doi Moi*, SOEs are required to be profitable. Enterprises that are not financially sustainable are likely to be merged with other companies, declared bankrupt and closed down. In order to achieve profitability, most SOEs were forced to significantly reduce the number of their employees. The problem of surplus labour has had an impact on the studied enterprises. SOE FMCG2, for example, is a large enterprise that has reduced their workforce substantially by 17.67 per cent during 1990–2007. In 1990, the firm had 1,523 employees, which reduced to 1,254 in 2007. This means the displacement of 269 employees. Similarly, SOE FMCG1 has reduced their workforce by 21.56 per cent, and SOE Auto4 by 23.42 per cent during the past 20 years.

Despite the substantial SOE labour force that has been restructured to date, case study evidence suggests that overstaffing, a legacy of the centrally planned system, is still evident in SOEs. An extreme example of overstaffing is evident in the comment of an HR manager. Reflecting upon the 12 accountants working in SOE Auto2, she was of the view that 'It was more than twice of what the company really needs'. Furthermore, overstaffing is a long-enduring problem for SOEs, as legal regulation imposes obligations on enterprises in their treatment of surplus workers. They are required to retrain existing ones for any new positions, allow employees to take extended leave, and put staff on reduced workload and pay and find or create suitable jobs for redundant workers (The 2002 Amendment to the Labour Code, Article 17). The government has also implemented a number of policies to assist surplus workers, such as financial incentives for enterprises who absorb surplus workers and a one-off payment to surplus workers who find other employment. Embedded in the socialist ideology for long, firms also believe that morally they are responsible for the well-being of their employees, which includes providing them with a continuous flow of jobs and income. Therefore, SOEs show great reluctance in hiring new labour, and instead opt for retraining their existing workforce to suit their new requirements. If surplus labour cannot meet the new labour requirements, it is a common practice to take surplus workers from other firms.

In the process of dramatic downsizing and equitisation, which began in the 1980s and late 1990s respectively, SOEs consistently display a very low level of new labour requirements and also a very low level of turnover rates. This finding seems to be controversial, given the generally low performance of the SOE firms and much less attractive salary package in SOEs. Employees remain with the state sector despite the fact that they often complain about the low salaries officially paid by the enterprises. Job openings in these firms also attract a large number of applicants. Top-level SOE employees benefit considerably from 'unofficial' income that is concealed; meanwhile, shop floor workers enjoy less demanding, less competitive and more permanent jobs. Furthermore, labour profiles in the state sector show that SOE employees tend to be older and less skilled; therefore, their mobility is more limited compared with that of the labour force in foreign invested sectors.

Source: Vo (2009: 41–47)

Once the issue of HR requirements via HRP of some form or other has been resolved, one implication may be the need for more HR. This is the topic of the second main part of this chapter.

2.8 Recruitment and selection

Recruitment is the process of contacting suitably qualified applicants (internal and external) for a vacant position and encouraging the suitable people to apply. Selection is the process of matching the attributes of candidates with the requirements of the job and then choosing the most appropriate applicants for the vacancies. Interestingly, in the early 1990s in the West, it was argued that the desire for a flexible, multi-skilled workforce in which team working was more prominent meant recruitment and selection was less about matching individual people to the fixed requirements of individual jobs at a single point in time and more about having candidates with a range of skills who were able and willing to work together. Consequently, immediate skills and background were less important relative to criteria such as willingness to learn, adaptability and ability to work in teams (Beaumont, 1993: 56). There are obvious implications in these ideas for employee resourcing which we will discuss later.

We saw in the earlier section of this chapter on HRP that job vacancies occur for a variety of reasons. These include internal growth within the organisation, as well as HR leaving their positions as a result of, for example, retirement, resignation, promotion, transfer and dismissal. How does an organisation go about filling any resultant demand with suitable HR? The case for systematic and effective procedures and methods seems to be incontrovertible given factors such as the:

- need to comply with laws, such as those concerning discrimination;

- mass of evidence demonstrating the costs of mistakes in recruitment;

- impact on the image and reputation of an organisation from having the 'wrong' recruits.

Legal intervention includes laws to both ban and institutionalise discrimination on the basis of gender, race and age. This include laws which impose positive discrimination, such as those that apply to the scheduled castes (*dalit* or lower castes) in India or *Bumiputras* (Malays and other 'sons of the soil') in Malaysia.

In parts of Asia recruitment has for a long time depended more on 'who you are' and 'who you know' rather than 'what you know' – an advantage which, as we saw, has only recently been identified in the West. Some Asian employers will seek candidates among relations or friends of existing staff or among other contacts. Therefore the most appropriate recruit might not be the one who has the most ability (see, for example, Weir and Hutchings, 2006).

However, if HRM is able to demonstrate that systematic recruitment and selection can contribute to organisational effectiveness, there will be a shift in the focus of selection. Lest the Western reader feels that selection based on ability is a Western innovation, it should be recalled that for over a thousand years the Chinese Empire's system for appointing senior officials was based on merit (passing examinations), while it was only in the mid-nineteenth century that ability started to replace social status as the primary method of making appointments in the British civil service and the army. The British army relied upon officers buying commissions until the greater effectiveness of the army of the East India Company, based on promotion by ability, was shown in the Crimean War and other conflicts.

2.9 Stages

There are several stages in the recruitment and selection process. This involves assessments of both:

- jobs (via job analysis or other factors); and
- candidates (via selection methods).

These phases and activities can be seen within a comprehensive recruitment procedure, as outlined diagrammatically in Figure 2.2.

Figure 2.2   A systematic approach to recruitment and selection

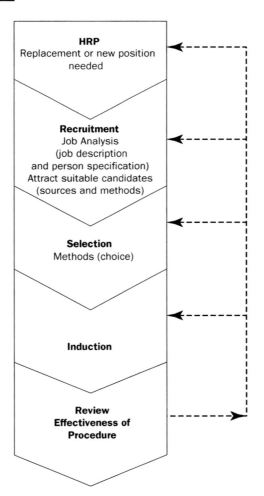

An initial question may be: what exactly is the post that needs to be filled and what does the job actually involve? After all, if we do not know this, how can we judge who might be the 'best' person to fill it? Thus, before recruitment begins, information on key elements of the job is needed. This involves job analysis and its output.

2.9.1 Job analysis

Job analysis is used to elicit what a particular job is about and what it actually involves.

Think About/Question 2.3

How would you discover what a specific job actually involves?

This can include a range of methods. Some of these are highlighted in Table 2.3.

Table 2.3 Methods of job analysis

Method	Characteristics
Work study	Examine each aspect of job
Questionnaires	Details of what job holder does
Interviews	As above
Work diaries	Detailing tasks completed each day
Critical incident reviews	Records kept
Observations	Supervisor's comments
Panels of experts	Ask what might be details of new jobs

2.9.1.1 Time and motion studies

One method of analysing jobs is work study, which includes 'time and motion' studies (as was noted in the first part of this chapter). The job analyst, who may be an insider (generalist or even specialist) or an outsider (consultant or contractor), studies selected employees 'at work', recording and measuring their activities over a sustained period of time. Each task is broken down into individual elements and the way in which these are carried out is examined microscopically. This is the basis for Scientific Management and Taylorism.

2.9.1.2 Questionnaires

Questionnaires are another method used in job analysis, and can be specifically designed or standard questionnaires bought in 'off the shelf'. The general approach is to discover the details of what the job holder actually does and the knowledge, skills and abilities the person is drawing upon to carry out the job. This is not as simple as it might seem at first sight as many facets of any job may easily be overlooked. One approach is to look at what is involved in the job in terms of the following:

- mental processes   –   planning, organising, decision making
- working methods   –   use of machines, tools, physical activity
- human relationships   –   with other employees and customers
- conditions   –   working hours, physical conditions
- other characteristics

For example, from the US, the Position Analysis Questionnaire seeks data on 194 job elements grouped into 27 dimensions and six categories, while the Management Position Description Questionnaire is a checklist of 208 items grouped into 15 sections related to concerns and responsibilities. The Work Profiling System has three overlapping tests, each consisting of 300 to 400 items analysed by computer to give a job description and profile of the 'ideal' recruit. However, as in much of HRM, there is need for a trade-off as these methods can be very time-consuming and expensive.

2.9.1.3 Interviews

Another method uses interviews, which have the same purpose as questionnaires and are often used in conjunction with them. They may be used to check questionnaire results and to discover further information about the content, context and requirements of jobs. Interviews may be held not just with job holders, but also with supervisors, subordinates, colleagues and customers.

2.9.1.4 Work diaries

Other methods include the keeping of work diaries, with details of tasks completed each day. Similarly, there can be critical incident reviews, where such events are logged and later reviewed.

2.9.1.5 Expert panels

If a job is new and therefore does not exist to be analysed, there is no job holder to investigate. So, a panel of experts is asked what the key tasks and skills of the future job are likely to be. The use of experts (either experienced workers or members of management) to assess job requirements is the system used most regularly in parts of Asia.

2.9.2 Job description

Where job analysis is used, the key elements in a job are outlined. These elements may then be written up as a statement – a job description – setting out what is involved in a job. A job description does not actually describe the kind of person who might be able to do the job; it is needed to develop a person specification. The possible contents of a job description are varied; in the West they often include the following:

- basic details (title, grade, location)
- reporting lines (which other jobs the post holder is responsible to/for)
- main purpose of the job
- contacts
- major duties
- expected deliverables or outputs
- expertise to be applied
- working conditions
- general circumstances

In contrast, in some parts of Asia, such job descriptions as do exist are usually very limited in their content.

2.9.3 Person specification

The information in the job description can be used to produce a person specification. This document lists and defines the attributes, often classified as either 'essential' or 'desirable', of a person who might be effective and content in the job. The person attributes can be grouped into major categories. Two of the most well known grouping methods are those by Rodger and by Munro Fraser, and are listed in Table 2.4.

| Table 2.4 | Categories of personal attributes |

Category	Personal attributes
Rodger's 7-Point Plan	■ Physical make-up ■ Attainment ■ General intelligence ■ Special aptitude ■ Interests ■ Disposition ■ Circumstances
Munro Fraser's 5-Point Grading	■ Impact on others ■ Acquired knowledge or qualifications ■ Innate abilities ■ Motivation ■ Adjustment or emotional balance

In some parts of Asia, except within international organisations, person specifications are very general, and would probably be unacceptable in the West. For example, saying 'attractive, female aged 18 to 21' or 'strong, healthy male aged 21 to 25' would be considered discriminatory in the West.

In summary, organisations and managers aiming to resource HR in a systematic and standardised way should make efforts to:

- see the job and its requirements in all its dimensions
- compile personal attributes that are essential to effective performance
- be aware of other factors that will impact on selection (such as political influences)
- list attributes that might improve performance as a basis to distinguish candidates
- be aware of building in prejudices of 'suitable' candidates (i.e. race, gender, age, etc.)

2.10 Sources and methods of recruitment and selection

How do organisations recruit the HR they need? There are several sources, divided into two groups: internal and external (as we saw in Chapter 1 and the ideas around different types of LM).

2.10.1 Internal methods

Think About/Question 2.4

What types of internal recruitment methods are you familiar with?

There are many common methods. They include the following.

2.10.1.1 Job bidding

This involves using current HR. Awareness of employment opportunities can be made by job posting via memos, emails, computerised bulletins, newsletters, staff vacancy notices, etc. As we will see later, in some parts of Asia existing HR are seen as the main source for new recruits and often a work unit or department will be dominated by people from particular places, even places a long distance from the location. Hence, Javanese are prominent in the Indonesian civil service, even in remote islands; Goanese or Keralites dominate sectors of Indian banks, and people from interior provinces of China make up most of the workers in manufacturing plants in Guangdong.

2.10.1.2 Promotion

Current HR may also be used as part of a promotion system and succession planning to fill vacancies. This includes the idea of being 'groomed', as the 'natural heir', or 'crown prince'.

The above approaches involve employee transfers and are sometimes underpinned by a HR skills database, allowing identification of suitable existing talent. However, in parts of Asia the 'database' is actually a series of connections – what the Chinese call *'guanxi'*, the Arabs *'wasta'*, the Malays *'orang delam'*, the Japanese *'kon'*, the Koreans *'inmaek'* and the Vietnamese *'quan he'*. Of course, if we think this a purely Asian phenomenon we should recall that the West has similar versions of the support network, such as the English 'old school tie'.

2.10.1.3 Unsolicited applications

Unsolicited applications and speculative candidates are another source of recruits. This source is a feature of the recruitment process in parts of Asia. People desperately seeking work will try any means to follow up on the possibility of employment. The disruption to business activities resulting from trying to deal with countless applications reinforces the preference to rely on informal means of recruitment. Many thousands of candidates regularly apply for a few jobs with some employers. Mail services in much of Asia are not sufficiently reliable to be used by recruiters or candidates so personal visits are often necessary, in turn causing very large queues to form outside the premises of a potential employer.

2.10.1.4 Employee recommendations and contacts

To avoid applications by 'unknown' people, applications can be sought not by advertising but by letting it be known that certain vacancies are likely to arise. This is common in parts of Asia. Contacts will submit lists of candidates or will recommend specific individuals. Existing HR can encourage family, friends and contacts to apply for positions. This may even result in a payment from grateful employers. There are a variety of terms for such processes, including 'kith and kin', where jobs are seen as being handed down over generations within families. Western examples included Ford truck drivers in the UK.

One benefit of this process is that it may impose a form of 'quality control' check on new staff. Another benefit is to limit the need for the scope of checks (such as security vetting, etc.) for some jobs. However, one 'cost' of such a source is that the most suitable candidates might not be within the reach of the contacts. In addition, this process can replicate the characteristics of the existing workforce, and also therefore be discriminatory.

2.10.2 External methods

> Think About/Question 2.5
>
> What types of external recruitment methods are you familiar with?

There are numerous external methods of recruitment. They include the following.

2.10.2.1 Referrals

These are registers kept by organisations of members seeking employment. Such organisations include trade unions, professional bodies and political parties.

As we have seen, however, some political organisations in parts of Asia may impose recruits on employers. So such organisations are rarely approached in recruitment matters because it is expected that they will have unsuitable recruits. However, if an influential person in the employer's hierarchy wishes to build up 'credit' in their network (Chen, 2004), that person will suggest taking recruits from the political party, trade union, or even a Chinese clan group or an Indian caste.

2.10.2.2 Agencies

A variety of agencies may be considered for use in HR resourcing, and include central government provision of 'labour exchanges' or employment centres. Many countries have these but, because they may not be considered to be that effective, a range of private sector agencies have also arisen. These include outplacement consultants who provide help to enforced redundancies. Then there are selection consultants and temporary recruitment agencies, which can be used to reduce employer administration as they recruit and select for positions.

HR provision agencies (labour agents), which supply set numbers and types of HR, are popular in South West Asia, Malaysia and China, particularly in the construction, domestic service and mass production industries. This is often where the number rather than the quality of 'labour' is what the employer seeks.

For more senior positions another type of agency exists – the executive search consultant, or 'headhunter' as they are colloquially known. These organisations actively seek promising candidates through networks of similar senior managers and specialists. Headhunters are used for top jobs, particularly in India and China, where those with ability and connections are highly sought, but are less well established in countries such as Japan, where those in top jobs are reluctant to move employers, or Pakistan, where there is an established elite with such good connections that they do not need an intermediary to arrange an introduction to another top job.

The reputation of some Asian HR agencies is poor. When advertisements are placed with labour exchanges or HR suppliers the response is likely to be huge, creating much work for those seeking to fill posts. The HR suppliers often extract a fee from the candidates just to be placed on a register, and a higher fee if they are appointed to a job. Some countries, such as the Philippines, have legislated against candidates being required to pay a fee, but with little impact on the practice. Governments have used registration of agencies as a means of control, but malpractices are still widespread.

2.10.2.3 Educational institutions

Schools and universities with their career services can be used in HR resourcing as they can offer guidance and some testing. In some countries, such as South Korea and Japan, some employers have very close relationships with individual universities, departments and even individual faculties, and focus their attention and recruitment on specific sources. Such employers often fit their recruitment into the annual cycle of the completion of education.

2.10.2.4 Retirees

Retired workers can sometimes be considered as a possible source of recruits. In the past few years older workers in Singapore have become a focus of attention in the wake of publicity over the demographic 'time bomb' (which we noted earlier; see 2.6.2) with falling birth rates and increasing participation in education. This predicted a shortage of workers, particularly of younger people; so, with encouragement from the Singapore government, organisations have developed alternative HR resourcing strategies, including attracting and retaining those who would usually reach retirement age. In the remainder of Asia retirees are rarely sought unless they have retired from a role which had useful contacts, such as a senior civil service or military position, in which case they are offered a so-called 'golden parachute' (in Japanese *amakudari*, or 'descent from heaven') in a job where they can use connections with former colleagues or reap a reward for previous favours – a situation that is also found in the West.

2.10.2.5 Foreign workers

There is a long tradition of using this source of HR in various countries – for example, Turkish workers who were a source of HR in West Germany during the 1950s and 1960s. The former European colonial powers also made use of this source of worker, which included sending expatriates overseas to work and using specific nationalities in certain sectors/jobs and countries, such as Chinese laundry men, Indian rubber tappers, Malaysian and Sikh security guards in Hong Kong. Later these former colonial powers became the destination of labour. For example, Pakistanis moved to the UK to work in industrial mills while Bangladeshis moved to Europe to open 'Indian' restaurants.

This is a prevalent source of labour in parts of Asia, from the Indian construction workers in Dubai, the Myanmarese hotel workers in Thailand, the Bangladeshi petrol pump attendants, the Indonesian construction workers in Malaysia and widespread use of labour from the Philippines in several Asian countries. These workers provide flexibility (numerically) for their employer to cope with the peaks and troughs of workloads.

The employment of foreign workers raises many issues. These include those of a moral and ethical nature, such as exploiting poor workers who are forced to work in dangerous workplaces or who are mistreated financially and physically, as well as draining developing economies of skilled HR, particularly those in IT and health care.

2.10.2.6 E-recruitment

The use of the internet for recruitment purposes is a significant contemporary development in Europe and North America and has potential in India, China and South East Asia. This is in terms of both employers and candidates advertising on the web as well as through 'cyber agencies'. Hunting for new jobs is one of the most popular online activities, as companies increasingly use electronic recruiting methods. The advantages of this method are cheapness and speed. Examples of jobs portals to assist in this e-recruitment, including some based in Asia, are shown in Table 2.5.

Table 2.5　　Examples of e-recruitment sites

Western

www.moster.co.uk
A 'career network' (more than 24,000 UK jobs), easy to search for jobs, create a CV and set profiles for email notification of jobs that match your criteria. Has a career centre, ranging from discrimination to redundancy.

www.fish4jobs.co.uk
Simple – asks two basic questions: (1) What job? and (2) Where? It then delivers returns from 29,444 jobs listed. Individual channels, which include secretarial, marketing and construction, have trade tips, with a career centre, a 'life coach' and 'legal doctor' on hand to help.

www.workthing.com
Dominant in the public sector, education, media, charity and permanent IT positions, thanks to its links with the Guardian Media Group. After registration, you can set up a range of different profiles, add your CV for

employers to download, and save interesting vacancies. Extras include email notification of suitable jobs (daily or instantly), a salary checker and help on making an immediate impression.

www.i-resign.com
This originally was an entertaining guide to quitting your job, which has expanded to become a fully fledged jobs portal. Old favourites remain, including Quit Countdown tips, resignation letter templates and the latest Big Quitters, but with a link to workthing.com.

www.jobsite.co.uk
One of the UK's largest online agencies (e.g. 97,000 jobs advertised in one month) and with 35 industries covered. Along with the usual tools, you can create four different covering letters, how to write a CV and read the latest news on your sector.

www.planetrecruit.co.uk
The best option for agency-only jobs, which is all it deals with. No thrills and no extra content, but an impressive range of jobs is covered (100,000) with a fast search facility.

www.stepstone.co.uk
A large number of jobs – 62,000 in Europe and more in the US. Searching job categories follows the Yahoo model – clicking on a title brings up further options or search by job title. CV registration and tailored emails are available.

www.gis-a-job.com
High job total (85,000) with search engine by sectors.

www.jobs.ac.uk
Dominant for academic jobs. Allows a choice of types of job to receive regular direct postings.

Asian

www.4icj.com
Directory of top jobs, recruitment, employment and career sites in Asia.

www.classifiedpost.com.hk
South China Morning Post classified site; mostly jobs in Hong Kong, but some in China.

www.executiveaccess.com
Executive jobs in Asia.

www.expatriates.com/classifieds/china/jobs
A site for advice on working abroad with a classified jobs section as well as other adverts.

www.futurestep.com
A subsidiary of Korn Ferry, the executive search/headhunter firm.

http://jobchina.net
For bilingual candidates, especially for joint venture businesses and projects.

www.jobsabroad.com
Sections on China and other parts of Asia; mainly geared to teaching jobs.

www.jobsdb.com.hk
Chinese and Hong Kong headhunters mainly use this site.

www.jobstreet.com
One of the leading internet recruitment websites in the Asia-Pacific.

www.timesjobs.com
Linked to the widely circulated and popular Indian newspaper.

Major newspapers in the Asian region often put their classified adverts online and these can be accessed through the relevant website. As we note below, host country national and local employers rarely use advertisements, but international employers and recruitment agencies do tend to use this medium.

2.10.3 Advertising

Another method of recruiting involves advertising the position. A variety of media are available, from the more general to the more specific. This includes press, local and national television and radio, cinema and internet websites. Then there are posters, career exhibitions, conferences, brochures, videos and open days, which might be considered as methods of attracting recruits.

Advertisements placed in parts of Asia rarely provide much in the way of job information; the contents are likely to be limited to job title, a brief list of duties and the application process – which is usually to a PO box or an agent who will handle the response. Salary details and the identity of the ultimate employer are rarely included. The intermediaries can 'mislay' or divert applications so that the best candidates are not always presented to the employer. Standardised application forms are rare, so letters of application are presented in a wide variety of formats which can be difficult to consider in an objective manner and are not easily used by IT systems. Unsuccessful applicants are not usually contacted, partly to save costs but also to save face – it is considered better not to hear than to be rejected, and it also avoids having to discuss the reasons for rejection.

Think About/Question 2.6

What are the advantages and disadvantages of internal and external recruitment?

There are numerous methods of recruitment; each has its advantages and disadvantages. Some of these can be seen in Table 2.6. Most organisations follow a mixed strategy, although they differ substantially in their preference for internal and external recruitment. At one extreme are those that promote only from within. At the other extreme all posts are advertised externally, although existing employees may apply.

Table 2.6   Advantages and disadvantages of internal and external recruitment

	Internal	External
Advantages	■ Improve morale/motivation ■ Chain effect of promotion ■ Potential talent is not ignored ■ Person knows the organisation ■ Faster/less expensive ■ Reduces training costs ■ Better assessment of abilities	■ Larger applicant pool ■ New ideas/contacts ■ Access to clients/'secrets' ■ Reduces 'in-fighting' ■ Cheaper than training ■ Not depleting existing HR stock ■ Publicity/PR of growth
Disadvantages	■ Not always the best person ■ Over-promotion ■ Disruption from HR mobility ■ No new ideas and skills ■ 'In-fighting' for promotions ■ Favouritism ■ Morale of unsuccessful	■ Expensive ■ Unknown candidates ■ Select those who do not 'fit' ■ 'We did it this way' attitudes ■ Longer adjustment times ■ Internal candidate morale ■ Publicity/PR of leavers

We can see an example of recruitment in practice in Asia in Text Box 2.4. This applies across a range of organisational types.

Text Box 2.4

Recruitment strategies in Vietnam

This section discusses the recruitment policies and practices of the investigated SOEs and MNCs. In particular, it examines how these companies utilised internal and external recruitment channels. Internal recruitment channels consist of recruitment within the companies and recruitment through joint venture (JV) partners in cases where the studied firms are JVs with Vietnamese SOEs. External recruitment channels consist of direct recruitment from the external labour market, recruitment by employment agencies and recruitment through personal networks. Although all the studied companies indicate the use of both external and internal channels of recruitment, SOEs have a much greater tendency to recruit internally based on internal promotions within the organisation and personal recommendation, while MNCs rely more on the external labour market for their recruitment.

Recruitment in SOEs

Before *Doi Moi* in 1986, the concept of an external labour market did not exist, as employees were assigned to enterprises by the government, except for a small proportion of the labour force who chose to enter the private sector. The government guaranteed permanent employment and lifetime welfare coverage in SOEs. The recruitment, allocation to firms and dismissal of employees were all subject to the official approval of state personnel departments. If an employee wished to transfer to a new company against the wish of his/her current company, the company could hinder the transfer by refusing to release the individual's personnel file. A personnel file contains the employee's personal information such as educational level, professional and salary ranks, political status and work history. Therefore, without the file, the employee cannot be allocated in the new enterprise, and face the risk of being cut off from the state welfare system. Furthermore, geographical mobility was tightly controlled by a system of residence permits, which allowed persons to legally reside and work in one area only. Transferring to another job or locality also involved dealing with civil authorities who controlled residence registration and food supply allocation. The two management systems, one at company level (employees' personnel files) and one at national level (residence permits), almost virtually eliminated labour mobility across firms and geographic regions, creating a tightly closed labour market, and also constituted a form of social and political control (also see e.g. O'Connor, 1996).

However, these rules have been relaxed, and now SOEs justify their R&S decision based only on the quality of candidates. In practice, SOEs have a clear tendency to recruit internally based on internal promotions and personal recommendations. To a much lesser extent, they also give out advertisements in newspapers to attract more candidates.

Recruitment through personal networks

The benefits of recruitment through personal networks are widely accredited. For example, DeWitte (1989) argues that people who are referred by other employees are better and more realistically informed about the job and culture of the organisation than those who apply through other sources. What is special in Vietnam is the intensiveness of the recruitment by this method and the underlying power of the entangled web of personal relationships.

Vietnamese personal networks can be best described as similar to the Chinese 'guanxi', which is understood as a special kind of relationship characterised by implicit rules of obligation and reciprocity (Yeung and Tung, 1996). The four main elements of guanxi are trust, favour, dependence and adaptation (Wong, 1998), which often influence decision-making (Wong, 1997). In a manner similar to guanxi, Vietnamese personal networks influence much of the business conducted in Vietnam. Those who are in charge of R&S functions in Vietnam are normally under an incredible level of pressure directly from their social circles and indirectly from those who belong to the social circles of these persons. Visits are paid, phone calls are made and even money changes hands to ensure that certain persons are on the recruitment list. One of the most oft-cited reasons for failing the recruitment process is 'I do not have any connection with them', as one blue-collar interviewed employee in MNC Auto4 explained why he failed to be selected for MNC Auto1, which was his first choice of employer.

The influence of personal networks is strong, and companies are willing to take advantage of them. Many enterprises give priority to hiring their employees' immediate family members (parents, spouse, children) and relatives. It is not unusual to see up to three or four members of a family (husband, wife, son/daughter, siblings) working in the same company in Vietnam. Employment based on personal contacts often has beneficial effects for the management, since sponsors do not normally recommend low-quality people for fear of losing their own reputation. However, Verma and Zhiming (1995) assert that relations might affect the implementation of HRM policies such as job assignment, reward policies, disciplinary action and conflict management. In addition, the refusal of applicants with better qualifications, but without connections, will finally lead to a deterioration of the quality of the workforce. How far such personal networks can affect the fairness and the quality of R&S in SOEs is hard to determine. But the truth is that in Vietnam in general, and in the investigated companies in particular, this is widely accepted by both the recruited employees and the recruiters as part of the game. Although companies claim that they try to limit the negative effects of personal networks through a selection process, they acknowledge the fact that the vast majority, if not all, of their new recruits have a direct connection of some kind with the companies' management board or existing employees.

Internal transfer and promotion

SOEs give priority to internal labour sources when it comes to targeting prospective candidates to fill vacancies in the office. It is customary that vacancies are posted internally before any advertisement is made externally. Promoting blue-collar employees to a position in the office, as a long service bonus, is a norm in SOEs. Priority is given to those who have been working with the company for a longer time, with little consideration to their potential fit to the new job. The decision to access the internal labour market brings in a number of distinct advantages. It is cost effective, preserves organisational culture, promotes loyalty and motivates current employees (Lauterbach & Weisberg, 1994). New employees who enter the organisation via internal recruitment sources have more realistic expectations than employees recruited via external recruitment sources (Moser, 2005). Furthermore, reliance on the internal labour market is a solution for labour surplus in the state sector.

Advertisement

To a much lesser extent, SOEs also use newspapers to attract a wider pool of candidates for office positions by posting advertisements. In this case, a company's established name and reputation is the key to attracting job seekers to respond to an advertised position. 'Wanted' signboards posted at the front gate are also used to recruit blue-collar workers. Companies may post recruitment notices in certain areas, especially to attract candidates who live in the immediate neighbourhood. This practice can benefit the company in some ways, such as by minimising vandalism and theft by poor locals and establishing a good relationship with the neighbourhood. Notably, the automotive industry has a clear preference for recruiting men for blue-collar positions. Employers do not like hiring women for several reasons. One reason is the potential financial loss associated with childbearing, but employers also show gender stereotype thinking and a lack of recognition of women's skills. Although prohibited by labour laws and other regulations, recruitment advertisements frequently specify 'male candidates only'. In some SOEs, where the labour legislations are expected to be respected, this overt discrimination still exists.

Recruitment in MNCs

In the Vietnamese context, due to the constraints of the Vietnamese labour market, which is short of highly skilled labour, MNCs utilise all channels of recruitment and maintain a balance between internal and external labour markets. Recruitment through personal networks is also very popular in foreign-invested firms despite the fact that it has been criticised as being biased and subjective.

Internal transfer and promotion

It appears that, as in their SOE counterparts, MNCs give priority to internal labour sources when it comes to targeting prospective candidates to fill managerial vacancies. It is customary that vacancies are posted internally before any external advertisement is made. MNC FMCG1, for example, emphasises developing the internal labour market to the extent that they refuse to recruit externally for vacant positions in the factory. External recruitment is only available at the head office for more transferable skills such as in sales, marketing and financial posts. Reliance on the internal labour market, as in the case of MNC FMCG1, might well be caused by the limited nature of the Vietnamese labour market, which is unable to provide firms with the skills they need, and by the relative novelty of the industry and technology, which requires a certain amount of training time for new staff to reach an efficient level of operation. Therefore, big firms tend to grow their own managers.

Recruitment through joint venture partners

In the past, at the start of operations, foreign partners in a JV often relied on the Vietnamese partner to recruit employees (both blue-collar and white-collar ones) for the new establishment. Attracted by higher earnings in JVs and motivated by the need to downsizing their own workforce, the Vietnamese partners would simply transfer some of their own employees to the JVs. Interviewees alleged that sometimes this lot included relatives or friends of the Vietnamese officials who might not be qualified for the job. These persons were transplanted directly into the new organisation without going through any selection process. Two main problems relate to recruiting employees from the Vietnamese partners in the JVs: they often do not have the right skills – production and management alike – and they are deeply embedded in the social structure of SOEs. These employees are more likely to perceive local companies as referents and value them as benchmarks (see e.g. Björkman and Lu, 1997). Therefore, appointing persons from the local partner is likely to negatively impact on the practices of the JVs.

As per the experience of the investigated companies, breaking the working habit of the former SOE staff is more difficult than simply terminating their contracts and recruiting new staff in their place. MNC FMCG1, MNC FMCG2 and MNC FMCG3 have experienced the conversion into ownership status with the significant increase in the foreign partners' shares. These companies believed that the old staff were incapable of coping with the challenge of the new organisational structure, due to their deep embeddedness in the old system. A blunt strategy of making redundancies was applied. Three continuous redundancy processes were conducted in MNC FMCG1 in 1997, 1998 and 1999. Around 14 managers, together with nearly 250 blue-collar workers from the 'old days', were targeted. The result is, at present, only one manager and about 50 workers, who were much younger and whose performances were rated far better than their cohorts, remain with MNC FMCG1. Similarly, MNC FMCG2 and MNC FMCG3 have deliberately dismissed managerial staff members who were the input of the Vietnamese JV partners when the foreign partners bought the JVs outright.

Even though the direct transfer of personnel from the Vietnamese partners has been popular within JVs established in and before 1995, it has gradually declined ever since. It seems that MNCs in Vietnam have learned not to recruit the bulk of managers, professionals and blue-collar workers from the local JV partners. They are now very careful in selecting employees with the appropriate attitudes and capabilities, who are willing and able to perform in the expected manner. This issue is now often stressed by MNCs during JV negotiations. Both parties in the Joint Venture Contract agree upon a precise number of people from the Vietnamese partners – most commonly for top management positions as stipulated in the Foreign Investment Law. The rest of the JV employees can then be freshly recruited from other sources. In fact, companies have recruited and selected workers from the Vietnamese partners under the strict condition that successful applicants must fulfil certain criteria and undergo the same selection process as any external candidates.

Direct recruitment

MNCs invite applications by advertising in newspapers and magazines, attending job fairs and recruiting directly from graduates of educational institutions. The most popular source of directly recruiting white-collar employees is advertisements in newspapers, as it is the most effective way of reaching the wider and more dispersed target groups. However, companies have experienced problems in both attracting high-quality applicants and dealing with the large numbers of applications through newspaper advertisements, which makes the processing time-consuming and inefficient.

Another source of direct recruitment of white-collar employees is universities. Companies actively seek skilled candidates in universities by organising a wide range of activities such as establishing direct connections with local technical schools and universities, offering the chance of factory visits for students, holding campus recruitment activities, providing scholarships, sponsoring student competitions and activities, and so on. However, interestingly, companies that conduct such activities aim at the longer-term objective of promoting their image among potential job applicants instead of the shorter-term objective of having a regular intake of new graduates. In fact, none of the investigated companies recruit fresh graduates on a regular basis or give them any priority in the R&S process. The main concern expressed with regard to hiring graduates is the high turnover rate in this group.

Recruitment by employment agencies

As mentioned in 3.2.1 [see Text Box 2.3], before 1998, in theory, foreign-invested firms were required to send their requests for labour to the local ESO. In 1999, Decree 46/1999 ND-CP allowed foreign employers to directly recruit Vietnamese employees if the ESO were unable to meet the supply requirement within 30 days of the receipt of such a requirement. However, it did not solve the main problem: the inefficiency of the ESO. Companies have complained that the labour sources provided by the ESO were plentiful in quantity but poor in quality, were very slow and failed to meet any urgent needs.

Therefore, as far as the recruitment of white-collar employees is concerned, the normal practice was to perform a 'fake movement' – called so by the interviewed HR practitioners. Companies would inform the ESO of their needs and, at the same time, conduct their own recruitment. When the selection process would come to the end, companies would refuse the list provided by the ESO, which normally only arrived at this time, on the basis of 'unsuitability', and would legally register their selected employees. This practice was popular among foreign-invested companies, with or without the unofficial consent of the local ESO. Interviewed HR managers noted that at some locations the local ESO showed their tolerance of this practice, while others were stricter, in which case the companies would face troubles when registering new employees who were recruited from outside 'the formal channel'. This resulted in a small fine per case. However, if the incident was repeated, companies might be faced with the possibility of a labour inspection. To overcome this problem, the investigated companies developed a counterstrategy. In case of an urgent need, the companies came to a verbal agreement with their new recruits to show their official joining date in the labour contract one or two months later to legalise the recruitment process. In this way, the companies took over the ESO's recruiting function while still acknowledging their administrative functions.

Since late 2002, foreign-invested firms have been allowed to directly recruit Vietnamese staff without having to go through the ESO. Even though the use of the ESO in recruiting skilled labour is extremely limited, all of the investigated companies acknowledged that the local ESO are the main source of blue-collar worker recruitment, and may have contributed up to 95 per cent of their blue-collar workforce. This is an economic and diplomatic decision. On the one hand, the local labour markets, which are abundant in non-skilled or low-skilled labour, provide firms with more candidates than they are able to handle. Taking help from the ESO saves time, because they provide shorter lists of candidates. Companies claim that they could receive a list of thousands of candidates if they do not provide the ESO with a limit. For example, MNC FMCG1 had asked the local ESO for 150 candidates for 100 vacancies, while MNC FMCG3 had asked for up to 500–600 candidates for 150 vacancies. Recruiting local persons through the local ESO to fill shopfloor positions also saves time. Companies save commuting costs, as well as recruiting costs, when compared with other recruitment methods. On the other hand, by using the local labour force, which helps to reduce underemployment and unemployment rates, and thus pushing up the local economies, companies maintain a better relationship with local authorities that may turn out to be extremely useful in their operations.

Another type of recruitment process is through employment agencies such as non-state 'recruitment consultants' and 'executive search consultants', commonly known as 'headhunters' in the Vietnamese labour market. This is however practised only by big firms for recruiting managerial and skilled workers. It seems to be much more popular with non-Asian MNCs than with Asian ones. MNC FMCG1 and FMCG5, for example, widely use this channel. Long-term contracts are signed with several headhunters with corporate discount rates. But some Asian MNCs, such as MNC Auto2 and MNC FMCG4, claim that they have tried their services, but reckon that even though employment agencies present their candidates within the agreed time span, the quality of candidates is 'not much higher than the average of the market'. Thus, they decided that using them is not cost-effective.

Source: Vo (2009: 47–54)

2.11 Selection

Once the closing date for applications, or at set intervals if there are no specific closing dates, is reached the selection of candidates can begin. This involves deciding whether applicants are suitable and then selecting 'the best', ideally by comparing and evaluating them against the yardstick of the job's person specification – although we have seen that this often includes factors outside those in a formal person specification. The selection process may conclude with the deliberations of an appointing panel or committee, which reviews the information and reaches a judgement.

2.12 Methods

Think About/Question 2.7

What selection methods are you familiar with?

There are many selection methods, ranging from the short and simple to the longer and more complex.

2.12.1 Application forms

Although not often used in parts of Asia, application forms use standard questions to extract and record details of background, experience and personal data. This data is often simple, assessed subjectively and used to eliminate those applicants seen as unsuitable. There are many types of application form, varying in length and format. In those parts of Asia where letters of application are used more often than application forms, the lack of systematic presentation of data makes sifting much more haphazard than is the case where standard forms are used. An interesting aspect of this is the tendency of some organisations to request handwritten letters. This is seen in France, where graphology is considered to be a useful selection tool, although many non-French employers also judge candidates by the clarity and form of their handwriting.

2.12.2 References

References are requests for information about the candidate from past employers or staff of schools/colleges/universities with knowledge of the candidate's character, and are used in support of other methods.

References can be used to check the validity of statements made and to elicit additional information as well as to testify to the character or to offer professional opinions. In the West, legislation and employment case law has created an increasing 'duty of care' in providing references, with factual evidence and support needed for what is presented as an informed view of the candidate's capability. References in some parts of Asia are usually informal and are used to establish a network or connection between the candidate and employer. The referee has given a commitment that the candidate is reputable and if he or she fails to work as expected, the referee loses face and so will be expected to put pressure on the recommended candidate to work well for the employer.

2.12.3 Interviews

A range of types and size of interview format also exists. Interview methods used (and misused) in Asia vary. This revolves around how many candidates are interviewed in an hour (15 to 20 would not be unusual in some countries), how long candidates wait before interview (most will be asked to arrive at the start of the working day even if they will not be interviewed for many hours), and how often review panels later add candidates who were not selected by interviewing panels. The possible interview methods include the following.

2.12.3.1 Unstructured

This is a commonly used format for interviews. It gives freedom to explore issues in some detail and depth in a free-ranging manner. This type of interview also allows interviewers to explore higher-level skills, such as conceptual reasoning. The use of this format, however, can make comparisons between candidates difficult and can produce complaints of unfairness as a result of candidates being asked different questions.

Yet, unstructured interviews are the main means of selection in parts of Asia. These interviews are often of very short duration and are used to support prior decisions or inclinations. In some areas of Asia the main purpose of an interview, and the wait before meeting the interviewer, is to establish the candidate's role as a supplicant who will be privileged to work for the organisation. The employer rarely sets out to present an attractive image to enhance the recruitment process or to 'sell' the attractions of the job, aspects that may play a role in the West in tight labour markets or difficult to fill positions. Demonstrating the power in the relationship, rather than identifying capability, is the purpose of the interview. The candidate's education and employment history is cursorily checked, and relationships and networks (to other employees and to political, kinship or social groups) are confirmed. Name-dropping (especially of prestigious educational facilities, prominent employers and important individuals) is an important part of the interview for middle- and senior-level jobs. Exceptions to the demeaning nature of selection will be made for high-prestige candidates whose status is far above those conducting the interview. Candidates who appear to be unusual, or who do not conform to the expected submissive manner, are likely to be rejected. In China, for example, candidates with 'unlucky' names will not even be selected for interview.

However, when interviews and other selection methods are demeaning, it is unlikely that the selected candidates will be motivated to work at their best for the employer. This outcome might be acceptable for workers on the most basic tasks, but not so for higher added-value work. In the medium and long term it is likely to be more effective to remove the demeaning interviews (and those who enjoy exercising power) and select employees who will enjoy being productive for the organisation.

2.12.3.2 Structured

These interview formats ask standard sets of questions and record responses, thus allowing the production of comparative data between candidates. This structure and process will assist in the required 'discrimination' between candidates for the final selection choice.

Structured interviews are rare in many parts of Asia and are used mainly by international employers, in particular those from the US who are used to an employment environment in which selection decisions are a potential source of litigation by aggrieved interviewees. Most local employers will be reluctant to interview all candidates in a standard way and managers will ignore instructions from HRM departments and managers to use such methods.

2.12.3.3 Mixed

These interview formats allow certain questions to be asked of all candidates. Other questions are specific to the particular individual. This format is usual in Singapore and Hong Kong, especially for managerial and professional positions. This style of interview is also the format which will, increasingly, be used by international organisations as management adapt to local conditions.

2.12.3.4 Individual and panel

The interview format may involve just a single interviewer. Alternatively, a small team, commonly three to five interviewers, may be used, usually with a mix of HRM staff and staff with knowledge of the specific requirements of the job to be filled. Recruitment for government jobs in parts of Asia, if not filled through quotas, will often use panel interviews, with a further review by a committee who will not actually meet the candidates. Panels and review committees are intended to remove bias, but often they introduce further levels of bias and 'politics' to the decision making.

2.12.3.5 Group

The applicant may be interviewed alone, which is more usual in the West. Alternatively, a number of candidates may be assessed simultaneously, particularly if large numbers are being considered for lower-level jobs. Labourers and factory workers are usually selected in this way by some Asian employers and by HR agencies. The group interviews sometimes are little more than the HRM equivalent of strolling around a market examining the goods available on all the stalls.

2.12.3.6 Telephone, video conferencing and email instant messaging interviews

This format can be used as a 'screening' mechanism (see Torrington et al., 2002) to make initial decisions on whether to move to a more time-consuming or costly stage in the recruitment process. Remote interviews are especially useful when it will be difficult to meet face to face because of time or distance constraints.

Although distances in some parts of Asia are huge, the lack of reliable long-distance communications and the preference to make candidates show willingness to meet employers' requirements mean that telephone, video and instant messaging interviews are not often used. Some Asian employers are especially aware of the existence of 'professional candidates' who will substitute for the applicant, so employers in some countries make sure they identify the candidate accurately.

2.12.3.7 Conducting interviews

In terms of the conduct of interviews, potential employers and candidates need to be prepared, organised and on time (much of the following is just as relevant for performance management and appraisal interviews, see Chapter 4). The interview should be a two-way process: the candidate is also evaluating the organisation while the candidate is being evaluated. Furthermore, however difficult it may be for some managers, it is the applicant who should do most of the talking and this may require the development of active listening skills in the interviewer. In the West, techniques and skills in areas such as recording information during and at the end of each interview, and an awareness of the legal and ethical issues surrounding interviews, are required. As we have seen, in parts of Asia the interview is often not an opportunity for candidates to consider the employer so there is less of a two-way process and less pressure on interviewers to be organised, succinct and persuasive.

Some common perceptions, sequences, protocols and questions in respect of interviews can be noted and put into a pattern, as seen in Tables 2.7, 2.8 and 2.9. Despite the importance of interviews, readers may wish to reflect on how closely such a pattern has been followed in their experience. This experience could be as an interviewer or as an interviewee.

2.12.4 Limitations of the 'classic trio' resourcing methods

Even in the West, a long and consistent history of research has produced a list of problems with the 'classic trio' of employee resourcing methods. To recap, these three are: (a) application forms; (b) references (both of which present the 'best case' and are open to being 'economical with the truth'); and (c) interviews (with biases, subjectivity, etc.).

There has been a growth of businesses that check the truthfulness of CV content owing to lack of honesty on the part of candidates. Companies may hire screening specialists, such as The Risk Advisory Group, to weed out untruthful CVs, although data protection and privacy rights of individuals need to be observed. It can also be a complex process if international background checks are required. Employers should be open about the nature of any discrepancies in CVs and allow them to be explained.

There were some high-profile cases in Singapore in 2007 when individuals were imprisoned for falsifying CVs and qualifications. Singapore may believe in rigorously enforcing its laws while in some other Asian countries this is not always the case. Even in terms of basic information, there are occasions in some parts of Asia when, without any intention to deceive, incorrect information is nevertheless given with

Table 2.7 Guide to conducting interviews

Before the interview	At the interview	After the interview
Who will conduct it?	Logical pattern	How and when will all be notified?
Panel members available and can meet prior	Understanding of way to be conducted	Arrangements to pay expenses?
References before or after?	Examine motivation and interest of candidates	
Other activities precede or follow?	Assess how candidates likely to fit in	
How many candidates, how much time for each?		
Accommodation needed?		
Asked to wait for result or to be notified later?		
Information to candidates on job, interview process		
Who will receive candidates and have all been notified?		
Room adequate/no interruptions		
Suitable waiting area		

Table 2.8 Interview structure: a recommended pattern

Stage	Objectives	Activities
Opening	➤ Put at ease ➤ Develop rapport ➤ Set the scene	◆ Greet by name ◆ Introduce yourself ◆ Explain purpose of interview ◆ Outline how purpose will be achieved ◆ Obtain assent to outline
Middle	➤ Collect information ➤ Provide information	◆ Structure making sense/logic to candidate ◆ Listening ◆ Answering questions
Closing	➤ Close interview ➤ Confirm future action	◆ Summarise interview ◆ Check no more questions ◆ Indicate what happens next and when

Source: Adapted from Torrington et al. (2002)

Table 2.9 Use of questions and statements in interviewing

Type	Example	Characteristics	Uses	Not useful
Open	'Tell me about ...'	Encourage to talk	Exploring and gathering information on broad basis	If talkative or if discipline is required
Closed	'How old are you then?'	Narrow, to establish a point	Probing single specific points	Gaining data on broad basis or where not well informed
Probing	'What exactly happened next?'	Follows open questions to establish details	Establishing and checking information already known or arising from open questions	Exploring emotionally charged areas
Reflective	'You feel upset about ...'	Powerful, repeat back statement	Encouraging to continue talking about problems or exploring deeper	Checking information
Leading	'You are sorry now aren't you?'	Indicates answer looking for and expected	Gaining compliance or acceptance of view	Gaining information about what they think or feel
Hypothetical	'What would you do if ...?'	Posing a situation	Getting to think in broader terms about topic	Need time to give reasoned reply
Multiple		Several questions in one	None	Never

Table 2.9 Use of questions and statements in interviewing *(Cont'd)*

Type	Example	Characteristics	Uses	Not useful
Non-committals ('lubricators')	'Yes', 'Ahah'	Listening, encouraging to talk	Indicating you are listening and want them to continue	Keeping talkative to a particular point
Inhibitors	'I see', 'Oh!'	Sharp halt	Signalling enough	Normal situations or emotional or frank discussion
Comparison	'Would you prefer weekly or monthly ...?'	Realistic and relevant comparisons	Explore and reveal own needs, values, etc	Comparisons are unrealistic or irrelevant
Summaries	'What we seem to have decided so far ...'	Draws together main points of discussion	Avoiding discrepancies about points, etc Gaining commitment	If used prematurely

regard to dates of birth, family and given names, all of which can vary with the result that different documents for the same individual may appear to be contradictory.

Given the enduring popularity (and use of the technique elsewhere, as in performance management and appraisals), it is essential to be mindful of some of the common biases in interviews.

Think About/Question 2.8

What problems might arise with using interviews as a selection method?

There are many problems with interviews which revolve around the participants (interviewers and interviewees) themselves and the biases and effects that may result. Some of these problems can be seen in Table 2.10. One example of stereotyping and a common misconception that can influence selection is the belief that disabled job applicants will suffer higher levels of sickness absence than non-disabled people. In practice, the research and data does not support such a proposition. A similar issue arises with older workers, again not proven by the research.

Table 2.10 **Biases in interviews**

Type	Characteristics/impacts
Non-verbal behaviour	Significant impact
Speed	Decisions made very quickly (within first few minutes)
Primacy	First impressions and information assimilated early on
Order of information	Favourable information early/later very influential
Halo and horns	Generalisation from one 'outstanding' characteristic (good or bad)
Expectancy	Positive/negative expectations formed from application form
Self-fulfilling prophecy	Questions designed to confirm initial impressions
Stereotyping	Includes comparisons with ideal applicant; implicit personality theory as a substitute for seeking specific information of applicant; characteristics are typical of members of particular group

Table 2.10 Biases in interviews *(Cont'd)*

Type	Characteristics/impacts
Prototyping	Favour particular type of personality regardless of job-related factors
Contrast	Preceding applicants create context in which evaluation takes place
Negative information bias	Perceived negative points sought, given undue emphasis over more positive ones
Similar-to-me	Preference to those perceived as having similar background, history, personality
Personal liking	Whether or not personally like candidate
Information overload	Judgements formed on only a fraction of data
Fundamental attribution error	Actions caused by aspect of personality rather than simple response to events
Trait attribution	Past behaviour is good predictor of future behaviour (omits mediating influences and circumstances)
Temporal extension	Behaviour at interview is typical of general disposition

Source: Adapted from Hakel (1982) and Taylor (1998)

Given the above, perhaps greater use of other selection methods should be encouraged. However, while they may be useful additions to the selection process, there are drawbacks with some of these other employee resourcing techniques that managers need to be wary of. Despite the weaknesses of the 'classic trio', some of the other methods are even less reliable. Indeed, it is disappointing that in some parts of Asia such unreliable methods (which include unstructured letters, unstructured interviews and group interviews) are still used.

2.12.5 Employment tests

Some methods that are used in the selection process have been shown to be better predictors of job performance than the 'classic trio'. Employment tests seek to measure specific characteristics, abilities and behaviour of candidates. The benefits of these methods include the fact that the test results are numerical and statistical, so allowing direct comparison of candidates based on the same criteria and producing explicit and specific results – although they may need to be interpreted and analysed, particularly in the case of tests of personal attributes. These tests provide 'hard' data which can be evaluated for their predictive usefulness in later years (i.e. comparing predicted with actual performance). Several tests to assist in employee resourcing are available; they include the following.

2.12.5.1 Ability tests

These tests involve a range of simulations or events. Some are paper or computer screen tests of numerical or verbal reasoning and other abilities. There can be work scenarios and actual tasks, such as being given a piece of real or simulated work to complete or a team problem-solving exercise. In several Asian countries the military use such tests as part of the initial assessment of recruits. Asian airlines, such as Cathay Pacific, use aircraft simulators to test candidates, who already have some flying experience, for aircrew jobs.

2.12.5.2 Psychometric tests of occupational personality

Occupational personality tests attempt to determine if the candidate has the 'right' kind of 'personality' for a job. In the UK a survey in 2000 found that 54 per cent of companies from a broad sweep of industries said they used such tests (*The Financial Times*, 2001). In the West the use of psychological tests varies by job level. For example, while used for 20 per cent of manual positions, this figure rose to between 70 and 80 per cent for management posts and 90 per cent for graduate entry positions (Newell and Shackleton, 1994).

This type of test is still rare in parts of Asia, although some international and national firms produce and administer tests in Singapore, Malaysia, India and China.

2.12.5.3 Assessment centres

A more reliable selection method is the assessment centre with its battery of tests. These tests compare candidates' performance in simulated problems, with focused or behavioural event interviews which seek a deep understanding of candidates in relation to the role envisaged for them. There can be a range of tests; indeed the number of techniques used is an advantage. The use of several trained assessors is essential. The assessors enable the pooling of tests and assessors' results. Tests can include, for instance, 'in-basket' simulations where candidates are asked to process and take action on an accumulation of memos, reports and letters, or team exercises involving building a small tower or bridge. Others tests include leaderless group discussions when a group response to a question is required. Individual presentations may also be used in the exercise, as may assigned leadership tasks.

Major employers in the West use assessment centres as they are recognised as better predictors than the 'classic trio' and other selection methods. In parts of Asia only a limited number of military organisations and international organisations (such as banks and oil companies) use assessment centres on a regular basis.

Think About/Question 2.9

What might be some disadvantages with employment tests?

There are several drawbacks with tests. These can be seen in Table 2.11 and also below.

A classic piece of research carried out by Stagner in 1958 (reported in Jackson, 1996) provides a further warning against the use of personality tests, even when they are used in the same culture as that in which they were developed. In Stagner's research, some 68 managers completed a personality questionnaire. At the end, each manager was presented with a written profile summarising the main characteristics of their personalities. The managers then completed a further questionnaire asking how accurate they believed their profile to be. Some 50 per cent ranked their profile overall as being 'amazingly accurate' and a further 40 per cent as 'rather good'. However, the researchers had tricked the

Table 2.11   Disadvantages of tests

Disadvantage	Characteristics
Responses	Faked for 'desirable' scores (especially where same tests used/practised)
Temporary factors	Produce variable results, e.g. because of anxiety, illness, etc.
Ethnocentric	USA (white, middle class, male) based comparisons as 'norm' and reference
Meaningful	Accuracy (Stagner's research)

managers by giving them all the same faked personality profile to assess, instead of genuine summaries of their own personalities. This shows that tests can appear to be a great deal more accurate and meaningful than they actually are.

2.12.6 Problems with using employment tests in Asia

A major problem with using tests developed outside Asia is that the tests may have unforeseen cultural expectations with them, and so may be biased against groups in Asia. For example, in some Asian educational systems students are taught to remember the 'right' answer, whereas most Western ability tests ask those being tested to find the 'right' answer without guidance from a teacher.

The occupational personality tests developed in the West are also based on different cultures. These will, for example, assume that classic theories, such as Maslow's (1970) hierarchy of needs or Cattell's (1946) theories of personality are universal, whereas most societies have different views of personal needs and personality (see Smith and Bond, 1998; Shweder, 2003). The external norm groups used for comparison in ability and occupational personality are also different from those in the West and almost no test providers have yet developed suitable norm groups for Asia. One example of the norm group issue was an Asian bank that used UK-developed ability tests to examine candidates for teller jobs. The norm groups from the UK were based on secondary school leavers, whereas in much of Asia tellers are university graduates. The candidates tested therefore produced scores much higher than the UK norms and the advice from the testing firm was that the people had too much ability and would soon be bored in the teller jobs. In the event, however, the candidates made effective and long-serving tellers.

We can see an example of selection practice in Asia in Text Box 2.5. This is seen across a range of organisational types.

Text Box 2.5

Selection in Vietnam

Selection strategies

This section discusses the selection strategies of the investigated SOEs and MNCs. It is argued that the selection process of SOEs is simple, subject to personal agenda and has a low level of reliability and validity.

On the contrary, MNCs strongly adapt to the limitations, constraints and opportunities they face in the Vietnamese labour market. There is evidence of MNCs shortening the selection process to meet with the contingency nature of R&S in the Vietnamese market and diluting global selection criteria to respond to a scarcity of labour at the skilled end, and of skills and knowledge at the low-skilled end, of the labour market.

Selection in SOEs

The first step of the selection process is to establish a selection and interview panel. The structure of the panel is probably the first sign of changes in the selection process within the state sector. Back in the 1980s, the management of the Vietnamese SOEs was under the supervision of the four committees, consisting of the Communist Party representative(s), the board of directors, the trade union representative(s) and the youth union representative(s). Often the trade union representative was either the managing director or the deputy managing director, and was therefore seen as closely linked to management (Fahey, 1995). The selection panel often consisted of representatives of these four committees.

However, since *Doi Moi*, the situation has changed. The new structure of the panel is quite similar across firms and industries. To maintain standards of selection, a panel of at least three (it can be up to four or five) is established, including one representative of the personnel/HR department, one functional head and one member of the board of directors. The composition of the panel clearly shows the tendency towards a devolvement of responsibility to line management, which in general is a new practice in SOEs.

A typical, simple process for selecting white-collar and blue-collar workers consists of reading a written application to make the first cut, then conducting interviews and finally a probation period for the newly recruited employee. For blue-collar workers, a manual dexterity test is normally required. In some companies, applicants do not need to go through any interviews. Candidates are required to produce a medical certificate before they start working. An illustrative example of the simple selection process is given by SOE FMCG3. After the initial screening and shortlisting process, which is based on the job description, interviews are conducted by a board comprising an HR manager, senior line managers and a vice director or general director. After the interview stage, the HR department asks the selected candidate to submit a medical certificate as an evidence of being in a healthy state to do the job. The process ends when the candidate presents the medical certificate and the labour contract is signed. Probation period varies from three to six months, depending on the position. No case has been reported where the candidate failed the probation. Interviewed managers have revealed that the selection costs are minimal for both white-collar and blue-collar workers.

HR managers have revealed that SOEs rely highly on interviews as a selection method. Interview questions are to ascertain an applicant's qualities such as logical thinking, general business awareness and, more importantly, attitude. Interviews are unstructured and no scoring key is used. The use of interviews in SOEs is believed to possess inherent problems and is not sufficient to identify the best candidates. More valid and reliable selection methods are absent in SOEs, as an HR manager noted:

> Although we are aware of different selection methods, such as ability tests, psychometric tests, assessment centres and other advanced methods of assessment used in MNCs, we only need a very limited amount of labour input, thus economically it does not make sense to adopt a systematic and costly selection process.

The use of more sophisticated selection methods could be quite costly if the organisations do not have any appropriately trained staff (which is normally the case) and instead have to acquire professional help from outside. However, as most applicants would be transferring from other firms in the same General Corporation, HR managers can informally collect information about the candidates from his/her current and former employers and colleagues before the interviews.

Before the interview, a copy of the candidates' CVs is given to each member of the interview panel. The majority of HR managers have revealed that it is a common practice to have some informal discussion within the interview panel before the interviews, in which not only the candidates' qualifications, skills and abilities but also their relationship with their sponsors (who either work in the company or have connections with those in power in the company) are discussed. In many cases, the selection decision is made before the interview is ever conducted.

Furthermore, the selection criteria have not changed since the days of the centrally planned economy. In particular, the selection criteria for managerial appointments are still based on education, personality, self-confidence, work experience and good attitude. The strongest emphasis is placed on the applicants' educational qualifications. It is noted that managing directors, vice managing directors and, in some cases, senior managers are appointed directly by a higher authority, namely the General Corporation management or the relevant ministry. The selection criteria in these cases are not published and focus on political reliability, education qualifications, previous working performance and personal connections/links of the candidates within the power circles.

Selection in MNCs

A typical process for selecting both white-collar and blue-collar workers includes at least four steps. The process consists of reading a written application to make the first cut, an interview, a health check and a probation period – not necessarily in this order. In the majority of cases, the companies may require different types of tests (including written test) and/or two rounds of interviews. For blue-collar workers, a manual dexterity test is normally required. An illustrative example of the extremely careful and rigorous selection process is given by MNC Auto3. The company's selection process includes a written test, which is designed, sent to and marked in the company's headquarters, a first interview before a panel of interviewers, a second interview approximately a week later, a physical examination, a drug test and a probation period for the successful applicant. The first interview is conducted by a local personnel manager and respective immediate superiors, which is supervised or joined by two or three expatriate managers. The second interview normally involves top managers, where a vice general director or a general director is often present. To be a blue-collar worker in MNC Auto3, a candidate has to pass a manual dexterity test as well.

Induction and probation are considered as an extension of the selection process. Firms have used the induction and probation period to re-emphasise the companies' values, especially in Japanese firms, and for further testing the new recruits in a 'real working context', as put by the MNC Auto2 HR manager. The probation period – typically three months – is actively used to further classify new recruits. It has a special meaning in the studied Vietnamese subsidiaries where selection criteria are diluted to match the knowledge floor of the local labour market. MNC Auto2 claims to use the probation period as a final selection device. The final interview with the general director is only held after the candidates pass the probation period. If the candidates do not perform well enough, their immediate supervisor can decide not to take them on and the selection process ends there. MNC Auto2 claims that around 5–6 per cent of candidates fail to get through probation and thus fail to be selected. Other companies have confirmed that the performance of new recruits in this period influences their decisions on the type of labour contract, and its specific terms, they will sign with the new employees after the probation period.

A rigorous and expensive selection process is not a collective practice in the foreign-invested sector. Operating in the same flourishing motorbike market, MNC Auto4 has no intention of following such a rigorous selection process. In the FMCG industry, MNC FMCG3 and MNC FMCG4 also adopt simple selection processes, especially for manual workers. Cost, time savings and the sort of candidates the company wants to draw from the labour market explain this low-cost strategy. They look for manual workers (packers) with good health, and as far as education is concerned, basic literacy is sufficient. The company therefore believes that selection of packers should be a simple and straightforward business. In comparison, the automotive industry and other factories in the FMCG industry need a higher skills level in their employees and adopt a more complex selection process accordingly.

It is evident from the case studies that 'foreign' tests are of little use to test the locals' knowledge. Instead, selection tests are designed by a group of Vietnamese staff on the basis of the following:

1. the knowledge they believe is necessary to perform the job's tasks;
2. the basic and/or advanced knowledge of the main subjects relating to the job the candidates are applying for (this part is based on the content of relevant subjects taught at high school, college or university);
3. the skills and/or knowledge that the companies wish the successful candidates to possess (these tests can be made to comply with the global format or can be totally localised).

With regard to the selection criteria, the MNCs show a high degree of similarity as they all lay emphasis on the job applicants' capability, work experience and job performance. In their global 'competence list', candidates for white-collar positions are rated based on educational and training experience, past performance, leadership, commercial awareness, teamwork spirit, communication, motivation, adaptability, resourcefulness, interest in position, knowledge, behaviour, command over English and so on. However, in Vietnam, some managers claimed that it is hard to measure some 'Western concepts', such as 'motivation' and 'resourcefulness'. They are not confident with these notions and are concerned that they cannot accurately rate candidates on these criteria. An interview with an HR manager at the regional level of the same company also reveals that marking candidate performance and filing selection results, in particular, and the selection practice, in general, are 'loose' in Vietnam because of the lax legal system regarding this issue. The interviewed expatriate provided an example that a subsidiary in Australia, for instance, has to be very careful in rating candidate performance, and keeping such data, to protect itself in case of any queries or lawsuits regarding issues such as 'equal opportunities', while it is not the case in Vietnam.

When the global selection criteria seem to be impractical, the investigated companies opt for more 'practical' criteria. It is found that regardless of their industries and their nationalities, companies make their selection decision mainly on the basis of two factors: language skills and attitude. However, the problem is that fake language accreditations are readily available, because they have become an 'entrance ticket' to companies, including those that have nothing to do with foreigners. Therefore, companies have begun to organise their own English tests to 'pick out those who possess tons of language degrees but cannot understand what they are asked in a speaking test' (MNC FMCG3 HR manager). As far as attitude is concerned, companies particularly look for those who show 'dynamism', 'swiftness' and, most importantly, 'the ability to learn quickly' – traits which are considered essential, given the low quality of labour input.

Last but not least, there has been an ongoing debate about the 'domestic brain drain', where the foreign-invested sector attracts more talented employees out of the domestic labour market than SOEs as they offer higher salary and benefits and better training opportunities (see e.g. O'Connor, 1996; Bonwick & Associates, 1999). This study acknowledges the existence of the phenomenon. For example, painters are a 'rare commodity' that the studied automotive companies seek, due to several practical reasons. As the size of the factories in Vietnam is relatively small, automotive factories are equipped with semi-automatic production lines, which means advanced painting techniques (cathode electro-deposit) are present hand in hand with less sophisticated ones (spraying). Different components of a product are made from different materials, and unfinished products are subject to minor scratches and marks. However, a single monotone colour coat of paint needs to be achieved on the surface of the finished product. This requires good painters, whose abilities lie between technical skills and the arts. Highly experienced painters of SOEs in the automotive industry are hunted by foreign-invested companies. In fact, two senior painters of MNC Auto2 were recruited from its Vietnamese JV partner, while one of MNC Auto1 was poached from MNC Auto2. It is not surprising that skilled professionals, after accumulating work experience in SOEs and becoming more desirable in the labour market, are likely to move to the foreign-invested sector for higher salaries, better training opportunities and more dynamic work environment.

However, the move from an SOE to an MNC is a calculation, with both pull and push factors that cannot be easily untangled. Top-level executives, with their movement to an MNC, can bring with them their valuable networks, contacts and experience, but they are often in their 50s and less inclined to move. Furthermore, as mentioned in Section 3.2.2 [see Text Box 2.3, *The unbalanced labour market*] , top-level SOE employees benefit considerably from 'unofficial' income that is concealed, meanwhile shopfloor workers enjoy less-demanding, less-competitive and more-permanent jobs (which also applies to white collar workers). The 'war for talents', created by rising salaries for the high-end segment of the workforce in Vietnam, is perhaps much more predominant in newly found and expanding industries such as the banking, finance and information technological industries.

Source: Adapted from Vo (2009: 54–60)

2.13 Recruitment and selection in practice

Variations in employee resourcing are noted in Text Box 2.6.

Text Box 2.6

European comparisons in employee resourcing

The interview process is the primary method of selection in Britain and France, although it is approached differently in each country. The British form of interview is structured and criterion-referenced in the belief that the more that is known about the candidate, the more valid and reliable will be the interviewer's judgement on that person. This approach is also seen in Scandinavia, Germany and Austria.

The interview process in France, on the other hand, is the complete opposite – unstructured and informal – the reasoning being that the more at ease the interviewee is, the higher the quality of his or her responses. This approach is echoed in Italy, Portugal, Luxembourg and Switzerland.

Additional methods, such as assessment centres and psychological testing, are employed in Britain as a means of reducing the inevitable subjectivity of the interview process. France, on the other hand, regards such methods as unnatural and prefers to supplement its interview process with handwriting analysis.

Source: Adapted from Torrington et al. (2002: 205)

However, selection may be more ad hoc and reactive than the earlier examples indicate. The level, sophistication, time and cost that organisations actually apply to employee resourcing vary. As we have seen, in parts of Asia the selection process is very rudimentary. The type of selection device used and the elaborateness of the procedures employed do vary according to the perceived importance of the job to the organisation. For example:

- Tests and interviews are often sufficient for school leavers applying for entry level jobs.
- Higher-level occupations may demand more personal and exhaustive approaches.
- The use of psychological tests varies according to job level.

We can also see some interesting examples in Asian countries, some of which are set out in Text Boxes 2.7, 2.8 and 2.9. The case studies in Appendix 3 also provide examples.

Text Box 2.7

Job mobility in China

Attitudes about employment in China have certainly changed since the 1970s mainly due to the new market-oriented reforms (Xinhua News Agency, 2003, http://www.xinhuanet.com). A land once known as the socialist "iron rice bowl," or a haven for lifetime employment, has become a revolving-door society leading to a job hopping crisis. Under the planned economy, China was a country where loyal workers served their state-owned employers until death. The employers used to cover all the housing and medical expenses for their staff, and if the employees decided to leave, they would lose everything, making them think twice about their decision. With the new reforms in place, however, the Chinese labor market has experienced significant changes. Among many others, medical care or housing expenses are no longer covered by the employers (Xinhua News Agency, 2003). Moreover, restrictions on labor mobility have been lowered, allowing the ambitious and talented employees to switch jobs, disciplines, and firms more freely to broaden their experience. Unlike their parents who were influenced by the Cultural Revolution – greatly valuing social status and loyalty; young Chinese workers of 2007 consider themselves free agents with endless opportunities. Rapid economic growth and an erosion of traditional values in China enable workers to live a more entrepreneurial lifestyle and find jobs that better balance their work and life (Xinhua News Agency, 2003). The top reasons for job hopping in China include better compensation and benefits, career development prospects, and job dissatisfaction.

While increased job mobility undoubtedly provides workers with exciting opportunities, the fast pace at which workers are changing employers has taken its toll on many companies. Company managers fear the time around the Chinese New Year, when many employees take their annual bonus and promptly say goodbye. While the amount of bonus can reach up to several times their monthly wages, some employees will leave if they are dissatisfied with their "13th month pay" (Lee, 2006). Those who plan to leave anyway for a different reason will wait just long enough to take their bonus and never come back. Increased employee mobility is generally regarded as having a negative impact on industry's performance. Job hopping tends to drive up training and recruiting costs for employers, disrupt business, and contribute to salary increases. Losing employees to competitors is particularly harmful for a firm because the resources possessed by these workers can be used against the former employer, thereby eroding its competitive advantage in the marketplace. When trying to solve the issue of employee retention, Chinese employers are being forced to come up with new strategies and re-evaluate how they measure up against their competitors. To recruit and keep a quality workforce in today's cut-throat labor market, employers are now required to provide new employees with personal attention, offer better training programs, and demonstrate room for advancement. For many Chinese firms, retaining high caliber workers also involves attracting employees with compensation packages that include competitive salaries and flexible benefits (Zuehlke, 2001). For higher-skilled jobs, Chinese enterprises have started offering some of the same incentives as in Europe or the United States: retention bonuses, stock options, and housing allowances (Lee, 2006). However, not all industries follow the traditional path and, instead of hampered production, show gains from the increased employee turnover.

Source: Vojtkova et al. (2009: 147–148)

Text Box 2.8

Recruitment and selection in China

Under the planned economy, Chinese workers were regarded as 'masters of the nation' and everyone was entitled to employment. Article 42 of the Constitution of the People's Republic of China stipulates, 'Work is the glorious duty of every able-bodied citizen. All working people in state enterprises and in urban and rural economic collectives should perform their tasks with an attitude consonant with their status as masters of the country'. To implement socialist ideology during the rule of Mao Tse Tung, urban citizens who were able to work were assigned by local labour bureaux, which registered their citizenship status (or *hukou*), to enterprises. Many workers in China's SOEs and COEs were assured of lifetime employment, better known as 'the iron rice bowl' (*tie fan wan*), in their work 'unit' *(danwei)* (Warner, 1995, 1996). The job allocation criteria consisted of political attitudes, age, gender and education (Shen and Edwards, 2004).

From the enterprise perspective, the *tie fan wan* system did not allow enterprises to use recruitment and selection processes, which are standard practices in Western enterprises (Warner, 1993; Zhu and Dowling, 1994). Therefore, a mismatch always occurred between the skills of the workforce and enterprise needs. To support the *tie fan wan* system Chinese enterprises did not have the right to fire or lay off employees for financial reasons. Dismissal of workers was allowed only if a worker had committed 'gross negligence', but this term was open to interpretation and dismissal was rarely used (Glover and Siu, 2000).

From the employee perspective, employees were assigned to *danweis* (work units) by local labour bureaux without being consulted themselves. Once they were assigned to *danweis*, employees were in any case tied to jobs because of the housing provision offered, which they would lose if they moved on. Because there was no concept of a labour market, employees were actually unable to leave or transfer to other *danweis* for personal reasons. Hence, these mismatches between employment and the needs and interests of employees occurred, often creating low morale for the professionally qualified (Granick, 1991).

The reform in employment relations has been a gradual process. Prior to 1986, government reform of the economy focused on economic activities, and employment relations were generally ignored. Until 1986, the *tie fan wan* employment system had existed, only to be gradually replaced by flexible employment and labour contracts. Labour contracts have two forms, individual and collective, covering many aspects of labour terms, such as the period of employment, wages, production tasks, labour discipline and penalties (Zhu, 1995; Warner, 1998; for more about labour contracts see Chapter 6). Between 1986 and 1995 – the year when the 1994 Labour Law came into effect – marked a trial period for labour contracts as the government was sensitive to the opposition of the majority of workers in SOEs and COEs. During that period, enterprises required only new recruits to sign labour contracts. Such a practice differentiated the contract workers who did not have the guarantee of long-term employment from the existing workers who still enjoyed permanent employment. Contracts can be terminated by the employer on grounds of poor performance during the probationary period, violation of company rules or enterprise bankruptcy (Markel, 1994). Often, contract and temporary (those who have not signed a contract but are not permanent) workers are not entitled to extensive enterprise welfare benefits (White, 1987).

Since the 1980s, the Chinese government has encouraged employers to decide the number and quality of their own employees. The 1994 Labour Law legitimised the massive dismissal of workers in enterprises that were declared bankrupt or in extreme difficulties. 'In case it becomes necessary for the employer to reduce the workforce during the period of legal consolidation when on the brink of bankruptcy or when it experiences business difficulties, then the employer shall explain the situation to its trade union or all employees thirty days in advance' (The 1994 Labour Law, Chapter 3, Article 27). Since the promulgation of the 1994 Labour Law, the labour contract system has been widely implemented in China. By the end of 1996, a labour contract system had become compulsory in both the public and private sectors (Dowling and Welch, 2004). Many employees have been forced to retire before they reached legal retirement age in order for the enterprise to control the size of its workforce. Such early retirement is called 'internal retirement' (*nei tui*).

According to the 1994 Labour Law, employees are allowed to take jobs outside of their own companies for a certain period, but retain employment status within the enterprise without receiving salaries (*ting xing liu zhi*). *Ting xing liu zhi* needs to be agreed mutually by the employee and the employer. Employees must return to the company or re-sign a contract when the agreed period has passed. In most cases, the employee should pay the company for retaining his/her employment status. *Ting xing liu zhi* has been practised mostly in SOEs, COEs and the public sector, but is declining in the wake of widespread privatisation. The government maintained a strong presence in employment relations during the 1990s (Morris, Sheehan and Hassard, 2001), but such influence or interference has declined since the late 1990s. Widespread privatisation has contributed to the implementation of labour contracts and the virtual death knell of the 'iron rice bowl' employment system. There is literally no single permanent worker in any Chinese industry. The deepening employment relations reform, represented by legitimising the laying-off of China's massive surplus workforce, has demolished Chinese workers' faith in socialist ideology by realising that losing jobs is inevitable and there is no 100 per cent secure employment anymore. Workers have become accustomed to the idea that the 'iron rice bowl' of job security and enterprise-provided welfare is a thing of the past (Morris et al., 2001).

A freedom to fire or hire has contributed to any given enterprise's control of the quantity and quality of the labour force. The 'two-way selection', that is, free selection of occupation and employees, has become more common. Knowledge, age, education and demonstrated managerial ability rather than pure political ideology and seniority are considered to be more important in the recruitment and selection process (Zhu and Dowling, 1998). The data from the case study of four privatised enterprises show that the recruitment channels are very diverse, although recruitment is only local and largely relies on individual recommendations due to a lack of a developed, across-region free labour market. For those medium or large-scale enterprises the frequently used recruitment channels include job fairs organised by local labour bureaux or employment centres (belong to local personnel bureaux), media advertising, recruitment agencies and employment services at universities. Enterprises normally use different channels for recruiting different employees. With recruiting managers or skilled employees, they tend to use job fairs or media advertising; when recruiting unskilled workers they normally use recruitment agencies or word of mouth.

Selection criteria have shifted from pure political ideology and seniority to *De* (political ideology, moral attitudes), *Neng* (ability and education level), *Qian* (working attitudes), *Ji* (performance and achievement), with a heavy focus on *Neng* and *Ji*. The 'soft' aspects, i.e. political ideology, which used to be the main selection criteria, are no longer relevant. For many marketable workers, changing jobs is no longer impossible and has become a fact of life. When choosing a job, although working conditions and pay are still major concerns, personal development in order to remain employable is something that many Chinese people now have to consider.

Nevertheless, Chinese workers are at a disadvantage when dealing with employers in regard to employment relations. There are many reasons for this. First, the enterprise reform legitimises closing down a large number of non-profitable enterprises and layoffs in overstaffed enterprises, thus creating a large surplus workforce. Second, regulations are lacking in regard to the prevention of unfair dismissals. Third, China still does not have a completely free labour market, which makes it difficult for ordinary laid-off workers to be re-employed. As the previous chapters emphasised, without a free labour market and a developed social security system, the huge reduction in China's workforce poses a threat to social stability.

Source: Shen (2007: 31–34)

Text Box 2.9

Recruitment and selection in Vietnam

Two major changes marked the breaking up of the lifetime employment system and have opened the gate for enterprises to enter the open labour market. The first change occurred in 1987, when the government issued Decision 217/HDBT, and later reconfirmed in Labour Code 1994, which stipulated that SOEs could hire workers according to criteria set by the enterprises. The enterprise could reject any recommended candidate if that person was not qualified or the recruitment was not needed by the enterprise. Employees can also be hired from other locations if they could not be found in sufficient numbers in the locations where the enterprise was situated. This freedom to recruit and select employees of firms, together with the abandonment of labour control by residence permit, and employment opportunities offered by newly emerged economic sectors, such as the private and foreign-invested sectors, increased labour mobility and allowed the emergence of an open labour market that would not have been possible in the centrally planned economy.

The second major change is the adoption of the labour contract system instead of permanent employment. The 1994 Labour Code formalised labour contracts as the basis for the employer–employee relationship. Labour contracts stipulate the work to be performed, working hours and rest breaks, wages, location of job, conditions on occupational safety and hygiene, and social insurance for employees (Labour Code 1994, Article 29). Since the introduction of the legislation, all newly employed workers in the state sector have been put on termed contract. The introduction of the labour contract system was a milestone in labour reforms because it revoked the long-standing tradition of lifetime employment and shifted the power of decision-making regarding the utilisation of human resources from the state to the enterprises.

Struggling to improve their efficiency, SOEs embarked on a process of restructuring, where most of them significantly reduced the number of their employees. Despite this substantial restructuring of the SOE labour force, evidence suggests that overstaffing, which is a legacy of the centrally planned system, is still evident in SOEs today. Furthermore, by law, SOEs are required to retrain and assign redundant employees to a new job, if possible. If a new job cannot be created, then the employer must pay an allowance to the employee for loss of work (Labour Code, 1994, Article 17). They are also expected to allow employees to take extended leave and to put staff on a reduced workload and pay before any redundancy can be made. This shows that currently SOEs manage their human resources based on both economic factors and political and social factors.

As far as recruitment is concerned, SOEs focus strongly on internal promotions and personal recommendations. To a much lesser extent, they also utilise advertisements in newspapers to attract more candidates. A typical process for selecting white-collar and blue-collar workers is very simple and consists of reading a written application to make the first cut, then interviews, health checks and a probation period for the newly recruited employee. For blue-collar workers, a manual dexterity test is normally required. SOEs rely heavily on unstructured interviews as a selection method, which has a low level of reliability and validity, and thus is not a sufficient method to identify the best candidates.

As far as selection is concerned, the selection criteria have not changed since the days of the centrally planned economy and are mainly based on educational qualifications and harmonious personal characteristics.

Nepotism is still prevalent in selection decisions. Furthermore, top-level positions are normally appointed rather than selected. This situation implies the need for objective selection criteria and sophisticated selection methods in the state sector.

In the Vietnamese context, due to the constraints of the Vietnamese labour market, which is short of highly skilled labour, MNCs utilise all channels of recruitment, including internal promotion, recruitment through joint venture partners, advertising in newspapers and magazines, attending job fairs, recruiting graduates of educational institutions, using employment agencies and personal networks. However, they rely more on the external labour market, especially direct advertisement, recruitment agencies and headhunters. MNCs show a high degree of localisation of recruitment practices by utilising personal networks and internal headhunting agencies to establish their candidate pools despite the fact that this procedure has been criticised to be biased and subjective.

Some MNCs have lived up to their well-known standards of possessing rigorous selection processes. With regard to the selection criteria, companies lay emphasis on a job applicant's capability, work experience and job performance in previous jobs. MNCs use a wide range of selection techniques, such as written examinations, psychometric tests and assessment centres. They are also strongly adaptive to the limitations, constraints and opportunities that they face in the Vietnamese labour market. There is evidence of companies shortening the selection process to meet with the contingency nature of R&S in the Vietnamese market and diluting the global selection criteria in order to respond to the scarcity of labour at the skilled end, and of skills and knowledge at the low-skilled end, of the labour market.

However, some MNCs, especially those in the FMCG industry, adopt very simple selection processes. Cost and time savings and the type of employees they attempt to recruit are the main reasons for this low-cost strategy. They look for manual workers with good health, and as far as education is concerned, basic literacy is sufficient. These MNCs therefore believe that selection should be a simple and straightforward business.

Source: Vo (2009: 152–154; 159–160)

2.14 Conclusion

In this chapter we have covered the initial key area of HRM – employee resourcing. This was in terms of HRP and the commensurate recruitment and selection process that this may require. The predictions are that HRP will be of limited use in some parts of Asia. This is partly because an unstated assumption in HRP is that the future has continuity with the past. The influences of environmental volatility, applicability for small firms and rapidly developing Asian economies reduce the use of HRP in some Asian countries.

However, to be useful, HRP should be seen not as a highly precise technique, but as a loose collection of ideas and tools which can be applied as necessary to the individual needs and circumstances of a particular organisation.

In terms of recruitment and selection, several key points were made. Recruitment methods can apply to existing and new HR and vary depending on the HR approach of the organisation (the flexible firm, and so on), and the level and types of HR sought and the normal practices in the country concerned. Furthermore, a set of questions quickly arises. These include the following.

- What is required to perform the job?
- What selection techniques have predictive validity?
- Is there a significant relationship between a predictor (for example, the interview rating of applicants) and subsequent successful performance in a job?
- Are these reliable (for example, consistency of the measure over time)?
- Are Western techniques in selection applicable in Asia?

No selection process provides a complete, accurate prediction of performance as jobs change and people develop, and techniques of assessment and measurement are imperfect. Nevertheless, a variety of methods can be used to compensate for prejudice or unreliability from a single source of assessment.

Evidence continues to suggest that many firms, especially in Asia, do not treat employee resourcing as seriously as they should. HRP is rudimentary. Letters of application or simple application forms for pre-selection and swift unstructured interviews for final selection continue to predominate in parts of Asia. Many organisations and managers continue to use these methods despite a long and consistent stream of research indicating low reliability and validity of many techniques as a method of selection. It is important that organisations plan their recruitment and selection strategy in advance and in relation to developing corporate strategy. However, in practice HRP is usually left to the last minute!

End of chapter tasks/questions
Based on the bank and airlines case studies in Appendix 3, using and applying information within this chapter

1. To what extent will a bank and an airline in India have the same type of staff resourcing plan?

2. Discuss the likely similarities and differences in the staff resourcing plans of a bank and an airline in India.

3. What are the similarities and differences in likely recruitment policies for pilots in each case study airline in Asia?

4. Why has each airline appeared to seek young females as recruits for cabin crew jobs?

5. How will the approach to HRM planning differ between a new airline and a long-established airline?

6. Why would banks use work study and airlines use benchmarking to determine how many staff they require? How could banks use benchmarking and airlines use work study to their advantage?

7. What types of recruit would banks and airlines in China be competing with each other to attract? How would they each persuade suitable candidates to join their industry?

8. What selection methods would be common to the recruitment of pilots in every airline and which would be used in specific locations?

9. What are the advantages and disadvantages of using psychometric tests to select foreign currency traders in the bank?

10. Discuss the likely basic attitudes to undertaking an activity involving some risk, at work, in the following occupations – investment banker, foreign exchange trader, retail banker, pension fund investor, pilot, airline commercial manager, aircraft engineer.

End of chapter tasks/questions

Based on the Wong Yu case in Appendix 3 ((B) HRM practices and changes in Asia: Case Study A3.3, Employee resourcing – Wong Yu Pharmaceutical and Textile), using and applying information within this chapter

1. What are the issues and problems within the company?
2. Suggest some solutions to these problems.
3. What do you think might happen next?

References

Aisbett, E. (2005) *Why Are the Critics So Convinced that Globalization Is Bad for the Poor?* NBER Working Paper No. 11066, Cambridge, MA: NBER.

Arbache, J., Dickerson, A. and Green, F. (2004) 'Trade liberalization and wages in developing countries', *Economic Journal*, 114: F73–F96.

Beaumont, P. (1993) *HRM: Key Concepts and Skills*. London: Sage.

Benson, J. and Zhu, Y. (1999) 'Markets, firms and workers in Chinese state-owned enterprises', *Human Resource Management Journal*, 9(4): 58–74.

Björkman, I and Lu, Y 1997, 'Human resource management practices in foreign invested enterprises in China: What has been learned?', in S. Stewart and A. Carver (eds), *A Coming of Age: Developments in Sino-Foreign Joint Ventures, Advances in Chinese Industrial Studies*, Vol. 5. London: JAI Press.

Bonwick & Associates (1999), Unpublished Vietnamese Salary Survey.

Cattell, R.B. (1946) *The Description and Measurement of Personality*. New York: World Book Co.

Chen, D.R. (1995) *Chinese Firms between Hierarchy and Market: The Contract Management Responsibility System in China*. New York: St Martin's Press.

Chen, F. (1995) *Economic Transition and Political Legitimacy in Post-Mao China: Ideology and Reform*. Albany, NY: State University of New York Press.

Chen, M. (2004) *Asian Management Systems*. London: Thomson.

Child, J. (1994) *Management in China During the Age of Reform*. Cambridge: Cambridge University Press.

Currie, J. and Harrison, A. (1997) 'Sharing the costs: The impact of trade reform on capital and labor in Morocco', *Journal of Labor Economics,* 15(3): S44–S71.

Davidson, C. and Matusz, S. (2004) *International Trade and Labor Markets: Theory, Evidence and Policy Implications.* Kalamazoo: W.E. Upjohn Institute for Employment Research.

DeWitte, K. (1989) 'Recruitment and advertising', in P. Herriot (ed.), *Assessment and Selection in Organizations: Methods and Practices for Recruitment and Appraisal.* Chichester: John Wiley.

Dollar, D. and Kraay, A. (2004) 'Trade, growth, and poverty', *Economic Journal,* 114 (February): F22–F49.

Dowling, P.J. and Welch, D.E. (2004) *International Human Resources Management: Managing People in a Multinational Context* (4th ed.). London: Thomson Learning.

Fahey, S. (1995) 'Changing labour relations', in B.J.T. Kerkvliet (ed.), *Dilemmas of Development: Vietnam Update 1994.* Canberra: Australia National University Department of Political and Social Change Research School of Pacific and Asian Studies.

Financial Times (2001) 'B&Q defends "brutal" use of psychometric testing', 21 April, p. 3.

Freeman, R. (2003) *Trade Wars: The Exaggerated Impact of Trade in Economic Debate.* NBER Working Paper No. 10000, Cambridge, MA: NBER.

Glover, L. and Siu, N. (2000) 'The human resource barriers to managing quality in China', *The International Journal of Human Resource Management,* 11(5): 867–82.

Granick, D. (1991) 'Multiple labour markets in the industrial state enterprise', *China Quarterly,* 126: 269–89.

GSO (General Statistics Office) (2008) *Statistical Yearbook of Vietnam 2007.* Hanoi: Statistical Publishing House.

Gunter, B.G. and van der Hoeven, R. (2004) 'The social dimension of globalization: A review of literature', *International Labour Review,* 143(1-2): 7–43.

Hakel, M. (1982) 'Employment interviewing', in K. Rowland and G. Ferris (eds), *Personnel Management.* London: Allyn & Bacon.

Hallak, J.C. and Levinsohn, J. (2004) *Fooling Ourselves: Evaluating the Globalization and Growth Debate.* NBER Working Paper No. 10244, Cambridge, MA: NBER.

Harry, W.E. (2007) 'Employment creation and localisation – the crucial human resources issues for the GCC', *International Journal of Human Resource Management,* 18(1): 132–146.

Jackson, A. (1996) *Understanding Psychological Testing*. Leicester: British Psychological Society.

Klein, M., Schuh, S. and Triest, R. (2003) *Job Creation, Job Destruction, and International Competition*. Kalamazoo: W.E. Upjohn Institute.

Lauterbach, B. and Weisberg, J. (1994) 'Top management successions: The choice between internal and external sources', *The International Journal of Human Resource Management*, 5(1): 51–62.

Le, D.D. (1997) 'Legal consequences of state-owned enterprise reform', in N.C. Yuen, N.J. Freeman and F.H. Huynh (eds), *State-owned Enterprise Reform in Vietnam. Lessons from Asia*. Singapore: Institution of South East Asian Studies.

Lee, Don. (2006) 'Job hopping is rampant as China's economy chases skilled workers,' *Los Angeles Times,* 21 February, C1.

Lee, S. and Wood, A. (2007) 'Changing patterns in the world of work in Asia', in J. Burgess and J. Connell (eds) *Globalisation and Work in Asia*. Oxford: Chandos.

Lucas, L. (2008) 'Blood types: Typecasting beats at heart of the culture', *Financial Times, Japan Survey*, 13 October.

Luebker, M. (2004) 'Globalization and perceptions of social inequality', *International Labour Review*, 143(1-2): 91–128.

Majid, N. (2004) *What Is the Effect of Trade Openness on Wages?* ILO Employment Strategy Papers 2004/18, Geneva: ILO.

Markel, D. (1994) 'Finally, a national labour law', *China Business Review*, 21(6): 46–49.

Maslow, A.H. (1970) *Motivation and Personality*. New York: Harper Row.

McGregor, A. (2009) 'The party organiser', *Financial Times*, 1 October.

MOLISA (Ministry of Labour, Invalids and Social Affairs) (2006) *Statistical Data of Employment and Unemployment in Vietnam 1996–2005*. Hanoi: The Publishing House of Social Labor.

Morris, J., Sheehan, J. and Hassard, J. (2001) 'From dependency to defiance? Work unit relationships in China's state enterprise reforms', *Journal of Management Studies*, 38(5): 69 717.

Moser, K. (2005) 'Recruitment sources and post-hire outcomes: The mediating role of unmet expectations', *International Journal of Selection and Assessment*, 13(3): 188–197.

Nakamoto, R. (2006) 'A labour force in decline', *Financial Times*, 6 November.

Newell, S. and Shackleton, L. (1994) 'The use of psychological tests for selection purposes by job grade', *Human Resource Management Journal*, 4, 1: 14–23.

Nguyen, V.H. and Tran, V.N. (1997) 'Government policies and state-owned enterprises', in N.C. Yuen, N.J. Freeman and F.H. Huynh (eds), *State-owned Enterprise Reform in Vietnam: Lessons from Asia*. Singapore: Institute of South East Asian Studies.

O'Connor, D. (1996) *Labour market aspects of state enterprise reform in Vietnam*, Technical Paper No. 117. Paris: OECD Development Centre.

Rama, M. (2003a) *Globalization and Workers in Developing Countries*. World Bank Policy Research Working Paper No. 2958, Washington DC: World Bank.

Rama, M. (2003b) 'Globalization and the labor market', *World Bank Research Observer*, 18(2): 159–86.

Rowley, C. and Yukongdi, V. (2009) *The Changing Face of Women Managers in Asia*, London: Routledge.

Shen, J. (2007) *Labour Disputes and their Resolution in China*. Oxford: Chandos.

Shen, J. and Edwards, V. (2004) 'Recruitment and selection in Chinese MNEs', *International Journal of Human Resource Management*, 15(4/5): 814–35.

Shweder, R.A. (2003) *Why do Men Barbecue?* Cambridge, Mass: Harvard University Press.

Smith P.B. and Bond M.H. (1998) *Social Psychology Across Cultures*. Hemel Hempstead: Prentice Hall.

Studwell, J. (2002) *The China Dream*. London: Profile Books.

Taylor, S. (1998) *Employee Resourcing*. London: CIPD.

Thornhill, A., Lewis, P., Millmore, M. and Saunders, M. (2000) *Managing Change: A Human Resource Strategy Approach*. London: Financial Times/Prentice Hall.

Torrington, D., Hall, L. and Taylor, S. (2002) *Human Resource Management*. London: Financial Times/Prentice Hall.

Vaughan-Whitehead, D. (ed.) (2005) *Working and Employment Conditions in New EU Member States: Convergence or Diversity?* Geneva: ILO.

Verma, A. and Zhiming, Y. (1995) 'The changing face of human resource management in China. Opportunities, problems and strategies', in A. Verma, T.A. Kochan and R.D. Lansbury (eds), *Employment Relations in the Growing Asian Economies*. London/New York: Routledge.

Vo, A. (2009) *The Transformation of HRM and IR in Vietnam*. Oxford: Chandos Publishing.

Vojtkova, L., Eisner, A.B. and Korn, H.J. (2009) 'Chinese cases: Job-hopping in Z-Park', in R. Alas (ed.) *Implementation of Changes in Chinese Organisations: Groping a Way through the Darkness*. Oxford: Chandos Publishing.

Warner, M. (1992) *How Chinese Managers Learn: Management and Industrial Training in the PRC*. London: Macmillan.

Warner, M. (1993) 'Human resource management "with Chinese characteristics"', *The International Journal of Human Resource Management*, 4(1): 45–65.

Warner, M. (1995) *The Management of Human Resources in Chinese Industry*. New York: St. Martin's Press.

Warner, M. (1996) 'Economic reforms, industrial relations and human resources in the People's Republic of China: An overview', *Industrial Relations Journal*, 27(3): 195–210.

Warner, M. (1998) 'HRM practices in international joint ventures versus state-owned enterprises in China', in Selmer, J. (ed.), *International Management in China: Cross-cultural Issues*. London: Routledge, 83–97.

Warner, M. (2004) 'Human resource management in China revisited: Introduction', *The International Journal of Human Resource Management*, 15(4/5): 617–34.

Weir, D. and Hutchings, K. (2006) 'Guanxi and Wasta: A Review of the traditional ways of networking in China and the Arab World and their implications for international business', *Thunderbird International Business Review*, 48(1) 1–12.

Whipp, L. (2008) 'Closed lives of those on fringes of the jobs market', *Financial Times Japan Survey*, 13 October.

White, G. (1987) 'The politics of economic reform in Chinese industry: The introduction of the labour contract system', *The China Quarterly*, 11: 365–389.

Winter, A. (2004) 'Trade liberalization and economic performance: An overview', *Economic Journal*, 114 (Feb): F4–F21.

Wong, Y.H. (1997) 'Insider selling to China: Guanxi, trust and adaptation', *Journal of International Selling and Sales Management*, 3 (2): 55–73.

Wong, Y.H. (1998) 'The dynamics of *guanxi* in China', *Singapore Management Review*, 20(2): 25–43.

Xinhua News Agency (2003) 'China's young seek to better themselves by job-hopping'. Available at http://english.eastday.com/epublish/gb/paper1/994/class000100006/hwz154380.htm (retrieved 20 December 2007).

Yeung, I. and Tung, R. (1996) 'Achieving business success in Confucian societies: The importance of "guanxi" (connections)', *Organisational Dynamics*, 25(2): 54–66.

Zhu, J.H. and Dowling, P.J. (1994) 'The impact of economic system upon HRM practices in China', *Human Resource Planning*, 17(4): 1–21.

Zhu, J.H. and Dowling, P.J. (1998) 'Performance appraisal in China', in Selmer, J. (ed.), *International Management in China: Cross-cultural Issues*'. London: Routledge, 115–36.

Zhu, Y. (1995) 'Major changes under way in China's industrial relations', *International Labour Review*, 24(3): 26–49.

Zhu, Y. and Warner, M. (2005) 'Changing Chinese employment relations since WTO accession', *Personnel Review*, 34(3): 354–69.

Zuehlke, L. (2001) 'Job hopping: The favorite pastime of today's work force?' Available at http://maysbusiness.tamu.edu/old/2001/01/jobcmt.html (retrieved 21 December 2007).

Employee rewards

3.1 Introduction

We have now covered the initial aspects of HRM – resourcing the organisation with people. This can involve planning requirements for HR and recruiting and selecting them. One factor that critically impacts on these aspects of HRM is that of employee rewards and its management (see White and Druker, 2000). For instance, HR resourcing difficulties, including the dimensions of attraction and retention, may be linked back to employee rewards. Rewards retain their importance for a range of reasons and reward practices attract widespread media, political and public attention, especially in cases where rewards seem to be too low or too high. These issues have been brought to the attention of an even wider audience with the fall-out from the post-2008 global financial crisis as the high reward practices in sectors such as banking have come under fresh scrutiny.

Later in this chapter we discuss rewards in terms of their link to 'performance', and how, and to what extent, these aspects can be built into HRM systems. This is also linked to ideas of HR flexibility and the flexible firm model (see Chapter 1 at 1.7.2.2). Indeed, while some forms of such performance-linked reward systems are not particularly new, there is a continuing interest in them from a range of bodies – not just businesses and other employers, but also governments and policy makers. For example, in parts of Asia the public sector offers low rewards but, at least until recently, it offered job security. As governments struggle to reduce bureaucracy and the number of their public sector employees through privatisation, technology and simplification or codification of laws, the combination of low rewards and low job security creates serious economic and political problems which could even threaten the existence of some governments (Harry, 2007). For example, the impact of high rates of youth unemployment and low pay in the Gulf Co-operation Council (GCC) countries led to the use of recent increases in oil wealth to award substantial pay increases to citizens in the public sector (around 70 per cent in the case of the United Arab Emirates).

The types of reward system and some of the related methods and issues will be examined in this chapter. Rewards are also one of those areas and issues that display wide variation in practice and in acceptance of certain levels, as well as internationally and comparatively. We will look at some of these practices and issues.

3.2 Overview

Employee rewards retain their relevance and importance for HRM for several reasons, which include the following.

1. Rewards interact with many other aspects of HRM – for instance, employee resourcing, such as attracting and retaining HR, and employee relations, including the involvement of trade unions in negotiations and disputes involving rewards.

2. Rewards also impact on other areas, such as organisational performance, as well as having a role in driving and integrating with strategy and reinforcing values (see Wilson, 2001) and enhancing employee motivation and commitment. Indeed, for some commentators, the decline of career systems and commensurate employee commitment is also linked to rewards, with the need now to focus more on broadly defined rewards to elicit employee commitment. Job security in Asia is declining, especially in the public and semi-public sectors; for example, the 'iron rice bowl' (guaranteed employment) of China has been broken. Even some Japanese firms, well known for lifetime employment, have found ways to dispose of surplus labour – even to the extent of removing all job responsibilities and letting staff sit and do nothing except look out of the window (known as '*madogiwazoku*', the 'window gazing clan') in the hope that they will be humiliated into resigning. Throughout Asia there are moves to reduce the number of employees who have security of employment and rely on temporary or 'contingent' employees, or those from other countries or other regions who have little expectation of being able to claim employment rights.

3. Overall, employee rewards are composed of numerous elements. Putting these together as a 'rewards package' can range from a simple

to a more complex mix of 'intrinsic' and 'extrinsic' rewards. A rewards package can include pay, benefits, promotion, praise, long-term security of employment, opportunities for development and training, for instance, with 'generalised investments' (see Galunic and Weeks, 2001). A possible framework by which to assess an organisation's portfolio of rewards could be made up of four types:

- salaries/wages
- bonuses/incentives
- benefits
- recognition programmes

The above can be seen in the two dimensions of: 'cash versus non-cash'; and 'all employees versus some employees' – that is, differentiated by performance (Wilson, 2001).

4. Rewards can form a large part of the cost basis of a business and may even be a method of competing between employers. This reward role does vary, even between countries, where some employers offer higher pay than employers in neighbouring countries – for example, Singapore and Malaysia, India and Nepal, or Hong Kong and neighbouring Chinese provinces such as Guangdong, where costs from higher pay would be expected to lead to businesses moving to cheaper neighbours. However, many employers believe that the higher wage costs are worthwhile as the HR are more productive or are capable of undertaking greater added value work which justifies the higher costs. For those organisations operating in highly competitive markets exposed to foreign competition, minimisation of labour costs could be critical to their survival. This has been an important factor in the Asian 'tiger' economies of South East Asia and is now important in Vietnam, China and India. However, this may be less the case in other sectors, such as private services, were there are often non-tradable (non-exportable) jobs. For instance, if the price of a haircut goes up because of increases in wages (imposed by a statutory minimum wage, for example), what would customers do since all other businesses would be paying the same rate and therefore charging the same price? Customers may try to reduce the number of visits for a haircut, but they are unlikely to go overseas for the service. Businesses may then even be encouraged to attempt to compete on the basis of quality rather than (low) cost if wages are standardised amongst all in the sector.

5. The area of rewards also attracts much public, institutional, government and media attention and comment. Debates around both the bottom (i.e. national minimum wage or extremely low pay for migrant workers) and top (i.e. top management and investment bankers' remuneration) of the rewards spectrum retain their salience and high profile. This area has become far more widely exposed with the post-2008 global financial crisis resulting in a plethora of examples of seemingly indefensible rewards practices, especially in the West.

6. Employee rewards remain highly varied internationally. For senior managers there are expectations of very high rewards and large differentials from employees in the US, whereas in other countries, such as India and Japan, this large differential is not so widely expected. There are also ideas of seniority-based pay in some countries, such as Japan and South Korea. Then there is the harmonised annual round of reward increases, such as 'shunto' (the 'spring livelihood offensive') in Japan, held every year since 1955, although this practice is now under some stress (*The Economist*, 2003).

Think About/Question 3.1

What do you think is the basis for a person's rewards? You can list these criteria or any methods you may use to assist in this. To what extent are they applicable for all jobs, organisations and countries?

One aspect of rewards is an increasing, albeit not new, focus on setting levels by linking rewards to contribution and 'performance'. This is by various links to different performances in diverse schemes. Ideas of adding greater performance (or 'variable' or 'at risk') aspects to rewards can create a volatile employee relations situation. The maxim 'what gets measured gets done' has relevance here as people may do what is rewarded and not what is needed.

Performance-based systems require several elements to assist in their success. These include:

- a clear understanding of measures, goals or standards and actions that people need to take
- challenging but achievable goals (Wilson, 2001)
- a short, robust and explicit link between performance and reward
- must 'fit' with prevailing personal, organisational and national cultures

You can look at the above and complete the questions set out in Case Study 3.1 below. Also, Hille (2008) provides the interesting example of Chungwha Telecom in Taiwan, which made changes to its rewards packages and the role of incentives and shares in that, while Guerra and Chung (2008) note issues surrounding executive pay.

Case Study 3.1

Rewards in a law firm

A leading US law firm had a pay system based on a requirement of 2,420 hours of 'chargeable time' to secure the bonus. This resulted in a high-profile PR fallout with client concerns and accusations, for example, of 'padding' and over-billing clients.

- Why do you think this happened?
- What new rewards system would you recommend and introduce? Why?

3.3 Rewards and integration

The links between business strategy and integration with HRM (as we discussed earlier in Chapter 1 at 1.7) can be seen here in reward elements. These linkages can be explicit, as seen in Table 3.1. Thus, there can be integrated reward systems, driven by business strategy. However, it does still need to be remembered that contingency theory (also discussed in Chapter 1, at 1.5.1) is important in rewards. In particular, variations can stem from the following factors: (a) organisational strategies and cultures need different reward strategies; (b) the usefulness of reward strategies and practices varies according to context, and (c) reward practices affect people differently.

Table 3.1   Integration in rewards

Business strategy	Reward strategy
Added-value by improving motivation and commitment	Introduce/improve PRP (individual, team, gain-sharing)
Added-value by improving performance and productivity	Introduce/improve PRP and performance management

Table 3.1   Integration in rewards (*Cont'd*)

Business strategy	Reward strategy
Competitive advantage by value by developing and using distinctive core competencies	Introduce competence-related pay
Competitive advantage by technological development	Introduce competence-related or skill-based pay
Competitive advantage by delivering better value and quality	Recognise/reward for meeting/exceeding customer service and quality standards
Competitive advantage by developing capacity to respond quickly and flexibly to opportunities	Provide rewards for multi-skilling and job flexibility Develop flexible pay structures (broad banding)
Competitive advantage by attracting, developing and retaining high quality HR	Ensure pay rates are competitive Reward for developing competencies and careers in broad-banded pay structure

Source: Adapted from Armstrong (1999)

3.4 Types of reward

Employee rewards can come in many varieties.

> Think About/Question 3.2
>
> What different components of rewards are you familiar with?

The broad aspects of rewards can be seen as comprising the elements shown in Table 3.2.

People require rewards for the services they provide for the organisation. In taking a job a person must work and forsake time which could be occupied with other activities. Therefore, organisations 'compensate' for the time lost and the efforts put in by individuals to carry out the tasks and duties of a job. This is why US organisations, in particular, refer to pay systems as 'compensation'. Compensation comes in two main forms: intrinsic and extrinsic.

Table 3.2 Elements of rewards

Aspects of rewards	Examples
Money	Salary, bonus and incentives, expenses
Benefits	Pension, cars, housing, insurance, leave, medical facilities
Work	Challenge, autonomy, environment
Development	Training, personal development, employability, job security

3.4.1 Intrinsic rewards

These rewards relate to the inner satisfactions experienced in carrying out the tasks and duties of a job. These satisfactions may be small or large, depending on factors such as the degree of interest in the work, conditions, opportunities and recognition. Intrinsic rewards may not usually be sufficient to induce someone to take a job and remain in it, although people may accept lesser extrinsic reward if the intrinsic satisfactions of a job are obvious and substantial.

Charity workers, such as those based in Malaysia and India, for example, may chose a vocation which pays less than they could expect from other career choices. Throughout Asia, working for a prestigious employer or a government department with status is considered to be a valuable intrinsic reward.

3.4.2 Extrinsic rewards

These have two major aspects: first, pay, which can be received in the form of wages, salary, bonuses, commissions, and so on, and, secondly, benefits, which can be other rewards that have a notional monetary value but are not paid in cash. There is a vast array of examples here, ranging from housing, car or transport, pension/provident fund, loans, insurance, medical facilities, meals, recreational and child care services, to the use of corporate facilities and resources.

In parts of Asia, housing – often job-related – is given to employees or a housing allowance is provided. This is especially so in the public sector, and it is also seen in South Asian banks and certainly throughout Asia for expatriates in managerial positions. In contrast, pensions, insurance and child care facilities are less common than they are in the West.

3.4.3 Rewards packages

As can be seen from the above, an organisation has several options when putting together the components of a total rewards package. Some key points should be made on this aspect of rewards:

1. There is a trend towards diversity in packages in the West, but in some parts of Asia reward generally means cash – and paid now. The package rarely includes stock options and 'transparent' profit shares.

2. The proportion of the total cost of rewards packages accounted for by benefits varies between (and within) countries, sectors and organisations. In parts of Asia benefits generally make up a higher proportion of the rewards package, despite employees' preference for cash or near cash, than is the case in Europe or the US.

3. There has been increasing complexity in the types of benefit, especially for senior management.

4. The trend has been for the proportion of benefits within packages to rise sharply, especially when housing and pension/provident fund contributions become a large part of the benefits package. In parts of Asia great value is placed on conspicuous symbols of success, so management staff will certainly wish to have a prestige car, club membership and an expense account to impress others. Furthermore, despite what has been noted about Asians valuing immediate cash, senior management will prefer these expensive obvious 'symbols' as well as less obvious cash.

We can see these ideas and issues in action. One Asian example, Vietnam, is described in Text Box 3.1.

Text Box 3.1

Rewards packages in Vietnam

Other incomes in SOEs

Other sources of income that SOE employees might receive include different types of allowances, benefits, bonuses and unofficial income.

Allowances

Allowances are normally estimated on the minimal salary level and include the following types:

Area allowance: This allowance is designed to supplement the income of employees working in remote areas where the climate is not favourable, and living and transportation conditions are harsh. There are 45 cities and provinces in Vietnam that enjoy area allowance. The average level of area allowance for the communes, wards and townships is 0.38 in comparison with the minimal salary level, which in other words means 38 per cent of the minimal salary level (GTZ, 2006: 19).

Hazardous, difficult and dangerous allowance: This allowance is to compensate those employees who work in hazardous and dangerous areas; it is not included in their salary. The levels of hazardous and dangerous allowance are 0.1, 0.2, 0.3 and 0.4 in comparison with the minimal salary level.

Mobile allowance: This allowance is to compensate those employees who work in professions requiring them to move frequently, causing instability in their life. There are three levels of mobile allowance: 0.2, 0.4 and 0.6 in comparison with the minimal salary level.

Responsibility allowance: This allowance is to compensate those employees who are directly involved in production, or who carry out their professional or operational work, while at the same time undertaking managerial tasks not included in their appointed position, or those tasks requiring high responsibility not accounted for in their salary. There are three levels of responsibility allowance: 0.1, 0.2 and 0.3 above the minimal salary level.

Special allowance: This allowance is provided to those employees who work on remote islands and bordering areas where the living conditions are extremely difficult. There are three levels, namely 30, 50 and 100 per cent of the minimum salary level, that are determined according to the consideration of the difficult living conditions in each commune.

Allowance for attraction: This allowance aims to attract people to come and work in new economic zones, far-off islands in which infrastructure (transportation, electricity, residence, school, kindergarten, hospital, etc.) is either lacking or insufficient. There are four levels of the allowance: 20, 30, 50 and 70 per cent of the post, grade or professional salary. The duration to receive the allowance depends on the actual difficulty (usually 3–5 years or more).

Benefits

Companies offer various benefits, as seen in Table 5.2 [table omitted]

Bonuses

Bonuses constitute an important part of the income for SOE employees in Vietnam. The government leaves the individual enterprises with much freedom to determine the amount in the revenue after paying taxes to the state. The fixed bonus is often in the form of a Tet (Lunar New Year) bonus. The 13th month salary bonus is very popular in the SOEs. In some cases, bonuses are divided on an equal basis, creating some egalitarianism. In other cases, bonuses are paid in accordance with the salary received by the individual employee; thus those who work longer and have a higher salary would receive more bonus. Besides this, employees might receive some small gift or cash on special days such as Mid-Autumn Moon Festival, Women's Day, Independence Day, etc. However, these types of bonus are not fixed and are dependent on the firm's performance and the viability of trade union activities.

Unofficial income

The concept of unofficial income, and related issues such as the generation of the unofficial income by enterprises and by employees in the state sector, emerged in the transition to a market economy in Vietnam (GTZ, 2006). These issues are complex, controversial and closely connected to the present low salary, allowance and bonus system. No official statistics are available on unofficial income.

The sources of this revenue can come from services provided to other agencies, organisations or individuals using the available resources, leasing space, equipment, facilities, fees from contract work, etc. SOE employees also enjoy unofficial income from individuals. CEOs receive gifts and under-the-table money in lieu of favours. The amount in the envelope depends on the role of the receiver and the political and/or economic benefit of the favour extended. For unlawful cases, the amount of money may be huge, up to billions of VND. Employees in lower positions can also receive 'facilitation payment' in the form of gifts or money for providing assistance in dealing with certain issues. Unofficial income received from individuals is extremely hard to measure; however, it is an ongoing issue in SOEs. Lucrative unofficial income enjoyed by employees in high positions is believed to be the real reason for them to stay with the state sector, when their official income might be 10 times lower than that of their colleagues in the foreign-invested or private sectors. Meanwhile, corruption is endemic in Vietnam. A 'Report of the Survey on Corruption in Vietnam' (2005) by the Vietnamese government reveals that 77 per cent of enterprises consider corruption to be the most significant socio-economic problem in Vietnam (Nigh, 2008). However, according to the World Bank's Vietnam Development Report (2006), Vietnamese firms attached a surprisingly low importance to corruption, with only a few of them rating corruption as a constraint on their business activities. One possible explanation offered by the World Bank is that entrepreneurs in Vietnam simply have learned how to 'live with floods', to the point where they do not see it as a significant constraint on their activities (World Bank, 2006: 48).

Other incomes in MNCs

Allowances and benefits

While salary practices are centrally designed, various types of allowances and benefits are left open to the subsidiaries to decide on what is suitable to the Vietnamese situation. Even though the value of these may vary significantly, companies appear to offer very similar types of allowances and benefits, which also resemble those offered by their Vietnamese SOE partners to their employees.

Bonuses

As far as bonus is concerned, the Labour Code indicates that the employer is responsible for paying a fixed bonus to those employees who have worked for more than one year when the company reaches 'break-even' point. The payment should not be lower than one month's salary and must be paid to all permanent employees.

All of the studied companies provide a fixed bonus in compliance with the Labour Code to all of their permanent/regular employees. Some of them provide much more than that required by law by providing an extra one month salary (14th month salary) as fixed bonus. A fixed bonus is paid either at the year-end or before Lunar New Year holiday (Tet holiday).

There is evidence that some companies, who are not objects of this research, do not provide any form of bonus and simply pay 12 months of fixed salary after reaching their break-even point. This obviously violates the Labour Law, but it does exist in practice.

In many cases, allowances/benefits and bonuses are used to adjust individual packages and, most importantly, to minimise the social and medical insurance costs, and to avoid the high personal income tax. Taking advantage of the ambiguous regulations regarding reward polices in foreign-invested companies, many firms developed a so-called '70/30 style' of remuneration package, in which companies and individuals come to a verbal agreement that the company pays 70 per cent of the agreed salary as 'fixed salary', while the remaining 30 per cent is in the form of non-salary payment (benefits, bonus). Applying this structure, companies only contribute to the social insurance and health insurance funds on the basis of 70 per cent of what they actually pay to their employees and accordingly avoid or reduce the high personal income tax. The '70/30 style' remuneration package gets the support of the higher income groups, namely professionals, managers and top executives, who aim at short-term benefits in terms of reduced income tax. It is because employees have to contribute 6 per cent of their salary (of which 5 per cent is for social security and 1 per cent for health insurance) to state-controlled funds, but they receive the same amount of money and the same kind of health services, regardless of their higher contribution. Therefore, social security and health insurance are seen as more for the benefit of the lower income group while the high-income groups only hesitantly contribute to these government-controlled funds.

However, a majority of big companies do not utilise this payment structure. Interviewed HR managers explain that this practice is based on the assumption that the related authority (company trade union, local trade union, local MOLISA, etc.) will turn a blind eye to this practice as long as the company does not violate the minimum payment level. However, in the event of being audited, the company must be able to verify their proportion of allowances/benefits and bonuses. Moreover, a cut in social security payments leads to a smaller pension paid to the employees in the future. Thus, the strategy is not for employees' long-term benefit, and can possibly cause labour relations problems for the company. In fact, the main reason for applying the 70/30 style is to reduce or avoid high income tax for managers and top executives.

Source: Vo (2009: 99–100; 102–103; 106–107)

3.4.3.1 Issues and problems

These developments in the area of rewards can create problems for management and the business. Employees generally do not value the 'worth' of the benefits components of a package as highly as their 'real' cost. This may be for a variety of reasons. It may be because the services are not needed or might be inappropriate: for example, benefits could include child and maternity leave for employees with no children, or insurance for someone whose religious faith forbids the use of insurance – these benefits are of no worth to such employees. Then there is the 'life cycle' question, when different types of benefit have varying levels of attractiveness over the career and increasing age of the person for whom they are provided. This can be observed in terms of the relative importance over a person's working life of benefits such as vacations, pensions and health care, where younger people prefer holidays and older workers prefer health care and savings.

A more generic problem has emerged in many economies with major traditional benefits, pensions and provident funds, which are more usual than pensions in parts of Asia. Developments such as the escalating costs of final salary pensions, the expense of provident fund contributions and the high volumes of early retirements in some public sector occupations have forced businesses to limit and withdraw final salary pensions and try to reduce provident fund contributions and for governments to struggle to meet the commitments made to public sector workers. This potential pension and provident fund commitment causes some Asian employers to keep basic pay low but use cost of living allowances (COLA), bonuses and benefits (which are usually not included in the calculation of pension and provident elements) to make up the rewards package.

3.4.3.2 Responses

One response to the management problem of this 'cost-appreciation' equation in benefits has been to move towards flexible benefits plans, or 'cafeteria benefits'. This system allows employees some choice of benefits and the ability to have a varying 'pick and mix' total rewards package. This process is aimed both at reducing overall costs and increasing the recipient's awareness of the 'real' costs of benefits. This is an attempt to link benefits more closely to motivation and performance.

Thus, HR are provided with a total benefits budget and a costed benefits 'menu'. From this list is created an individual total benefits package – for example, taking a larger chunk of the package in up-front benefits (such as pay) vis-à-vis deferred benefits (such as pension) or more of one type (such as childcare) over another (such as a car). This construction of individual, customised benefit packages can be undertaken on a regular basis. However, as with much in HRM, this increasing complexity may come with additional costs to the organisation, not least in terms of the time involved. One possible way to mitigate some of the problems here is to outsource rewards calculation and provision to bespoke providers in this field. Partly as a consequence, flexible benefits have been implemented less in some parts of Asia where 'take it or leave it' is the usual choice. Nevertheless, there are some Asian examples, such as the flexible benefits system in the South Korean public sector (Yu, Walder and Rowley, 2008).

3.4.4 Levels

Reward systems and packages can differ at both various levels and locations within the same organisation. These range from the more collective, such as occupation or industry level, company or enterprise, plant, business unit, section or department level, down to the more individual packages. These rewards can be negotiated in different ways, such as with collective bargaining, and agreements can be made covering longer or shorter periods.

3.5 Determinants

We now move on the complex and emotive area of what actually determines the size of a total rewards package.

> **Think About/Question 3.3**
>
> What are the reward levels based on of Chief Executives of companies, barristers, professional footballers, teachers, nurses and fire fighters? To what extent are they 'fair' and 'equitable'?

A constant problem area that produces much angst and publicity is the amount of remuneration given, especially at either end of the high-to-low rewards spectrum. The media reports both 'scrooge payers' and 'fat cats', a situation that is even more difficult to handle for the organisation if it is seen simultaneously as both a 'scrooge' to most staff with 'fat cats' in high places; it is also inconsistent in terms of the criteria used to justify reward levels.

A classic instance of the double standard argument involves assertions that, on the one hand, there is the need to 'pay for the best' while, on the other hand, there is the need to 'pay what the market indicates'. Furthermore, there is no real market for senior managers; the vast majority remain home country nationals – for instance, only one in five of US corporations operating outside the US actually has a non-US national on the board. There has been more recent backlash against very high reward levels, even in the bastion of such practices, the US: Jack Welch, the feted ex-boss of GEC, was forced to renounce some of his retirement package (including the use of private jets) from mid-2002.

What are such reward levels based on? Is anyone worth the hundreds of millions of dollars paid to some US senior executives? It is worth taking a moment here to jot down the justifications you would use for why you are paid what you are. Can you group these reasons into criteria?

> Think About/Question 3.4
>
> What general factors do you think help to determine rewards levels in a country?

We can see some of the disparate issues in this area of rewards in the Asian example in Text Box 3.2.

Text Box 3.2

Factors influencing reward systems in Vietnam

The Vietnamese business environment poses two main constraints on company reward systems, namely the legislation regarding remuneration policies in state and foreign-invested firms and the labour-market imperfections.

As far as legislation is concerned, the government regulates state sector and foreign-invested sector with two different sets of laws. In the state sector, the government stipulates the principles for developing the salary system (employee specifications, salary scales and salary tables), minimum salary and salary ratio. Under the pressure of rising living costs and inflation and competition from the private and foreign-invested sectors, in recent years the government has increased the minimum salary level several times. Most recently, Decree 166/2007/ND-CP, proposed by the Ministry of Internal Affairs, Ministry of Labour, War Invalids and Social Affairs (MOLISA) and the Ministry of Finance on adjusting salary and social subsidies and reforming the salary management mechanism, raised the minimum salary level to 540,000 VND (about 33.75 USD) per month, effective from 1 January 2008. This salary is based on a maximum of eight hours per day, six days per week and is equivalent to a daily salary of 22,493 VND (about 1.4 USD). Even with the new regulation, the minimum salary level in SOEs is lower than that of MNCs. Furthermore, SOEs are required to consult enterprise trade unions and their salary systems have to be registered with higher authorities, namely General Corporations and the local labour authority.

On the other hand, foreign-invested companies are free to apply either their own reward system or the Vietnamese one (Circular 11/LDTBXHTT, Article 2a). The question of increasing or decreasing the minimum salary in the foreign-invested sector has long been debated. During the period from 1990 to 2007, the Vietnamese government reduced the minimum salary level in foreign-invested companies three times, from 50 USD to 30 USD per month. This shows that the government favoured the idea of maintaining a low minimum salary level. Some arguments support this move. First of all, the minimum salary level in the foreign-invested sector has already been shown to be higher than that of the state sector. Any increase in the minimum salary in the foreign-invested sector will worsen the brain drain process from SOEs to foreign-invested firms. Inevitably, more qualified and competent workers have been attracted by joint venture enterprises, due to the wage difference between these two sectors. Second, a low minimum salary in foreign-invested companies is a must in order to compete with neighbouring countries for foreign capital. In the past, some of the neighbour nations had, at times, an even lower minimum salary of 27 USD, in contrast to Vietnam's minimum salary of 50 USD. Considering Vietnam's young population, with more than half of it in the working age, a low income is argued to be better than to be unemployed or under-employed.

However, in 2007, under great social pressures caused by rising waves of strikes in labour-intensive foreign-invested companies, the government issued Decree 168/2007/ND-CP that raised the minimum salary in this sector up to 50 USD again. Recently, there has been a change in government attitude towards salaries in the foreign-invested sector. In particular, the rate of increase of the minimum salary for workers in the foreign-invested sector is kept lower than that of the state sector. The aim is to reach the same level for all enterprises, following Vietnam's WTO commitments (non-discrimination between forms of business). It is expected that by 2012, Vietnam will have a common minimum salary for all enterprises (Personal interview with MOLISA conducted in 2007).

Furthermore, foreign-invested firms are required to make some contribution to two publicly managed funds: social insurance and medical insurance. Employers are to contribute 15 per cent of gross salary for social security (employees contribute 5 per cent) and 2 per cent for health insurance (employees contribute 1 per cent). The system was recently overhauled, positively affecting high-income earners. The Law on Social Insurance, which came into effect in January 2007, caps salary at 20 times the minimum wage for contribution purposes. For higher-paid employees, who might earn 60 or more times the minimum wage, this reduces contributions significantly in comparison to the past.

As far as the labour market is concerned, at the skilled end of the labour market, companies encounter the problem of lack of qualified and skilled candidates in some fields such as computing, marketing, human resource management, etc. This is a ubiquitous problem in Southeast Asia as a whole (Hainsworth, 1993; Kuruvilla and Venkataratnam, 1996). In this context, job-hopping in a bid for a higher salary has become popular. The labour market thus puts upon companies certain pressures in designing their remuneration package to retain their employees, or at least the valuable ones. Moreover, most interviewed companies consider high personal income tax for local staff as the biggest constraint to their salary policies. Since 1994, the government has reduced the rates of personal income tax several times. However, companies still claim that the Vietnamese tax rates are very high and effectively place a barrier to the upward progression of Vietnamese employees, as they advance to positions of authority within an organisation.

Source: Vo (2009: 88–90)

Levels of reward often depend on external and internal factors as well as the relative strength of the individual employee and market forces. These include a range of factors, which can be grouped into the following.

3.5.1 HR individual characteristics

First, there are the individual characteristics of the person concerned. These include elements such as age and experience, as well as qualifications, skills and performance. While age considerations are not allowed to be a factor in much of the West, in parts of Asia age and length of service are major influences in setting pay – the young have low pay and the older (while still able to work) receive higher pay. This raises a fundamental question: are rewards given for 'contributions', 'services rendered' or 'value-added' by the person concerned? There is then the aspect of a person's 'potential' to be considered. These are commonly the first factors to be used to justify levels of reward.

3.5.2 LM characteristics

Second, there are a range of LM factors that can come into play at different times and with various degrees of relevance. These include not only labour supply and demand, but also interventions in the LM, such as competitive pressures, the 'cost of living', and so on. An example of competitive pressures in the LM can be seen in relation to key IT specialists leading up to the expected 'Millennium Bug' in the late 1990s. The higher reward levels within China (as between Shanghai compared to Xian) is an example of the cost of living argument.

Yet, as we know, LMs are not 'perfect'. They can be 'sticky' and operate 'imperfectly' (see Chapter 1, 1.7.2.1). Furthermore, there can be interventions which distort 'pure' LMs. These include (a) trade unions, with their collective bargaining forcing reward rates higher than would exist otherwise, and (b) the state by, for example, using pay policies, introducing minimum wages and equal pay, or encouraging certain types of reward system (such as profit sharing).

3.5.3 Job characteristics

A major set of reasons often used to justify reward levels concerns the type of job itself. These include the responsibility and skill requirements of the particular position and also relativities (differences in levels of pay between different types of job) compared to other jobs. These relativities are based on comparisons. These comparisons can be made with other people, in the same or different jobs, inside and outside the organisation and specific LM, and also socially (such as with family, friends, relatives or historical comparator groups) and relativities of these jobs with other jobs in the past.

This argument about relativities is linked to what is called the 'going market rate'. The going market rate sets the 'floor' level of rewards for a job. People will begin to leave the organisation if the current rate received is felt to be too far out of line with the market rate. Relativities, like absolute levels of pay, result partly from competitive forces in LMs, interventions on the part of trade unions and governments and administrative decisions within organisations, such as the use of job evaluation.

3.5.4 Job evaluation

An important technique used to justify the level of reward is to base it on job evaluation. One of the fundamentals of a good rewards system is that employees believe it to be 'fair' and, above all, it is 'seen to be fair'. Rewards should recognise that some jobs are more demanding or difficult than others and the more demanding or difficult the job the better it is rewarded relative to other jobs in the organisation. Yet, fairness can still be sought. How can fairness be attained and differences justified? The classic way is to calculate rewards via job evaluation.

Job evaluation is the process of determining the 'worth' of a job to an organisation. This process internally compares the relative 'value' of jobs. It is used to *compare jobs*, not to assess a single job in isolation from others. The purpose is to assess the relative difficulty or responsibility of a number of jobs so as to put them into ranked categories, which might then be used as the basis of a rewards system which is seen to be fair and orderly. Therefore, another way to justify rewards is to say that the level has been set for the job itself and that this has been done 'objectively' as the result of job evaluation. Job evaluation has other important roles, such as its use in 'fairness' (or at least being seen to be fair) and as a defence by businesses in discrimination claims where it is claimed that those doing work of a similar nature are paid at different rates.

Think About/Question 3.5

What methods would you use to evaluate jobs for the purpose of rewards?

The following (both non-analytical and analytical) methods of job evaluation are some of those more commonly used. They are, as in much of HRM, better seen as systematic, rather than scientific, processes and they range from the simpler and less costly in time and money to the increasingly complex and expensive. As ever, there is a trade-off between cost and sophistication.

3.5.4.1 Ranking

Ranking is the least systematic method of job evaluation and is the one often used in parts of Asia. Here jobs are simply ranked in order on the basis of given criteria. These criteria may include market value, responsibility, difficulty, criticality to organisational success, skill required, and so on. The ranked jobs are then divided into grades and a rate of pay fixed for each grade is attached.

However, because this system is subjective and arbitrary, it can create dissatisfaction amongst those employees who feel that the system is unfair or is manipulated by the bosses. Also, the extent of differences in criteria, such as difficulty and responsibility, are not readily established with this method.

3.5.4.2 Grading (job classification)

This approach to job evaluation is similar to ranking except that classes or grades are established first, and jobs are then placed into these pre-formed grades. Jobs are usually evaluated on the basis of the whole job using one factor, such as difficulty. Although grading is more systematic than ranking, there does remain a largely subjective dimension and, therefore, it can cause disgruntlement among employees. Yet, this is a common means of evaluating jobs in parts of Asia and is usually established using very subjective criteria.

Some of the developments in the area of rewards have an impact here. One such development that has attracted much attention in the West and among international firms in Asia is 'broadbanding'. This is an attempt to retain the positive features of traditional pay scales while reducing its less desirable aspects, such as tendencies to focus on promotion over performance, an unwillingness to undertake duties associated with higher grades and the inability to offer higher salaries to new employees. Basically, broadbanding involves retaining some form of grading system, but with a reduced number of grades or salary bands and with pay variations within them based on performance rather than the nature of the job. However, there is a desire to retain a skeletal grading system as this gives order to the structure and helps to justify differentials.

3.5.4.3 Points rating

More systematic methods of job evaluation include points rating systems, where each job is evaluated according to a standard set of criteria. Such systems can be obtained 'ready made', with consultants able to provide generic, off-the-shelf systems. There are many examples of factors and factor plan weightings. The International Labour Organisation has produced a list of factors used most frequently. Criteria can include requirements in terms of education, skills, experience, planning and co-ordinating, initiative, judgement and decision making. Each of these different criteria might earn a number of points within an established range depending on the level required by the job. The points earned under each heading are then added together to give a total for the job. The total determines the grade into which the job is placed.

Points rating is the most commonly applied job evaluation method in the West and is used by many international organisations in Asia as it is seen to be more objective and fair. Therefore, it is commonly used to assess comparable worth issues in disputes on equal pay because it allows for comparisons across job categories and types of employment.

> **Think About/Question 3.6**
>
> What might be some of the problems with using job evaluation to set reward levels?

There are various problems with job evaluation to consider and remember. Some of the more general can be seen in Table 3.3.

Table 3.3   Issues with job evaluation

Issue	Characteristic
Time	Increasingly costly to raise 'objectivity'
Level	Too high or too low
Factor	Which chosen and weights critical

First, this method may lead to reward systems where pay is determined by administrative, rather than LM, considerations. One consequence is a danger that rates for some types of HR may be either inadequate for recruitment, retention and motivation, or rates are unnecessarily high.

Second, the specific factors chosen and how they are exactly weighted is fundamental and critical, not least as it can produce the outcome desired. For instance, factors may well be biased and even discriminatory, which in the worst case scenario are self-serving, producing the result that organisations want to be achieved, often justifying why some jobs (often done by men) are paid more than others (often done by women).

This can be clearly seen in the case in Table 3.4. The first example, using Factors (A), seems to 'justify' why maintenance fitters should be paid more than company nurses. After all, 'objective' job evaluation has been used in this endeavour, has it not? Given the gender segregation of work, it is obvious what the implications of this are. However, the second example using the same two jobs, but using different Factors (B), now indicates that they should be paid the same!

As we have just seen, the area of employee rewards, rather than being easy and simple as initially presented, is actually complex and often a minefield, with not just legal, but motivational and even PR aspects to it. Once we start to delve below the surface of employee rewards, there is little that is robust, objective or consistent. To make these matters worse are some of the recent trends in this area. One approach taken in an attempt to resolve for management some of the issues raised above is to

Table 3.4 Job evaluation using different job factors (each scored 1–10)

Factors (A)	Maintenance fitter	Company nurse
Skill ■ Experience in job ■ Training	 10 5	 1 7
Responsibility ■ for money ■ for equipment and machinery ■ for safety ■ for work done by other	 0 8 3 3	 0 3 6 0
Effort ■ lifting requirement ■ strength required ■ sustained physical effort	 4 7 5	 2 2 1
Conditions ■ physical environment ■ working position ■ hazards	 6 6 7	 0 0 0
Total	**64**	**22**

Factors (B)	Maintenance fitter	Company nurse
Basic knowledge	6	8
Complexity of task	6	7
Training	5	7
Responsibility ■ for people ■ for materials and equipment	 3 8	 8 5
Mental effort	5	6
Visual attention	6	6
Physical activity	8	5
Working conditions	6	1
Total	**53**	**53**

Source: Adapted from EOC (1985)

try to link rewards to performance. After all, surely no one will object to those who work harder being rewarded for their endeavours and getting paid more than those who work less hard, will they? This brings us to the second main aspect of rewards – the area of performance-related rewards.

3.6 Performance-related rewards

There are two bases for these rewards. They are as follows.

3.6.1 Time-based systems

The basic wage or salary paid is negotiated on the basis of the actual time spent in attendance on the job or at the place of work. Even today, payment for many jobs is made in this simple way. Additional payments can be made above the standard rate for working, for example, overtime, shifts, weekends, unsociable hours, and so on.

Within these systems is the incremental pay scale. People are paid for the time they spend at work regardless of the effort they put in and, in this case, they are also paid an additional amount or increment each year that they work for the employer usually within the job grade. This is supposed to encourage employees to stay with the same organisation for a long period of time, rewarding long service and so result in a stable workforce. There is also an implication that people will become more knowledgeable and effective in their job while they work for more years to gain experience. Another advantage is that it is simple and easy to calculate pay. A version of this was the prevalent form of reward system for full-time male workers in large firms in some Asian countries such as Japan and South Korea, where it is known as 'seniorityism'. This had cultural underpinnings, not least that esteem and wisdom are seen to come with age. However, the system was also aimed at reducing labour mobility so that the employers had a return on an investment in training and development (see Chapter 4 for more on this).

An important characteristic of time-based systems is that there is little about them to motivate employees to actually perform better. Also, employees can sometimes control and manipulate these payment systems to suit their own interests. It can encourage not only 'clock watching', but also an overtime culture, as this reward is paid at a premium to normal wages. At the end of their service employees are on their highest level of pay, but their most productive time was probably much earlier in their career.

In countries where an end-of-service payment is made (often a month's pay per year of service), employers use this form of employee-enforced savings as working capital and at the end of the usual 30 or 40 years of employment some employers fail to pay out the amount owed. This has led to a strong preference for 'cash now' as opposed to deferred reward, not only in parts of Asia but also in some Western countries where the anticipated pensions or provident fund entitlements have not always been honoured.

3.6.2 Performance-based systems

It is these management issues and problems that have created the fertile ground for the search for alternatives in rewards. The idea of incentives in rewards is not particularly new. Nevertheless, managers continue to seek a method and formula for linking rewards to performance so that effectively it can be put on a type of 'automatic pilot'. This leads to disputes when employees do not agree the method or formulae used. For example, staff of an international investment bank based in Hong Kong greatly resented their performance being 'standardised' with those based in Paris where the working hours and productivity were considered to be much lower. The capacity for hard work over long hours is found in parts of Asia. However, 'standardisation' using such Asian norms would be resisted in the West.

Performance-related pay (PRP) is the more topical version of this idea, although with a significant difference, for instance: 'Incentives are used to stimulate performance, while performance pay is to reward it ...' (Torrington and Hall, 1998: 618). Indeed, there has been some shift in payment systems towards providing rewards for some form of performance (or 'variable pay' or 'pay at risk'). Such systems reward individuals, groups or organisational units on their performance contributions. Performance-related rewards is an all-embracing term which includes rewards that recognise personal contributions and provide employees with opportunities to participate in the financial success of the organisation.

3.7 PRP schemes

PRP has several aims, which – along with the obvious objectives of improving motivation and performance as well as recognising differential contributions – include trying to attain strategic goals and reinforce organisational norms. PRP is based on some form of appraisal of the job holder against inputs (traits, skills) and/or outputs (objectives). This can take a number of forms. The schemes can be related not just to individual, but also to team, group and plant-wide performance. However, businesses need to ensure that participation in team rewards does not conflict with rewards offered by individual schemes. If there is tension or conflict, individuals, especially in the West, may decide it is more profitable for them to work alone rather than participate in joint team efforts. In parts of Asia there will be great pressure to have group rewards rather than rewards based on individual contribution. This is mainly because the community spirit is greater in some parts of Asia than it is in the West where the individual is considered to be more important than the group. In parts of Asia loyalty and personal needs are thought to be more important than individual contribution or capability. However, among the younger generation of workers, particularly among the elites in India and China, 'greed' rather than 'need' seems to be the prime motivator; in this respect, therefore, there does seem to be some convergence between Western and Asian expectations of PRP.

Think About/Question 3.7

What types of PRP scheme are you aware of?

A variety of PRP schemes exist. They include the following.

3.7.1 Payment by results

Historically, the most widely used incentive scheme has rewarded employees according to 'results', such as the number of units of work produced or reduced time taken to produce the units – the more you produce, the more you are paid. One example of this reward system is piecework, which is the standard form of payment in factories in China, India, Pakistan and other Asian countries. Alternatively, the incentive can be paid for time saved on the 'standard time' in performing a specified operation, as derived from work study (which we covered in Chapter 2).

Yet, there is a need to cater for problems such as external influences depressing output by, for example, machine failure, raw material delays and demand fluctuations. A solution to these issues was measured daywork. In this reward system, instead of variable rewards corresponding to output achieved, employees are paid a fixed sum so long as they maintain a predetermined and agreed level of working.

Again, some of the drawbacks of this form of system are apparent, such as speeding up to achieve the given output in a shorter time span – an example being a large-scale bakery where the speed of part of the line (i.e. the conveyor belt through the ovens) is increased to achieve the output, but now over a shorter time period. There may well then be quality problems arising from such changes.

3.7.2 Skills-based

This reward system seeks to reward employees for the skills, or competencies, which they acquire. Its most obvious benefits are to encourage multi-skilling and functional flexibility, while simultaneously indicating the organisation's commitment to HR development (see also Chapter 4). Most reward systems of this nature reward people with additional increments to their base pay once they have completed defined skill modules. Obviously, such a system needs close monitoring and managing to ensure that the skills learned and rewarded are actually the ones needed by the organisation. This form of reward system is more established in the West and is less common in parts of Asia, where (as will be seen in Chapter 4) some employers can sometimes be reluctant to increase the skill level of employees in certain sectors and levels.

3.7.3 Performance bonuses

These reward systems include temporary increases to base pay that are tied to specific performance outcomes. There are a plethora of methods, which include the widely used practices of paying a commission on sales and tipping for service. Another common method is for an organisation to set up competitions to achieve particular targets (for instance, an increase in sales) and to reward those who achieve those targets. This reward system may well have the effect of improving productivity, but unless all employees feel they have the opportunity to win, some may feel it is not worth the bother of making the extra effort. Rewards need to be managed efficiently or employees may well end up feeling cheated for the extra efforts made, with obvious effects on their future performance as well as on employee relations.

Another issue is that in some Asian societies individuals do not want to stand out ahead of their peers, so rewards based on competition within workgroups are not welcomed. In general, some Asians consider that harmony is more important than individual reward, so competition between workers is considered to be disruptive while competition between groups is accepted. A good example of group competition was seen when the Malaysian government chose Japanese and Korean construction firms each to build one of the Petronas Twin Towers that dominate the Kuala Lumpur skyline – the two firms competed on quality and speed to complete its own tower ahead of the other.

3.7.4 Instant or 'spot' bonuses

These reward systems recognise exceptional contributions. They may even take the form of senior managers walking around the workplace with an open cheque book to give instant rewards. These bonuses need to be set realistically and not awarded on an arbitrary basis, otherwise employees may feel that favourites are getting the rewards and others are neglected.

3.7.5 Profit sharing

There are a number of ways in which rewards can be linked to profit levels. Cash-based schemes represent the traditional and most common arrangement, whereby employees are paid a cash bonus, calculated as a proportion of annual profits. Such a system is found among some Asian employers who may give amounts such as one month's ('the 13th month') pay as a bonus to all employees in a good year. Gainsharing is a variant, and this, importantly, can apply to non-profit making organisations. Here the bonus relates to costs saved rather than profit generated. This form of reward system is rare in Asia but is more common in the West.

3.7.6 Stock options

Rather than cash, shares can be awarded to employees. This group of rewards is provided in an increasingly complex manner in the US and UK, in particular. Some businesses may offer lower-level employees the opportunity to buy shares in their companies at preferential rates. This is seen as a way of encouraging employees to 'think like owners' and, therefore, to work harder to increase the value of 'their' business and 'their' shares in it. Few Asian companies use these systems, although it could be argued that the communist work organisations in China, Vietnam and North Korea hope for their workers to act like owners.

3.7.7 Employee involvement

The systems described above lead us to another area – the role and use of types of reward as forms of employee involvement (see also Chapter 5). In 1992 the European Union (EU) Council of Ministers adopted recommendations concerning the promotion of 'Participation by Employed Persons in Profits and Enterprise Results'. Initiatives have already been taken in the UK and France to encourage profit sharing. Share ownership has been a continuing influence on these developments in the EU. Employee involvement, perhaps because of its socialist and communist links, is not encouraged in some parts of Asia, although Japanese organisations have welcomed and rewarded employee involvement in improving processes.

3.8 Difficulties with PRP

There can be enormous difficulties in introducing, running and managing PRP schemes.

> **Think About/Question 3.8**
>
> What problems do you think might arise with PRP schemes?

The choice of scheme and its success are related to the extent to which a variety of factors are met. Some of these can be seen in Table 3.5 and below. Critically, it is often the case of 'what gets measured gets done'.

Table 3.5   Factors to be considered in PRP

Factor	Characteristics
Measure	Level at which performance can be objectively measured
Ability	Change actually results in better performance
Timing	Lag between performance and reward
Co-operation	Extent between individuals or departments
Commitment	Management committed and able to communicate goals
Involvement	In scheme design (e.g. targets set seen as important)
Trade unions	Agree/oppose (e.g. impacts on goals/collective bargaining)
Acceptance	Employees accept and understand plans
Corporate culture	Not in conflict with culture (e.g. UK public sector)
Employee culture	Sensitive to cultural values of employees (e.g. Asian)
Calculation	Easy and direct reward for effort made – 'line of sight'

Figure 3.1 The line of sight model

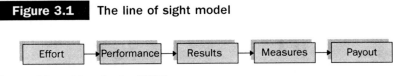

Source: Adapted from Lawler (1990)

Important aspects of PRP include the freedom and ability to actually increase performance, clear attribution of the source of any increased performance and short time to the reward. A key requirement of any contingent reward scheme is that people should have a clear 'line of sight' (see Figure 3.1) between what they do and what they will get for doing it. This concept expresses the essence of expectancy theory: that motivation takes place only when people expect that they will receive worthwhile rewards for their effort and contribution.

However, the time gap between increased performance and any reward may not actually operate as prescribed. For instance, the rewards through shares may be a long time coming, and the size of such rewards may also be small. In profit-related schemes both the 'ability to influence' and the time lag factors come into play. For example, any extra performance may not result in any improvement in share prices, which are affected by many factors other than just employee performance. Not only may the individual have very little influence on shares or profits, but the time gap between any enhanced performance and reward received for it may be very long and tenuous. Furthermore, the actual amounts paid out under such schemes may be fairly negligible. All these have obvious implications for motivating HR.

The problems of rewarding people using PRP and incentives across occupations and sectors, and links to motivation, are apparent. Assessing performance objectively remains difficult. It remains a perennially difficult task for management in a whole range of areas of HRM, including performance appraisals, training and development (see Chapter 4). One possible way forward is to develop a more sophisticated and nuanced range of criteria. Such an approach is the Balanced Scorecard method (Kaplan and Norton, 1996) whereby measurements are put in place to answer the four questions set out in Table 3.6.

Table 3.6 Questions and perspectives using the Balanced Score Card in rewards

Question	Perspective
How should we appear to our shareholders?	Financial
How should we appear to our customers?	Customer
In which business processes must we excel?	Internal
How will we sustain our ability to change/improve?	Learning and growth perspective

Source: Based on Kaplan and Norton (1996)

In sum, there are advantages and disadvantages to both of the main categories of reward system, neither of which is a complete solution to management and organisational problems. These are compared and contrasted in Table 3.7. This again indicates the contingent nature of employee rewards, as is often the case in HRM.

Table 3.7 Advantages and disadvantages of different reward systems

	Advantages	Disadvantages
Incremental System	◆ Simple, easy to calculate ◆ Reward service, stable workforce ◆ Experience gained is rewarded	◆ No incentive to work harder ◆ Slow progress for high fliers ◆ No incentive at top of scales
Results System	◆ Extra effort is recognised ◆ Less productive is penalised ◆ Encourage performance ◆ Appearance of fairness	◆ Results must be attributable ◆ Output must be measurable ◆ Effort/output link needs consistency ◆ Subjectivity in measures

3.9 Rewards in practice

Employee rewards can be seen in practice in a variety of areas. Set out below are some examples in the form of strategically related rewards and top management pay; also considered are variations in employee rewards in terms of PRP within organisations, attempts to spread PRP to non-private sector organisations, and international variations and examples.

3.9.1 Strategic employee rewards

Rewards can be used strategically. One example can be seen in Case Study 3.2 concerning Richer Sounds, the UK hi-fi music equipment retailer, as explained by Marchington and Wilkinson (2002). An Asian example is Smartphone of Hong Kong, where high quality customer service is a crucial part of the company's business plan and staff are expected to treat all customers well.

Case Study 3.2

Strategic rewards in action

Richer Sounds is a prominent British home entertainment retailer, best known as a hi-fi, home cinema and flat screen TV vendor, operating online and through a chain of 48 stores across the UK. The business is 100 per cent owned by Julian Richer, the founder and managing director. Richer Sounds formally began trading in 1978 when, at the age of 19, Julian opened his first shop. Initially known for selling budget audio equipment in a 'pile it high and sell it cheap' fashion, in recent years it has moved upmarket and expanded its range from just audio products to encompass TV and home cinema equipment. The company also instituted a corporate rebrand, redesigned its logo and literature and instituted a programme of facelifts, expansions and relocations of its stores. The core philosophy is to provide personal expert service at low prices – the motto is 'Biggest Brands, Best Prices, Expert Advice and Take It Home Today'. The stated aim is to beat competitors' prices, including those on the internet. Shops tend to be on the edge of main shopping areas in order to keep costs down.

Customer service is considered important and is the company's driving philosophy. Each store provides 'freepost' cards that are sent directly to Julian Richer, who responds personally to any negative feedback. Employees are encouraged to help customers to buy

---

products rather than simply go for the 'hard sell'. The company's basic principles are: 1) quality products (branded names); 2) value for money; 3) customer service. The company understands that while the first two can be controlled from head office, the third is very much in the hands of ordinary branch employees.

Rewards are seen very broadly with both (a) payment, and (b) a recognition (i.e. non-financial) aspect to its approach. Pay is above average for the retail sector, with the basic rate supplemented by commission, profit-sharing and customer-service bonus. A customer-service index is calculated with individuals being assessed on several indicators, the main one being customer feedback on service quality. Customer receipts include a questionnaire which invites customers to assess the level of service provided by the salesperson, who is identified by payroll number on the form. The individual's bonus is related to feedback, with both additions and deductions, which are totalled up monthly.

Non-financial recognition is important in motivation for the company and it has an array of incentives designed to make working more satisfying and enjoyable. For instance, staff who perform well receive 'gold aeroplane' badges as a recognition of their achievements, while wooden spoons are awarded for acts of stupidity. Additionally, a suggestion scheme has a small financial component, but the main element is a day trip on the Orient Express luxury train for the best two suggestions each quarter. Furthermore, branches also compete in the 'Richer Way League'. This is based on customer service standards and profits and has the use of a Rolls-Royce or Bentley motor car for a week as the prize.

Richer Sounds is known for empowering employees to make a difference to the company. Its suggestion scheme has been acknowledged as one of the most successful in terms of the number of suggestions per employee and has been the model for other businesses, including the Halifax Bank and Asda supermarkets. The company also received recognition from Business in the Community for its contributions to charity, one of the most generous donors (in percentage terms). In 2002 Richer Sounds was judged as the best British-owned company to work for by *The Sunday Times*. It has also been recognised by the government-backed Investors in People scheme.

Source: Adapted and developed from Marchington and Wilkinson (2002)

Rewards can also form part of a wider performance management system in Asia; this can be seen in South Korea (see Yang and Rowley, 2008) or China (Poon, Wei and Rowley, 2009).

3.9.2 Top management pay

A fundamental aspect of any reward system is that employees feel that the pay system is fair, reasonable and equitable. There is a widespread and increasingly vocal debate about top management pay, which often grows much faster than general pay increases. This has led to hostile public opinion and press coverage (using the derogatory term 'fat cats'). The issues revolve around how top management remuneration is set, how it is linked to 'performance' and how it rewards 'success' (or not). This debate involves not only the total amounts, but also the disparities with the rest of the organisation's workforce.

In 2007, for example, the earnings of US executives included the following:

- William McGuire (United Health) – US$1.1 billion
- Hank McKinnell (Pfizer) – US$213 million
- Bob Nardelli (Home Depot) – US$210 million
- Dick Grossa (NYSE) – US$187 million
- James Kitts (Gillette) – US$165 million

In 1997 in the US the average total direct remuneration of CEOs was 326 times that of the average employee (compared to 19 times in the UK). US average annual compensation (in real terms) of CEOs as a multiple of average worker pay was, in 1970, 39 times at US$1.3 million, but by 1999 it was 1,000 times higher at US$37.5 million. The fall-out of the post-2008 global financial crisis has also brought many other examples into the open, including the £700,000 annual pension for life from the age of 50 for the ex-head of one failed bank.

In some Asian countries, such as Japan, the multiple of CEO to average worker's pay is far lower than in the West. There are some examples – for instance, Pakistan – where the multiple is much closer to that of the US. If non-cash benefits, such as golf club membership, are included, then in parts of Asia multiples are higher between the highest and the lowest paid in an organisation. Hong Kong and China already have differentials in excess of 500 between the pay of CEOs and average workers. This is not just because average workers have low pay but because Chinese CEOs (especially in banking and investment) receive rates of pay similar to those of international top managers.

During 2007 the Singapore government increased salaries for ministers and top civil servants to become among the highest in the world. The President of Singapore is now paid almost S$4,000,000 (US$290,000) a year, which is getting close to the US$400,000 paid to the President of the US – who governs a much larger country. The rationale of the Singapore government is that, to attract and retain the best talent, high rewards are justified. One may wonder what is the rationale of Western countries such as the US and UK, which pay politicians and civil servants much less than industrialists and bankers. Part of this may be to reflect on the notion of intrinsic rewards as well as deferred rewards, such as pension, security, lucrative later jobs and the patronage/honours system.

3.9.3 Use of PRP by HR level

There is also varied use of PRP schemes by organisational hierarchies, which can be seen in Table 3.8.

Table 3.8   Variations in use of types of reward (%)

Reward type	Managerial	Manual	Non-Manual
Performance-related	52.4	12.9	32.4
Profit-related	14.8	6.7	12.4
Profit-sharing	9.5	4.8	9.1
Bonus scheme	38.6	24.8	28.6
Skill-based	4.3	10.0	4.8
Competence-based	4.9	3.3	2.3
Payment by results	8.6	2.4	3.3

Source: Adapted from Torrington and Hall (1998)

3.9.4 Use of PRP by organisations

Contemporary examples, in the West and in some international organisations in Asia, involve attempts to introduce more performance-related elements into the pay of both the private sector, such as retail banking, and the public sector, with groups such as health workers, teachers and the police force.

While, at first sight, these PRP initiatives may seem eminently desirable, it does not take long to see some of the problems and management issues that may arise. Even if we take the use in retail banking, how is performance measured? Is it based on 'sales'? If so, of what and by whom? Not only may distortions and product mis-selling occur, but 'churn' (i.e. where customers use products for only a short period of time) may arise. Some employees may have no opportunity to achieve sales given the nature of their job. In the public sector, the same issues arise in an environment determined by the ethos of a 'service' and professionalism rather than pay for performance.

3.9.5 International variations in rewards

Think About/Question 3.9

What variations in employee rewards between countries are you aware of?

There are many differences internationally between rewards (also see White and Drucker, 2000: Chapter 9). Reward systems remain varied between countries. We will give a few examples of these variations. In Japan the '*nenko*' system of seniority pay gives greater emphasis to an employee's seniority within the organisation. Similarly, in South Korea a system of 'seniorityism' was prevalent. In China there was the 'one big pot' reward system, especially in the large state-owned enterprises (SOEs). While these SOEs have declined, shedding 25 million workers between 1998 and 2001, there are still 50,000 SOEs employing 50 million people using variations of the 'big pot' system. The changing patterns of rewards in Asia can be seen in Wei and Rowley (2009). The use of rewards in MNCs in Asia (US and Japanese in Vietnam) can be seen in Vo (2007). Some examples of Asian reward systems can be seen in Text Boxes 3.3 and 3.4.

Text Box 3.3

The basis of rewards in China

The decision taken and supported by the China corporate management team was to change the way employees of the Guangzhou Enterprise were rewarded. The principle that was considered was "rewards by performance and position." This was clearly a significant departure from the old way of doing things. The old way of granting everyone the same absolute quantum was a legacy which was brought forward from the state-owned days where the concept of fair treatment was equated with equal treatment, regardless of personal background or individual capability or responsibility weightage or contribution. This thinking is very much aligned to post imperial China's era of Communist ideology, which emphasizes collectivist values and systems.

Source: Chin Seng Koh (2009: 157)

Text Box 3.4

Reward systems in Vietnam

SOEs

Prior to *Doi Moi*, SOE managers had virtually no discretion over workers' salaries. Salaries were calculated according to a government pay scale, based on educational level, grade and length of service. The salary and rank of an employee were determined by the length of service and political attitudes, and bear no relationship with the economic performance of either the firm's or the individual's performance. The variation in the grades was small in order to achieve egalitarianism. Given their lack of accountability and the egalitarian salary system, employees were not obliged or encouraged to perform well. Ultimately, this led to the notoriously low productivity and inefficiency of SOEs.

In the wake of the *Doi Moi* period, the government has given special attention to the remuneration policies in order to reinvigorate the state sector. Linking compensation to enterprise performance was the first important step in compensation reform. SOEs now have the right to select the method of payment of salary (Labour Code 1994, Article 58), in line with their operating situation and the quality and result of the work performed (Labour Code 1994, Article 55). The government only imposed a floor income but not an income ceiling. Wage differentials within the state sector between skilled and unskilled workers have been increased.

These changes were seen as a big move towards monetising salary, and replacing and abolishing the system of subsidised distribution (GTZ, 2006). However, SOEs are not totally free to set their own remuneration system as the government still determines and promulgates minimum salary levels for each region and each industry (Labour Code 1994, Article 56) and stipulates the principles for formulation of salary scales, salary tables and labour rates (Labour Code 1994, Article 57). Case studies show that while salary systems remain within the government's framework, there is evidence of different incentive mechanisms. Investigated SOEs have successfully developed and adopted a dual salary system consisting of two parts, namely a 'hard' salary, which strictly follows the government's salary schemes, and a 'soft' salary, which is sensitive to firm's performance and individual's performance. The 'soft' salary enhances the effectiveness of the salary system and helps to increase productivity.

The current salary system is criticised for being too complex and burdened with too many salary schemes, grades and steps. Furthermore, employees can gradually proceed through salary schemes and ladders without the need to improve their performance, and thus seniority is still a weighting factor in determining payment. More importantly, the SOE salary is notoriously insufficient for employees to maintain an average standard of living. In this situation, SOE employees must find other jobs to supplement their income, leading to low productivity and limited work stimulation in the state sector. Corruption is also another consequence.

MNCs

Foreign-invested companies are free to apply their own reward system to their Vietnamese subsidiaries, with the condition that they meet the minimum salary level in the foreign-invested sector set by the government (Circular 11/LDTBXH-TT, Article 2a). However, they are faced with an imperfect labour market, which has an abundance of low-skilled labour at one end of the market and a shortage of skilled labour at the other end. Companies commonly encounter the problem of lacking qualified and skilled candidates in some fields such as computing, marketing, HRM and so on. In this context, job-hopping in a bid for a higher salary has become popular. The labour market has thus placed upon companies certain pressures when designing their remuneration in order to retain their employees, or at least the valuable ones. On the contrary, one of the biggest attractions of investing in Vietnam is the abundance of a cheap low-skilled labour force. The minimum salary in this sector is USD 50 per month.

Compensation practices are highly centralised in terms of the defined position in the salary market, the permitted salary range and the compensation structure, which heavily stresses individual performance. Salary structures heavily emphasise individual-performance-related payment. Additionally, companies also offer stock options and individual/team incentives. There are, however, instances where centralised policies have been adapted into practices and procedures in a manner that is suitable to the local situation and preferences, as in allowances and benefits, a fixed bonus and the adoption of the '70/30' reward style to avoid or reduce high personal income tax and labour costs.

However, there is evidence of MNCs utilising an extremely simple reward system. For example, MNC FMCG4's salary system is divided into two categories: white-collar employees and blue-collar employees. The wage of a blue-collar employee is calculated based on their working days per month. Meanwhile, for white-collar employees, the only reference used to establish the starting salary and the increasing rate is the market average level. The salaries of the professionals and upper levels are negotiated on an individual basis with the consultation of expatriate managers, most often with the general director. The extremely simplified salary structure, at the time being, functions fairly well, in the context of a small-sized subsidiary.

Source: Vo (2009: 155–156; 161–162)

India presents a further example. The Indian Railways system of rewards is based on long-developed public sector comparator groups with slow progress up the salary grades. The Indian government has appointed a Sixth Central Pay Commission to consider reward systems for its 1.6 million staff.

Task 3.1

Devising a rewards system

As a government adviser you have been contacted to examine the advantages and disadvantages of the rewards system in the Indian Railways. You have been asked to devise and justify a move from national systems to encourage more local flexibility and performance.

Produce your report.

It is expected that the Central Pay Commission, will recommend substantial increases in pay and a reduction from the current 50+ grades (previously there had been over 500 grades), will reduce the difference between the maximum and minimum of the various grades and allow faster movement up the grades. The staff of Indian Railways seek comparison with the private sector – especially banks, customer contact centres and IT firms (where staff have benefitted from internationalisation of pay scales) rather than state and central government comparator groups.

In the US it is common to give very high rewards and bonuses to individual managers. Pay differentials between employees and managers used to be much greater in the US and UK than in many Asian countries, but some sectors in India and China now have levels of differentials more similar to those in the US and UK. Equal pay is of much greater concern in the West than it is in Japan, South Korea and China where women employees have traditionally had a separate status which is lower than that of male employees (Rowley and Yukongdi, 2009). Collectively bargained rewards remain more important in some countries, such as South Korea and Japan, than in others, such as Indonesia and Thailand, and also for some sectors, such as manufacturing, than for others, such as the hospitality industry.

Employee rewards are affected, therefore, not only by individual performance, but also by national criteria. Such criteria can be cultural, such as a society's expectations (for example, for high pay amongst US managers) or more egalitarian. Government strategies, as in Singapore, can sometimes deliberately make labour costs comparatively high to force employers to move up the added value chain. We will return to these themes in Chapter 6.

On the subject of international rewards, the following guide to international compensation systems has been developed by Milkovitch and Newman (1996). The first part contains the following four segments.

1. *Economic*: completive dynamics/markets; capital flow/ownership; taxes

2. *Employee*: demographics; knowledge/skills; attitudes/preferences

3. *Organisational*: strategic intent; technology innovation and work roles; autonomy and information flows

4. *Institutional*: culture/politics; social contract; trade unions and employer federations

The second part is to examine strategic similarities and differences between countries by six criteria:

- objectives
- internal alignment
- external competitiveness
- employee contribution
- advantages
- disadvantages

3.10 Conclusion

The subject of employee rewards continues to be as important and emotive an issue especially in some of the rapidly changing Asian countries such as India and China, where high pay for managers and owners has increased while millions of workers exist in poverty. There are attempts to 'justify' pay levels by reference to a range of factors, which includes an attempt to be more 'objective' by using more 'rigorous' forms of calculation, such as job evaluation, not least as a defence against claims of bias and discrimination in those countries that have passed legislation forbidding forms of discrimination.

There are two basic types of rewards system: those in which the key variable is either (a) time or (b) output. They are not mutually exclusive; hybrids are quite common. Changes occur and fashions come and go over time in the area of remuneration. Different rewards systems may be used for different grades of staff, especially between management and shop floor workers. However, there have been general moves towards paying for performance.

Reward systems vary significantly between and across sectors and countries. In recent years, in the West, major issues around pay have been associated with PRP and equal pay. With the growth of international corporations, structuring an equitable reward system for employees from different countries is a major concern.

Case Study 3.1

Rewards in a law firm

Please refer to section 3.2 for the facts of this case study

The main problem was the classic failure even to look at the basic tenet of a rewards system (i.e. that the targets set should be achievable). Yet, was this number of billable hours a realistic target? How many hours per week were actually required – for example:

– 46.5 hours every week for 52 weeks?
– 50.4 hours every week for 48 weeks?

As a response, the company replaced this with a totally different rewards system: a move from hourly-based to an assessment based on seven categories:

- respect and mentoring;
- quality of work;
- excellence in client service;
- integrity;
- contribution to the community;
- commitment to diversity; and
- contribution to the firm as an institution.

What issues may arise with this new system?

End of chapter tasks/questions
Based on the bank and airlines case studies in Appendix 3, using and applying information within this chapter

1. If employees' pay is linked to profit, what implications will this have for recruitment and retention for the bank in each location?

2. What are likely to be the main motivators of staff in an airline? How would the motivators be different between airlines in China, India and the GCC?

3. Why would an Indian aircraft engineer expect different pay and benefits from employment in India and in the GCC?

4. How would job evaluation be applied differently by the three airlines in the case study?

5. Would the bank have the same system of pay differentials in each location in which it operates? Discuss what would remain the same and what would be different and why these differences would occur.

6. What system of performance management and assessment will each airline find it best to use and why would they make the system selection?

7. What are the advantages and disadvantages of the bank using the same system of performance management and assessment in each location?

8. How will the view of long-term incentives differ between a bank and an airline?

9. How would the view of a range of incentives vary between China, India and the GCC?

10. How might the ratio of male to female employees vary between different jobs in a bank and an airline?

11. How would these gender ratios vary in China, India and the GCC?

References

Armstrong, M. (1999) *Employee Rewards*. London: CIPD.

Economist, The (2003) 'Japan's wage round: Heading down', 8 March, 72.

EOC (1985) *Job Evaluation Free of Sex Bias*.

Galunic, C. and Weeks, J. (2001) 'Investments that build on human nature', *Mastering People Management, Financial Times* P.5, 12 November, 10–11.

GTZ (2006) 'Salary systems in Vietnam'. Available at http:// www2.gtz.de/ vietnam/download/salary_system_in_vns_public_administration_en.pdf (accessed 17 December 2007).

Guerra, F. and Chung, J. (2008) 'Fear of falling executive pay', *Financial Times*, 6 January, 11.

Hainsworth, G.G. (1993) 'Human resource development in Vietnam', in M. Than and J.L.H. Tan (eds), *Vietnam's Dilemmas and Options: The Challenges of Economic Transition in the 1990s*. Singapore: Institute of South Eastern Asian Studies, 157–206.

Harry, W.E. (2007) 'Employment creation and localisation – the crucial human resources issues for the GCC', *International Journal of Human Resource Management*, 18(1): 132–146.

Hille, K. (2008) 'Incentives shift for Taiwan's tech workers', *Financial Times*, 25 September.

Kaplan, R.S. and Norton, D.P. (1996) *The Balanced Scorecard: Translating Strategy into Action*. Boston, MA: Harvard Business School Press.

Koh, Chin Seng (2009) 'Case 7 – Change in bonus payment system' in R. Alas (ed.) *Implementation of Changes in Chinese Organisations*. Oxford: Chandos.

Kuruvilla, S. and Venkataratnam, C.S. (1996) 'Economic development and industrial relations: The case of South and Southeast Asia', *Industrial Relations Review*, 27(1) 9–23.

Lawler, E. (1990) *Strategic Pay: Aligning Organizational Strategies and Pay Systems*. San Francisco: Jossey-Bass Publishers.

Marchington, M. and Wilkinson, A. (2002) *People Management and Development: HRM at Work*. London: CIPD.

Milkovitch, G. and Newman, J. (1996) *Compensation*. Chicago: Irwin.

Nigh, V. (2008) 'Lubricating the system', 16 May–7 April at Missouri Department of Agriculture, weblog post, *Doing business in Vietnam Seminar*, Ag Business Development Division, 7 April. Available at http://dbivietnam.blogspot.com/2008/04/lubricatingsystem.html (accessed 10 September 2008).

Poon, I., Wie, Q. and Rowley, C. (2009) 'The changing face of performance management in China', in C. Rowley and F. Cooke (eds) *The Changing Face of Management in China*. London: Routledge.

Rowley, C. and Yukongdi, V. (2009) *The Changing Face of Women Managers in Asia*. London: Routledge.

Shen, J. (2007) *Labour Disputes and their Resolution in China*. Oxford: Chandos.

The Socialist Republic of Vietnam (2005) *Report of the Survey on Corruption in Vietnam 2005*. Hanoi: Government of the Socialist Republic of Vietnam.

Taylor, R. (2001) 'The truth about work', *The Financial Times*, 25 January.

Torrington, D. and Hall, L. (1998) *Human Resource Management*. Harlow: Prentice Hall.

Vo, A. (2007) 'An investigation into the transfer of HRM policies and practices of US and Japanese companies based in Vietnam', in J. Burgess and J. Connell (eds) *Globalisation and Work in Asia*. Oxford: Chandos.

Vo, A. (2009) *The Transformation of HRM and IR in Vietnam*. Oxford: Chandos.

Wei, Q. and Rowley, C. (2009) 'Changing patterns of rewards in Asia', *Asia Pacific Business Review*, 15.

White, G. and Druker, J. (2000) *Reward Management: A Critical Text*. Abingdon: Routledge.

Wilson, T. (2001) 'Rewards that work', *Mastering People Management*, *Financial Times* P.4, 5 November, 2–3.

World Bank (2006) 'Vietnam Development Report 2006', Report No. 34474-VN. Available at http://www-wds.worldbank.org/external/default/WDSContentServer/WDSP/IB/2005/12/02/000160016_20051202141324/Rendered/PDF/344740VN.pdf (accessed 3 April 2008).

Yang, H. and Rowley, C. (2008) 'Performance management systems in South Korea', in A. Varma, P. Budhwar and A. DeNisi (eds) *Performance Management Systems: A Global Perspective*. London: Routledge.

Yu, G., Walder, N. and Rowley, C. (2008) 'The impact of flexible benefits and employee satisfaction', *International Journal of Society Systems Science*, 1(1): 67–83.

Employee development

4.1 Introduction

We have covered the initial areas of HRM in terms of employee resourcing and employee rewards. One area integrally linked to both of these is employee development: once the HR plan has been completed and HR recruited, how do organisations develop these HR and ensure their work is carried out well? A whole set of management and business issues emerge, ranging through the rationale, amount, type and assessment of employee development. As in many of the areas and activities of HRM, there are a variety of practices, from the more simple to the more complex, and these development practices remain difficult areas. Acknowledgement of the issues and their complexity is at least a useful start.

This chapter tackles the area of employee development in two major parts. First, the area of HR training is analysed, with its main issues, methods and purposes. Second, performance management and appraisal – the direction and measurement of how someone is working in terms of the methods and issues involved – are covered. These two aspects of HRM are intricately linked, and should be seen as such, not least as the latter can be a method of discovering the need for, and evaluating, the former.

4.2 Overview

Employee development is an important area for HRM in both the literature and its practice. For example, employee development is one of the crucial HRM polices to achieve important HR and organisational outcomes in HRM models (see Chapter 1). It is often prescribed that investment in employee development produces a range of beneficial outcomes, for both employees and organisations. Yet, measuring these outcomes robustly and with confidence can be difficult.

Investment in employee development is often taken as a 'good thing' in that it is something that the 'best' businesses surely should do. Linked to this is an area of increasing commitment (especially if long-term career systems are declining) through training as a 'generalized investment' (Galunic and Weeks, 2001). Another part of the issue, as in much of HRM, is the need to somehow 'prove' the benefits and results of training expenditure. This issue, which includes the 'when', 'where' and 'how' of evaluation, is a persistently problematic and difficult area. Another issue in the area of employee development concerns the fact that it is often a long-term investment with delayed paybacks. This is especially problematic in economies and businesses that may have short-term perspectives. At the same time, organisations may suffer from 'poaching' – the loss of trained staff to non-training competitor businesses – especially to those organisations which have saved costs by not investing in training.

In the West there has been recognition and criticism of the poor training provision in countries such as the UK for a very long time. This criticism concerns not only volume, but also the fact that 'academic' qualifications fail to give sufficient practical skills for the workplace. There have been numerous initiatives since the nineteenth century to improve the situation. In the UK these include National Vocational Qualifications (NVQs) – a system, developed in the 1980s, of narrow and trade-related vocational qualifications and standards of occupational competence, with the emphasis on practical skills. NVQ-type qualifications are now emulated in some Asian countries, especially those of South East Asia, which recognise the importance of skilled artisans and technicians.

For some commentators, the non-interventionist market force approach pushed the prime responsibility for training onto employers and the micro-level (Thornhill et al., 2000: 180). Therefore, one might expect training to be central to businesses. Yet, this may not always be the case. For instance, training may well be peripheral and, rather than invest in their ILM, employers may simply resort to the ELM to 'buy-in' the skills needed using money saved by not training existing employees. How does this compare with the situation in other leading economies? Training systems in different countries vary significantly. This has implications for the quality of production and the competitiveness of organisations.

4.2.1 Asian ways of learning and developing

Asian ways of learning, and hence training, have developed in ways that are different from the industrial societies of the West. In Asia learning is less experiential (where students learn by their own discovery) and depends more on being given the 'right answer' by the teacher or trainer. Also, many Asian languages are not based on an alphabet, so are less conducive to student-building knowledge, and more on having to be taught meanings – as with the Chinese characters, which are complete words in themselves. Many Asian countries were rural and agricultural until recently, so there has been more reliance on learning from others' experience and learning from elders. Such societies are also more risk averse than industrialised and post-industrial societies as individuals and families have less wealth and fewer reserves and risk has far greater consequences than in the case of rich states with their social security safety nets. The result is that innovation and trying new ways of working will often be avoided unless success is assured.

Some Asian organisations see training as a long-term investment, while others see it as a cost and, therefore, tend to neglect training. Employers may fear increasing the capability of the employees to the level that they become attractive to other employers and/or the employees ask for higher pay. One example of the extremes to which employers will go was found in Multan in Pakistan where the local cotton mill owners successfully resisted the provision of secondary education because the young people would be able to get jobs away from the area and deprive the mills of low-skilled, low-wage workers.

Individuals in parts of Asia also either see training as important or of no use in a situation where connections and fate will lead to career success or failure. Chinese, Sri Lankan and Indians, particularly those raised in middle-class homes, seem especially to value education and training as a means to improve their career prospects. Family members will often combine resources to finance those with the best prospects who will be expected to help other family members in the future. An interesting comparison (Kambayashi, Morita and Okabe, 2008) shows that the reasons for business education (enrolling for an MBA) in Japan was to become acquainted with the staff of other organisations and discover what they were doing in their companies – whereas in the US it was to change jobs or advance careers. Others in Asia believe that 'connections' or 'fate' are more relevant to career success, so in turn neglect education and training. For some Asians, especially those living in rural areas, education (except at the most basic levels) and training are beyond the resources of individuals and families. For some Asians work will be in family enterprises or cottage industries employing very few workers – the small organisations that will depend on passing on skills from old to young with little opportunity for learning or development of new expertise.

How do we explain the variations in employee development provision between businesses and across countries, and the skill shortages in some locations and an apparent surplus in another? The number of well-qualified citizens of the Philippines with not enough jobs to be filled is one example. As we will see later in this chapter, the levels of government encouragement of employee development spending by businesses also vary. We will look at these issues, the implications and types of provision and assessment. For instance, to what extent do training approaches suggest a universal model? Why do some businesses use 'internal' ('on the-job') training while others use 'external' ('off-the-job') training?

Interesting and international examples of such areas can be seen in Taylor (2006), Clarke (2008), Pfeifer (2008) and Kwong (2009). Indeed, the latter provides an interesting case of Taiwan, with examples such as Capital Finance and Sun Securities and their upgrading of skills and government company subsidies. It also notes the history of government-funded training and education leading to companies, such as AVO (one of the world's largest flat-panel display makers) and Chunghwa Telecom, having sizeable training departments. We can see a further Asian example in Text Box 4.1, covering training types and programmes in Vietnam.

Text Box 4.1

Training types in Vietnam

Training programmes in SOEs

On-the-job training, the majority of which is conducted in the workplace as part of the normal experience of employees, is the most popular training method in SOEs. On-the-job training mainly focuses on technical workers and involves learning through the assistance and supervision of an experienced and senior employee, normally the production line leader, who helps the trainee learn some useful knowledge and skills that are directly applicable to the trainee's production lines. This type of training has benefits in that it is customised and encompasses real work experiences. Relying on in-house resources, on-the-job training is also cost-effective and is thus preferred in SOEs. Workers, in general, are ranked in terms of technical skills from first to seventh grade, the latter being the highest skill level. They are expected to upgrade their skills gradually, by passing the 'Upgrading Technical Skills Examinations' that are held regularly. To pass these examinations, SOEs provide their workers, especially those who hold pivotal positions in the production lines, with some short in-class training courses (1–2 days) which are specially designed to cover some theoretical aspect of production. These examinations motivate workers to develop and improve their skills and raise their employability. However, no penalty is charged if workers fail the examinations; in fact, those who fail are still allowed to remain in their positions. Thus, upgrading skills is left to each individual's endeavour.

SOEs recognise that their severe shortage of qualified managers is posing a serious problem at present and will continue to do so in the immediate future. As a result, professional and managerial staff members are offered more training opportunities than workers. Across the case studies, around 60–65 per cent of the training budget is invested in training professionals and managers. Training programmes cover the following fields: business administration, government policy studies (e.g. tax policies), English, informatics and political training. Training courses are not offered on a regular basis but are dependent on the availability of trainees, trainers and, most importantly, funding. They are organised either by the company or by their General Corporation. Training is conducted by trainers from universities, external consultants or relevant governmental agencies (e.g. tax policies courses are taught by the Tax Policy Research Institute, and business administration courses by the Vietnam Chamber of Commerce and Industry). The majority of these courses are reserved for department heads and upper-level employees.

Overseas training opportunities are very rare and mostly restricted for directorial and top managers. Often, these managers are sent on business tours to visit foreign enterprises and learn from their operations. The duration is about 7–10 days. In many cases, the cost is covered in equipment selling/buying contracts with the foreign partners, in which training is a part of the deal. Overseas travelling/training opportunities are highly sought after and still considered as 'rewards' to key employees. Therefore, the selection criteria are highly subjective and are set at the sole discretion of the top executives of the company and their General Corporation (see also Quang and Dung, 1998).

To limit training budgets, SOEs encourage their employees to embark on self-study. Companies provide support by partly reimbursing their tuition fees (normally 50 per cent). The most popular methods still are in-service training and specialised training for graduate and postgraduate levels and supplementary studies for high school and lower levels. Employees attend these classes in the evening after work. Companies might allow their employees to take leave for studying purposes. However, in general, the understanding is that studies must not interfere with their obligations at work. Although co-ordinated and implemented by universities, these training programmes suffer serious deficiencies and learning quality is greatly neglected (Quang and Dung, 1998). In practice, programmes are shortened to reduce learning time as much as possible, teachers are overpowered by the student-managers and examination results can be corrupted. The quality has become so low that it has given rise to a popular adage 'as ignorant as specialised training students, as stupid as in-service training ones'. However, these training programmes are still very popular as they provide employees the chance to attain the minimum level of education required for their positions or an extra degree, which would be viewed favourable in promotion competitions, at a low cost, in terms of both finance and time investment. In many cases, obtaining a degree/certificate is the main objective, rather than upgrading one's skills and knowledge.

As discussed in Section 6.3, in-service training, specialised training and supplementary studies were popular prior to *Doi Moi*. Recently, with the renovation and expansion of the educational system, more options are now available to the public. Employees can invest on high quality E&T programmes, offered either by local educational institutions or by foreign-invested ones. Some choose to undertake a second university degree or master degree. Management degrees, such as Master of Business Administration, have been very popular. Compared to the cost of in-service or specialised training, tuition fees for these degrees are much higher. However, enrolments have been increasing steadily, evidencing the real demand for business and managerial skills.

Finally, retraining is an important part of T&D activities in the state sector. In the old centrally planned economy, the compulsion imposed on enterprises by the government to employ more than the necessary number of staff led to over-employment in SOEs. Since *Doi Moi*, SOEs' restructuring has led to mass redundancies. Most of the redundant employees have low-level, outdated and over-specialised skills, which hinder their mobility and employability in the new labour market. The government requires all downsizing SOEs to provide retraining to their laid-off workers so they can be redeployed to other functions in the same company or can regain employment somewhere else. On the one hand, retraining successfully preserves the state sector's reputation in securing jobs for their employees. However, on the other hand, it causes stagnation and prevents the injection of 'new blood' into the SOEs' labour force, as revealed by SOE Auto3's HR manager:

> Many of these employees have managed to retain employment relationships with the enterprise. We put people on the retraining schemes with the view that their skills will be upgraded and, more importantly, relevant to our company. Afterwards they might still work for us on non-permanent contracts or they will find a job somewhere else nearby. ...We see all the old faces.

Training programmes in MNCs

Training programmes in MNCs often start with the very basics of business education in the curriculum. Employers provide broad-based foundation training for their staff as a basis for further training provided later. MNC Auto1, for instance, has implemented a 'learning tree' training scheme with roots (basic business skills: stage 1), trunks (functional skills and advanced business skills: stage 2) and leaves (management and leadership skills: stage 3). In the first stage of this programme, 100 per cent of staff is required to participate to ensure that all employees have basic business awareness and speak the same business language. In the next stages, the company seeks to develop potential managers only, where intensive training programmes are tailored to prepare them to assume managerial posts. Similarly, MNC Auto3 developed a model of on-the-job training in six steps, which covers the company's whole workforce. Step one is for the lowest level of employees, while step six is for managerial staff members. The six steps aim to upgrade employees' skills and knowledge from the very basic level, such as to complete routine repeatable jobs under detailed instructions and regular supervision, through to using their own judgement and creativity to complete tasks with limited supervision.

Managers and professional/technical staff undertake more external training programmes than internal ones. Internal training mode is mainly on-the-job training for clerical, sales and production employees. Normally, companies establish a regular relationship with training providers to cater for basic training needs. Employees are required to actively pursue training by choosing courses to suit their personal development needs (courses are available on a 'first come, first served' basis) or taking them as a compulsory requirement for their current or new posts. Many of these programmes are taught overseas or by foreign experts so that Vietnamese managers can gain international exposure and experience. Some of them are required to take international assignments as part of their training programmes.

Non-Asian MNCs, such as MNC Auto1, MNC FMCG1 and MNC FMCG2, also offer 'shadowing opportunities', where high potential local employees tag along and observe expatriate managers from HQ full time. Mentoring is also used as a training strategy. However, effective formal mentoring relationships may not be formed easily in Vietnam due to the lack of expatriate managers and the cultural differences that form a gap between mentors and mentees. In addition, the demand in terms of time for mentoring programmes has a negative effect on expatriate managers' business effectiveness. Thus, the popularity and success of mentoring programmes are limited in the studied firms. This finding complements the argument that Western mentoring policies have trouble being transferred to the Asian context, and mentoring relationships that are developed naturally are more effective than mentoring that is created by formal means (Weldon and Vanhonacker, 1999).

Compared to their SOE counterparts, training methods in MNCs are more diverse and advanced. One of the most recent approaches adopted by MNCs is e-learning and blended learning. E-learning uses company intranet to deliver training courses to employees, and thus allows Vietnamese employees to gain access to a well of knowledge available to the company's global workforce. However, as a type of education where the medium of instruction is computer technology without personal interaction, e-learning has certain weaknesses, such as the lack of instructor interaction (Bouhnik and Marcus, 2006; Flamholz and Cheung, 2007). In the Vietnamese context, e-learning might not be optimal as the workforce does not have a strong knowledge platform to make good use of the company's global resources.

Blended learning aims to overcome the inadequacies that evolve from e-learning, by incorporating two or more methods for delivering training (Bersin, 2004; Mackay and Stockport, 2006). Typically this would include e-learning along with a mixture of other training methods such as on-the-job training or classroom-style training. One increasingly popular style of a blended learning programme involves combining both e-learning and manager-led on-the-job training. This style of training has proven to be liked by Vietnamese employees and to be more efficient than a singular classroom or e-learning program. Employees can learn and apply their training more immediately in a real work environment and can gain increased levels of motivation as the relevance of training to the job is clearly demonstrated. Blended learning also transfers the responsibility of learning to the individual, provides more immediate feedback from the supervisor and offers greater flexibility in the pace and timing of delivery (De Jong and Versloot, 1999; Lewis, 1997; Holton et al., 1997).

Besides the formal T&D channels, companies are aware of and use informal cultural aspects of management development to create a common language and shared attitudes across their operations globally. Non-Asian companies focus on policies such as an in-house top management programme and management forum, where participants are executives from all regions of the world and have contributed greatly to a strong global culture. By contrast, Asian corporations encourage employees to identify themselves within the corporation by emphasising the company's philosophy. In addition, e-forums, e-networks and e-learning, which are very popular in the studied firms, contribute greatly to creating a global culture and transferring 'soft skills'.

In the Vietnamese market, companies are faced with a dilemma – they could spend a fortune on training and developing their management staff only to see them leave the company (newly equipped with skills that make them more desirable in the market) for higher paying employers, in many cases a competitor company. As skills are scarce within and across industries, job-hopping to accelerate salary is popular. While some companies have a practical viewpoint on this matter, others think twice before determining their training budget. The MNC FMCG2 HR manager said:

> When talented and ambitious people are equipped with new knowledge and skills that they learnt in a multinational company, they become a precious commodity in the labour market; you should expect that they might want to move on.

On the other hand, MNC Auto3 claims they are unwilling to bear the training costs for managers because of the perception that such employees are highly individualistic and inclined to switch jobs whenever a more attractive opportunity becomes available. Moreover, each industry is narrow enough, so the list of talents within it is widely known to insiders. The production manager of MNC Auto1 can easily name top/key performers in MNC Auto2 or MNC Auto3. The competition for high-quality staff is fierce. MNC Auto1's regional sales and marketing manager used to be MNC Auto3's sales and marketing manager. He was one of the pioneers in assisting the country director in setting up MNC Auto3's operations in Vietnam. MNC FMCG3's production manager used to work for MNC FMCG4. Furthermore, there is clear evidence of spillover effects caused by employees who used to work for foreign MNCs and then subsequently moved to local firms. In some other cases, possessing local connections and newly acquired knowledge, Vietnamese managers leave MNCs and start their own businesses in the same or related industry, providing services to their former employers.

Preventative strategies have been applied to keep trained managers with the companies and reduce the regretted turnover rate. Some companies provide training and education programmes and/or financial support to managers' education only on the condition that they are bound by a legal contract with the company to stay for at least three to five years after the programme, otherwise, hefty fines would be applied. MNC Auto3, on the other hand, offers highly firm-specific training courses (such as the company's New Circle Leader, Training Within Industry, Company Philosophy higher level, etc.), which greatly improve the chance of getting acknowledged and promoted within MNC Auto3 but are of little help in seeking jobs elsewhere. No 'normal' degree or certificate has ever been given. The company thus limits the ability of their employees to use the knowledge gained in the company to advance their positions in other companies.

Source: Vo (2009: 117–119; 123–126)

Key questions in the area of employee development include the following. Is simply spending money on training necessarily a 'good thing'? How do businesses know what their training needs are? How does training expenditure become justified? Why are training budgets often one of the first areas to be cut when costs are to be reduced? This is linked to what is called 'training needs analysis', which is a medium- and long-term endeavour to identify what the organisation needs in terms of training and is therefore vulnerable to short-term cost cutting exercises.

We can see some of these issues in Case Study 4.1.

Case Study 4.1

HRM issues at ACT

ACT is a small, thriving electronics manufacturing and distribution company. Set up in 1987, the company produces components for the PC assembly market. Growth has been rapid, with a lot of new business won on its reputation for product innovation and high quality. The company employs 150 people at a greenfield site in the South East of England. It is now planning a further expansion of its facility to take advantage of new markets which are opening up in Europe and beyond, and is considering expanding production in Asia.

Although the company is a success, the managing director (MD) is feeling uneasy about the way in which the company is currently managing its human resources. There are two areas in particular that have given cause for concern: (1) the way in which non-technical training is organised, and (2) the capabilities of his management team.

Organisation of training

ACT has always invested heavily in training. The MD is convinced that ACT's reputation is mainly attributable to its highly trained workforce. In the past, training was confined to technical areas. However, with the expansion of ACT it has been necessary to develop training to provide additional skills in areas such as administration, finance, marketing, team-building and communication.

There is no HRM department in ACT. Training has been left to the line managers to organise. With technical training this was not a great problem. It was always well organised, consisting of mainly 'on-the-job' training and day-release courses provided by the local college. However, now that training is to be extended into non-technical areas, the MD is having increasing doubts about the effectiveness of the training organisation within ACT. A recent incident serves to highlight this. Walking through the production department a few weeks ago, the MD spotted a memo and a list on the notice board. It was written by the department manager and alongside the memo was a very 'glossy' brochure from an external training consultancy advertising a wide range of administration and supervisory courses. The memo invited staff to study the brochure, select a course they felt would benefit them and add their name to the list. The MD studied the list. Many of the courses that people were applying for appeared to the MD to be somewhat peripheral to the needs of their job at ACT. Furthermore, he realised that if everybody who was applying actually went on the courses selected a very serious hole would appear in the training budget! He quickly removed the memo and brochure and made a mental note to have a word with the manager concerned.

As the MD walked back to his office, he reflected on the incident. There was no doubt in his mind that something would have to be done to ensure that training was organised in a more structured and professional way. The company has to ensure that it obtains a return on its training investment.

Calibre of the management team

The management team consists of three board directors, four department managers, and four supervisory staff members (see organisation chart below).

With ACT's rapid expansion, emphasis has always been on product design, quality, achieving high levels of output and maximising sales. What has become more obvious is that, in the rush to achieve business growth, the development of core management skills has been neglected. Without these skills the MD fears there will be a real threat to the future survival of the company. A couple of examples highlight the MD's concern:

- In the boardroom none of the directors seems capable of discussing and dealing with strategic issues. For instance, the other day the MD wanted to discuss both the exploration of new markets in Europe and the sourcing of components from the Asia-Pacific to reduce production costs for ACT, or even expanding its operations in Asia. However, the meeting was quickly taken up with a discussion about the technical details of the latest semi-conductor design!

- The departmental managers are all good engineers and are respected by the workforce for their technical capabilities. All of them have grown with the company and promotion has largely rested on the possession of sound technical skills. Yet, the department managers seem unwilling to delegate and 'step back' from the day-to-day running of the company. The other day the MD heard one of supervisors complaining about the level of interference she was experiencing from her departmental manager. The supervisor said: 'He won't keep his nose out. He takes all the decisions so I just let him get on with it.' The MD has also noticed that some of the supervisors are too 'laid back' with the workforce, while others seem to be managing through a culture of fear and intimidation.

The MD has tried to communicate his concerns at management team meetings, but his managers keep avoiding the issue. When he presses them, they become defensive and withdrawn. The MD is approaching retirement age and wants to resolve these issues before he retires.

ACT Organisation Chart

Source: Adapted and developed from Beardwell and Holden (1997)

Task

Imagine you are a member of a firm of management consultants who has been approached by the MD for advice and guidance. You have been asked to review and make recommendations that will improve the way in which training is organised and evaluated and develop managers to achieve organisational goals.

You have also been asked to suggest which one country in North East Asia (Japan or South Korea) or South East Asia (Malaysia or Vietnam) in which ACT could expand production and advise on the main HRM practices (resourcing, rewards, development) for the new factory.

Produce your report.

4.3 Training

We note the uses of training and the tensions in this area next.

4.3.1 Uses

There are a variety of uses for training.

> Think About/Question 4.1
>
> **What should businesses use training for?**

Some of the various uses for training are indicated in Figure 4.1.

Figure 4.1   Possible uses of training

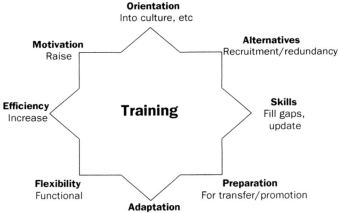

4.3.2 Tensions

The area of training and development is one of those areas where most people normally agree that it is a 'good thing' and 'the more the better'. After all, how can anyone argue against such assertions? Yet, one needs to take account of several issues in this area that revolve around the numerous tensions within training and its measurement.

First, there is tension between 'economic utility' versus 'inherent value' in training that needs to be noted and remembered. For some, it is argued that training must be shown in clear and practical ways to meet the needs of the business. Therefore, there has been increasing interest in attempts to evaluate the outcomes of training investment from this economic utility perspective. Alternatively, there is much debate on the inherent value of training and developmental opportunities. These take the beneficial outcomes on 'trust'. Obviously, the measurement of 'utility' and 'value' issues are less of a priority in this second approach.

Second, there is debate and tension concerning the view that, for certain occupations and professions, there is a known body of knowledge and set of generic skills versus ambiguity in the area. For example, for management professionals, as with accountants, lawyers, medical doctors, and so on, is there is a set of skills they must all have?

Third, the degree of 'planning' in training is an important and hotly debated issue with further tensions. For some commentators training is seen as a planned process, as work-related learning, which can be seen as the systematic development of the attitudes, knowledge, skills and behaviour patterns required by an individual in order to perform adequately a given task or job. For other commentators training can be less planned and can be informal. Again, issues such as evaluation are differentially dealt with in the former compared to the latter process. This also leads us to the area of management development.

Fourth, there is a distinction and tension between training and management development. We will not go into this is great detail here; rather we will treat them as broadly similar. However, it is worth noting quickly some of the more distinctive features of management development.

4.4 Management development

An initial question concerns the debate as to whether there are management skills that can be developed. It was famously argued in a classic work (Katz, 1955) – which has a continuing legacy – that there is a set of core skills employed by managers which were inborn personality traits, but could be developed. A broad, very general three-category typology of skills – technical, human and conceptual – was proposed, the level and mix of which in a manager was seen to evolve over levels and types of managing (see Figure 4.2).

Technical skills are the understanding of, or proficiency in, specific activities requiring the use of specialised tools, methods, processes, procedures, techniques or knowledge. As people move from their

Figure 4.2 Types and evolution of managerial skills and development requirements

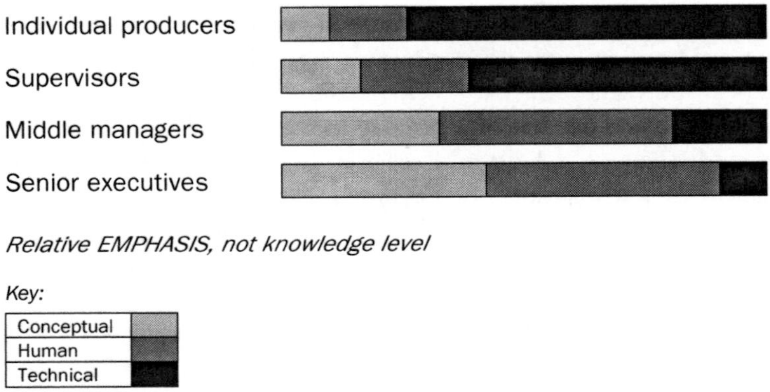

Individual producers

Supervisors

Middle managers

Senior executives

Relative EMPHASIS, not knowledge level

Key:

Conceptual	
Human	
Technical	

Source: Adapted from Katz (1955)

technical specialisation and into managerial positions, they also move towards the use of specialised knowledge bases and cognitive processes. One reason why managers must have technical skills is that these skills allow them to train, direct and evaluate those performing specialised tasks. Human skills are the ability to work co-operatively with others, to communicate effectively, to resolve conflict and to be a team player. Some researchers argue that these are the skills that managers most lack and thus need the most development. Conceptual skills are the ability to see the organisation as a whole or having a systemic viewpoint. While technical skills focus on things and human skills focus on people, conceptual skills focus on ideas and concepts. It was acknowledged that, while each skill category was discussed independently, the skills are interrelated when applied to managerial problems.

Management development is concerned with encouraging managers to improve their skills. Particular emphasis is often given in such programmes to important aspects of general management such as leadership, decision making, team work, communication, innovation and change.

For some commentators, management development improves managerial effectiveness through a planned and deliberate learning process. However, this may overemphasise the importance of deliberate planning in the process. As we noted earlier, there is a debate about the formality versus informality dimension, as in management development. The relationships between these can be seen in Figure 4.3.

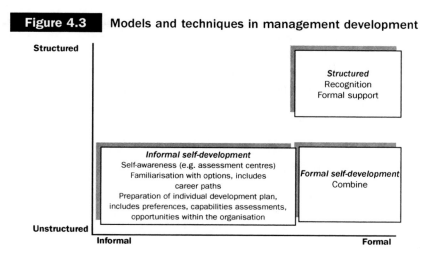

Figure 4.3   Models and techniques in management development

4.4.1 Formal development

Some writers see management development as being provided in a formal, top-down and highly structured manner. The emphasis, therefore, is on formal programmes. This sort of approach is associated with such factors as corporate 'universities', training departments, well-publicised programmes, integrated systems of appraisals identifying needs and candidates, and so on. Structured learning includes formal, directed, structured methods, which in turn include centrally provided programmes through which all managers progress in order to rise up the ranks. Yet, there are some problems and questions to consider with this approach. These include the following:

- Are the courses offered the ones that are most needed?
- Are courses offered to those who would benefit most from them?
- Are managers reluctant to admit 'weaknesses' that need rectification?
- Do managers argue they are too busy, or that the courses are irrelevant or insufficiently 'practical'?

4.4.2 Informal self-development

On the other hand, and in contrast to the above, there is a more informal model of management development. Here development is more decentralised and places greater emphasis on self-development. This is achieved through informal, unstructured ways of learning. Indeed, it has been argued by some commentators that, given the varied nature and range of managerial work and an individual's strengths and weaknesses, formal approaches may actually be inappropriate. Also, this sort of informal approach can be both cheaper and have motivational impacts, for example, stemming from devising an organisation's own management development plans, 'owning' problems, and so on.

4.4.3 Formal self-development

Another group of commentators have tried to combine the merits of the above two approaches – self-development plus guidance and organisationally provided support mechanisms. Examples of this sort of approach include the following. First, there is mentoring, which consists of using a system of experienced 'tutors', often senior managers, who take a relatively long-term interest in the development of the specific individual, to guide and provide orientation. There are many examples of organisations and jobs using such a system, including UK universities where a junior or new colleague may be allocated a specific senior person. This type of system has obvious advantages, not least in terms of cost-effectiveness and speed of inculcation of the person into the organisation. However, there are the equally obvious, but often overlooked, problems, which include those relating to the mentor allocated who may not have the requisite inclination, skills, training or time to undertake what might turn out to be an onerous role.

A second example of this approach is action learning (Revans, 1972). This has a focus on 'questioning insight' over traditional 'programmed knowledge'. With this approach, the problem needs to be 'real' and 'significant' to both the learner and trainer, and the main vehicle is often an action project. This is a process of 'learning by doing'. There are several approaches here, although a common theme is the view that management is a 'cluster' of practices best upgraded by direct exposure to problem-solving situations. This approach moves beyond debating possible solutions for problems to trying out the more favoured options. Furthermore, learning continues beyond the 'implementation' of solutions as it uses analysis of why something worked as it did. One method here is to organise business exchanges so that a manager experienced in one part of an organisation is transferred to another part to solve a particular set of problems thereby bringing a difference of experience and freshness of approach.

4.5 Factors shaping provision and effectiveness

Several factors are seen to shape the provision and effectiveness of training. These include those outlined in Table 4.1, amongst others.

Table 4.1   Factors shaping provision and effectiveness

Factors	Examples
Top management commitment	▪ Attendance on programmes ▪ Appointment of respected executives to training posts ▪ Allocation of resources to training function ▪ Not first target for cuts
Strategic connection	▪ Overseeing by senior executives (signal to others) ▪ Investment + strategic status allocated, i.e. senior management job to help managers
Nature of managerial work recognised	▪ Extent 'in tune' with nature of managerial work ▪ Fragmented/disparate activities; prefer action to contemplation; communicate directly; short time horizons
Varied needs and capabilities of managers	▪ Much work done as member of teams ▪ Fit in with this and motivation, needs and potential of individuals
Long-term, ongoing commitment	▪ Not just seen as 'one-off' to solve particular problem ▪ Not ad hoc
Systematic	▪ Allows standards reached, fewer mistakes, economic use, resource use ▪ Right training identified, implemented and evaluated

Further to the formality dimension, management development (and for that matter training) can be viewed within a framework of 'stages'. One of the more useful frameworks here is the 'levels of maturity' model (Burgoyne, 1988), as shown in Figure 4.4. Of course, as with many models we can question the actual applicability of this in terms of whether it applies equally to all firms, sectors and countries, its sequential nature and possible reversals, speed of movement between stages, and so on. In brief, these stages are as follows.

Figure 4.4 Levels of maturity in management development provision

1. No systematic management development	2. Isolated tactical management development	3. Integrated and coordinated structural and development tactics	4. A management development strategy to implement corporate policy	5. Management development strategy input to corporate policy formation	6. Strategic development of the management of corporate policy
No systematic or deliberate management development in structural or developmental sense. Total reliance on natural *laissez-faire* uncontrived processes of management development.	There are isolated and ad hoc tactical management development activities of either structural or developmental kinds, or both, in response to local problems, crises or sporadically identified general problems.	The specific management development tactics which impinge directly on the individual manager of career structure management, and of assisting learning, are integrated and coordinated.	A management development strategy plays its part in implementing corporate policies through managerial human resource planning, and providing a strategic framework and direction for the tactics of career structure management and of learning, education and training.	Management development processes feed information into corporate policy decision-making processes on the organisations' managerial assets, strengths, weaknesses and potential, and contribute to the forecasting and analysis of the manageability of proposed projects, ventures and changes.	Management development processes enhance the nature and quality of corporate policy-forming processes, which they also inform and help implement.

Source: Burgoyne (1988)

1. No systematic development
2. Isolated tactical development
3. Integrated and co-ordinated structural and development tactics
4. Development strategy to implement corporate policy
5. Development strategy input to corporate policy formation
6. Strategic development of the management of corporate policy

A critical aspect of the area of training is in terms of any evaluation of the results against planned purposes and objectives. A host of issues surround this topic. We outline these areas next.

4.6 Determining and locating training

One problem is how to foresee what critical new skills will be needed by an organisation? In surveys of managers and businesses the same areas tend to come up, such as the need for quality and customer service, internationalisation, communication and motivation, management of change, leadership, etc. Yet, these have been perennial issues from at least the late 1970s (see, for example, Peters and Waterman, 1982; Kanter, 1984). This indicates the difficulties of using practitioners to produce a map of the future – they may too often simply reflect familiar, fashionable and current concerns.

Similarly, as some Asian economies have been growing rapidly since the 1960s it has been very difficult for employers to predict what their needs will be in terms of skills, attitudes and behaviours. Since some Asian governments, such as those in China and India, have given up most aspects of central planning control of the economies, it has been left, generally, to the market to determine the required numbers of workers, skills, etc. However, HRM staff are unlikely to be aware of wider potential needs in society, nor are they likely to be aware of business needs unless they are involved in strategic planning, which they may not be (see Chapter 1).

Furthermore, training does not exist in a vacuum. Rather, it can be seen within a 'system' and 'cycle' (see Figures 4.5 and 4.6). The system can be complex. The cycle is often not followed in its entirety.

Figure 4.5 The training system

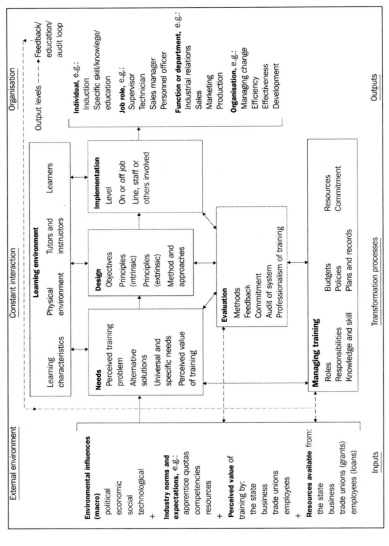

Source: Anderson (1993: 20)

Figure 4.6 The training cycle

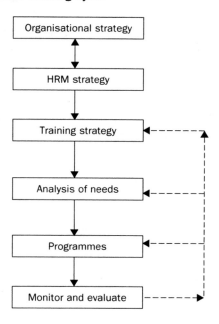

4.6.1 Training needs analysis

Is it simply good enough just to spend money on training on the assumption that all training is a 'good thing' and must produce some benefit? There are several questions and issues here. For example, is the training:

- given and, importantly, seen as a 'reward'? In many rich Arab countries, for example, people demand to be sent on employer-paid-for 'training' programmes in attractive locations with little learning expected;

- taken as an implied criticism? In South Asia, for example, staff are expected to bring all necessary knowledge and skills to a job, so if they need training they are not fit to do their job;

- simply using up the training budget? In some sectors if the allocated budget is not used it is forfeit and next year's budget will be cut;
- actually needed? The training may not be needed but the organisation does not realise this to be the situation. This can flow from neglecting to carry out a training needs analysis and lack of strategic planning.

> **Think About/Question 4.3**
>
> What factors might indicate a need for training in an organisation?

The factors that indicate a training need include looking at performance and assessing if any shortfall in achievement is caused by deficiencies related to training. A useful way of examining training needs is to look at the sources of those needs. Some of these can be seen in Table 4.2.

Table 4.2   Sources of training needs

Primary	Secondary
■ Requests	■ Workflow and materials
■ Diaries	■ Quality and complaint
■ Questionnaires	■ Accident rates
■ Interviews	■ Employee appraisals
■ Evaluation of past training	■ Attitude surveys

In determining training needs, there are questions and issues to think about, which include the following.

- What types of training are required to achieve organisational goals?
- Which jobs and which HR should be targeted?
- Are skills required simple, basic skills (language, numeracy)?
- Are skills required more complex (inter-personal, leadership, creative)?
- Are there trends that indicate the groups to be targeted (women, ethnic groups)?

Thus, an organisation first needs to determine its training requirements, with a focus on twin levels:

- Organisational – for example, HRP, plans for new technologies, products (see Chapter 1).
- The job – for example, job requirements via job descriptions, job analysis, person specifications (see Chapter 2).

4.6.2 Designing programmes and delivery

Impacts on training design and development come from key factors. For example, subject/methods, tutor/learner, resources/environment, and so on, all have impacts. Questions and issues in relation to this include the following.

- Where should it take place? This can be on-site or in separate locations.
- What types of programme? These can be provided in-house or by external consultants.
- What type of media? The range includes interactive computer programmes, DVDs and books.

A framework is to locate these on two dimensions. This concerns the differing amounts of:

- direction: self-directed and participative versus trainer-driven and less participative;
- base: individual versus group.

Think About/Question 4.4

What might be some of the advantages and disadvantages of these different delivery methods?

Each dimension and form has a set of advantages and disadvantages for employee development delivery. Usually these advantages and disadvantages are related to complexity and the numbers to be trained. Some of these can be seen in Table 4.3.

| Table 4.3 | Advantages and disadvantages of delivery methods |

Method ➤ *Direction* (more/less) ➤ *Base* (individual/group)	Advantages	Disadvantages
Lecture	✓ Volume of information to large numbers simultaneously ✓ Prepared in advance	✗ Lack of participation ✗ One way
Role play	✓ Develop inter-personal skills ✓ Confidence in protected environment	✗ May not be taken seriously ✗ Too nervous/embarrassed to perform
Group discussion	✓ Free exchange of knowledge ✓ Airs varying views/options	✗ Wander from subject ✗ Important points not covered
Video	✓ Real situation ✓ Information to group at once	✗ Little involvement ✗ One way
Projects	✓ Scope for creativity/initiative	✗ Needs to be of direct interest
Case study	✓ Examine situation in detail ✓ Removed from work pressures ✓ Different views	✗ Seems too easy ✗ Other/more complex issues in real life
Computer-based	✓ Work at own pace ✓ Immediate feedback ✓ Relearn at convenience	✗ Nervous of technology ✗ Isolation ✗ Technology
Guided reading	✓ Work at own pace ✓ Saves time	✗ Not encourage research/new materials ✗ Availability
In-tray exercise	✓ Experience issues arising ✓ Own/directed pace	✗ Need realistic issues ✗ Time needed

Source: Adapted from Foot and Hook (1996)

4.6.3 Implementation and methods

This area includes the routine and, crucially important to success, the administrative arrangements for training. These range from booking programmes, rooms, accommodation, meals and equipment, through to the event itself and carrying out the training. This training itself can be categorised into two broad types, as follows.

4.6.3.1 On-the-job training

The British term 'sitting next to Nellie' (i.e. learning from an experienced person) sums up one approach to on-the-job training (see Storey and Quintas, 2001), although expert systems (often computer-based, but sometimes in the form of written documents) are a more modern way of passing on skills by those considered to be the most knowledgeable in a work process. These are used to quickly improve capability in routine or standardised work. The common types of on-the job training include the following.

- Job rotation – moving from job to job, each at similar skill levels
- Shadowing – working alongside an experienced worker
- Apprenticeships – working with skilled persons, often combined with training away from work

4.6.3.2 Off-the-job training

The main approaches to this method of training include the following.

- Face-to-face – lectures, presentations and workshops
- Programmed or distance learning – using manuals/units
- Computer-based and interactive teaching – use of IT

> **Think About/Question 4.5**
>
> What are the main advantages and disadvantages of on-the-job and off-the-job training that you are aware of?

The advantages and disadvantages of 'on' versus 'off' the job training need to be recognised. These can be seen in Table 4.4. However, the broad methods are not mutually exclusive as both can be employed in integrated and co-ordinated programmes with 'blended' training.

Table 4.4 Advantages and disadvantages of 'on-the-job' versus 'off-the-job' training

	On-the-job	Off-the-job
Advantages	√ Doing the 'real thing' √ Experience handed down √ No special facilities needed √ Relatively inexpensive √ Trainers know the organisation √ Mixing with others across organisation	√ Experienced/planned trainers √ Experienced/planned/latest courses √ Free from workplace distractions/pressures √ Groups may be cost-efficient √ Mixing with people from other firms
Disadvantages	✗ Trainer abilities, motivation, time ✗ Insular, latest knowledge missing ✗ Trainees unwelcome – seen as obstacles ✗ Cover for absent trainers ✗ Less productive when training ✗ Difficulties settling back into job	✗ Relevance/transfer back to workplace ✗ May not be bespoke, tailored, targeted ✗ 'Re-entry', settling back into 'real' work ✗ Costly, e.g. accommodation, replacements ✗ Seen/treated as a 'jolly'

Think About/Question 4.6

When would you use on-the-job and off-the-job training? Which training methods would you mainly use, and why, for the following?

- Banking sector: branch manager; teller.
- Aviation sector: pilot; cabin crew; baggage handler.

4.6.4 Trainers

The main roles and responsibilities in training can be distinguished roughly between activities that are:

- strategic – for example, corporate plan, HR plan, training policy, training plan; and
- operational – for example, training needs analysis, training design, training implementation and evaluation of the results of training.

Trainers fall into categories and require a variety of skills. These include the following.

- Consultant/problem solver
- Designer/learning expert
- Implementer/instructor/teacher
- Administrator/manager/arranger

The varied aspects of this job include the following.

- Direct training/instructing
- Organising/administrating
- Managing element
- Advisory service to management

4.7 Evaluation

One of the most important, but often neglected, aspects of training is evaluation. This is largely as a result of the difficulty of actually measuring improvements meaningfully. Questions and issues here include the following.

- Was the training programme a success?
- How did the programme succeed in meeting the objectives and goals set? For instance, what improvements have there been?
- Has any change in performance actually resulted from the programme?

4.7.1 Issues and problems

There has been a shift in emphasis, in Asia also, towards 'cost effectiveness', especially in employee development activity, and towards the ability to demonstrate quantifiable results from such investments. In some organisations, including those in Asia, if there is no clear benefit from training and development, there is no investment. Wealthier organisations (and governments) often use training and development, especially foreign-based training, as part of the rewards package (see Chapter 3), with little actual training or learning involved.

It can be difficult to evaluate training as 'results' may not be observed immediately, and may be more medium- or long-term. Many HRM practitioners and academics note the difficulty in establishing a link between the incidence of training and performance. There is then the issue of the counter-factual – how do we know what might have happened without any intervention? This is an area that is often neglected and not adequately studied.

Think About/Question 4.7

How would you assess an organisation's training? What difficulties might you expect in doing this?

These are numerous ways to assess training. Some of the questions and issues in the area of training and development programme validation can be noted, some of which can be seen in Table 4.5.

Table 4.5   Training assessment – methods and difficulties

Assessment	Difficulties
Feedback questionnaires ('smile sheets')	■ What were the aims and objectives of programme? ■ When are these given?
Specific interview/ discussion	■ Where is impact expected? ■ Is it: individual's job; department; organisation?
Examine and test	■ When is impact expected and assessment timing? ■ Is it: during/end of programme; after return to work?
Observation and note changes	■ Who evaluates? ■ Is it: trainee; trainee's manager; tutor?
Performance data and measures	■ How to calculate 'costs' and 'benefits'? ■ Is change the result of programme?
Tutor notes	■ Do they have inclination/time? ■ Bias
HRM activities (appraisals)	■ Not the focus ■ May not be allocated time or indicates 'weakness'

4.7.2 Possible routes to evaluation

Methods exist to try to evaluate employee development programmes. One of the most well known is Hamblin (1974) – a multi-level method, composed of different levels of objectives and effects: reactions, learning, job behaviour, organisation, ultimate objective/effect (see Table 4.6). Examples of applying Hamblin can be seen in Tables 4.7 and 4.8.

Table 4.6   Training evaluation

Objectives	→	Effects
1. Reactions		Reactions
2. Learning		Learning
3. Job behaviour		Job behaviour
4. Organisation		Organisation
5. Ultimate value	←	Ultimate value

Source: Hamblin (1974)

Table 4.7   Training evaluation using Hamblin's levels

Level	Evaluation characteristics	Method examples
1. Reactions	◆ Ask about experience, parts useful/less so ◆ Elicit views on speakers, facilities, organisation, improvements	➤ Questionnaire ➤ Interview and discussion
2. Learning	◆ Test what learned as result (e.g. end of course) ◆ Assess degree acquired knowledge, skills, abilities aimed to deliver	➤ Test ➤ Exercise

| **Table 4.7** | Training evaluation using Hamblin's levels (*Cont'd*) |

Level	Evaluation characteristics	Method examples
3. Job behaviour	◆ Degree knowledge/skills used back at work ◆ If no result here, probably deemed failure ◆ Failure due to work culture or management attitudes mitigating against displaying new skills ◆ New skills best displayed in receptive environment	➤ Observation ➤ Self-assessment ➤ Questionnaire – manager ➤ Questionnaire – trainee ➤ Interview ➤ Performance appraisal
4. Organisation	◆ Effect on functioning ◆ Improvement in output, quality, productivity, waste, etc. ◆ Focus on areas of concern giving rise to training ◆ Less concerned with behavioural changes, more with change in performance via key indicators	➤ Effective indicator ➤ Performance data ➤ Complaints/rejects ➤ Sales/productivity ➤ Accidents ➤ Absenteeism ➤ Labour turnover
5. Ultimate value	◆ Some effect on performance ◆ Difficult to measure contribution or make judgement as to whether satisfactory	➤ As above ➤ Difficult

Source: Adapted from Bolton (1997)

| **Table 4.8** | Evaluating the impact of training |

Location	Instruments	Stage	Characteristics
Self	Observe behaviour	Reaction	During/end of programme
Line manager	Interviews	Immediate	Extent objectives achieved
Department	Questionnaires	Intermediate	Impact on job performance
Organisation	Performance data	Ultimate	Department/company impact
Designers	Feedback methods	Reaction	Reactive

Source: Adapted from Hamblin (1974); Bee and Bee (1994)

Other possible frameworks of evaluation include the Bee and Bee (1994) version, or the whole system (Morris, 1984). This is comprehensive, as seen in Figure 4.7.

Figure 4.7 Training evaluation: the whole system

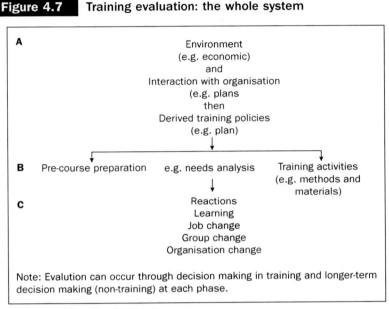

A

Environment
(e.g. economic)
and
Interaction with organisation
(e.g. plans
then
Derived training policies
(e.g. plan)

B   Pre-course preparation   e.g. needs analysis   Training activities
(e.g. methods and
materials)

C
Reactions
Learning
Job change
Group change
Organisation change

Note: Evalution can occur through decision making in training and longer-term decision making (non-training) at each phase.

Source: Adapted from Morris (1984)

4.8 Training in practice

In the UK there has been a succession of attempts to try to 'fix' the training problem, with more contemporary government initiatives, which include the Tomlinson inquiry (2003) and Leitch Review (2006), again trying to end the long line of failed initiatives designed to raise the prestige and quality of skills training. The woeful lack of training is not a new problem. It has been recognised by policy makers since at least the late nineteenth century. The UK is particularly weak in vocational education, especially in comparison to the more academic education seen as the route into university and 'better' jobs. This has been linked to a raft of causal factors – from the class system, through to seeing vocational qualifications as somehow 'second class' and only what you do if not 'bright' enough for 'proper' qualifications, to the perceived second rate nature of manufacturing vis-à-vis sectors such as services and finance. This is often brought into stark contrast by comparing the UK with other countries, which we return to later.

One example concerns NVQs. This UK competency approach was institutionalised with the development of a framework of NVQs. Yet, there are varied meanings for 'competency'. First, it is an underlying characteristic of a person that results in effective and/or superior performance in a job. Second, it is the ability to perform the activities within an occupational area to levels of performance expected in employment. Third, it is the integration of knowledge, skill and ability and to apply them with an understanding to a work activity and is assessed via performance.

For Torrington and Hall (1998) the basic idea of competency-based training is that it is:

- criterion-related, directed at developing ability to perform specific tasks directly related to the job you are in or for which you are preparing;

- expressed in terms of performance outcomes and specific indicators.

Yet, despite numerous initiatives, including the Management Charter Initiative and Investors in People, UK companies are generally perceived to lag behind many of their international competitors. The UK training culture is seen as 'voluntarist, finance rather than industry oriented, class based with public/private education' (Beardwell and Holden, 2001).

4.9 International comparisons in training

The amounts spent and types of vocational education and training provided vary across countries. Even within Asia this is the case (see Rowley and Warner, 2004). In some Asian countries training is neglected. A survey in 2000 of more than 1,000 Thai companies, including the country's top 200 largest firms, found that 75 per cent did not train employees to improve their technical capacity (Kazmin, 2003). Some employment in Asia is within family workplaces or cottage industries, which by their nature (low skilled activities, employing few workers, with little spare capital and often remote from vocational education facilities) lack the capacity or willingness to upgrade the skills of their employees. Young people in Asia may be desperate to learn, but opportunities can be rare and depend on the location and citizenship of those potential trainees.

4.9.1 Germany

We use this as an example of 'the best' European system of training. The country's vaunted system of extensive and developed training has apprenticeship programmes lasting approximately 3.5 years. This is funded through a mixture of state financing and employers' contributions. Although costly, the system produces qualified employees, enhances loyalty and reduces the costs of dysfunctional turnover. However, some have expressed concerns that the system is becoming too inflexible. It has a dual system: in-company training (practical); vocational school (theoretical) and many apprenticeships. There are excellent technical colleges and universities. The training culture is labelled as 'directed/functionalist: industry orientated, particularly engineering' (Beardwell and Holden, 2001).

4.9.2 Japan

There is a high level of training, especially in large companies, based on an expectation that those trained will stay with the employer for most of their career, thus repaying the investment in training over a long period of employment. New employees often have between one and six months' training on starting with a company. Training tends to be carried out in-house. For example, over 75 per cent of new regular employees and 52 per cent of non-regular employees receive training on starting with a company (Beardwell and Holden, 2001). On-the-job training is the main method, although a reflection of the trend towards more professional orientation to business is more business and adult 're-education' (Kambayashi, Morita and Okabe, 2008). There is also a system of pre-employment education for college graduates. The aim of this is to facilitate the transition from college to work, to inform about the organisation's culture and norms and cultivate a spirit of harmony and teamwork. Although there have been rapid changes in the education system as a result of declining numbers of young people in the population, high schools still take up to 90 per cent of pupils up to 18 years of age, so there are few young people seeking employment. For those not entering university there are two-year college courses which offer vocationally specific training. For most there are four-year university courses which were once considered to be a period of relaxation after the rigours of high school education but which are now, because of the competition for declining numbers of students, trying harder to provide worthwhile levels of education. The training culture has been described as 'directed/voluntarist: central and local government set and enforce training standards; meritocratic – top companies take from top universities; lifetime employment and training in large companies; self-development emphasised' (Beardwell and Holden, 2001).

4.9.3 China

SOEs and the town and village enterprises that arose with the opening of the economy to private business from the early 1980s lacked the resources and vision for training. Such organisations tend to arrange training by 'the sitting by Mrs Ma' style of learning from more skilled, usually older, workers. A clever or well-connected person passes critical national examinations and gains access to higher education but usually in topics approved by the government. Most professors in Business Schools, for example, are actually qualified in economics rather than in management. Until recently, very few Chinese people studied management topics. An insight into the training situation in China can be seen in Text Box 4.2.

Text Box 4.2

Low satisfaction with training in China

Under the planned economy, Chinese urban employees were classified into two groups: *workers* and *cadres*. Workers were blue-collar employees who were administered by the Ministry of Labour. Cadres were white-collar staff administered by the Ministry of Personnel. Training for workers was primarily in the form of post-employment apprenticeships and such training was compulsory. The supervisor was also called 'master' who actually was a lifelong mentor as well. Training programmes for blue-collar workers focused on improving working skills. Training for cadres was conducted by Communist Party-sponsored schools at different levels. Only those who had promotion potential were selected for training at Party political schools. Although training for cadres was not compulsory, nobody could afford to miss out, as it was considered critical and sometimes a prerequisite for promotion.

Taking training in schools of the Communist Party was a good networking opportunity for trainees as well and networking assisted in developing *guanxi*. Political studies were the focus of training for cadres. Training costs for both workers and cadres were met by the enterprises.

Since the economic reform, the training system for workers has been changed from compulsory apprenticeships to on-the-job training and optional part-time education. On-the-job training is limited and usually focused on briefings for new recruits and training on new regulations on products. Even less training is provided in POEs as enterprise managements usually regard training for new workers as a necessity, but on-the-job training is costly and causes disruption to production. The inadequate training provision is also due to the fact that firms do not have enough resources and time to implement systematic training when rapid economic expansion occurs, and a lack of commitment to employee development (Shen and Darby, 2006; Verburg, 1999; Warner, 1996). When training is provided, firms typically give priority to technical issues rather than management skills (Child, 1994; Shen and Darby, 2006; Wilhelm and Xia, 1993). Normally, employees in successful SOEs and COEs are free and encouraged to take up part-time education. Some generous enterprises even pay education expenses. However, encouragement for study is usually rare in POEs. There is also usually no training analysis or training audit. Limited training provisions have resulted in a lack of high-calibre employees and been a source of discontent for many Chinese workers.

Source: Shen (2007: 343–35)

4.9.4 Hong Kong

The economy has high-quality schools and universities along with strong vocational training facilities. This may be something of a surprise in a place that prides itself on its free-market forces approach to business. Skills training is sufficient to do a job, but there is also training to upgrade skills, replace foreign managers and technicians and to deal with the rapid expansion of production which, in many industries, was expanding by 10 per cent a year up to the post-2008 global financial crisis. Government and residence restrictions prevent individuals (except the well connected and well educated – these are often the same) from moving work location or job-hopping. Even those organisations which recognise the need for more training are unable, because of the pace of change and expansion, to allow staff to move from productive work to have time off for training.

However, the Chinese capacity for hard work means that many workers study for long periods outside working hours to increase their capability. A declining proportion of young people in the population, as a result of demographics and the one-child family planning, means that more productive use has to be made of potential HR. Rapid changes in economic development and a need to meet demand for increases in living standards means that the requirement for training is recognised, but the sheer scale and pace of change means that training is demand led rather than supply driven, with shortfalls for many skills and over capacity of skills that are no longer needed. The training culture is seen as voluntarist with some government direction.

4.9.5 Vietnam

An insight into the training situation in Vietnam can be seen in Text Box 4.3.

Text Box 4.3

Training in Vietnam

Factors influencing companies' training and development strategies

The Vietnamese E&T system can be classified as a unitary system (Maurice, Sellier and Silvestre, 1986), where achievement in formal education is regarded as a crucial indicator of competence and ability, and only 'failures' enter the state's practical training, which suffers from low prestige and a scarcity of funding. Education has long been seen as a means of achieving higher income and upward social mobility and of gaining respect. There is strong resistance to undertaking vocational and technical education and training (VOTECH) where instead, continuing the general education is preferred, as it opens the door to university entrance (Beresford, 1988). VOTECH is considered widely inferior to university education in the Vietnamese society. Although government's investment in VOTECH is improving slowly, the fact remains that it is extremely poor. In 2002, the budget for VOTECH accounted for only about 5 per cent of the total budget for E&T. In 2003, it increased to 6 per cent, and in 2004, to 6.5 per cent (Nguyen, 2006: 8). The weak vocational training system has become a constraint to the sustainable development of the country, as the majority of jobs most needed in Vietnam's transitional economy require technical skills (Nguyen, 2007).

Furthermore, a chronic mismatch exists between the output of the education system and the input of the companies (Duoc and Metzger, 2007; Hargreaves et al., 2001). Three main factors contribute to this problem. First, graduates from the E&T system lack practical experience and skills, and thereby fail to meet companies' selection requirements (MOET, 2001). Up to 80 per cent of graduate students have to be retrained by employers to match the requirements of labour inputs (Nguyen and Truong, 2007: 142). Although Vietnamese students are well versed in theory, their ability to apply theory to the work situation is extremely limited. Graduates from the Foreign Trade University, for example, during their four-and-a-half-year course, were exposed to real life experience only once at the end of their course in the form of company visits to write their graduation thesis. As the current curriculum is not related to practical training needs (Hargreaves et al., 2001), students must be re-trained before actually being assigned the work. Secondly, the labour market data in Vietnam is scarce (Duong and Morgan, 2001). As a result, training and education providers are not fully aware of the types and number of workers in demand. Thirdly, there is a total lack of formal and professional career guidance and counselling for students. Vietnamese students get career guidance from their parents, relatives and friends. Decisions are based on general perceptions of what are considered as prestigious careers (such as lawyers, medical doctor) or 'in fashion' careers, rather than on realistic occupational information, the needs of the industry, personal abilities and employment expectations. This results in the widespread situation where graduates choose fields of study that are not suitable for them, and later switch their career path and work in fields that are different from their university degrees.

When the economy develops along a new direction towards a market oriented one, the old management style becomes inadequate; instead of that, there is increasing demand for competent business managers. Until the 1990s, business and management education was almost non-existent and the experience of Vietnamese enterprises with market mechanisms was extremely limited. Now, more than two decades after *Doi Moi*, the shortage of appropriate managerial expertise still exists in the country as a whole, but is felt most acutely in SOEs. In their surveys with leading MNCs operating in Vietnam, William Mercer identified that management and person-related skills continue to be the weakness of Vietnamese employees. Kim (1996) describes this as a defect in the 'human factor' and predicts it could be the biggest obstacle to Vietnam's economic progress.

Due to the weaknesses in the E&T system, the workplace is expected to be the other major source of skill formation and training in Vietnam. Incentives are offered to enterprises in the form of tax exemption to encourage in-house training for their employees (Education Law 1998, Labour Law 1992). In theory, the law provides scope for the integration of training into business strategies and HRM systems. However, without imposing a floor level of training budget and a proper inspection, monitoring and enforcing mechanisms in place to ensure a consistent implementation of the law, ultimately, the level of investment on human development is still dependent on each company.

Training and development in SOEs

This section looks at T&D activities in the state sector. It argues that under increasing pressure to improve organisational efficiency, SOEs have introduced some fundamental changes into their HR function; however, T&D systems in SOEs have not advanced far from the old days of the centrally planned economy. Their activities suffer from limited financial resources, low-quality training courses, out-of-date training methods and a lack of systematic approach to training.

Prior to the economic reform, the concept of an external labour market was non-existent and employees were assigned to enterprises by the government, in many cases, without regard to the match between an employee's skill and knowledge and the firm's demands. At the workplace level, bounded by the centrally controlled system, bureaucratic rules and procedures and secured by the lifetime employment system, SOE employees were not motivated to learn and develop new skills and knowledge. The training offered to workers was mainly on the job, focusing on enhancing productivity and improving organisational health and safety. Meanwhile, short courses to strengthen employees' political beliefs were widely available, and employees were required to attend these courses if they wished to be promoted. This bureaucratic system created a gap that was expected to be filled by three main channels of education, namely in-service training (*dao tao tai chuc*), specialised training (*chuyen tu*) and supplementary studies (*bo tuc van hoa*). These national training programmes were the only sources available to SOE employees from which to gain the extra education they needed to fulfil their tasks and/or were a prerequisite for future promotion.

As far as T&D for managers is concerned, the opportunities were extremely limited. This was because SOEs were considered merely as production units, whereas any necessary management function was centralised and controlled by the government. SOE managers therefore were not trained in business management, as the skills were deemed unnecessary. Furthermore, overseas training opportunities, mainly within the old communist system, were very rare and granted to top cadres as a reward for their contributions rather than on the basis of training needs. On those rare occasions, the selection criteria for training opportunities were mainly based on the cadres' position, seniority and political attitude.

The economic reform has challenged the operation of Vietnamese SOEs. The companies have realised that poor T&D systems lead to poor employee attitude, low commitment and high levels of employee turnover, which can be critical to business operations (see also Neupert, Baughn and Dao, 2005). Recently, the training and re-training of employees at the workplace level have witnessed some slow yet fundamental changes. First, the role of training provider has shifted from the central government to enterprises. Secondly, the selection criteria for the training of an employee now emphasises less on position, seniority and political attitude, and is instead more in-line with job demands and requirements. Thirdly, a much wider range, and higher quality, of training programmes are offered to employees. However, the legacies of the past, together with the fact that T&D remains a low priority on the list of 'pressing issues' that management must attend to, have resulted in low training budgets and a weak T&D function in SOEs.

The extent and nature of training

To start with, workforces with low skill levels seem to be common in SOEs. SOE FMCG4's labour profile can be used to illustrate this point. According to the company's statistics on the quality of its labour force, SOE FMCG4 had 324 employees in 2004. Only 17.6 per cent of the workforce had university or college degrees, the remaining 82.4 per cent had medium or below-medium skills level. Although all managerial staff members and professionals have university or college degrees, the majority of blue-collar workers have lower degrees (high school or vocational ones). Interestingly, more than 20 years after *Doi Moi*, political training is still considered very important, with 83 per cent of professionals and upper level personnel having attended and achieved certificates for these courses. This figure reveals the importance of political training and attitude, in general, in promotion and career development opportunities in the state sector. Language ability (mostly English) has become a new requirement, not only in the foreign-invested sector but also in the state sector. New recruits in SOEs now need to have at least a B-level English certificate (intermediate level) even though their jobs have little, if any, to do with language. However, only 4.9 per cent of the workforce actually has any English language certificates. Noticeably, none of the managerial staff have any kind of business administration degree. Interviews with other SOEs reveal that the situation of the low skills level is common in the state sector and may be worse in smaller and less well resourced enterprises.

Most Vietnamese SOEs recognise the importance of employee T&D; however, they are faced with the chronic problem of having very limited financial resources for these activities. HR managers report difficulties in obtaining funds and getting approval for training courses. The average training cost per employee ranges from USD 14 to USD 21 per annum, which is about 7–19 times lower than the cost incurred by MNCs operating in the same industries. This suggests that although there has been an improvement in training activities, currently SOEs still lack commitment to employee development and pay little attention to nurturing and retaining talents through T&D opportunities.

Training and development in SOEs – conclusions

Prior to the economic reform, bounded by bureaucratic rules and procedures, and secured by the lifetime employment system, SOE employees were not motivated to learn and acquire new skills and knowledge. Training offered to workers was mainly on the job as required by the production lines that they were assigned to. Meanwhile, political training was widely available. The lack of training resulted in low productivity and poor product quality.

Even after *Doi Moi*, workforces with low skill levels still are common in SOEs. Case studies show that SOEs only invest limited resources on T&D for their managerial staff. The activities suffer from limited financial resources, low-quality training courses, out-of-date training methods and lack of systematic training systems. Training contents are conveyed through old methods of training, and are thus often repetitive, boring and irrelevant. Workers are offered further technical on-the-job training and are expected to pass technical grade examinations, which are held regularly. These examinations motivate workers to develop and improve their skills and raise their employability. However, no penalty is imposed on workers who fail the examinations. In fact, those who fail the test are still allowed to remain in their positions. Thus, upgrading skills is left to each individual's endeavour. Meanwhile, a larger proportion of the training budget is devoted to professionals and managers. High-quality training opportunities are mostly offered to top executives and managers as a form of rewards. A wide range of training courses are recorded;

however, management training courses are still primarily concerned with familiarising managers with the government's law and regulations rather than offering them opportunities to learn modern management concepts and methods. Obviously, this creates pressure on managers to undertake further training by themselves at their own expense. Finally, SOEs demonstrate a lack of systematic approach to training with no training-need analysis, poor training design and implementation and no training evaluation process. There is also a lack of commitment to training and involvement by senior management in the training processes.

Training and development in MNCs

MNCs recognise the lack of skills and qualifications in Vietnam's labour force and, especially, the need for management training. They make a significant effort and investment to train their management staff, as this is a key to retaining local managers. In general, T&D programmes are centrally controlled, especially during the early years of establishment. Management training programmes in Vietnam need to start with the very basics of business education in their curriculum. Compared with their SOE counterparts, training methods in MNCs are more diverse and advanced, such as the use of e-learning and blended learning. Besides the formal T&D channels, companies are aware of and use informal cultural aspects of management development, such as emphasising the company's philosophy, management forum, e-forums, e-networks and so on, to create a common language and shared attitude. In order to encounter high turnover rates and poaching, companies develop strategies such as legally binding their staff for a certain number of years after providing them training or firm-specific programmes.

On the contrary, T&D in some Asian MNCs are limited to meeting production needs and focus heavily on technical knowledge while neglecting people management skills. Furthermore, in all Asian subsidiaries in Vietnam, job rotation is not a popular practice. Although rotation for workers in production lines is more popular, Vietnamese managers in these companies are often seen as stuck in narrow specialisms. This shows that MNCs' investment on T&D is dependent not only on the host country's situation, in this case the Vietnamese labour market situation and the output of the educational system, but also on the MNCs' HRM strategies, such as global staffing strategy, and business strategies.

Source: Vo (2009: 112–115; 156–157; 162)

4.9.6 India

There is little training available for many workers, except for that needed to undertake the immediate work. With few exceptions, there is still great conservatism among management, workers and trade unions, with some reluctance to change working methods or improve standards. Organisations exposed to international competition, such as the high-profile customer contact centres and IT specialist firms which are regularly referred to by the Indian and foreign media, are among the few exceptions. For most Indians the customer services provided by their local suppliers have changed little in the past four decades and the skills and attitudes of most staff have not improved. The education system, with some highly notable exceptions, is of a low quality and has made little attempt to embrace new technology or ways of learning. A rapidly expanding population with large numbers of young people entering the labour force means that there is little drive for making more productive use of HR. Individuals and families organise their education and training direction and have a preference, especially in the middle classes, for medical, engineering and IT disciplines. The training culture can be described as ad hoc/voluntarist: government reluctant to make changes in education and training standards and employers are reluctant to invest in training.

We can see some of the issues in Text Box 4.4.

Text Box 4.4

Skill shortages in India

Offset against the huge pools of surplus labour that define the Indian economy in general are the employability demands of the BPO sector. Each component of the sector requires tertiary level education in a society where literacy rates hover around 65 per cent for the population as a whole and at 45 per cent for females. Jobs in IT minimally require a tertiary degree in engineering, computer science or mathematics, while call centre and data processing operations insist upon a bachelor's level degree and high levels of proficiency in spoken and written English. Paradoxical as it may seem, it is currently a seller's market for labour in this particular enclave economy. It is estimated that by 2012, the labour power requirements for the off-shore Indian IT/ITeS markets, as well as domestic and captive IT/ITeS support requirements, will add up to 4–6 million workers (KPMG, 2004). While India could be one of the few countries with a qualified surplus labour pool by 2020, there is a possibility of a shortage in terms of skilled personnel for IT/ITeS to the tune of about half million workers, even in the medium term, that is, by 2009. (KPMG, 2004: 19; Taskforce, 2003: 6).

The employable labour shortage is already impacting on the performance of the Indian IT/ITeS industry today in terms of attrition levels and wage trends (see below). The question here is of quality, not quantity. While it is estimated that approximately 17 million people will be available to the IT industry by 2008 (Nasscom-j, 2005), the problem relates to their employability and trainability. 'The issue of manpower gap is not as much about institutional seat availability as about the nature of skills and training provided in these institutions' (Taskforce, 2003: 6).

According to one report, 'Different categories of work at the agent level ... will require specific qualifications. These must be supported by some necessary delivery-related skills, such as language skills, analytical skills, computer proficiency, customer service orientation and behavioural traits' (KPMG, 2004: 34–36). While these are common requirements for CSRs anywhere in the world, in the context of India, staff need to be equipped with additional skills, such as language neutralisation, cross-cultural skills and familiarity with products that are not commonly used in India, such as credit cards. For high-end R&D work, Indian employers are constrained by the low base of available PhDs, the low enthusiasm of higher educated staff for R&D activities and the low growth in R&D staff (KPMG, 2004: 53; Saini and Budhwar, 2004).

To address the manpower requirements, the Ministry of Communications and Information Technology's Taskforce on meeting the HR Challenges in IT and ITeS (2003: 12) recommends addressing the entire development lifecycle of human resources, from attracting the right people through to education, certification, deployment and retraining. This requires close co-operation and co-ordination between governments, education institutions, industry bodies and individual firms. NASSCOM, the industry body, has already moved to establish a common certification system for some of the standard skills. For example, it recently launched the NASSCOM Assessment of Competence (NAC) for potential employees in the BPO industry as an industry standard assessment program with the aim of ensuring the transformation of a 'trainable' workforce into an 'employable' workforce (The Hindu, 2005b). Some states, such as Karnataka and Andhra Pradesh, have already moved to establish centralised testing and certification for potential employees in the industry (KPMG, 2004: 65–66). However, the breadth and depth of skills and competencies required for the industry are of such a nature that the scope for effective standardisation of skill testing and training will be quite limited. Therefore, KPMG (2004: 63) recommends a hybrid model with base-level common testing and certification supported by company-specific programs.

One of the leading BPO firms that we studied is engaged in educating the public and local colleges in enhancing the employment reputation of ITeS work, tarnished by the social stigma of working unsocial hours and allegations of sweatshop-like conditions. Other companies are also following suit with open-days for the parents of young staff to see first-hand what the ITeS industry is all about. To spread employment networks beyond tier one cities, such as Bangalore, Delhi and Hyderabad, the ITeS companies are also moving to set up facilities in tier two cities as well. Additionally, some Indian ITeS companies have started attracting 'non-employed' people, such as retiring army personnel, teachers and housewives (KPMG, 2004: 73)

Source: Thite and Russell (2007: 82–84)

4.9.7 Gulf Co-operation Council (GCC)

The oil and gas resource rich states of the GCC have very different problems from those of some other parts of Asia. The wealthy GCC countries rely greatly on foreigners to undertake work which nationals are reluctant to engage in. Although certainly there are poor GCC nationals, there are many even poorer foreigners willing to work for less money and with greater restrictions upon them. Over 80 per cent of the workers in Qatar and the United Arab Emirates (UAE) are foreigners. This access to cheap foreign labour has meant that when skilled HR are needed, these are bought in already trained and any foreign worker whose skills are no longer sufficient will be sent home. Organisations, with very few exceptions, particularly in the oil and gas industries, have no history or tradition of training except to give overseas trips as a reward to national employees. However, concerns about the dependence on foreigners, regular troughs in government oil income and a rapid increase in the population of young nationals has led to a desire to provide vocational education – for example, GOTEVOT (Government Organization for Technical and Vocational Training) in Saudi Arabia and the Higher Colleges of Technology in the UAE. Training levies are imposed on employers of foreigners to pay for the training of nationals. The required skills are bought in and rarely are citizens fully trained to undertake job requirements. Some related developments – such as the greater education of GCC women and the use of their skills as in home working using IT – are noted in Rowley et al. (2010). The training culture can be labelled as government directive (often not enforced), and avoidance of training by private sector.

4.10 Variety in training provision

It can be seen that there is a great variety of attitudes and approaches between countries (and between organisations, especially between large and medium/small sized) in their training provision and underpinnings and supports. Part of this variety is due to the level of state and government intervention in the training system, and the overall training culture engendered.

Think About/Question 4.8

To what extent should training provision be left to the 'free market' and organisations? What might be the long-term implications for organisations and the economy of low training and skills?

The implications of these different levels of provision and approach are more than of academic interest. For instance, provisions have implications in terms of having critical roles in producing different forms of competition and economic performance. Some of these can be seen in Table 4.9.

Table 4.9 Implications of different types of training provision

System	Characteristics	Causes	Implications
Voluntary	■ Laissez faire ■ Market provides if shortages	◆ Free markets ◆ Free riders ◆ 'Hire and fire'	➢ Skills shortages and poaching ➢ Greater numerical flexibility ➢ Competitive downward spiral ➢ Simple, low value-added production
Compulsory	■ Directed ■ Force all to train or contribute	◆ Interventions ◆ Institutions ◆ Redundancy limits	➢ Skills provision ➢ All contribute ➢ Greater functional flexibility ➢ Complex, high value-added

We now move to the second major part of the chapter, which concerns employee performance appraisal. This will be examined in terms of the methods, techniques and international perspectives in this area.

4.11 Performance appraisal

Employee performance appraisal involves several aspects. These include the following.

- The processes and procedures of evaluating performance in the job
- Regular assessments to determine how well the employee is doing
- Records and discussions of performance levels
- Central HR control and co-ordination
- The resultant findings used in other HRM areas (e.g. HRP, training)

However, it needs to be recognised that tensions and critical evaluation are involved in the area of appraisal, in the following categories.

1. Between measuring past performance versus future potential. Performance appraisal generally looks more to the past and performance management tends to look more forward in an active way.

2. Between different schools of thought which emphasise the importance of methods, systems and procedures versus the skills of managers. The latter school of thought is gaining some popularity – for instance, in some organisations skills in appraisal may now be seen as a basic managerial attribute.

3. Between the extent to which different issues are deal with simultaneously. To what extent are evaluation issues (such as pay and promotion) discussed at the same time as development issues (such as measures to improve performance, objectives and career development).

4. Between closed systems and open systems. Organisations sometimes gather performance data by means such as 'mystery customers' and computer monitoring. There are ethical issues in this type of data gathering such as the question of whether there are rights to privacy at work. This is especially important as appraisal is normally considered to be built on trust.

4.12 Methods and techniques

A range of methods and techniques exist for carrying out appraisals. With these systems there is the common trade-off in HRM between, on the one hand, more speed, ease and cost of limited data and, on the other hand, slowness, complexity and the expense of producing comprehensive data.

> **Think About/Question 4.9**
>
> What types and methods of performance appraisal are you aware of?

The main methods include the following. They have some common and specific advantages and problems, which we will return to later in this chapter.

4.12.1 Work standards

This is one of the simplest methods. Here the person is judged, for example, by the number of units of output produced over a given period – for instance, 100 items produced or 100 customer calls answered in a particular period of time. This is a common method of performance appraisal used by some Asian organisations.

4.12.2 Comment boxes

With this method the appraiser answers questions about the performance of the employee. Often the appraiser is not required to grade the appraisee according to predetermined scales and is allowed to describe in his or her own words how the person has performed. This system is found in Asia, but where there can be some reluctance to rate an individual's performance accurately.

4.12.3 Checklists

This requires the appraiser to check off 'yes' or 'no' to questions about the appraisee concerning various aspects of employee performance. This method is also popular in parts of Asia.

4.12.4 Ranking

Here there is less discretion for the appraiser, who must place in rank order, from highest to lowest performing, all those employees being appraised. This is resisted as a method in parts of Asia, but it is found in some organisations, especially when used to rank foreign workers.

4.12.5 Forced distribution

Here appraisers rate people on a forced distribution of categories – for instance, 10 per cent low; 20 per cent low average; 40 per cent average; 20 per cent high average; 10 per cent high. This can be seen in Table 4.10. Again, the appraisers' discretion is constrained with this method, so it is less used by Asian organisations, although international employers regularly use this system to compel local managers to make judgements about performance.

Table 4.10 Example of forced distribution

High	Next	Middle	Next	Low
10%	20%	40%	20%	10%
Names	Names	Names	Names	Names

4.12.6 Rating scales

Here various attributes of performance are listed (for example, accuracy, knowledge, quality of work) and the person is evaluated on each of these dimensions (usually from the job description) individually (see Chapter 2). A scale is often used – for example, 1 poor; 2 below average; 3 average; 4 above average; 5 excellent. An overall score is then calculated, so there is some ease of interpretation. An example of a 5-point rating scale can be seen in Table 4.11. When formal appraisal systems are used in Asia, this is one of the oldest and most popular methods.

Table 4.11 Example of rating scale

Criteria	Scale				
	Poor	Average	Good	Very good	Excellent
Time keeping	①	②	③	④	⑤
Appearance	①	②	③	④	⑤
Communication skills	①	②	③	④	⑤
Relationships with subordinates	①	②	③	④	⑤
Relationship with seniors	①	②	③	④	⑤
Organisation skills	①	②	③	④	⑤

4.12.7 Critical incidents

This method is a procedure for collecting observed incidents that are seen as important or critical to performance. A list (or log) of incidents is compiled, with details of examples of positive and negative employee performance recorded and kept. High-performing employees are identified as those performing well during many critical incidents. It is considered that adequate, but not exceptional, employees are those involved in only a few critical incidents.

4.12.8 Behaviourally anchored rating scales (BARS)

These appraisal methods specify definite, observable and measurable behaviour. The format uses critical incidents to serve as 'anchor statements' on a scale. The form contains defined performance dimensions, each with critical incident anchors (examples of actual behaviour on the job, not general descriptions or traits). The appraiser then rates the person against these predetermined factors. An example can be seen in Table 4.12. These methods are used less often in some parts of Asia because of their complexity and need for judgement. However, the advantages of such methods include developing the following.

- Validity of each of the main duties (obtained from job descriptions)
- Agreement over suitable descriptions for each category of behaviour
- Economies of scale if many people have the same job description

Table 4.12   Example of BARS performance dimension

Performance dimension scale development under BARS for the dimension 'Ability to absorb and interpret policies for an employee relations specialist' (Rated 1–9).

This **employee relations specialist** could be expected to:		
	9	Serve as information source concerning new and changed policies for others in the organisation

Table 4.12   Example of BARS performance dimension (*Cont'd*)

Be aware quickly of program changes and explain these to employees	8	
	7	Reconcile conflicting policies and procedures correctly to meet HRM goals
Recognise need for additional information to gain a better understanding of policy changes	6	
	5	Complete various HRM forms correctly after receiving instruction on them
Require some help and practice in mastering new policies and procedures	4	
	3	Know there is a problem, but go down many blind alleys before realising they are wrong
Incorrectly interpret guidelines, creating problems for line managers	2	
	1	Be unable to learn new procedures even after repeated explanations

Source: Adapted from DeCenzo and Robbins (1999)

4.12.9 Behavioural observation scales (BOS)

Like the above technique, this method uses critical incident techniques to identify a series of behaviours in the job. However, the format is different in that, instead of identifying behaviours exhibited during the rating period, the appraiser needs to indicate on a scale how often the person was actually observed engaging in the specific behaviour under review. An example of this method can be seen in Table 4.13. Because of its complexity this method is less common in some parts of Asia.

Table 4.13   Example of BOS performance dimension

Sample BOS items for the performance dimension 'Communicating with subordinates' (Rated 1–5).

Criteria	Almost Never				Almost Always
Puts up notices on bulletin boards when new policies or procedures are implemented.	1	2	3	4	5
Maintains eye contact when talking to employees.	1	2	3	4	5
Uses both written memos and verbal discussion when giving instructions.	1	2	3	4	5
Discusses changes in policies or procedures with employees before implementing them.	1	2	3	4	5
Writes memos that are clear, concise and easy to understand	1	2	3	4	5

Total Performance Level:
5–9:   Below adequate
10–14:   Adequate
15–19:   Good
20+:   Excellent

Source: Adapted from Fisher et al. (1999)

4.12.10 Peer

With this method, colleagues and co-workers at the same level assess each other's performance. This is increasingly popular in the West where team working has been encouraged. One advantage of this method is that it is based on actual experience in the workplace. In some Asian cultures, however, seeking the views of colleagues and co-workers at the same level risks losing power and respect. Asian group loyalty would lead almost all peers to rate each other highly.

4.12.11 Subordinate

With this method, employees are asked to rate their bosses. There have been experiments with this method at DuPont, Nabisco, Mobil, GE and UPS in the US, and BP in the UK. This method is seen as more 'democratic' and useful in improving channels of communication. In much of Asia there would be not only loss of 'face', but also loss of power, respect and loyalty in using such a system. Therefore, this method is rarely acceptable in parts of Asia.

4.12.12 Self-appraisal

One of the more recent methods to take off has been self-appraisal. To try to seek more differentiation in rankings with such formats, people can be asked to rank different aspects of their performance in relation to other aspects. In Asia it is found that there is a range of responses to self-appraisal so that it is expected that, for example, the Malaysian or Taiwanese would be modest in their assessment, while the Pakistani or Indian would be more generous in their self image. There are also variations by sector and in organisations so that, for example, investment bankers will be more inclined to rate themselves highly, while social workers are more inclined to say that they could do better.

4.12.13 360-degree appraisal

This is one of the latest trends in this area in the West. This method involves as many different people as possible in performance evaluation. This can range from subordinates to peers to managers, customers and clients. As most Asians are unwilling to be rated by peers or subordinates, this technique is less common in parts of Asia, although some international organisations attempt to impose the system.

4.12.14 Management by objectives (MBO)

This method was traditionally used more for professional and managerial grades, but is still found in many organisations at lower levels. This is seen particularly when performance management and assessment (PMA) is used. There is commonly a cycle, which may include the following stages.

1. Discussion – forms are completed as the basis for initial discussions.
2. Agreement – reached on objectives/goals to strive to achieve during the period.

3. Training and development – needed for achievement of objectives.

4. Modification – as a result of changed circumstances (corporate policy, environment).

5. Review – at the end of the period to see if goals have been met and fresh goals set.

Better managed Asian organisations tend to use some form of MBO; those most concerned with improving performance use PMA.

4.12.15 Interviews

While we have seen that there are many types of performance appraisal, those that involve an interview at some stage are common. Interviews are an important part of the process, not least as they are integral to the communication and feedback that is often involved. Some of the same points that apply to employee selection interviews (see Chapter 2) can be followed as ground rules for performance appraisal interviews. These can be seen in Table 4.14. Problems are encountered, however, when evaluating the performance of an individual, irrespective of the interview style.

Table 4.14 Interview structure

Stage	Characteristics
1. Preparation	➤ Armed with all facts ➤ Sure how to proceed ➤ Clear purpose and aim
2. Purpose and rapport	➤ Agree purpose ➤ Agree structure of meeting ➤ Check pre-work complete
3. Factual review	➤ Review facts about performance in period ➤ Appraiser reinforcement
4. Appraisee views	➤ Asked to comment on performance ➤ What has gone well/less well, liked/disliked ➤ Possible new objectives
5. Appraiser views	➤ Add own perspective ➤ Recognition and constructive criticism ➤ Questions about what said
6. Problem-solving approach	➤ Discussion of differences ➤ Discuss how to resolve ➤ Consider developmental training needs
7. Objective setting	➤ Agree what actions to be taken ➤ Who takes them

Source: Adapted from Torrington and Hall (1998)

4.13 Potential problems with performance appraisal

> **Think About/Question 4.10**
>
> What problems might there be with performance appraisals and their conduct in Asia?

There are numerous potential problems with appraisals, both general and specific to certain methods. These include those noted in Tables 4.15 and 4.16 as both common biases found in appraisers and generic problems with each system of appraisal.

Table 4.15   Biases in performance appraisals

Issue	Characteristics
Supervisory bias	Range (i.e. race, gender, cultural)
'Halo and horns'	One good/bad event influences whole judgement
Temporal	First/last event outshines all others
Strictness and leniency	Give high or low marks
Central tendency	Gives middle marks

Table 4.16   Problems with performance appraisal methods

Method	Problems
Work standards	▪ Responsibility for output not neatly divided between employees ▪ Jobs involve bundle of tasks to disentangle or relate to output
Comment boxes	▪ Allows bland comments ▪ No easy comparisons (between appraisers, employees, periods)
Checklists	▪ Questions pre-set ▪ Merely go down list
Ranking	▪ Supervisor bias and halo effect ▪ Difficulties in merging rankings between appraisers ▪ Not helpful in communication, motivation and training matters
Forced distribution	▪ A group may not conform to these fixed percentages ▪ Assumes there are good/bad performers in all groups

| Table 4.16 | Problems with performance appraisal methods (*Cont'd*) |

Method	Problems
Rating scales	▪ Qualitative information not generated ▪ Little value with respect to training, communication or motivation ▪ Supervisor bias, halo effect, central tendency, leniency/strictness
Critical incidents	▪ Demanding – maintaining critical incidents log may be neglected ▪ Difficult to quantify and interpret log (so comparing employees)
BARS	▪ Costly and time consuming ▪ Long time to obtain agreement on descriptions for every job ▪ Only takes account of existing performance, not future potential
BOS	▪ Costly ▪ Time consuming
Peer	▪ Rivalry or jealousy ▪ Prejudice can distort, although larger groups reduce this ▪ Reluctant to express honest opinion ▪ May not know about all aspects of the job ▪ Cultural issues
Subordinate	▪ Rivalry or jealousy ▪ Prejudice can distort, although larger groups reduce this ▪ Too frightened to express real opinion ▪ Reluctance to accept views of subordinates ▪ Cultural issues
Self-appraisal	▪ Difficulty in analysing own performance ▪ Unrealistic views of how well/poorly done ▪ Tend to overrate themselves ▪ Unwilling to admit weaknesses ▪ May underplay strengths ▪ Cultural issues
360-degree	▪ Time and costs ▪ Willingness of others to complete ▪ Above problems
MBO	▪ Expensive on time and produces uncertain outcomes ▪ May not produce comparative data for rewards/HRP use

There has been a trend for the use of performance appraisal techniques to spread down organisational hierarchies. Part of this is linked to objectives being set at the top and cascaded to lower levels. However, we can also question their use in their traditional bastions across the whole organisational structure.

Think about/Question 4.11

To what extent are appraisals applicable to all types of employee in an organisation?

Some commentators argue that, because appraisal sits uneasily with the ethos that characterises the attitudes of most professional groups, it is an inappropriate approach to take if an organisation wishes to maximise its performance (Fletcher, 1997). There is a 'professional ethos' which, it can be argued, contrasts with the principles of appraisal, which emphasise wholly conflicting characteristics. This can be seen in Table 4.17. Similar points are made concerning other professionals, such as university professors, teachers, doctors and lawyers, who carried out work with autonomy via 'professionalisation' while, in contrast, white-collar corporate workers had less of this and were more vulnerable because it is often '... required that they identify, absolutely and unreservedly with their employers' (Ehrenreich, 2006: 25).

Table 4.17   Performance appraisals in professions

Professional ethos	Appraisal characteristics
• Level of autonomy and independence of judgement • Self-discipline, adherence to standards • Possession of specialised knowledge/skills • Power and status based on expertise • Operating and guided by code of ethics • Answerable to governing professional body	• Hierarchical authority and direction from superiors • Administrative rules and following procedures • Definition by organisation of standards and goals • Demand primary loyalty be given to organisation • Basis of power on one's organisational position

Source: Adapted from Fletcher (1997)

In short, appraisals can yield individual-level information crucial to HRM and its practices (such as HRP and training). However, performance appraisal systems require precise planning and meticulous execution to be of real value. Appraisals should be approached in a proper manner. The appraisers need to focus on performance and be objective; the actual appraisal needs to be easy to conduct, consistent and reviewed to introduce improvements. The appraisee's immediate supervisor or manager is usually the person most often involved in the appraisal process. There are many appraisal methods, and these vary in suitability between organisations, employees and time. Poor, inexpertly or unevenly applied appraisals can lead to a sense of a 'witch-hunt', lapse into favouritism, lose their purpose and value, and may be seen merely as an increasingly time-wasting, bureaucratic 'hoop to jump', creating widespread resentment. Indeed, for many managers appraisals are seen in the following ways.

- 'Owned' by the HRM department
- Simply another task forced on them
- Of little value and interfere with 'real' business of running the organisations
- Do not consider the opportunity and transaction costs involved
- Irrelevant with search for naïve universalism at the cost of contingent reality
- Cause employee resentment and difficult future working relationships

4.14 International comparisons in performance appraisal

Think About/Question 4.12

What issues might arise with appraisal systems when used in different countries?

Some of the general problems with appraisals have been noted by various researchers in relation to MNCs. These include the following. In many Arab and South Asian countries, assertive women may receive biased ratings if expected to play more 'subservient' roles, especially in public. In other parts of Asia, if using 360-degree or peer appraisals where young workers are asked to rate older subordinates, the cultural value of 'respect and esteem' may bias rating. There are also other country-based differences, for example, employees from Taiwan, when compared with similar workers in the US, are more likely to give themselves lower rating in self-evaluation forms (see Farh et al., 1991). Americans, and Western employees generally, usually give themselves higher self-assessed ratings than those given by their bosses; the reverse is true in China. One explanation is that the more individualist culture in the West encourages higher levels of self-confidence. In more collectivist cultures, there is a greater emphasis on solidarity, interdependence and inter-group harmony. This may lead employees to underestimate their value. However, Shen (2009) gives an example of employee satisfaction with performance management, particularly with more objective performance appraisal criteria and execution.

Other research has shown difficulties with appraisals internationally; see the reports in Taylor (1998). For example, staff of Singapore Airlines in Thailand were reluctant to highlight bad points. Other examples included a Chinese reluctance to assert their own views directly to superiors and East and South Asian countries with continued diffidence to appraisals because of the heritage of SOEs and rewards of loyalty and political status along with unease with subordinate involvement.

The values on which employees are appraised also vary between countries. Organisations should be sensitive to these so as not to underestimate the contribution of various individuals and groups of employees. International organisations need to adopt appraisal systems that recognise these differences.

We can see the issues in this area in the cases of China and Vietnam in Text Boxes 4.5 and 4.6. These issues can be seen in a range of organisational forms.

Text Box 4.5

Performance management in China

During the planned economy, an organisation's and individual's performance had no financial and strategic implications; pay was not related to performance and poor organisational performance did not lead to bankruptcy. As a result, performance management involving strategic performance planning, assessment and review processes were irrelevant to Chinese enterprises. Organisational performance assessment was only for the purpose of selecting 'excellent organisations' in order to promote the Party's line. Therefore, organisational performance was not assessed against profits and sales, but the implementation of government's production quotas and conforming to the Party's principles. Performance appraisals for individuals were carried out very rarely and often were conducted for particular individuals who were considered for promotion and transferring to another department or organisation. It was common practice of an existing organisation/department to write a performance report for an individual facing transfer to another organisation/department.

If the transfer took place between two departments in the same organisation, the performance report was passed directly between the two departments. If the transfer occurred between two organisations, the report might be posted to or brought by the individual to the new organisation. In the case of personnel transfer, appraisals were conducted secretly by senior managers not involving the appraisee himself. So the appraisee did not know the appraisal outcome at all. The criteria for cadre appraisal emphasised political loyalty, seniority and the ability to maintain harmonious relations with peers and subordinates (Easterby-Smith, Malina and Lu, 1995). Those for workers included technical skills in addition to the criteria of cadre appraisals. In the case of promotion, appraisals were conducted by the organisation/department at enterprise level or the local organisation/department level of the CCP. Peer appraisal in the form of group discussions was the major appraisal method. Hence, the results of appraisals depended largely on the relationship (*guanxi*) with leaders and colleagues.

Since the economic reform, performance appraisals have been one of the most important HRM practices (Easterby-Smith et al., 1995; Shen, 2004; Zhao, 1994) and are directly linked to pay for individual workers. The distinction between blue-collar workers and cadres has been diminishing. Management by objectives (MBO) has been common practice for most Chinese enterprises. Performance goals are set at the beginning of a certain period, e.g. annually, quarterly or monthly; the frequency of setting goals depends largely on type or niche of industry. Normally, manufacturing industries tend to set goals more frequently than other industries and often assess performance against quantity and quality of production units.

In general, the appraisal criteria are also *De, Neng, Qing* and *Ji*. However, Chinese firms are paying less and less attention to 'soft' aspects of performance criteria, such as party loyalty, positive working attitude and sound moral practices, especially when assessing ordinary workers. There is an emphasis on 'what have you done for the firm' rather than how one would go about it. The performance appraisal procedure includes self-assessment, peer group discussion and a superior's final comments (Zhu and Dowling, 1998). Although there is an emphasis on 'democratic' soundings of opinions, which is directly linked to Chinese culture, such as the importance of harmonious peer and subordinate relationships (Easterby-Smith et al., 1995), many firms tend not to pay attention to peer opinions. The results of performance appraisal usually remain confidential because management feels reluctant to pass on any negative information to appraisees, so that direct confrontation is avoided and 'face' can be saved. The lack of openness, transparency, the influence on management development and objective standards in Chinese performance appraisal practices has provoked large-scale scepticism and resistance to the implementation of performance appraisals. Moreover, according to Benson et al. (2000), Chinese enterprises often focus on conformity and compliance with rules by emphasising discipline, punishment, restrictions and personal loss of face rather than cultivating employee commitment.

Nevertheless, the case study of four privatised firms reveals a change in the conduct of performance appraisal and the use of appraisal results. Appraisals are used to determine pay and improving efficiency of the firm, but have little to do with employees' career development, for instance, feedback is rarely given for identifying any problems, or not provided at all. Appraisals are often conducted between individuals and their direct managers. Peer assessment is rare; instead, the supervisor or line manager usually conduct face-to-face appraisal with the employee. Small and medium POEs usually adopt the production unit-based appraisal system for production workers and a comparison of work plan and work completion system for non-production employees including managers and office workers. The major appraisal criteria were quantity, quality of products and working hours for production workers, the proportion of task completion, and complaints of workers regarding non-production employees. Goal setting and appraisals are conducted frequently, usually on a monthly basis. The production manager was assessed against the overall production outcome of the department. Apart from these criteria, POEs also consider whether workers had complied with the firm's regulations. In order to improve efficiency and encourage competition, appraisals in POEs are often conducted in a 'cruel' manner, revealing appraisal results to all employees. Under normal circumstances, the worst performing employee is likely to be sacked. Such practices put a lot of pressure on employees.

Source: Shen (2007: 36–37)

Text Box 4.6

Performance management in Vietnam

Performance management in SOEs

This section examines and compares the PM systems in SOEs under the centrally planned economic system and after *Doi Moi*, across five main functions of a PM system, namely setting performance objectives, monitoring performance, evaluating performance, providing feedback, and planning for future performance. It argues that PM in the state sector has gradually shifted from a politically oriented bureaucratic process towards an equitable system that emphasises individual achievement. However, the PM system still neglects identifying training needs to improve current performance and preparing for future career development opportunities.

PM under the centrally planned economy

Prior to *Doi Moi*, PM was an important element of personnel administration in Vietnam. Performance appraisals were usually conducted once or twice per year, facilitated by the administration department. PM, during this period, was a lengthy and highly hierarchical process, involving staff at all levels of the company, including the employees, the production lines, the departments, the company's board of directors and the representatives of mass organisations (see Table TB4.6.1). There was an intensive intervention from mass organisations. Any PM decision had to be made with the concurrence and under the supervision of the 'Four Committees', consisting of the Communist Party representative, the board of directors, the trade union representative, the youth union representative, and sometimes the women's association representative.

Table TB4.6.1 The hierarchical process of PM in SOEs under the centrally planned economy

Step	Level	Content
Step 1	Employee	Self-evaluation
Step 2 (applied for blue-collar workers only)	Production team	<ul><li>Review employee's self-evaluation</li><li>Compare among team members</li><li>Approve or revise self-evaluation</li><li>Report to the production manager</li></ul> Evaluation was conducted in an open performance review meeting attended by all team members, production team heads and representatives of mass organisations.

Table TB4.6.1	The hierarchical process of PM in SOEs under the centrally planned economy (Cont'd)	
Step	**Level**	**Content**
Step 3	Department/ production lines (1)	▪ Review employee's self-evaluation ▪ Compare the performance with other members of the department (white-collar workers) or production line (blue-collar workers) ▪ Approve or revise previous evaluation ▪ Report to the trade union committee At the departmental level, evaluation was conducted in an open performance review meeting attended by all members, department heads and representatives of mass organisations. At the level of production lines, participants include production line heads and representatives of mass organisations.
Step 4	Trade union committee	▪ Administration staff members collect the performance rating from departments and production lines ▪ Report to trade union committee ▪ Review departments' and production lines' overall ratings ▪ Compare performance across departments and production lines ▪ Advise performance rating distribution for each department and production line ▪ Evaluation reports were then returned to departments and production lines
Step 5	Department/ production lines (2)	▪ Revise evaluation rating of all employees in their departments and production lines according to the instruction given by the trade union committee ▪ Report to the company's performance appraisal committee At this stage, the evaluation decision was made in a closed meeting, attended by department heads or production line heads, their deputy heads and representatives of mass organisations.

Table TB4.6.1	The hierarchical process of PM in SOEs under the centrally planned economy (*Cont'd*)	
Step	**Level**	**Content**
Step 6	Performance appraisal committee	■ Administration staff members collect the performance rating from departments ■ Report to the company's performance appraisal committee, which comprised the board of directors and representatives of mass organisations ■ Final decision was made ■ All individual performance ratings were made public ■ Complimenting titles were granted (Excellent Employees, Competitive Soldier, Labour Hero)

Performance criteria were vague and included factors such as political attitude, work attitude, work performance, technical skills, co-operation and personal (harmonious) relationships with colleagues, especially with the managers, etc. Two non-performance criteria, namely political attitude and work attitude, were commonly used for evaluation of employees' performance. In this way, performance appraisals were subject to vagueness and were thus open to individual interpretation. However, it is very important to note that although PM lacked well-defined and measurable criteria and other appraisal techniques commonly used in Western market economies, PM in SOEs could be highly objective as the companies allow 'democratic' voicing of opinions in performance appraisals, which means that opinions from a wide range of employees are gathered in order to achieve a 'democratic' evaluation of an employee's performance. Although the PM system operated in a hierarchical order, in which the decision of the committee at a lower-level needed approval of the immediate higher-level committee, the evaluation of an individual's performance was conducted in the open and in the presence of the employee and all of their colleagues, and the results were made public. These practices allowed an objective view of an individual's performance from multiple sources.

Finally, the role of PM during the centrally planned economy in SOEs should not be neglected. It was considered an important element of personnel administration, as employees' performance, especially those of cadres, was recorded in their personnel file, which would move with them from organisation to organisation. Although PM did not have an immediate influence on payment, it played a vital role in the life of SOE employees as it formed the basis for job promotion, desirable transfers and the distribution of welfare benefits such as, and most importantly, allocating heavily subsidised or free housing.

PM since *Doi Moi*

Since the economic reform, SOEs have been under great pressure to remain economically viable and competitive, and as a result have revised their PM systems with the aim of breaking the old practices of egalitarianism, which did not distinguish between high and low performers and did not link performance to rewards. There have been some attempts to adopt Western PM practices. However, changes have only been partially successful, and PM systems still serve more an evaluation purpose rather than a developmental purpose.

Setting performance objectives

Before the reform, SOEs were directly controlled and managed by the government. Both managers and employees paid little attention to production targets, knowing that operating profits were pre-determined in the plan and losses were made up from the government budget expenditure (Vu, 2002). Now, as a legacy of the centrally planned economic system, organisational objectives are not normally conveyed to low positioned employees and there is a very weak link between organisational objectives and individual performance objectives. SOE employees are only vaguely aware of company plans; thus, they neither consciously strive to achieve common organisational goals nor attempt to link their individual performance objectives with that of the company. Noticeably, the majority of firms reported that no individual performance objectives are set biannually or annually. Employees are expected to 'fulfil their tasks as reasonably expected', as put by Auto SOE3's vice managing director. Furthermore, motivation to perform is not high in an environment where underperformers are not likely to be penalised or fired and the recruitment of new talents is restricted, given the limitations in recruitment and selection activities faced by SOEs.

SOE FMCG1, however, is an exception, where the company aligns company business objectives and individual objectives using Balanced Scorecards to set business objectives and successfully engage their employees in this process. It is noteworthy that the company is a pioneering case in Vietnam that applied new practices in PM and its success proves that SOEs can potentially learn and use best practices in PM as a management tool.

The previous PM system in SOE FMCG1, the performance appraisal criteria system, did not reflect the company's strategic priorities, and employees were not directly responsible for their work unit/department/firm's performance. In December 2003, the company started the equitisation process and more than ever before, embarked on the task of achieving commercial success. The company's board of directors realised that the performance criteria were difficult to accurately measure, and that the PM system had become a formality that provided no real value. In 2001, inspired by the success of foreign-invested firms in the same industry, and urged by the need to align performance and payment, the management decided to adopt Balanced Scorecards, with some assistance provided by a consulting firm.

The board of directors and the top management team agreed on the company's strategic objectives and incorporated these objectives into a company-level Balanced Scorecard. The companies share their business objectives and targets, embodied in the company's Balanced Scorecard, with their employees and actively encourage them to suggest strategies by which these targets can be achieved. The company's Balanced Scorecard was then cascaded down to all departments, work units and employees, who then developed their own Balanced Scorecards in a manner that was in alignment with the company-level objectives. An individual's performance plan was then prepared by the employee and approved by his/her direct manager and assigned for the next 12 months. Individual scorecards view organisational performance from different perspectives such as finance, cost, customer satisfaction, growth, etc. As a result, company employees had clearer objectives, measures and performance targets. Their efforts and performance determined the levels of pay, benefits and bonuses they received. In this way, the company motivated and linked individual performance to company objectives and achievements. The company so far has achieved some improvements in vertical and horizontal alignment, as a result of its Balanced Scorecard implementation.

Monitoring performance

Depending on the company, PM is held once a year at fixed intervals. The final-year performance review is backed up by mid-year review and regular check-ups by heads of department or production lines. In a relationship-based society like Vietnam, regular check-up is a norm. Direct supervisors, and colleagues in the same work unit, often notice first hand any changes in an employee's work performance and the reasons thereof. Reciprocating good deeds, such as offers to cover some work, change shifts, etc. to help colleagues achieve their objectives in difficult times are common. This practice not only helps managers to identify performance problems before they become serious, but also provides the employees with a support mechanism – which is said to be important in the Vietnamese context. However, regular check-ups and interim performance reviews are better understood as informal discussions and daily interactions than formal reviews.

Measuring performance

Performance criteria are quite similar across the studied SOEs, as revealed in the companies' standardised performance appraisal sheets. While the appraisal criteria are different for each company, they, in general, consist of four broad areas, namely work achievement, work attitude and effort, collegial relationship and potential for further improvement. An overall grading from excellent, good, pass or poor is required for the first three categories. PM process still is a highly hierarchical process, as depicted in Table TB4.6.2.

Table TB4.6.2   **The hierarchical process of PM in SOEs after *Doi Moi***

Step	Level	Content
Step 1	Employee	Self-evaluation
Step 2 (applied for blue-collar workers only)	Production team	▪ Review employee's self-evaluation ▪ Compare among team members ▪ Approve or revise self-evaluation ▪ Report to the production manager Evaluation is conducted in an open performance review meeting attended by all team members and production team heads.
Step 3	Department/ production lines (1)	▪ Review employee's self-evaluation ▪ Compare the performance among members of department (white-collar workers) or production line (blue-collar workers) ▪ Approve or revise previous evaluation ▪ Report to the company's administration/HR department At departments, evaluation is conducted in an open performance review meeting attended by all employees and department heads. At production lines, evaluations are reviewed by production heads.

Table TB4.6.2	The hierarchical process of PM in SOEs after *Doi Moi (Cont'd)*	
Step	Level	Content
Step 4	Administration/ HR department	▪ Administration/HR department collects the performance rating from departments ▪ Review departments' and production lines' overall ratings ▪ Compare performance across departments and production lines ▪ Advise performance rating distribution for each department and production line ▪ Evaluation reports were then returned to the departments and production lines
Step 5	Department/ production lines (2)	▪ Revise evaluation rating of all employees in their department and production lines according to the instruction given by the administration/HR department ▪ Report to the company's performance appraisal committee At this stage, final evaluation ratings are decided in a closed meeting, attended by department heads or production line heads and deputy heads.
Step 6	Performance appraisal committee	▪ Administration/HR staff members collect the performance rating from departments ▪ Report to the company's Performance Appraisal Committee, which comprised the board of directors and representatives of the trade union ▪ Final decision was made ▪ All individual performance ratings were made public ▪ Complimenting titles were granted (Excellent Employees, Competitive Soldier, Labour Hero)

Compared to their own systems prior to *Doi Moi*, political attitude and the ability to maintain a harmonious relationship with co-workers, colleagues and managers are still highly valued. These appraisal criteria are vague, hard to measure and open to individual interpretation and favouritism. On the other hand, the 'performance' criteria, which are used to evaluate an employee's work effectiveness and real contributions to the organisation, have been given much more attention since the economic reforms. However, in the majority of cases, with the exception of SOE FMCG1, the performance measurement is based mainly on the completion of tasks specified in the individual contract, irrespective of the company's performance.

There is little change recorded at the shop floor level for blue-collar workers. A worker's performance is assessed mainly on the basis of their production quantity and quality. Quantified workload, tools and machine maintenance, labour discipline, and safety are the areas assessed. To a lesser extent, co-operation demonstrated that personal relationships with colleagues, especially with the leaders, are also important to have good results. In contrast to the PM process for white-collar workers, performance is rated mainly at the level of execution.

It is noteworthy that since *Doi Moi*, the PM process has been separated from the intervention of mass organisations, such as the party, the trade union, the youth union and the women's associations, although trade union representatives are still informed of the final performance-rating decisions. Nonetheless, the importance of working attitude, in general, and political attitude in particular, are still predominant in SOEs. To be promoted to top positions, preference is given to an employee who is a Communist Party member, or at least a potential party member who is under the party's consideration and supervision. 'Red does not mean leader, however to be a leader, you must be red' is still a common expectation in SOEs.

Since *Doi Moi*, the major purpose of performance assessment is shifted to linking payment to individual performance. Although sincere attempts to link performance to payment are recorded (emphasis on performance rather than seniority and attitude, the introduction of pay for performance, etc.), it is evident that the old practice of egalitarianism still lingers on. Of an organisational workforce, normally more than 70 per cent is rated in the top two performance levels in a four-level rating system, namely excellent, good, pass and poor. The forced distribution of performance ratings, which can be used to control the numbers of employees above or below a specific level, is not utilised in SOEs.

In a relations-based society like Vietnam, employees are inclined to invest personal time and resources to cement harmonious working relationships with key managers and their peers, sometimes at the expense of their personal gain. Such investments may include elaborate gifts, private parties, family visits, offer to cover work for sick colleagues without extra pay, etc. It is uncommon for Vietnamese employees to show their dissatisfaction with the lack of an equitable rating distribution in case it hurts their working relationships. Being sick, injured or unfortunate events befalling on immediate family members, such as death or critical illness, are, in many cases, accepted as excuses for substandard performance and might not result in being penalised in performance rating and, thus, payment. On the other hand, there are reported cases of female employees, who have just returned to their posts after maternity leave, willingly accepting a lower performance-rating level in order to 'be fair' to other hard-working peers. Similarly, high performers, who have remained at the highest performance-rating level for a couple of years or more, voluntarily accept a lower rating to 'give a chance' to those behind them.

Providing feedback

The exchange of formal performance feedback is an imperative element of the PM system. As mentioned above, SOEs exercised 'democratic' voicing of opinions in performance appraisals, where opinions from all employees working in the same department or production line are gathered in order to achieve a 'democratic' evaluation of an employee's performance. However, Vietnamese employees have a non-confrontational style of communication, as they try to minimise the loss of face and preserve harmonious relations. Negative feedback and areas for improvement are normally provided and recorded in vague terms only (e.g. working attitude needs to be improved, performance can be enhanced), where more detailed feedback is preferably given in informal talks in some private place out of the working hours.

Interviewed managers revealed that they are hesitant to criticise chronic low performers as it would do more harm than good to their work units and harm the harmonious working environment. Further, the current state sector's employment system, which favours long-time employment, makes it very difficult for managers to dismiss these employees. With few exceptions, performance appraisal meetings are usually considered a formality. Negative feedback is only received indirectly when production lines/departments are sometimes forced to downgrade some employees' performance ratings as instructed by the company's performance appraisal committee.

Planning for future performance

In theory, performance appraisals should include not only short-range goals, such as justifying merit increases and identifying candidates for promotion, but also long-range goals, such as detecting employees' training needs to improve future performance and identifying their career development aspirations and opportunities (Foot and Hook,

1996). When performance feedback indicates that an employee did not attain their objectives due to insufficient capabilities, it is their manager's responsibility to help the subordinate to identify their training needs, and provide suitable training to fill in the capability gap. Discussing long-term career plans and opportunities, within the scope of PM, also have positive effects on employee motivation and loyalty.

It is evident that although SOEs use PM systems to justify pay for performance and salary increases and identify candidates for promotion, all of which are considered short-range goals, they do not use this tool to implement any long-range goals. It is evident that SOEs show more emphasis on the assessment of past performance than on planning future development. Although all the studied SOEs claim to have training programmes for their employees, it is generally considered the employees' responsibility to be appropriately trained (see also Chapter 6). There is a very weak link, if any, between the results of an employee's performance appraisal and any training and development opportunities they might receive in the near future. In practice, career planning and development are hardly discussed during the performance appraisal process. To advance in their career, individual employees must seek out and take advantage of opportunities offered by the organisation's career development programmes, or, in the majority of cases, seek courses and training programmes outside the organisation, where they must pay for themselves. There is neither a formal procedure for replacement of, nor career path made by managers and/or the HR department, for employees.

Performance management in MNCs

This section examines the PM practices of the studied MNCs. It shows that in the foreign-invested sector, PM practices are diverse. A wide range of advanced PM tools and techniques, including the use of Balanced Scorecards, SMART objectives, 360-degree feedback and forced distributions, are found in non-Asian firms. However, in Asian MNCs, PM is characterised by a top-down performance objective setting, an informal and regular performance review, and performance appraisals conducted strictly top-down and allegedly suffering from favouritism and lack of openness.

Setting performance objectives

The studied American- and European-based MNCs report systems of top-down alignment. The company's objectives are cascaded down to department's, team's, manager's and employees' objectives. Each employee is required to set their own performance objectives based on their team and manager's objectives. Each objective needs to be provided with a measurement of success and achieved within a deadline. Employees then hold a discussion with their manager on their objectives, measures of success and timings, and make the relevant changes. The manager's approval must be obtained before the performance objectives are logged into the system, either in the hard copy kept by the HR department or in soft copy stored by the company's HR information system.

Balanced Scorecards are a popular PM tool. The Balanced Scorecard of MNC Auto1, for instance, is built on a regional/global one. It includes five key business priorities: volume revenue and market share, cost and business structures, product programme and execution, quality and customer satisfaction, and people and safety (Figure TB4.6.1). This allows headquarters to measure how each subsidiary is performing with a similar measurement system and common criteria. Each department in the subsidiary develops its own business plan which is linked to the company's Balanced Scorecard. Individuals and teams in departments throughout the company then translate the higher-level strategic objectives into personal and team objectives.

Figure TB4.6.1 **MNC Auto1's Balanced Scorecard**

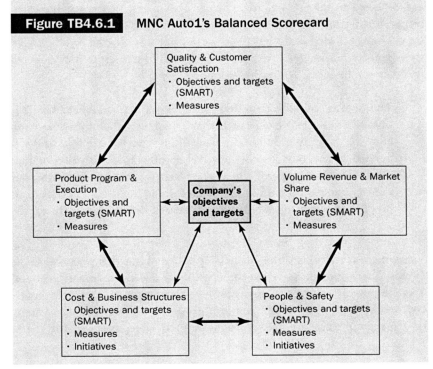

In order to clarify as much as possible an individual's objectives and responsibilities, companies use SMART objectives. SMART objectives are set to stretch and be specific (objectives should be challenging and state exactly what will be achieved); measurable (objectives must be quantifiable so that performance can be checked); aligned (there must be a clear link between the objective and the business Balanced Scorecard); realistic (while objectives should be challenging they should also be achievable); time-target (objectives should specify a completion date and milestones). Even though MNC FMCG3 does not use the Balanced Scorecard and SMART objectives, there is an extensive use of measurable objectives. In essence, there is one principle controlling the setting of individual objectives: to use measurable objectives to achieve clarification in individual objectives by supporting a more precise ranking of employees and ultimately linking performance to the incentive and reward systems.

The studied Asian MNCs also report a system of top-down alignment. The top-down process, however, ends at departmental heads in the office and production line heads in the factory. While the targets set for the production area are relatively fixed, there is a certain degree of flexibility in setting individual objectives in the office area. White-collar employees are expected to take 'fringe tasks' when they arise. In some companies, target setting is a one-way process, with little engagement of the subordinates. Individual objectives are set but not written down, which significantly damages the reviewing process. One interviewed professional in MNC Auto4 has stated:

> The setting of objectives has been extremely one-way. He [her immediate supervisor] sets the department's objectives and allocates tasks to individuals. We will do what we are told to do. It is hard to say that you do not feel comfortable with this or that objective. He might feel you are not heartily enthusiastic with your job or, worse, you are not capable of doing it. Also, you should be prepared to pick up any work that turns up unexpectedly on the way ...

Vietnamese employees differ in their opinions about this practice. Some express their objections, while some willingly accept it. Expatriates and Vietnamese top managers provide comments, which are later cross-checked by the author with lower-level employees as accurate, that many of their employees are happy to have their objectives set for them.

Explanations could include the passive attitude rooted in the Vietnamese education style, respect for hierarchical order and the typical Vietnamese non-confrontational attitude.

Monitoring performance

Companies normally review an employee's performance once or twice per year in accordance with their headquarters' accounting and financial practices. The annual and six-monthly PM is often backed up by interim assessments. Besides maintaining mid-year and annual performance reviews, Asian managers are said to rely more on informal discussions and daily interactions than on formal reviews and resulting discussions to rate their Vietnamese subordinates. Performance coaching and counselling, if necessary, are offered in non-Asian firms. When significant variation in performance is considered a warning sign of an underlying problem, companies offer the chance to discuss and assist employees. In this case, however, whether the employee chooses to follow the counselling process or not, he/she is still expected to achieve the specified performance objectives.

Measuring performance

The performance evaluation criteria used in MNCs consist of a number of factors such as work performance, knowledge of the job, quantity and quality of work, managerial and leadership skills, teamwork, etc. They are normally set at the MNC's headquarters. For example, MNC FMCG3 uses global performance evaluation criteria, which include two main criteria, namely leadership qualities and work results. Leadership qualities consist of building talent, collaborative, decisive, innovative, inspirational and visionary. While the qualities are the same for everyone, the descriptive behaviours for how the qualities are demonstrated vary with the employee's roles. Work results are assessed against the performance objectives set at the beginning of the performance appraisal cycle.

Performance evaluation, which is based on a combination of employees' performance results and behaviours (working attitude), is not an exclusive pattern that only occurs in Vietnamese SOEs; MNCs, including non-Asian firms, evaluate individual behaviours too. The performance rating form of MNC FMCG1 requires a lengthy rating of individual critical behaviour, which includes attendance at work and other plant activities; adherence to plant safety/security standards and practice; confronting improper behaviours; adapting personal behaviour to become a part of the work team; recognising and utilising the contributions of people from diverse backgrounds, gender and level in the organisation, etc.

Individual reviews for professionals and managerial staff are more complicated than for blue-collar workers. For the former group, interviews with the employees and their immediate supervisors are conducted individually, while the evaluation of blue-collar workers is carried out in a meeting with their team, in which each team member's performance is discussed openly in the presence of their colleagues. Simple as they are, open discussions and individual reviews always exist at the shopfloor level. In most of the case studies, performance reviews are linked directly to their pay (see section 'Pay for performance' in Chapter 5).

In MNCs, advanced PM tools and techniques are widely applied, which is illustrated by the use of the 360-degree feedback technique used in the US and European firms and forced distributions of performance ratings in all US firms. The premise behind the 360-degree feedback is that the best way to understand and improve one's performance is to gather and process feedback from multiple sources that are in contact with one's services, which include their peers, supervisors, customers, etc. (Stone, 2008). The 360-degree feedback is applied solely to top management, which means about less than 10 employees in each company are subject to this type of performance review. The implementation of top-management 360-degree feedback is managed at the regional level. The list of raters is chosen randomly from the employee's relationship map. They then access the form on the intranet, fill in and send it electronically to the regional headquarters. The HRM department in Vietnam is not directly involved in this process except inasmuch as they provide the employees with sufficient 'competence' to take part in this process by organising in-house performance seminars beforehand.

The distribution of performance ratings is seen as a sharp tool not only to evaluate individual performance but also to create competition to push up performance among employees. It is noted that while using distributions of performance rating is also a popular practice in Vietnamese SOEs, the 'forced' element is what makes some MNCs different and more aggressive in their attempt to link performance and the pay system (see Table TB4.6.3). The flexibility of the distribution varies among firms. Some firms keep a firm grip on the top performer's end, while others pay more attention to the 'needs improvement' end. Forced distributions also influence an employee's future career with the firm. High performers in these companies are promoted to a higher position

Table TB4.6.3	Performance rating distribution system applications in MNCs	
	Forced distributions	
Company	**White-collar employees**	**Blue-collar employees**
MNC Auto1	A (5%–10%), B+, B, C. 'Looser' forced distributions are applied for blue-collar workers.	
MNC Auto2	S (special), A, B, C. No forced distribution is imposed. However, normally S and A occupy 5%–10%. A global forced distribution system is being considered.[a]	
MNC Auto3	A, B+, B–, C. No forced distribution is imposed by headquarters. However, company distributes rankings as follows: normally A accounts for about 3%, B+ 10% and B– 20%.	
MNC Auto4	1, 2, 3. No forced distribution is imposed, although the percentage of 1 is normally around 5%–10%.	
MNC Auto5	A, B, C. No forced distribution is imposed.	
MNC FMCG1	1 (15%–20%), 2 (65%–70%), 3 (15%).	
MNC FMCG2	Exceptional (15%), meet expectation (80%), below expectation (5%).	Ratings are the same as white-collar employees. However, forced distribution is not applied.
MNC FMCG3	Exceed expectation (20%), meet expectation (70%), less than average (10%), not rated (for temporary workers).	Ratings are the same as white-collar employees. However, forced distribution is not applied.
MNC FMCG4	Ratings are conducted but no forced distribution. There are four ratings: outstanding (91–100 marks/100), very good (81–90 marks), satisfactory (71–80 marks), needs improvement (61–70 marks) and non-satisfactory (below 61 marks).	
MNC FMCG5	There are three ratings: exceptional, meet expectation or below expectation. Forced distribution is applied; however, the information on the distribution is not communicated to employees. All ratings are solely decided by expatriate managers.	
MNC FMCG6	Ratings are conducted but no forced distribution. There are four ratings: outstanding, very good, good, competent and underperforming. However, the number of 'high potential' within the outstanding group is limited to 1 or 2 only.	

[a] Questionnaire with regional headquarters

when the opportunity arises. On the other hand, employees who fall in the lowest group might be faced with counselling, improvement plans, etc. and are not able to resign their labour contracts with the companies if they are in the bottom group for two or three consecutive periods.

The 360-degree feedback includes upward rating which is unfamiliar, and might be considered as incompatible, in a hierarchical society like Vietnam. Meanwhile, the forced distributions system promotes competition among colleagues, and thus can damage their harmonious relations. Presumably, the transfer of these technologies into the Vietnamese subsidiaries could be faced with strong reactions and even refusal from the local employees. However, in practice, no particular constraints on the implementation of the 360-degree feedback and forced distributions are recorded, except for the high cost of education involved in the 360-degree feedback process, especially as the examiners are expected to be chosen from a multiple of sources that may include external ones.

This smooth transfer might be a result of the newly liberated business system at the macro-level, and a cultivated 'foreign culture' in the studied firms at the micro-level. The breakdown of the centrally planned economy, leading to the collapse of the communist model of an egalitarian approach of income distribution, makes the 'capitalist countries' methods of distributing principles', which are strongly based on individual performance, more acceptable to the society in general and employees in particular. Vietnamese employees have come to consider performance-related payment as an important dimension of modern PM practices. At the company level, employees have a positive perception of American/ European standards of 'fairness' and 'straightforwardness', which reflects a common perception about the way Westerners conduct business in general. This is seen as a refreshing and welcome work environment. Many managers assert that they will not work for SOEs (again), because they are nurtured in, and get fond of, this work environment, as one manager of US FMCG3 recounted:

> I used to work for another MNC, and then I had my first child. My husband and I decided that I should move to a SOE to reduce the workload and have more time with my family. However, I left after six months. I suppose I got used to a foreign invested company's working atmosphere. I'm no longer sensitive and patient enough with personal networks, unnamed and untransparent rules and all those things ... I'm tired of bending my back and lowering my head. So, here I am in MNC FMCG3. The workload is even heavier ... but I'm happy to be here.

Providing feedback

PM systems in the non-Asian MNCs are consistently marked by a high level of employee participation in the process and the openness of the process. Evaluation of individual performance is open for discussion, and if employees disagree with the performance evaluation rated by their supervisors or colleagues, they can voice their concerns and ask for a re-evaluation. Immediate supervisors and HR managers are responsible for organising interviews to 'check and balance' evaluations to minimise unfairness or favouritism. The final ratings are decided by both parties.

On the other hand, the PM process in Asian-based MNCs involves no face-to-face discussion. Vietnamese interviewees state that the process lacks openness, and the fairness of the process is dubious and can be subject to favouritism, especially in the case of white-collar workers where the assessment of employees is solely done by direct supervisors. Interviewed managers report that their bosses have the final say in their rankings, and it is not unusual that they use this right to upgrade or downgrade the rankings significantly, based on their personal view of the employees. In fact, this practice has significantly reduced Vietnamese managers' trust in the meaningfulness of the PM process that they themselves conduct. Many of them consider the process as a documentary requirement and/or a judgemental tool rather than a developmental tool. The halo effect (Cooper, 1981), which means the tendency to let one rating dimension influence all rating dimensions, is evident in these two companies. The HRM plant manager of MNC FMCG4 says:

> Even if I do not fulfil my target this year, but my boss believes in my potential, I'm still rated very highly. I suppose they have different perspectives, based more on their perception of a particular person.

In the same line of argument, MNC Auto3's salary specialist adds that the system allows for favouritism in the workplace, where the assessment is on surface behaviour rather than on long-term performance. She says:

> They [managers] have a rather fixed perception about each of their employees. They do have their 'favourites' ... One of my colleagues played a game once on his computer during the working time, and our boss caught him in action. After that, nothing could change his idea about him [my colleague], even though for sure he has not been the only one who plays games in working hours. There was a

rather uncomfortable atmosphere after that between his boss and him ... The guy felt it and he probably thought it meant the end of his career in this company. He left two months ago, roughly four months after the incident.

Although the practice of top-down appraisal, which heavily depends on managers' personal evaluations, is in line with some aspects of Vietnamese culture, such as respect for authority and hierarchical orders, Vietnamese employees in general are dissatisfied with this PM practice. This may be explained by the fact that this practice is contrary to the customary Vietnamese practice – which has been predominant in SOEs for decades – of 'democratic' voicing of opinions in performance appraisals. Thus, the relationship between national cultural traits and their influences on firms' behaviours is indeterminate and complex. In this case, respect for authority and hierarchy is traditionally implemented in a fashion that stresses openness and 'democratic' participation in decision making.

Mendonca and Kanungo (1990) believe that performance appraisal practices with a more confrontational mode of feedback during the appraisal discussion may not be effective in developing countries where 'face saving' is important. Weldon and Jehn (1993) argue that Chinese managers and professionals are more concerned about collective welfare and harmonious relations than personal gain. The findings of this research in the investigated MNCs reveal that this is not necessarily the case. Relating to the performance review discussion, difficulties involved in providing and receiving direct criticism in Vietnam are acknowledged. Interviewed expatriates admit that they sometimes have to 'tone down' their criticism, if they have any, to their local employees. Criticism, which is considered harsh, rude or unfair, may deteriorate the manager-subordinate relations. The situation can get worse in the Vietnamese context where unfair criticism would be faced with nothing but silence from the side of the Vietnamese employee. Moreover, word of mouth, which is popular in a Vietnamese workplace, might also be the cause of misconceptions about the manager and result in the deterioration of relations between that manager and other Vietnamese employees who are close friends or relatives of the employee. A Japanese MNC's subsidiary, which is one of the pilot case studies of this research, reports a case of the Vietnamese employees boycotting a Japanese manager, due to his 'improper manner' to the Vietnamese subordinates. This led to a refusal to extend his work contract in Vietnam.

Nevertheless, it is argued that the problem of direct criticism is more a potential than a real difficulty, and that cultural values are not overwhelming constraints to the implementation of PM, as long as expatriates and local managers are sensitive enough towards the issue. The MNC FMCG1 plant director states that he has good and thorough discussions with Vietnamese employees, which also covers negative issues. His success may be explained by the fact that this expatriate has managed to build a good relationship with locals during his five-year stay in Vietnam. His subordinates add that the positive result is due to the manager's amicable nature and a certain degree of tolerance for a 'foreigner' by the employees.

Planning for future performance

It is evident that MNCs not only use PM systems to achieve short-range goals (merit increase, pay for performance and promotion) but also use this opportunity to set long-range goals. PM systems in the majority of MNCs provide an equitable and transparent framework for constructive discussions between supervisors and employees about past performance efforts, identifying personal strengths and weaknesses, giving recognition to significant achievements, defining strategies to address identified performance issues, career aspirations and a long-term professional development plan.

Based on this discussion, training and development relevant to individual performance areas, professional aspirations and longer-term organisational needs are offered to employees. Some companies report the use of performance planning to address issues relating to the immediate improvement of the current job tasks, and career planning to deal with the individual's skills and preferences to fulfil their career aspiration in the future. While the basic responsibility for training and development planning rests with individual employees, the organisation's role is to develop an environment for personal growth, provide training and development opportunities and promote internally whenever possible. Based on the results of the PM process, some companies, such as MNC Auto1, MNC FMCG1, MNC FMCG2 and MNC FMCG6, provide employees of great potential with coaching services, regular non-judgemental feedback and encourage employees to do their best (see also Chapter 6).

Performance management in SOEs – conclusions

Prior to *Doi Moi*, PM was an important element of personnel administration in Vietnam. PM, during this period, was a lengthy and highly hierarchical process, involving staff at all levels of the company.

Any PM decision had to be made with the concurrence and under the supervision of the 'Four Committees', namely representatives from the Communist Party, the board of directors, the trade union, the youth union and sometimes the women's association. Appraisal criteria strongly emphasised non-work related criteria, such as good moral, political attitude, work attitude, co-operation and harmonious relationships with colleagues. Political status (e.g. being a member of the Communist Party) and attitude were the most important criteria in promotion assessment. However, it is important to note that although PM lacked well-defined and measurable criteria, as well as other appraisal techniques commonly used in Western countries, performance appraisals could be highly objective as the companies exercised 'democratic' voicing of opinions, especially for blue-collar workers, which means appraisals were often conducted in the open and in the presence of the employee and all of their colleagues, and the results were made public.

Since the economic reforms, PM in SOEs has been in a gradual transition from a politically oriented bureaucratic assessment towards an equitable system that aims to break egalitarianism by linking performance to compensation and placing stronger emphasis on individual merit and achievements. The PM process has been separated from the intervention of mass organisations, although trade unions are still informed of the final performance rating decisions. Employees can no longer take for granted that they will receive the same treatment regardless of their productivity. Instead, the new performance appraisal system places strong emphasis on competence and performance criteria, which are used to evaluate an employee's work effectiveness and real contributions to the organisation, and has been given much more attention since the economic reforms. Although solid attempts to link performance to payment have been recorded, the old practice of egalitarianism still lingers. Vietnamese employees show reluctance in enforcing equitable rating distribution if it hurts their working and personal relationships. PM systems still serve more as an evaluation purpose rather than a developmental purpose.

Performance management in MNCs – conclusions

In the foreign-invested sector, PM practices are diverse, with distinctive practices recorded in MNCs of different nationalities. In non-Asian firms, the PM process is closely linked with financial measurements and individual performance. A wide range of advanced PM tools and techniques are found, including the use of Balanced Scorecards, SMART objectives, 360-degree feedback and forced distributions. The end-of-year or six-monthly PM is often backed up by interim assessments and performance coaching and counselling, if necessary. PM processes are marked by a high level of employee participation in the process and the openness of the process. It is noted that the 360-degree feedback includes upward ratings, which is unfamiliar and might be considered as incompatible in a hierarchical society. Meanwhile the forced distributions system promotes competition among colleagues, and thus can damage their harmonious relations. Presumably, the transfer of these practices to the Vietnamese subsidiaries could be faced with strong reactions and even refusal from the local employees. However, in practice, no particular constraint on the implementation of the 360-degree feedback and forced distributions has been recorded.

In Asian MNCs, a PM system of top-down alignment of performance objectives is popular. The process allegedly suffers from favouritism and lack of openness. Besides maintaining mid-year and annual performance reviews, managers rely more on informal discussions and daily interactions than on the formal reviews and discussions to rate their Vietnamese subordinates. Performance appraisal is strictly top-down, and supervisors' decisions are considered as final. The PM process involves no upward evaluation and little face-to-face discussion. Although top-down appraisal practices are in line with some aspects of Vietnamese culture, such as respect for authority and hierarchical orders, Vietnamese employees in general are dissatisfied with this practice as it opposes the Vietnamese customary practice of 'democratic' sounding of opinions in performance appraisals, which has been predominant in SOEs for decades.

Source: Vo (2009: 65–85; 154–155; 160–161)

4.15 Conclusion

Employee development is a key area of HRM with the potential to make a large impact on the business. There has long been criticism in the UK of its training and management development. While, in Asia, some countries (for example, the 'Tiger' economies) and organisations have performed spectacularly well as a result of their investment in training and employee development, others have neglected this investment and suffered the consequent loss of productivity. Complaints continue (for example, in South Asia) of a lack of vocational qualifications and an academic focus, failing to give school leavers sufficient skills for the workplace. Management development has also become the subject of activity and initiatives.

The importance of training varies significantly across countries. There is often a lack of investment, especially in times of recession. We can distinguish between strategic and pragmatic use of training over the long and short term. Despite the need to link training initiatives to corporate strategies, many firms still neglect training when developing strategy. Training has tactical links with HRP and performance appraisals and is a key instrument in implementation of HRM systems and processes.

The perennial problem of training remains evaluation. This links to who should pay for this training? It could be organisations: do they benefit and will the market provide the resources? Or alternatively, states, which will give training parity to different academic routes in funding/esteem and reduce poaching by employers who have neglected training?

Employee performance appraisal is expensive, but is spreading even in Asia. Methods vary in their suitability, for example:

- Simple and easy methods with the emphasis on evaluation (rating scales) for some employees
- Methods with a developmental emphasis (e.g. MBO) for managerial employees
- Cultures of organisations (e.g. private versus public sector important)
- Cross-cultural contexts are critical

Appraisals can be a complicated procedure. They need to be seen to be fair and consistently and sensitively applied to have real value to management and businesses.

Finally, this work on employee development links back to Chapter 1. The creation of flexible firms is likely to need a flexible workforce, usually created through a wide range of employee development activities. We have in this chapter indicated the limits to views on universalism and 'one best way', and the importance of contingency and context, as well as the limits to ideas of HRM's strategic input and integration.

End of chapter tasks/questions

Based on the bank and airlines case studies in Appendix 3,
using and applying information within this chapter

1. How are the approaches to training and development of staff likely to differ between banks and airlines?

2. Airlines always have to train pilots in their company operating procedures and often have to train on the specific aircraft type used, but none of these Asian airlines undertake basic pilot training. Why is basic training not undertaken?

3. How would the approaches to training and development differ between the airlines in China, India and the GCC?

4. How would two young Chinese graduates – one seeking to be an airline pilot, the other seeking to be a commercial banker – manage their learning and development to construct a successful career path in their chosen industry?

5. How will the airline maximise the benefits from training or from not training (i.e. recruiting ready-trained staff) their own pilots?

6. How can the bank leverage competitive advantage from management development in each location in the case study?

7. What are the key elements to be considered in a training needs analysis in each location in which the bank operates?

8. What are the advantages and disadvantages of standardising or localising training needs analysis within a bank?

9. How will PMA be integrated into training within each of the different airlines?

10. How is the training and development policy of the bank likely to differ depending on the nationality of the employee?

References

Anderson, A. (1993) *Successful Training Practice*. Oxford: Blackwell.

Beardwell, I. and Holden, L. (1997; 2001) *HRM: A Contemporary Approach*. Harlow: Prentice Hall.

Bee, R. and Bee, F. (1994) *Training Needs Analysis and Evaluation*. London: CIPD.

Benson, J., Debroux, P., Yuasa, M. and Zhu, Y. (2000) 'Flexibility and labour management: Chinese manufacturing enterprises in the 1990s', *The International Journal of Human Resource Management*, 11(2): 183–96.

Beresford, M. (1988) *Vietnam Politics, Economics and Society*. London/New York: Pinter Publishers.

Bersin, J. (2004) *The Blended Learning Book. Best Practices, Proven Methodologies, and Lessons Learned*. San Francisco: Pfeiffer.

Bolton, T. (1997) *Human Resource Management: An Introduction*. Oxford: Blackwell.

Bouhnik, D. and Marcus, T. (2006) 'Interaction in distance-learning courses', *Journal of the American Society for Information Science and Technology*, 57(3): 299–305.

Burgoyne, J. (1988) 'Management development for the individual and the organisation', *Personnel Management*, June.

Child, J. (1994) *Management in China during the Age of Reform*. Cambridge: Cambridge University Press.

Clarke, J. (2008) 'In-house training can build on cross-border learning', *Financial Times*, 10 November.

Cooper, W.H. (1981) 'Ubiquitous halo', *Psychological Bulletin*, 90: 218–244.

DeCenzo, D. and Robbins, S. (1996) *Human Resource Management*. New York/Chichester: John Wiley & Sons.

De Jong, J.A. and Versloot, B. (1999) 'Structured on-the-job training: Report of a multiple case study', *International Journal of Training and Development*, 3(3): 186–199.

Duoc, T.Q. and Metzger, C. (2007) 'Quality of business graduates in Vietnamese institutions: Multiple perspectives', *The Journal of Management Development*, 26(7): 629.

Duong, L.B. and Morgan, W.J. (2001) 'The contribution of vocational education and training to the integration of refugee returnees in Vietnam', *Compare*, 31: 93–111.

Easterby-Smith, M., Malina, D. and Lu, Y. (1995) 'How culture sensitive is HRM? A comparative analysis of practice in Chinese and UK companies', *The International Journal of Human Resource Management*, 6(1): 31–59.

Ehrenreich, B. (2006) 'Gizza a job', *Guardian Weekend*, 4 March, 19–25.

Farh, J., Dobbins, G.H. and Cheng, B.S. (1991) 'Cultural relativity in action: A comparison of self-ratings made by Chinese and US workers', *Personnel Psychology*, 44: 129–467.

Fisher, C., Schoenfeldt, L. and Shaw, J. (1999) *Human Resource Management*. Boston, Mass.: Houghton Mifflin.

Flamholz, A. and Cheung, T. (2007) 'Classroom application of an integrated eLearning system', in C. Montgomerie and J. Seale (eds), *Proceedings of World Conference on Educational Multimedia, Hypermedia and Telecommunications 2007*. Chesapeake, VA: AACE, 2203–2208.

Fletcher, C. (1997) *Appraisal: Routes to Improved Performance*. London: CIPD.

Foot, M. and Hook, C. (1996) *Introducing Human Resource Management*. Harlow, Essex: Addison Wesley Longman Ltd.

Galunic, G. and Weeks, J. (2001) 'Investments that build on human nature', Mastering People Management, *Financial Times* P.5, 12 November, 10–11.

Hamblin, A.C. (1974) 'Evaluation and control of training', *Industrial Training International*, 9 (5): 154–156.

Hargreaves, E., Montero, C., Chau, N., Sibli, M. and Thanh, T. (2001) 'Multigrade teaching in Peru, Sri Lanka and Vietnam: An overview', *International Journal of Educational Development*, 21(6): 499–520.

Hindu, The (2005b) 'NASSCOM programme for future BPO workers', 14 October.

Holton, E.F. III, Bates, R.A., Seyler, D.L. and Carvalho, M.B. (1997) 'Toward construct validation of a transfer climate instrument', *Human Resource Development Quarterly*, 8: 95–113.

Kambayashi, N., Morita, M. and Okabe, Y. (2008) *Management Education in Japan*. Oxford: Chandos.

Kanter, R. (1984) *The Change Masters*. New York: Simon & Schuster.

Katz, R.L. (1955) 'Skills of an effective administrator', *Harvard Business Review*, 33.

Kazmin, A. (2003) 'A Buddhist boot camp for Thailand's elite', *Financial Times*, 8 January, 14.

Kim, T.H. (1996) *Vietnam's Economy: The Period 1945–1995 and its Perspective by the Year 2020*. Hanoi: Statistical Publishing House.

KPMG (2004) 'Strengthening the human resource foundation of the Indian IT enabled services industry', Report by KPMG Advisory Services Private Limited in association with NASSCOM under the aegis of the Department of IT, Ministry of Information Technology and Communications, Government of India.

Kwong, R. (2009) 'Taiwan's workers opt for more qualifications', *Financial Times*, 2 April.

Lewis, T. (1997) 'America's choice: Literacy or productivity', *Curriculum Inquiry*, 27(4): 391–421.

Mackay, S. and Stockport, G. (2006) 'Blended learning, classroom and e-learning', *The Business Review*, 5(1): 82–88.

Maurice, M., Sellier, F. and Silvestre, J.J. (1986) *The Social Foundations of Industrial Power*. Cambridge, MA: MIT Press.

Mendonca, M. and Kanungo, R.N. (1990) 'Performance management in developing countries', in A.M. Jaeger and R.N. Kanungo (eds), *Management in Developing Countries*. London: Routledge.

MOET (Ministry of Education and Training) (2001) *The Vietnam Education Development Strategic Plan for 2001–10, 2001*. Hanoi: Education Publishing House.

Morris, M. (1984) 'The evaluation of training', *Industrial and Commercial Training*, March/April.

Nasscom-j (2005) Available at http://www.nasscom.org/articleprint.asp?art_id=4728 (accessed on 29 November 2005).

Neupert, K.E., Baughn, C.C. and Dao, T.T.L. (2005) 'International management skills for success in Asia: A needs-based determination of skills for foreign managers and local managers', *Journal of European Industrial Training*, (29)2: 165–180.

Nguyen, V.T. (2006) 'Vocational training in Vietnam', in *Proceedings of the Asia-Pacific Programme of Educational Innovation for Development (APEID)*, Bangkok, Thailand, 6–8 December 2006 Available at http://www.unescobkk.org/fileadmin/user_upload/apeid/Conference/papers/3B4_paper_Ngyuen_Viet_Thang.doc (accessed 11 September 2008).

Nguyen, N.A. and Nguyen, T. (2007) 'Foreign direct investment in Vietnam: An overview and analysis of the determinants of spatial distribution across provinces', MPRA Paper 1921, University Library of Munich, Germany.

Peters, T. and Waterman, R. (1982) *In Search of Excellence*. New York: Harper Row.

Pfeifer, S. (2008) 'Training's most formidable force', *Financial Times*, 16 October.

Quang, T. and Dung, H.K. (1998) 'Human resource development in state-owned enterprises in Vietnam', *Research and Practice in Human Resource Management*, (6)1: 85–103.

Revans, R. (1972) 'Action learning: A management development programme', *Personnel Review*.

Rowley, C. and Warner, M. (2004) 'HR development in the Asia Pacific', *Journal of World Business*, 39(4): 308–310.

Rowley, C., Scott-Jackson, W., Kariem, B., Porteous, A. and Harb, A. (2010) 'Maximizing women's participation in the GCC workforce: The example of home working', *Effective Executive*, XIII(8): 46–67.

Saini, D. and Budhwar, P. (2004) 'HRM in India', in Budhwar, P. (ed.), *Managing Human Resources in Asia-Pacific*. London: Routledge.

Shen, J. (2004) 'A model of international performance appraisal in the context of Chinese MNCs', *International Journal of Manpower*, 25(6): 547–63.

Shen, J. (2007) *Labour Disputes and their Resolution in China*, Oxford: Chandos.

Shen, J. (2009) 'The implementation of a new employment relations system and employees' responses in a Chinese manufacturing enterprise', in R. Alas (ed.) *Implementation of Changes in Chinese Organsations*. Oxford: Chandos.

Shen, J. and Darby, R. (2006) 'International training and management development in Chinese multinational enterprises', *Employee Relations*, 28(4): 342–62.

Stone, R. (2008) *Managing Human Resources* (2nd edn). Milton, Queensland: John Wiley & Sons.

Storey, J. and Quintas, P. (2001) *HRM: A Critical Text*. London: Thomson.

Taskforce (2003) 'Taskforce on meeting the human resources challenge for IT and IT enabled services'. Government of India, Ministry of Communications and Information Technology. Department of Information Technology. 18 December 2003.

Taylor, A. (2006) 'McDonald's chips away at image as poor employer', *Financial Times*, 20 April.

Taylor, S. (1998) *Employee Resourcing*. London: CIPD.

Thite, M. and Russell, B. (2007) 'India and business process outsourcing', in J. Burgess and J. Connell (eds) *Globalisation and Work in Asia*. Oxford: Chandos, 67–92.

Thornhill, A., Lewis, P., Millimore, M. and Saunders, M. (2000) *Managing Change: A HR Strategy Approach*. Harlow: FT/Prentice Hall.

Torrington, D. and Hall, L. (1998) *Human Resource Management*. London: FT/Prentice Hall.

Verburg, R. (1999) 'Developing HRM in foreign-Chinese joint ventures', *European Management Journal*, 14(5): 518–26.

Vo, A. (2009) *The Transformation of HRM and IR in Vietnam*. Oxford: Chandos.

Vu, Q.N. (2002) 'State-owned enterprises reform in Vietnam', PhD thesis, Canberra: Australian National University.

Warner, M. (1996) 'Economic reforms, industrial relations and human resources in the People's Republic of China: An overview', *Industrial Relations Journal*, 27(3): 195–210.

Weldon, E. and Jehn, K. (1993) 'Work goals and work-related beliefs among managers and professionals in the United States and the People's Republic of China', *Asia Pacific Journal of Human Resources*, 31(3): 64–70.

Weldon, E. and Vanhonacker, W. (1999) 'Operating a foreign-invested enterprise in China: Challenges for managers and management researchers', *Journal of World Business*, 34(1): 94–107.

Wilhelm, P.G. and Xia, A. (1993) 'A comparison of the United States and Chinese managerial cultures in the transitional period: Implications for labour relations and joint ventures', *The International Journal of Organizational Analysis*, 1(4): 405–26.

Zhao, S.M. (1994) 'Human resource management in China', *Asia Pacific Journal of Human Resources*, 32(2): 3–12.

Zhu, J.H. and Dowling, P.J. (1998) 'Performance appraisal in China', in Selmer, J. (ed.), *International Management in China: Cross-cultural Issues*'. London: Routledge, 115–36.

Employee relations

5.1 Introduction

This chapter is concerned with the area of employee relations. Here, unlike some other commentators, we do not make a hard distinction between the terms *industrial relations* (IR) and *employee relations*, which we take to include all aspects of work and the work environment. The area of IR and then employee relations were key areas feeding into the development of personnel management, and then into HRM. The field has critical impacts on HRM, through the political process as well as employer and employee organisations (such as trade unions), and includes labour market changes and legislation. In parts of Asia politics and employee relations are often strongly linked. This discussion forms the first half of this chapter, dealing with its early development, definitions, a system, strategy, perspectives, partnership and the future.

In the West (especially in the European Union), a key aspect of the employee relations area – not least because it is seen to be both a 'cause' and a 'cure' for 'poor' employee relations – is employee involvement. A spectrum of practices is often lumped under the rubric of this elastic concept, ranging from industrial democracy through to financial participation. A more contemporary guise is the idea of workplace partnerships. However, the use of employee involvement as a solution to help in business and management problems often comes too late in the HRM strategy and processes, with it being ad hoc, used merely as a 'bolt on' and some sort of organisational 'life belt'. This area forms the second major part of this chapter, where employee involvement is examined in terms of forms and practices with the related issues that these raise.

5.2 Overview

Employee relations as a subject frequently arouses very mixed reactions. Why is this? For some commentators attitudes are influenced by a range of factors, which include 'frames of reference' and 'perspectives' in employee relations. Trying to interpret employee relations issues and events, especially disputes, in terms of the 'facts' of the situation to arrive at an explanation of the causes is not easy. Yet, surely 'the facts speak for themselves'? With sufficiently close attention given to collecting detailed information can we not come across some objective explanations? We will look at these issues in the first part of this overview.

The origin of employee relations is in IR, with its antecedents arising in the late nineteenth century 'labour problem', with its 'Two Faces'. On the one hand, there was labour militancy, conflict and economic disruption; on the other hand, there were issues of poor pay and poor working conditions. The best 'solution' to this problem was seen by many as collective bargaining, to which IR became closely linked. The IR area remained marked by pragmatism and its scope largely reflected the practical concerns of management, public policy and governments. From the 1950s to the 1980s the area became almost synonymous with trade unions and strife. Managing this strife was a major and time-consuming concern of personnel specialists and line managers, as well as governments as, for example, in South Korea and Japan.

Drawing on a wide variety of theories and data from economics, history, sociology, law, politics and organisational behaviour, employee relations is concerned with all aspects of the employment relationship. It was argued that in every country there was an employee relations 'system' involving three groups or parties: workers and their organisations; employers, managers and their organisations; government and agencies concerned with work (see Dunlop, 1959 and Figure 5.1). Every system creates a complex set of rules to govern the workplace; these rules, and the context in which they operate, will be considered in more detail later in this chapter (see 5.4.1 and 5.4.2).

The idea of 'good' and 'harmonious' employee relations is often proposed as 'normal' and the key to success. This can be seen in some of the 'Asian Tiger' economies. Why does this harmony seem so elusive and the subject of debate? If we look at employee relations in Asia there is great diversity in structures and practices. The role of employee organisations as one group in the employee relations system has been hotly debated, especially in the US. Nevertheless, even in American HRM models (see Chapter 1), trade

Figure 5.1 The ER system

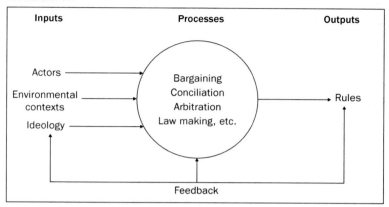

Source: Dunlop (1958)

unions are considered by many to be both 'stakeholders' and 'situational factors'. In the same framework, employee influence is given as a 'HRM policy choice' while 'laws' are another situational factor. Indeed, the idea of employee involvement, and more recently ideas of 'partnership' with labour/trade unions, is not new. The ideas of HRM processes and procedures to reduce or resolve conflict are also of long standing.

We can see some of the issues regarding employee relations and disputes in the Asian example in Text Box 5.1.

Text Box 5.1

Employee relations in China

'Labour dispute' is generally regarded as any controversy concerning terms, tenure, or conditions of employment, or concerning the association or representation of persons in negotiating, fixing, maintaining, changing, or seeking to arrange terms or conditions of employment, regardless of whether the disputants stand in the relationship of employer and employee. Whether individual or collective in nature, labour disputes take place between two parties in employer-employee relations, in which employees exercise their labour rights and fulfil their labour duties. Labour disputes in China refer particularly to disputes arising or relating to employment or labour contracts between employers, which can be either SOEs or POEs, and individual employees of any nationality within mainland China (Mo, 2000).

Workers in today's China have become more vulnerable and marginalised than at any time since 1949. China's economic reform has drastically changed employment relations and, in fact, has permanently ended the harmonious employment relations that used to exist. While enterprises have ignored most of their responsibilities in looking after their workers' social and economic needs, they have virtually been given a carte blanche regarding employment. Profit-oriented enterprise management strategies often result in abusing such power. Consequently, there are widespread violations of workers' rights, labour disputes and a high level of discontent among ordinary workers.

With the help of legal aid and information centres, the Chinese workforce, which used to be docile under the 'iron rice-bowl' system (Walder, 1986), has begun to understand and now agitate for their own legal rights in different ways. In spite of facing retaliation from employers, such as losing jobs or work unit housing, or even criminal charges, desperate workers have no other choice but to fight for justice. Their struggles are reflected in many forms, from appealing to unions and local government, work stoppages and strikes. Other more violent collective actions are emerging, such as street demonstrations and protests, blocking main roads and government buildings, beating up enterprise managers and smashing or sabotaging enterprise properties. At the beginning of the economic reform, workers were reluctant to act in this way. Gradually, discontented workers have become more prepared to do so. Workers have also proved adept at using the proletarian rhetoric of the Maoist period to press for social justice in the new economic environment and phrasing their demands in class terms, which the authorities find uncomfortable to deal with (Chen, 1995; Sheehan, 1998). The widespread labour disputes are a major source of social instability, which is perceived by the CCP as the major threat to its nearly six-decade-long rule in China. With employment relations becoming more complex, labour disputes become more equally complex in terms of their forms and causes, making it increasingly difficult for the CCP to solve.

There has been widespread violation of workers' rights and labour disputes in China during the past two decades. Labour disputes increased an astonishing 1.544% from 1994 to 2005. As the reliability of official statistics is always in question, the number of labour disputes reported in government data including the aforementioned labour and social security statistical yearbooks might be less than the actual number. However, it is almost impossible to ascertain the full scale of labour disputes in China. There are considerable regional variations in the occurrence of labour disputes and it has become evident that regional differences are closely associated with the scale of the regional economy, the restructuring of SOEs and development of non-SOEs. Guangdong, Jiangsu, Zhejiang, Shandong, Shanghai, Beijing, Sichuan and Liaoning are the most heavily affected regions. In 2005, 65.8% of labour disputes reaching a number of 206,700 occurred in these regions.

Labourers make grievances felt in many ways, ranging from passive resistance such as declining labour enthusiasm, committing suicide by individuals, hunger strikes, appealing to enterprise management and to local authorities and bringing cases to arbitration committees and people's courts, and to active mass protests, work stoppage strikes, street demonstrations, surrounding government buildings and blocking roads. During the past decade, employees tended to appeal directly to local authorities or bring their cases to arbitration committees without dealing with enterprise management. When going to local authorities does not persuade local governments to take matters seriously, appealing to local authorities sometimes easily turns into mass protests and demonstrations. Although most labourers tend to work through official channels including tripartite consultation, arbitration and litigation to resolve their labour disputes, collective violent actions have happened frequently during the past decade because the dialogue channel between workers and managers is largely blocked; today's society does not provide Chinese people with individual rights and legal ways to protect themselves. Collective actions, in the form of demonstrations, strikes and petitions, help increase the social influence and accelerate the hearing of cases. Many labour disputes occur during the same period of time. Frequent protests have also helped to focus central government attention on labour relations problems.

Collective labour disputes are unorganised, largely localised, isolated and sporadic in nature due to a lack of collective power (Chen, 2000; Choi, 2003; Mok et al., 2002; Morris et al., 2001; Taylor, 2000). Most incidents have remained isolated and short-lived, lacking strong leadership. The past few years, however, have seen increasingly better organised collective actions. Most of the organisers are serving Party members and/or mid-level cadres whose interests were also affected; they therefore become involved in order to find a solution to disputes. Workers have also tried to contact other enterprises so that the dispute action spreads. Instigators are always arrested by Chinese authorities.

The occurrence of labour disputes is attributed to the lack of clear regulations on and unlimited power granted to management over employment relations. According to Western labour standards, violations of workers' rights in China occur in almost every aspect of HRM, such as employment rights and justice, recruitment and selection, training, wages and benefits, working hours, working conditions, and the social security protection system. While labour disputes involve almost all aspects of employment relations, non-payment or delayed payment, job loss and industry accidents are the three major causes. Many financially impoverished or bankrupt firms are unable to pay unemployment allowances (redundancy benefits) for 'selling-off employment' or unable to pay social insurance or provide medical benefits. Migrant workers employed in POEs are paid very poorly and are more likely to suffer from wage defaults.

Given the undeveloped labour market and inadequate social security system, massive job losses resulting from restructured or bankrupted SOEs has made a considerable number of workers have no other choice but take action in the form of protests and demonstrations. Moreover, industry accidents resulting from poor working conditions and working overtime, inadequate compensation for work injury and being paid a pittance for working long hours are the major causes of labour disputes. A lack of training is also, though not serious, a cause of labour disputes. Management corruption and mismanagement sometimes fuel the anger of already disgruntled workers. To a certain extent, local governments are responsible for the worsening working conditions in FIEs and POEs as they usually give tacit consent to these unlawful practices in order to attract investment. A small number of labour disputes have been lodged at arbitration committees by employers. Such cases involve mainly violations of labour contracts and damage to enterprise equipment.

While labour disputes have increased considerably in all types of enterprises, the economic ownership impacts on how labour conflicts occur, actual working conditions of people, and the characteristics of the labour force. Although pay-related labour disputes, including non-payment or delayed payment of salaries or wages, social insurance and other compensation, happen very often in all kinds of enterprises regardless of SOEs, COEs, FIEs, POEs or others, situations in POEs are relatively worse and in non-profit state organisations are usually better. Workforce reduction-related labour disputes resulting from SOEs' restructuring and bankruptcy occur most often in SOEs. Dismissal-related labour disputes occurred the least often in POEs. This can be explained by the fact that there is an expectation of lower employment in the long term. Training appeared be a less significant cause of labour disputes. Fewer labour disputes were caused by a lack of training in POEs but more occurred in

FIEs because employees in FIEs usually have higher expectations than in POEs for receiving training and personal development. Labour disputes caused by industrial accidents happened most frequently in POEs and FIEs, and particularly in East Asian-invested FIEs.

Source: Shen (2007: 45; 60–61)

Among other issues, there may be disagreements in employee relations. If there are disagreements, how can we attempt to prevent and resolve them?

Some of the issues and processes in this area are illustrated by the examples in Text Box 5.2.

Text Box 5.2

Dispute resolution processes

In the post-2006 global 'credit crunch' and economic downturn situation with its commensurate impacts on business and employment, it may seem to many that managers can more easily blithely assert their prerogative and take hard line 'take it or leave it' positions in negotiations and dealing with staff. Hence, there is no need for ways to resolve disagreements and disputes as they will not occur. In any case, it may be argued by some people that, with enough time and goodwill, all disagreements and disputes can be settled and resolved.

However, the above situation and scenario may not always be the case. If neither side can walk away, as is obviously often the case with the high costs to both sides that would be incurred, the disagreement or dispute needs to be resolved. Therefore, dispute settlement and its processes can be seen as assisted continuation of negotiation and related to conflict – they are an intervention process and adjunct to collective bargaining (Rowley, 2002a; 2002b). From a unitary perspective, dispute settlement may be viewed as irrelevant (Rowley, 2001a; 2001b). However, one inherent outcome of managing people from a pluralist (or radical) perspective is conflict (Rowley, 2002c). Of course, there can be a range of conflict types, but here we are more concerned with the more formal and visible forms. Once this type of conflict, leading to a dispute, occurs, then some sort of settlement and resolution will be needed.

If informal and internal ways to settle disputes fail, there is stalemate or an impasse is reached, then resort to varied forms of more formal processes may be usefully considered. Again, such processes can be internal, or externally facilitated, and also range from ad hoc to more permanent systems and from voluntary to prescribed and compulsory, even as parts of procedural agreements. However, while some disputes can be handled by law or labour courts, others require assistance from intervention by a neutral, third party in processes such as conciliation, mediation and arbitration.

Indeed, there can be publicly supported and funded systems of dispute settlement. These supports vary between, and have a long history across, countries, sectors/industries and times, with varied preference for certain types and levels of voluntary vis-à-vis compulsory elements over time and juncture (i.e. wartime) of each type.

In the UK, for example, there was an early 19th century system of compulsory and binding arbitration. The 1896 Conciliation Act then allowed government appointed arbitration (voluntary, except during wartime) to settle disputes. From 1919 the Industrial Relations Court was used by government to refer disputes to if both sides agreed. Renamed the Industrial Advisory Board in 1971, this body was replaced by the Central Arbitration Committee (CAC) in 1976. The independent, albeit government funded, Advisory, Conciliation and Arbitration Service (ACAS) can appoint arbitrators or refer matters to the CAC. ACAS remains the UK's main provider of dispute settlement assistance of the types in its name. Similar ideas of state-encouraged dispute resolution systems can be found in other parts of the world, for example, from the US, to Australia and Switzerland and Ireland.

Varied intervention types

The main types of dispute settlement process can be seen on a spectrum, ranging from at one end conciliation, with mediation in the middle and arbitration at the other end. These can be seen diagrammatically in Figure TB5.2.1. While each of these types of intervention involves neutral, mutually accepted third parties, but who these are, what they do

Figure TB5.2.1	A spectrum of processes and features in dispute resolution

```
                    Conciliation ---------------- Mediation ------------- Arbitration
                    LOW          ---------------- Strength ------------- HIGH
    Features:
    Intervention
    Discretion
    Proactiveness
    Solutions
```

and the type and 'strength' of intervention, discretion, and so on, all vary, as it shown in Figure TB5.2.1.

Conciliation

Conciliation is a process that involves independent, neutral third parties acting as messengers and interpreters in identifying causes of differences and the relative significance and importance (from 'easily traded' to 'deal breakers') of issues and positions of both parties in order to help develop ideas and mutually acceptable solutions. Agreement to any possible solutions remains the parties' own; joint decision as conciliators do not, *per se*, impose or recommend solutions. Provision of conciliation may be from private or public facilities. In the UK the best-known supplier is ACAS. Conciliation is undertaken by its full-time staff, almost all civil servants. This UK system is voluntary and arises via the parties' requests, procedural agreements or ACAS volunteering its services, in disputes.

Mediation

Mediation is a process that involves an independent, neutral third party assisting parties to resolve differences and come to some agreement and end the dispute. Mediation is more proactive than conciliation as mediators may now suggest their own ideas and proposals for a resolution. However, such solutions are non-binding on the parties. The parties may accept, reject or alter the ideas and proposals in solutions. In the UK, such mediators are drawn from an ACAS list, whose members are often academics.

Arbitration

Arbitration is the method and process of resolving disputes by referring them to an independent, neutral third party but now with both parties having agreed beforehand to abide by the arbitrator's decision for settlement. Basically, the arbitrator(s) hears the arguments of both sides and decides on them.

Arbitration is often criticized because of tendencies it may engender and encourage. One of these is the 'flip-flop' effect, with decisions being awarded alternately to one side and then the other side each time a dispute is referred to arbitration. This switching is irrespective of the merits of the particular case on a particular occasion and is an attempt to maintain the image of arbitrator neutrality and impartiality by being not seen as favouring only one side with decisions.

Another detrimental tendency is to 'split the difference' in decisions, which encourages more intransigence and extreme positions in offers and demands from both sides and a seemingly even wider gap between the parties' positions. Therefore, only the lowest offers and highest demands from each side are given and tabled as both parties know that while these 'extremes' will not be agreed, it may maximize the median and 'real' result if the demands and offers are split in arbitration. Thus, the parties 'real' positions are not clearly set out by either side.

Some possible solutions to these issues of 'splitting' decisions have been developed, such as the idea of so-called 'pendulum arbitration'. This process only allows arbitrators to choose between each side's final offers and demands in their entirety with the 'splitting'. An additional benefit of such pendulum arbitration is that this method encourages less extreme positions in the parties' final offers and demands before they go to arbitration as neither side can afford to risk being seen as 'unreasonable' as this will not attract the arbitrator's decision (i.e. the 'pendulum') their way. A further by-product of this moderating influence is that, in turn, this psychology can encourage voluntary dispute settlement as parties will be closer together in offers and demands before actually going to arbitration.

Yet, there are issues and problems with pendulum arbitration, not least that the decision implies that one side is totally 'right' and the other side is totally 'wrong' in a dispute in all the offers and demands. Critically, the system does not allow for classic negotiating, with its trade-offs and compromises over issues between parties. Indeed, often there is rarely a simple choice between offers and demands, but rather complex packages and also with conflicting views and evaluations of any data used and presented (Kennerly, 1994), as 'the facts' often 'do not speak for themselves'. In sum, 'The 'winner takes all' concept underlying pendulum arbitration is incompatible with the principles of compromise and flexibility underlying the negotiation process ...' (Salamon, 2000: 485).

We have distinguished and outlined the three main types of dispute resolution process. However, in practice, the dividing line between dispute resolution processes is less robust; rather it is thin and easily blurs. For instance, the process of mediation may be similar to conciliation, or it may be more formal and similar to arbitration, except with no final binding award.

Issues for management

There are several key, often conflicting, issues and considerations around dispute settlement and its processes for management and business. These include the following Table.

Table TB5.2.1	Key issues for management in dispute resolution	
Some processes (conciliation and mediation) avoid giving third parties power to resolve disputes on what might be uncongenial terms.	versus	Third parties do not have to live with the consequences of their actions or decisions.
Processes force both sides to re-examine cases which can make some movement, and hence settlement, possible.	versus	Can become addictive, 'chilling' important processes such as negotiation, making earlier settlement less likely as parties simply wait to go to dispute resolution.
Third parties approach issues with fresh minds and can bring their own suggestions and proposals for resolutions.	versus	Third parties may not have expert enough knowledge of the area and issues.
'Permanent' third parties can be appointed to boost knowledge of the area and issues.	versus	Independence can decline as third parties can go 'native' with long exposure to the area and issues.
Processes have powerful 'public relations' dimensions, being used to shift blame and responsibility for settlements onto others and outsiders, rather than as a 'failure' by the parties themselves.	versus	Actual calling for dispute resolution can be seen as a sign of weakness and undermining the authority of the parties themselves.

Nevertheless, despite these issues, the benefits of such processes in dispute settlement are obvious. After all, disagreements and disputes will need to be settled and resolved as amicably and agreeably as possible in some fashion. Also, some amicable and 'see as fair' settlement is needed to avoid festering resentments and future disputes erupting. Given this, dispute resolution will remain important for management.

Source: Rowley (2009)

There are examples of dispute resolution processes around the world. These include the US, Australia and Switzerland (see Salamon, 2000) as well as Asia. Some interesting examples are provided in Text Boxes 5.3 and 5.4 covering the resolution of disputes in China and Vietnam.

Text Box 5.3

Labour dispute arbitration in China

Alternative dispute resolution is attracting increasing attention in market economies, such as the United States, as a means of allowing both unionised and non-unionised employees to discuss their grievances in the presence of outside third parties (Hagglund and Provis, 2005). Labour arbitration is one major alternative dispute resolution mechanism for settling conflicts outside litigation in court and has been advocated by practitioners and scholars in the areas of industrial relations and human resource management. Due to the declining influence of the political and administrative mechanisms and the complexity of litigation for resolving labour disputes, more reliance is placed on labour arbitration, an issue which has received almost no attention in the Chinese industrial relations literature. Research in this area therefore is scarce and has not yet recognised the reality of labour arbitration in China during the past three decades. This chapter analyses the characteristics of Chinese labour arbitration by looking at key issues, including: (a) how the labour arbitration system has developed and been implemented in China, (b) labour arbitration procedures, recruitment of arbitrators, (c) the role of arbitration in settling labour disputes, and (d) limitations of the labour arbitration system.

Arbitration in the market economy

Arbitration is the process by which two adversarial parties submit their claims to a third party, who is supposed to be independent, disinterested and unbiased. The arbitrator then decides in favour of one of the claimants or issues a decision that is a compromise between the two competing positions. When the parties have agreed to abide by the arbitrator's ruling, his decision is final and binding.

Although the result of a labour arbitration hearing may not please the parties, the outcome is usually preferable to continuing a strike or other action that in the long term benefits nobody. If the employer and employee cannot reach a mediated agreement, they can agree, by giving written permission, for the mediator to make a final and binding decision. The mediator will explain to the parties that once he or she makes a decision, that decision is enforceable and cannot be challenged. Normally, there are penalties for breaching such decisions. In the United States, a party cannot later seek another determination in an employment relations agency or federal or state court. If either or both parties do not want the mediator to make a decision, the problem may be taken to the court. Unlike mediation, where mediators sometimes provide ideas, suggestions, or even formal proposals for settlement, arbitrators listen to the arguments of both sides, review whatever evidence has been presented, and make a decision.

In market economies, arbitration is not a process regulated by the legal system but a form of 'handshake diplomacy'. However, if both parties submit their positions to a mutually agreed upon arbitrator in good faith, they are expected to abide by the resulting ruling. A good arbitration system should be impartial, independent, immune and neutral. According to Bishop and Reed (1998), an impartial arbitrator is one who is not biased in favour of, or prejudiced against, a particular party or its case. An independent arbitrator has no close financial or professional relationship with a particular party or its counsel, and should be neutral in dealing with disputes.

According to Song, Zhao and Li (2003: 180), arbitrators 'are at the core of the arbitration system because they guarantee the quality of arbitration'. The ideal arbitrator should be independent, unbiased and have adequate expertise and knowledge in order to deal with cases effectively and fairly. Therefore, 'the selection of the members of the arbitral tribunal is probably the single most important step in the arbitration process, yet is one that can be fraught with unknown consequences' (McLaren, 2003: 233).

Arbitrators may be selected either by the parties, by independent appointing authorities (trade association, arbitral institution, etc) or by a 'list system' (McLaren, 2003: 234) as in market economies such as the United States. When a 'list system' is used, each party from a list is recommended or published by the arbitration committee. The arbitration committee then appoints an arbitrator(s) in accordance with the two parties' preference. The benefits associated with the list-appointed method are that, firstly, it offers the parties some control over the selection process, and secondly, possibly a less partisan panel because the opposing party's agreement is required for all the arbitrators (McLaren, 2003: 236). Where the party-appointed method is used, each party offers the names of arbitrators and reaches agreement on their appointment through negotiation, or each party nominates an arbitrator and they jointly select the third arbitrator. This method enables the parties to exercise maximum control and leads to parties having increased confidence in the arbitral process (McLaren, 2003). The disadvantage of this method is that it may compromise the neutrality of the arbitrators. Relying on an institution to appoint arbitrators effectively reduces control of the process by the parties (McLaren, 2003).

The development of the labour arbitration system in China

The first legislation on arbitration matters in China appeared in 1912, and in 1921 the Commercial Arbitration Department was established by the Beiyang Government (1912–28) (Song, Zhao and Li, 2003). Commercial arbitration was covered by existing arbitration regulations. In 1950, one year after taking power on mainland China, the triumphant CCP established a labour arbitration system. The Ministry of Labour issued rules for labour arbitration commissions in municipalities and regulations on procedures for resolving labour disputes. During the 1950s, China transformed most privately-owned enterprises (POEs) into state-owned enterprises (SOEs) and collectively-owned enterprises (COEs) and the latter became the dominant form of production in the Chinese economy. According to socialist ideology, workers are the owners of SOEs and COEs, and labour disputes would not occur as they owned the enterprises. 'Even if there was any dispute, it ought to be resolved through various administrative and political means for settling internal differences, rather than any formal or informal proceedings' (Mo, 2000: 21). Subsequently, the labour arbitration commission was abolished in 1957. From then on there was no labour arbitration in China until the economic reforms of the late 1970s were underway.

With the expansion of the economic reform and resulting widespread labour disputes, there was a growing need for a system whereby disputes could be resolved. The arbitration of labour disputes, as an institutional channel, was regarded by the Chinese government as a helpful mechanism to minimise social unrest (Lee, 2000). In 1987, the government re-created the arbitration mechanism for the settlement of labor disputes within the SOEs and then, in 1993, extended the labour arbitration mechanism to other enterprises. However, China officially adopted the labour arbitration system in 1995 when the 1994 Chinese Labour Law was promulgated and implemented. Shanghai established the first street-level labour dispute arbitration committee in Beizhang Street in 1996. By the end of 2001, the Beizhang Street Labour Dispute Arbitration Committee (LDAC) had established 33 arbitration advisory points in residential areas. In 2001 alone, it dealt with 52 labour dispute cases. Since then, the LDAC system has been adopted by most industries in Shanghai. Workers usually seek resolution of disputes through labour arbitration and labour litigation rather than trade unions; 58.5% of disputes had been dealt with through arbitration in Shanghai from 1996 to 2001, with an annual growth rate of 67% (SHMTUC, 2002). Between January and June 2001 dispute resolution organisations in

Shanghai received a total of more than 30,000 arbitration requests, and the majority of them involved non-SOEs and non-COEs (SHMTUC, 2002). Table 8.1 [*omitted*] shows labour dispute arbitration cases in enterprises of different economic ownership in Shanghai in 2001.

The situation in Shanghai reflects China's situation nationally. By the end of 2001, the government had established about 3,300 labour dispute arbitration committees above the county level, with about 20,000 full-time and part-time arbitrators acting as the backbone of the system (Fox, Donohue and Wu, 2005). By September 2005, 232,000 labour arbitration committees (LACs) had been established nationally in the unionised organisations, covering 59,407,000 employees. By the end of 2005, 8,891 regional and industrial TACs and 115 labour arbitration institutes had been established (the ACFTU, 2005). However, the Labour Law does not cover government servants, workers at non-profit and social organisations, labourers engaged in farming activities, or housemaids. Nonetheless, the reality is that labour arbitration committees still deal with disputes involving these groups.

The number of dispute cases dealt with by labour arbitration nationally increased from 47,591 in 1996 involving 189,120 employees to 260,471 in 2004 involving 764,981 employees. In 2005, the LACs at the organisation level dealt with 193,000 and settled 42,000 labour disputes. The regional and industrial LACs dealt with 65,000 and settled with 51,000 labour disputes (ACFTU, 2005). From 1996 to 2004, labour disputes settled by arbitration exceeded those settled by mediation channels in 27 provinces, autonomous regions or municipalities throughout the country (China Labour Statistical Yearbooks 1997–2005; China National Statistics Yearbooks, 1997–2005). In the same period workers involved in collective labour disputes that went to arbitration increased by 418% from 92,203 to 477,992. Collective disputes involving more than 30 employees accounted for 60.61% of the total workers involved in labour disputes.

There are many reasons why a large number of labour disputes have been submitted to arbitration. As mentioned in the last chapter, from the perspective of employees, the major issues concern pay, dismissal resulting from revocation or termination of labour contracts, insurance and welfare, changed labour contracts, and injury in the workplace. From the employers' perspective, the foci of labour disputes are two-fold: firstly, an employee's resignation (normally skilled workers or managers) without the permission of the employer; and secondly, damage to factory equipment by workers.

According to Thireau and Hua (2003), less educated workers tend to take their grievances to the government's Visits and Letters Offices that are run by the cities' labour bureaux, People's Congresses or Party organs, while the more educated and skilled employees more often take their cases to legal arbitration. Cases brought by employers to arbitration are relatively fewer than those requested by workers. The arbitration cases applied by employers accounted for an average rate of 6.51%. Table 8.2 [omitted] summarises labour disputes that were dealt with through labour arbitration, and provides statistics of arbitration applicants for the period 1997–2004.

Source: Shen (2007: 107–110)

Text Box 5.4

Resolving labour disputes in Vietnam

Before applying any disciplinary measures to employees, the management is required to inform, discuss and agree upon the matter with the executive committee of the trade union. However, the nature of the so-called discussion or negotiation between union and management on labour issues is dubious. Most of the time, the management simply informs the trade unions about what decision has been made. It is not unusual for the unions to be on the same side as the management when solving labour conflicts. Union and management both show intolerance to social delinquency, such as prostitution, drug use, possession and others. In these cases, unions play the role of a 'middleman' to convey the management's message, as MNC Auto1 union president insists: 'The union officials contribute to convince the employees of a harmonious management–employee relationship.'

According to an incomplete statistic of VCGL (2002), during the period from early 1995 (since the Labour Law was enforced) to mid-2002, 472 collective strikes took place, of which 262 happened in foreign-invested companies, accounting for 55.5 per cent of strikes occurring in Vietnam. Labour strikes are highly concentrated in firms invested by Taiwan, Korea and Hong Kong, which normally operate in labour-intensive industries. Up to 2002, they were responsible for 71.43 per cent of the total strikes. Taiwanese firms have been the most notorious with 109 strikes, accounting for 41.6 per cent of the incidents in the foreign-invested sector and 23.1 per cent of the total strikes in all sectors. Most of the strikes occurred in the industrialised provinces or cities such as Ho Chi Minh City, Dong Nai, Binh Duong, Ba Ria Vung Tau, Ha Noi and Hai Duong.

Interestingly, 100 per cent of these strikes are illegal. This is because regulations governing the use of strike as a weapon severely reduce the possibility and legality of labour militancy. First of all, in most cases, these strikes were organised by the workers themselves, with all the unions standing by, which make these strikes illegal, regardless of the fact that they followed the right procedures and processes (The Labourer, 1 January 2002). The fact that only 60 per cent of foreign-invested companies have a union established in their organisations means that for 40 per cent of foreign-invested companies – the most turbulent labour environment, especially in firms invested by Hong Kong, Taiwan and Korea and operating in labour-intensive industries – the right to strike does not apply. Secondly, strikes are prohibited in certain enterprises of public service and enterprises that are essential to the national economy or national security and defence, as indicated in a list issued by the government (The Labour Law, 1994, Article 174). Thirdly, workers must give two weeks' notice prior to any industrial action to allow time for mediation. Strikes can only be used as legal weapons after the failure of conciliation attempts of the company's Labour Conciliation Council and Labour Arbitration Council at the provincial level (The Labour Law, 1994, Article 171). Fourthly, when it is apprehended that a strike may constitute a serious threat to the national economy or public safety, the prime minister has the power to issue a decision to suspend or to stop the strike (The Labour Law, 1994, Article 175). The government has so far shown a considerable degree of determination in disposing of any so-called illegal representatives of employees.

Many are of the opinion that the reasons why the recent labour strikes have been organised by the workers themselves, bypassing the trade unions, are the general lack of understanding of the labour laws and the belief that strike is the quickest way to solve labour disputes. In fact, this is only one side of the coin. The reality of these strikes showed clearly that the unions' involvement was too weak. Almost all the unions were unable to perform their full range of functions, with some union leaders unwilling to voice the concerns of workers, fearing that it may affect their jobs.

Source: Vo (2009: 143–145)

5.3 Employee relations

We can trace the antecedence and development of employee relations, which could be said to have existed ever since people interacted in the labour process.

Think About/Question 5.1

To what extent is labour-management harmony the key to organisational success?

5.3.1 Definitions

Some definitions of IR are narrow – as, for example, those of the influential early pioneers of the topic, such as Flanders (1970) and others. For these writers, IR was about the institutions of job regulation and the rules governing employment. Thus, IR was seen as being about job regulation and collective bargaining, and often narrow sectors and workers – industrial, male, manual workers and their organisations, trade unions. Yet, this reduced IR to the study of formal bargaining structures and procedures, which is somewhat limiting.

In contrast, for other commentators, the starting point for IR was the 'exchange relationship' – the buying and selling of 'labour'. In particular, the basic disparity of bargaining strength between the 'buyer' and 'seller' of labour actually makes conflict inevitable. These commentators, for example, considered that IR was the process of control over work relations (Hyman, 1975). Yet, while this is interesting and it broadens out the field, employee relations covers more than just this: it involves the study of both structures and actions.

However, there are broader views of employee relations, which view it as being concerned with all aspects of the employment relationship. It includes the study of individuals, groups and their unions and associations, employers and their organisations, and the environment in which these parties interact. It is this idea of organisations and environments which we turn to next.

5.4 Concept of a 'system'

In every country an employee relations system, a subsystem of the economic and political system, exists. This involves the following three groups or parties (see Figure 5.1 in section 5.2).

- Workers and their organisations
- Employers, managers and their organisations
- Government and agencies concerned with the workplace and work community

Furthermore, the concept of an employee relations system can be applied at different levels, as follows.

- National (different countries)
- Industry (different sectors of production or services)
- Group, firm and plant (particularly given the importance of international corporations)

Think About/Question 5.2

What might be the purpose and 'output' of an employee relations system?

5.4.1 Rules

Every employee relations system creates a complex system of rules to govern the workplace and work community. These rules may take a variety of forms – for example, agreements, statutes, custom and practice – but their essential character is to define the status of the parties and to govern their conduct. These rules are fundamentally of two kinds:

1 Procedural – the methods and procedures to be used, such as those involved in settling disputes.
2 Substantive – dealing with, for example, rates of wages, hours of work, and so on.

The system's rules may be created in a variety of ways – through laws, collective bargaining, or imposed unilaterally by one of the parties.

> **Think About/Question 5.3**
>
> What might impact on the operation of an employee relations system?

5.4.2 Context

The parties and the system do not operate in a vacuum but within an environmental context comprising the following aspects.

- Political and legal factors – i.e. the power relationships and status of the parties
- Economic factors – in particular, labour markets and product markets
- Social factors – including culture and values
- Technological factors – i.e. methods and resources applied to production

If rules are the output of the system, the input to the system is the value and objectives of the three parties. The subject matter of employee relations, therefore, involves the three parties of the system and their organisation, objectives, relationships and interactions within the environment in which they operate.

While a classic piece of work, Dunlop's (1959) writing attracted much criticism, some of which stems from his own time and place of 1950s American pluralism. Dunlop argued, for example, that in each employee relations system there was an underlying, shared ideology (of consensus) which was expected to lead to stability in the system. However, the emphasis on stability and consensus makes it difficult for the model to explain dynamic change. Thus, Dunlop's work was criticised for being too static, overly conservative, ignorant of behavioural factors, and more concerned with solving, rather than seeking, the sources of conflict.

5.5 Strategic choice

Criticisms of Dunlop led some writers to build on his approach. They introduced into the area the important concept of 'strategic choice' and the idea of applying it at three levels (see Figure 5.2).

Figure 5.2	Strategic choice in industrial relations		
Nature of decisions			
Decision level	*Employers*	*Unions*	*Government*
1. **Strategic:** Macro or global level for the key institutions	The strategic role of HR: policies on unions; investments; plant location; new technology; outsourcing	Political roles (e.g. relationship with political parties and other interest groups); union organising (e.g. neutrality and corporate campaigns); public policy objectives (e.g. labour law reform); economic policies (e.g. full employment)	Macro-economics and social policies – industrial policy
2. **Functional:** Employment relationships and IR systems	Personnel policies and negotiations and strategies	Collective bargaining policies and negotiations and strategies	Labour employment standards law; direct involvement via incomes policies or dispute settlement
3. **Workplace:** Individuals and groups	Contractual or bureaucratic and individual employee workgroup participation	Policies on employee participation; introduction of new technology; work organisation design	Regulation of working rights and/or employee participation

Source: Kochan et al. (1984)

These levels are as follows.

Strategic

This level comprises the strategies, values, structures, and so on of the parties. Here we may ask questions such as how business strategy affects employee relations. For example, we might compare a business strategy that emphasises product differentiation and innovation against one seeking to minimise labour costs (see the earlier points in Chapter 1). In much of Asia, especially in South Asia, politics and employee relations are closely linked. Political groups use employee relations as a means of putting pressure on governments or opposition. In Asia we can compare the focus on labour reducing costs in countries such as Vietnam with the deliberate policy of driving up the cost of labour to encourage higher added-value jobs, such as in Singapore.

Functional

This level represents the actual process and results of contract negotiation. The discussion of strikes, bargaining power and wage determination feature prominently here. An Asian example of the functional level is the Japanese '*shunto*' annual pay negotiations which take the form of ritual posturing between employers' and employees' representatives.

Workplace
This level illustrates the activities in which employees, their supervisors and their union representatives engage in administering the labour contract and adjust to changing circumstances and new problems on a daily basis. Here there are issues such as managing conflict, motivation, participation and supervision of individual workers, as well as the structuring of work into jobs, groups or teams. The use of ex-military HR managers in countries such as China and Pakistan, with their supposed experience of managing people, shows the importance of managing the day-to-day workplace issues.

5.5.1 Goals and expectations

Importantly, this model is driven by the goals and expectations that people have of work. How people go about achieving their goals is through the organisational structures and processes. It is through these structures and processes that parties interact and make choices that, together with forces in their environment, determine the extent to which their goals are met.

Without a safety net of wealth or government support, some Asians work to gain the means of survival, including basic goods and services, for themselves and the family. For example, the provision of organisation-supplied accommodation by employers – such as the Indian railways, Chinese SOEs, Malaysian utility companies, South Korean manufacturers in Malaysia and contractors in the GCC – gives a needed source of shelter but comes at the risk that the of loss of a job (or involvement in an industrial dispute) will lead to loss of that shelter as well as loss of income.

5.5.2 Options and choice

This model emphasises the range of options that management, labour and government have in responding to environmental changes (such as increased competition or changes in technology). Although the environment is vitally important there is also, it is suggested, a degree of choice at all three levels.

Another useful addition is the idea of strategic choice and employee relations decisions being of a 'third order' (Purcell, 1987). This presents employee relations as 'downstream' of other strategies for organisations. This can be seen in Figure 5.3.

Figure 5.3 Three levels of strategic decision making

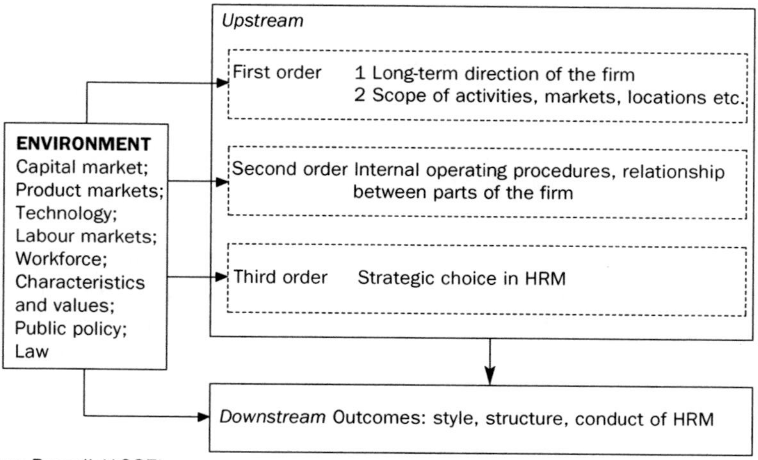

Source: Purcell (1987)

5.6 Frames of reference

An important development for employee relations concerned the work and ideas on the fundamental perspectives taken by people on the basic structures and roles of organisations.

> Think About/Question 5.4
>
> How are workers in (a) the West and (b) Asia likely to view the authority structures of the enterprise and management?

Within an organisation, are we 'all in it together', part of a team harmoniously pulling in the same direction with similar ambitions, desires, and so on? If so, how do we explain some of the conflicts and disagreements in relation to work? The seminal work of Fox (1966) explained that two views may be taken of the enterprise and managerial conceptions of its authority structure, i.e. on the nature, function and legitimacy of trade unions. These are as follows.

5.6.1 Unitarist perspective

In the unitarist perspective the organisation has a unified authority structure with common objectives and values – that is, there is one source of authority and focus of loyalty: 'a team'. Thus, it can be argued here that people:

> strive jointly towards a common objective, each pulling his weight to the best of his ability. Each accepts his place and his function gladly, following the leadership of the one so appointed. There are no oppositionary groups or factions, and therefore no rival leaders within the team? Nor are there any outside it; the team stands alone, its members owing allegiance to their own leaders but to no others.
>
> (Fox, 1966: 3)

This unitarist perspective is a common view of some Asian managers and government authorities. However, the role of trade unions and employee conflict in parts of Asia suggests this is less the perspective of all actors in the system.

5.6.2 Pluralist perspective

In the pluralist perspective the organisation is seen to consist of a coalition of individuals with diverse objectives and values. Here it can be argued that:

> In place of a corporate unity reflected in a single focus of authority and loyalty, we have to accept the existence of rival sources of leadership and authority.
>
> (Fox, 1966: 4)

So, organisations are made up of sectional groups with divergent interests, and this limits the degree of common purpose. For example, management has to balance various interests, which include shareholders, directors, customers and employees.

This pluralist perspective is less common in some parts of Asia among managers and government where rival thought is considered by some to be much more threatening than it is in the West (Harry and Nakajima, 2007). However, the existence and role of trade unions and conflict in parts of Asia, such as South Korea and Malaysia, suggests that pluralism is a perspective held by others.

In addition to these views, it is worth noting here another perspective – a radical view, which is a modification of Marxist analysis. This perspective denies that there can be any common interest in the employment relationship. Maoists in parts of India and Nepal and the Communist Party of North Korea maintain this perspective while the Communist Party in China has tended to ignore the issue during its pragmatic dealings with the factors impacting on economic growth. This radical view maintains that only the leadership of the Communist Party can determine the 'correct' path in employee relations and there is no need for intervention by other participants.

With the pluralistic view, it follows that some conflict is inherent in the very nature of employee relations. It is, therefore, as important for management to accept that some conflict of interest is inevitable as it is for unions and employees to accept that there are some common interests – in particular, contribution to the survival and success of the organisation. With the growing acceptance in the West, after the 1950s, of this sort of proposition, collective bargaining became increasingly considered by many as the best method to resolve these differences of interest.

The core thread running through employee relations is that labour is more than a commodity to be exchanged in the open competitive market and more than a set of 'human resources' to be allocated to serve the goals of the firm (Blyton and Turnbull, 1998). Rather, because workers bring their own goals, expectations and aspirations to the workplace, employee relations must also be concerned with how the policies governing employee relations, and the work itself, affects workers and their interests, as well as the interests of the firm and the larger society (Blyton and Turnbull, 1998). Nevertheless, conflicts should be limited in scope and frequency since the parties' goals are interdependent and common and at least some are shared. The essence of effective employee relations is, therefore, one in which the parties successfully resolve issues arising from their conflicting interests and successfully pursue joint gains in cases where they share common interests.

5.7 Individualism versus collectivism

There are other useful perspectives to consider in employee relations. One such approach is to view employee relations in terms of individualism versus collectivism and its variants. By individualism we mean the degree to which management asserts the individual nature of the relationship with employees within employee relations. By collectivism we mean the amount of collective focus in the relationships within employee relations. This view also allows the production of a set of employee relations regimes at societal level.

Furthermore, not only are there these different perspectives in employee relations, but their prevalence over time, and across different countries, has varied. This can be usefully seen if we make a broad brush coverage of history over the last two hundred years of industrialisation in order to locate developments and ground the more contemporary situation. We present such views next.

5.7.1 Liberal individualism/laissez faire

Along with industrialisation in the West during the nineteenth century was the idea of liberal individualism or laissez faire. With this it was believed that everything should be determined by the free play of markets. Thus, employment contracts were freely entered into by relatively equal people capable of pursuing their own best interests. Any combination of workers or employers would adversely affect this free market mechanism, which, if left to itself, would ensure the greatest possible good for all. The anti-combination feelings were strongest in the US where the government acted to prevent or reduce combinations of workers or employers aimed at protecting 'customers' from monopolies of labour or production. While this is an historical model, it has contemporary relevance, particularly in terms of World Trade Organisation values concerning free markets.

5.7.2 Liberal collectivism

From the late nineteenth century liberal collectivism developed. This was 'liberal' in the sense that the role of the state was limited. Simultaneously, this was 'collective' in the sense that parties were free to organise and engage in collective bargaining.

5.7.3 Corporatism

After the Second World War, and particularly following the 1960s, there developed a greater degree of government involvement and co-operation between the employee relations parties. This was seen in various examples – which included incomes policies and the establishment of tripartite mechanisms involving government, employer and employee representatives – in a number of countries. From the late 1970s such approaches declined. On the one side opposition grew to the view that unrepresentative trade union 'barons', not elected politicians, were now running countries in 'shady deals' with politicians. On the other side some wanted a return to 'free' collective bargaining and the end of trade union use in macro-economic policy, as in keeping inflation under control via incomes policies. Some countries have maintained elements of corporatism – for instance, the Scandinavian system, versions in South Korea from the 1990s and the succession of social partnership agreements in Ireland and Australia since the 1980s (see Salamon, 2000).

5.7.4 Individualism/neo-laissez faire

From the 1980s such corporatism was weakened with a revival, not so much of liberal collectivism, but essentially of individualism or neo-laissez faire. This was seen in the UK, but less so in some other countries, especially in Europe. Pro-trade union support and legislation was repealed and replaced by anti-trade union laws in a 'step-by-step' approach which whittled away union strengths in the UK. By 1997 the UK employee relations legal terrain was dramatically different from that of the earlier period.

5.7.5 Social democratic individualism

In the UK, after 1997 and the return of the Labour Party to government, there was a re-evaluation in terms of employee relations. On the one hand there has been much criticism that Labour was all 'style over substance' and that little has changed. This is seemingly supported by Labour's pronouncements that the previous Labour legislation would not be fundamentally overturned and that the UK benefited from a flexible labour market, which it needed to maintain. Yet, on the other hand, there is increasing vocal criticism by business interests of the so-called over-regulation of the economy, part of which concerns the regulation of employment matters. The post-2010 election situation in the UK is still in its early stages.

5.7.6 Government approaches

There are several models that use dimensions of varying trade union power and political ideology. The models, historically developed in the West, have relevance in contemporary situations – for example, liberal individualism in the past and in the 1980s in the UK, corporatism from 1945 to the 1980s in the UK, in Scandinavia since the 1930s, in post-war Japan, and now developing some aspects in South Korea and other Asian countries. We give an example of one such model in Figure 5.4.

Figure 5.4 Governmental approaches to employee relations

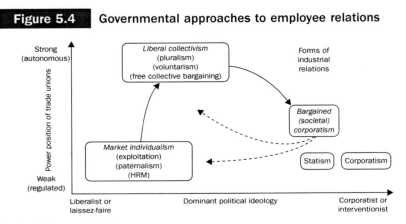

Source: Salamon (2000)

5.8 Partnership

Following Labour's 1997 election victory, as mentioned above, there was renewed interest in ideas of so-called workplace 'partnership' and deals. These were trumpeted as the way forward for employee relations, especially in the context of 'New Labour' in the UK. A range of employers and trade unions signed such agreements, and they received endorsement and encouragement from senior politicians. There had been some developments during the previous 18 years whereby some businesses and management had tried to change and recast 'traditional' employee relations. This was labelled by some commentators as 'The New IR'.

The 'New IR' changes involved reconfiguring trade union recognition and bargaining arrangements in order to try to obtain 'simplification'. For instance, in companies where multiple unions had been recognised, there were attempts to move to either 'single table bargaining' (with all the different unions bargaining together) or 'single union recognition' (with commensurate de-recognition of the other unions). If the organisation or particular operation was new, a single union-only recognition was offered from the start. This recognised union would then represent everyone in the company, in a similar way to some Asian enterprise unions, such as those in Japan.

We present some Asian examples (Japan, South Korea and Malaysia) of trade unions, types and structures in Text Boxes 5.5, 5.6 and 5.7.

Text Box 5.5

Trade unions in Japan

This section surveys the reorganization of Japan's labour union movement in the 1980s. Two major national centres, Sohyo (General Council of Trade Unions of Japan) and Domei (Japanese Confederation of Labour), dominated Japan's postwar union movement. Sohyo, affiliated with the World Federation of Trade Unions, was a 'left-leaning' national centre for organized labour, whose membership mainly comprised government and other public sector workers' unions including the National Railway Union. Domei was a conservative national centre affiliated with the International Confederation of Free Trade Unions. It drew its membership mainly from private sector unions. After the dissolution of Domei and two other minor national centres in 1987, a new national labour federation, Rengo (Japan Private Sector Trade Union Federation) was formed. Rengo comprised 55 industrial federations and 5,390,000 workers. Two years later, after years of public sector privatisation in Sohyo, it dissolved and many of its affiliates followed suit and joined a new unified national centre Rengo (Japanese Trade Union Confederation). The new Rengo comprised 74 industrial federations and 7,980,000 workers representing the interests of both public and private sector workers. A small number of Sohyo's unions formed Zenroren (*Zenkoku Rodo Kumiai Sorengokai*, National Confederation of Trade Unions) or Zenrokyo, as competing national centres.

With the birth of the unified national centre Rengo, expectations were that unions would gain greater political power but the Rengo was, in reality, a conservative organisation dominated by the major private sector industrial federations rather than a nationally representative organisation for all workers. The deregulation of labour rules was further accelerated in the 1980s as legislation was passed which continued to deregulate labour practices. The Law for Dispatch (Labour Hire) Workers was passed in 1985 with the law at first only applying to 26 professional jobs. This increased the scope for employers to offer and utilise short-term employment contracts. Changes to the Labour Standard Law (LSL) in 1987 allowed employers to use flexible working time practices, but this could apply to a limited range of jobs. Successive changes to the LSL and Law for Dispatch Workers widened the range of jobs where the laws could apply. Next, this chapter will discuss the changes that have occurred since the 1980s and the impact this has had on the employment structure in the following sections.

While unions are expected to prevent any further degradation in employment conditions, their potential effectiveness is limited. Japan's unions are largely enterprise-based where only regular employees are eligible for membership. Almost all enterprise unions in large companies have reached union-shop agreements. However, while there is significant disparity in the pay and conditions between regular and non-regular workers, their job content is virtually indistinguishable. In this way, members of enterprise unions are becoming a type of privileged worker. The privileges enjoyed by one group of workers at the expense of another has led to worker disenchantment with unions. Currently, the Japanese enterprise unions stand at a crossroads; they have become a kind of pressure group for regular employees in common with the old craft guilds. That said, they could try to encourage contingent employees to unionise and aim for improving overall working conditions which include them.

Source: Hisano (2007: 279–280; 290–291)

Text Box 5.6

Trade unions in Korea

Union types and structure

The single union national centre of the FKTU was challenged after 1987. Enterprise unions in industrial complexes started providing physical and financial support to one another to mutually increase their bargaining power, giving rise to collective labour associations that encompassed an entire region. Such regional trade union associations, or Councils, started out in Seoul and gradually spread to other major industrial complexes in the region. The new unions launched ten regional and seven occupational trade union councils in 1988 for worker solidarity, transcending the borders of enterprise unions. Councils focused on information exchange and mutual support among enterprise unions in a region or sector and were organized one after another. The Councils launched the Korea Trade Union Congress (KTUC, *chunnohyup*). The KTUC was suppressed by the government and its leaders were arrested as multiple unions were still illegal.

The FKTU's cooperative attitude toward government and management resulted in a significant number of unions breaking away and joining the Korean Council of Trade Union Representatives (KCTUR, *chonnodae*) in protest. The KCTUR was an emerging nucleus of the labour movement, while the KTUC was weakening under government suppression. The KCTUR comprised numerous occupational trade union councils and large-scale enterprise unions, becoming the foundation for the KCTU, with 862 unions and 420,000 members (26 per cent of total union membership). The combined councils founded a national centre step by step: the Korean Council of National Trade Unions in 1989, the Korean Council of Trade Union Representatives in 1993 and the KCTU in 1995.

As multiple unions, even at the national level, were still illegal, the government tried to prevent this new national centre forming. The KCTU was not registered as an authorized union; but, while the KCTU was not *de jure* legally authorized, it was *de facto* recognized, as demonstrated by the fact that its leaders took part in the Presidential Commission on industrial relations reform in 1996 and in the Tripartite Commission in 1998. With the labour law revisions in 1998 authorizing multiple unions at the national (or industrial) level, the KCTU gained legal authorization from 2000. The KTUC remained highly critical of the cooperative and non-democratic style of the FKTU and advocated a hard-line stance and democratic operation totally independent from management. The confrontational stance of the KCTU made it attractive to workers and it expanded. In 2004, out of 1,537,000 total union members, the FKTU had 780,000 (56.5 per cent) and the KCTU 668,000 (43.5 per cent).

The TUA (1953) did not regulate the structure of unions. However, between 1964 and 1987 the structure was affected by the government in a succession of legal revisions. The TUA revised in 1963 intended to create an industrial union system, seeing it as easier to control, and so restricted enterprise unions. However, policy changed and a revised TUA in 1973 deleted the clauses supporting industrial unions. The TUA revised in 1980 enforced enterprise unions more expressly as these alone were permitted, and industry-based unions were prohibited. The major reason for this was to weaken union power. Enterprise unions could affiliate with an industrial federation, but it was not an industry-based union movement. The TUA was revised again in 1987, deleting provisions permitting the establishment of unions only at the enterprise level, and allowing industry-based unions in order to guarantee workers rights of association and collective bargaining. Nevertheless, an enterprise union system prevailed until recently.

The establishment of industry-based, or at least occupational, unions had been an objective of the labour movement, not least as enterprise unions were limited in organizational power and economy of scale in operations and budgets, with weak financial standing inadequate to support activities.

By 1996, however, only four trade unions were industry-based at the national level, with just 91,000 members (5.7 per cent of total union membership). The conversion of enterprise to industry unions was initiated by the KCTU and started with the Korean Federation of Hospital Unions becoming the Korean Health and Medical Union in February 1998. Prior to this the Korean Teachers and Educational Workers Union was launched in 1989 as a single-industry union, but was not legal until 2000. The National Medical Insurance Union (currently the Korea Social Insurance Union), the Journalists' Union, the Banking and Financial Union, and the Railroad Workers Union, followed in transition to industry unions.

In terms of occupational unions, in 1994 the National Science and Technology Union and the Regional Health Insurance Union were the first, followed by the Mutual Credit Fund Union in 1996 and the National Universities Employees' Union, the Democratic Union for Bus Services, and the Research and Professional Union in 1997.

With the Asian Crisis and consequent layoffs and unemployment, both union centres strengthened efforts to build an industrial or occupational union system. Hundreds of enterprise-level metal workers unions joined in the Korea Metal Workers' Federation of the KCTU, forming a metal workers' industrial union in 2000. However, transformation to industrial or occupational unions faces opposition. For example, leaders of the powerful enterprise unions with large memberships in the manufacturing sector have been reluctant to concede their strong power and bargaining rights, while management are also opposed.

The strategy of the KCTU is to convert enterprise unions to industrial unions as soon as possible, however. In December 2005 industrial unionists accounted for about 30 per cent of total union membership, rising by May 2006 to 54.2 per cent, a majority for the first time. In June 2006 three powerful automobile enterprise unions (Hyundai, Kia and GM-Daewoo), which had been strongly opposed, declared they would transform themselves into a metal industry union in 2006.

This organizational transition has been one of the strategies adopted by unions to achieve economies of scale through mergers and consolidation to keep pace with the changing external environment. Globalization, rapid technological development and enhanced labour market flexibility are driving the evolution of the labour movement. This organizational conversion is also a shift from the existing decentralized collective bargaining structure toward a more centralized one. The effect of such change on the internal politics of unions, management and industrial relations remains to be seen.

The Korean government retained the long tradition of single unionism by prescribing only a single union at all (national, industrial, occupational, enterprise) levels. The main rationale was that multiple unions would compete and fight for the initiative of the labour movement and that resultant splits and conflicts would cause confusion and disorder in industrial relations.

However, many union leaders have strongly supported multiple unions. To reinforce the autonomy and accountability of labour and management and to achieve more democratic industrial relations, labour-related law revisions in 1996 permitted multiple unions for higher (national, industrial, occupational) level organizations in 2000 and unit business establishment level in 2002. The methods and procedures for collective bargaining, such as unifying the bargaining channel between labour and management, were to be developed. Thus, a multiple union system at enterprise level was postponed by five years in 2001 and by a further three years in 2006.

Development, structure and strategies of trade unions

Prior to 1987 the FKTU and its member unions were tightly repressed by the government. Policies and activities were generally subordinate to government, from which the FKTU received financial support. Thus, unions had little autonomy and were criticized for being 'yellow' unions. However, from the late 1970s a stronger, independent labour movement began to emerge. This movement resulted in wildcat strikes and the connection with the political democratization movement. Democracy provided opportunities for forming new unions and resulted in the KCTU.

Unions have acquired a full degree of liberalization and autonomy since 1987, with independence from government and management. The FKTU particularly has tried to reform itself to compete with the KCTU. Even though the FKTU is more cooperative than the KCTU with government and management, it still enjoys full autonomy.

There are three trends in the activities and strategies of Korean unions. First, union leaders have begun to realize that in order to survive in the competitive international market the antagonistic relationship between the labour and management should be converted to a more collaborative one. Confrontation and distrust between the two parties can help discourage business investment and destroy jobs. In 2006 the FKTU President joined the Minister of Industry and Resources and many business people in 'road shows' trying to attract foreign investment into Korea. It was the first time union leaders had tried to attract foreign investment with government and business leaders.

Second, there are some trends of convergence in the activities and strategies of unions. The two national level unions are trying to promote industrial unionism to improve the organizational power of the labour movement. Thus, long-rooted enterprise unionism is being gradually transformed. Uncoordinated decentralization based on enterprise unionism is being changed towards more centralized industrial unionism. However, because of the long tradition of enterprise unionism, it may be a difficult, slow change. The trend toward industrial unionism is an attempt to harmonize the decentralization and centralization of union organization. Also, behind the scenes there has been dialogue between the two national level unions to unify them, but it will take a long time for a unified national union to result because each national centre wants to subsume the other.

Third, Korea has tried to encourage social dialogue among labour, management and government since 1998 with the conviction that a consensus-building mechanism is necessary to create 'win–win' IR. After the social pact in 1998, the Korea Tripartite Commission failed to meet the expectations of labour, management and government. Nevertheless, each party is trying to develop social partnerships in various ways.

Until the 1970s Korea had adopted the strategy of protecting infant industries. As such industries began to gain international competitiveness, Korea opened its markets to the world. Especially from the 1980s, such an open-door policy was a key policy direction. In the process of joining the OECD and restructuring the economy after the Crisis, the speed of openness accelerated. Korea opened its financial markets and now several financial institutions are owned by foreign investors. The share of exports and imports as a part of GDP – 70.3 per cent in 2004 – indicates a high degree of openness in the Korean economy, implying substantial levels of competition in global markets.

Since the Korean market is exposed to a high degree of competition, it is not easy for employers to pass on wage increases in prices. This is a commonly made and historical argument. Instead, employers in large companies tend to pass on rises to subcontractors, which reduces the contractors', often SMEs, profits and wages. This is one of the reasons for the wide wage gap between large firms and the SMEs.

It has often been argued that Korean economic development was underpinned by a Confucian work ethic and its values, which produced characteristics such as emphasis on education, leadership in government and consensus formation, which later mixed with Western Christian ethics to produce '... an amalgam of family or collective-orientated values of the

East and the pragmatic, economic-goal orientated values of the West' (Lee 1993: 246). Additionally, there was the '... close, sometimes collusive ties between government and private capital ...' (McNamara 2002: 2).

Until the early 1990s most Korean employers who were the first generation of company founders were authoritative and labour exclusive, preferring top-down decision-making processes. These attitudes resulted in massive labour disputes and confrontations with angry and defiant unions post-1987. Employers were not accustomed to having dialogue and negotiations with unions. They were antagonistic to unions and felt their control threatened by calls for participation in business management, wage increases and payments during disputes.

Confronted with union collective activities, employers recognized that they had to jointly respond and formed the Korean Association of Industrial Organisations in 1989, representing employers in responding to unions. It failed in responding successfully and ceased its activities in 1992, and the Korea Employers Federation (KEF) became the counterpart to the unions at the national level. For example, annually the KEF suggests for employers basic guidelines and strategies for collective bargaining and positions on enactment and revision of labour-related laws, tries to persuade the government, politicians and the public and negotiates with unions.

In response to wage increases and strong unions, most employers followed labour market numerical flexibility strategies. They adopted labour cost-saving approaches, such as speeding up automation, improving wage flexibility by introducing performance-based pay systems instead of seniority-based systems, global outsourcing, downsizing by layoffs, freezing new regular employment and using temporary employment, outsourcing non-core jobs by establishing small independent companies within firms, moving-out production to low-wage countries, and reducing domestic investment and increasing foreign investment. The results are a decrease in stable jobs and an increase in unstable employment, early retirement, high (especially youth) unemployment and a deterioration of earnings distribution. On the other hand, some employers have adopted a labour-management partnership strategy by sharing information and engaging in dialogue with employees. In these companies some trade unions had 'no labour disputes' declarations and even accepted wage setting without collective bargaining.

Source: Rowley and Yoo (2008: 49–51; 58–60)

Text Box 5.7

Trade unions in Malaysia

Union types and structure

Martin's (1989: 113) typology of union movements is based on three distinctive positions that trade unions may occupy in relation to a state or to a political party. Trade unions may be dominated by the state (*ancillary* position); they may dominate it (*surrogate* position); or they may neither dominate nor be dominated (*autonomous* position). A union may be said to be in an ancillary position when major union bodies are characteristically subordinate or subservient to either a political party or the state, or both. In the case of the surrogate position, unions dominate the party or the state. This domination may ultimately take the form of union bodies acting in place of party or state by displaying qualities, espousing purposes and discharging functions normally associated with parties or states.

The autonomous position does not necessarily imply complete independence of parties and state; rather, it is better seen as being intermediate between the ancillary and surrogate positions. In this position, unions are neither clearly subservient to, nor clearly dominant over, either party or state. These three positions, given that there are three nominally distinct organizations involved, yield five categories, that is, party-ancillary, state-ancillary, party-surrogate, state-surrogate and autonomous. It would appear that in Malaysia, where a state employer dominated IR system exists (Kuruvilla and Venkataratnam 1996), the state-ancillary position is the most appropriate classification.

As stated by Todd and Peetz (2001), overall Malaysia's IR remains firmly within a 'control' rather than a 'commitment' framework. Malaysian unions are generally small, fragmented and regional. This is due largely to the strict requirements of the Trade Union Act 1959 (TUA), and in particular the manner in which a union is defined as:

Any association or combination of workmen or employers ... whose place of work is in West Malaysia, Sabah or Sarawak ... within any particular establishment, trade, occupation or industry or within similar trades, occupations or industries ...

The implication is that membership is limited to any one of the three geographical regions, that is, workers in Peninsular Malaysia may only join a trade union all of whose members work in Peninsular Malaysia, and the same applies to workers in Sabah and in Sarawak.

Further, the law has ensured that unions remain fragmented in their respective establishments, trades, occupations or industries. Therefore, unions of a general nature cannot be formed except in a particular establishment. The Director General of Trade Unions (DGTU), therefore, has very wide powers in respect of the registration of unions via ascertaining similarity of trades, occupations or industries. This has far-reaching consequences. One of the most important examples is that employees in the electronics industry may not be represented by the union of electrical workers as in the opinion of the DGTU the electronics industry is not similar to the electrical industry (Rowley and Bhopal 2006).

The rights of workers and employers under the IRA include the right to form, assist in the formation of or join a union and participate in its lawful activities. The union can represent its members in disputes as long as they are employees. However, certain categories of public officers are not eligible to join or be a member of a union. These include members of the police, prison service, armed forces and public officers engaged in a confidential or security capacity. Public officers holding any post in the managerial and professional group may unionize if they are so allowed in writing by the Chief Secretary to the government. This further emphasizes the extent of executive control over unionization in the public sector. The DGTU has the discretion not only to register a union or not, but also to cancel or withdraw the certificate of registration issued to a union under several circumstances, and may order suspension of union branches.

Unions can be classified under the following categories: private sector employees' unions, public sector employees' unions, unions in statutory bodies and local authorities, and employers' unions. Unions in the private sector can be further classified as either national or in-house (enterprise) unions. While national unions attempt to cover all workers in the same trade, occupation or industry, the same employer employs all members in in-house unions (enterprise unions).

Membership of the Malaysian Trades Union Congress (MTUC) consists of unions of employees in various trades, occupations and industries. Accordingly, it does not qualify for registration as a union under the Act. It is registered as a society under the Societies Act 1966, although it seems to have received *de facto* acceptance as the national representative of employees in IR matters (Wu 2006; Maimunah 2003). The MTUC, whose membership comprises both private and public sector unions, represents workers on tripartite bodies such as the National Labour Advisory Council (NLAC) and the Employees Provident Fund Board. It is affiliated to the International Confederation of Free Trade Unions. Individual unions can also be affiliated to international federations, for example, the Public Services Union is affiliated to the Public Sector International Federation.

Collective bargaining can take place between a single employer and a trade union or between a group of employers and a union. Multi-employer bargaining is found where employer's associations exist, for example, the Malayan Commercial Banks Association, which represents many of the larger banks, bargains with the National Union of Bank Employees (NUBE), which represents non-executive bank employees. According to Maimunah (2003: 175), in terms of numbers of workers covered, multi-employer bargaining is more significant, although the majority of agreements are made between unions and a single employer.

When different groups of employees in the company belong to separate unions, then employers carry out bargaining with these different unions. For example, many banks bargain not only with NUBE, but also with the Association of Bank Officers Malaysia. Malaysian Airlines negotiates with four unions, namely the Malaysian Airlines Employees Union, Peninsular Malaysia for non-executive graded staff, the Malaysian Airlines Executive Officers Union, Sabah, the Airlines Workers Union, Sarawak, and the Malaysian Airlines Executive Staff Association (Maimunah 2003: 175).

What do unions do?

The main services that unions provide for members are bargaining and representation. Collective bargaining provides a means for unions to defend and improve members' welfare through better, safer and healthier working conditions. Maimunah (2003: 163) explains that in Malaysia collective bargaining mostly focuses on economic issues. It could be expanded to include a host of other areas relating to the welfare of workers, especially in the areas of safety and productivity schemes. The outcomes of collective bargaining provide a measure of job security, status, self-respect, better working conditions and greater control of their working lives (Wu 2006: 145).

Unions offer legal representation if their members have problems at work. They may also consider and decide upon strikes, lockouts and similar industrial action affecting members. Unions also offer advice on labour disputes, protect against unfair labour practices such as unlawful dismissals, provide advice and training for laid-off workers and promote social and educational welfare. The NUBE (2006) organizes family days and activities such as various tournaments for members. Further, it provides for personal accident insurance cover and a retirement fund. In addition to this, it plays an active role in creating awareness in regard to broader issues such as social protection, the outsourcing of jobs and the privatization of water. However, very few unions have the resources and capability that the NUBE has, such as using the internet to reach out to its members. Its e-bulletins are informative and serve to inform members of current activities, issues and injustices, and generally promote the interests of the union and its members.

All collective agreements, which must specify the duration of the agreement, which cannot be less than three years, have to be taken cognizance of by the Industrial Court, that is, recognized as a binding, valid document enforceable by it. Such agreements are deemed to be an award and become binding on the parties and on workers who are employed or subsequently employed in the undertaking to which the agreement relates, regardless of whether they are members of the union or not (Section 17, IRA). The Industrial Court could refuse to recognize agreements that were unfavourable to national economic development interests. In 1991, some 379 collective agreements were taken cognizance of. Only in 1995 and 1997 did the number go slightly beyond 400. Since 2004, there has been a noticeable decline in the number of collective agreements taken cognizance of, from 369 in 2003 to 263 in 2005 (figures provided by the Industrial Court Department, 20 July 2006).

Administrative controls limit the right to strike. Once conciliation or mediation proceedings commence strikes should stop. Furthermore, bargaining on matters deemed managerial prerogatives are not allowed by legislation, thus ensuring that disputes regarding these subjects do not result in conflict. There were only four reported strikes in 2002 (involving 506 workers and 1,638 workdays lost) and three in 2004 (involving 279 workers and 3,262 workdays lost) (MHR 2006).

Ayadurai (in Leong 1991: 96) attributes the weakness of the labour movement to 'the incompetence of the labour leaders ... the fear or hostility ... of employers to unions, ... and the attitude or policies of the government' which since 1980 has become more unsympathetic, if not hostile, towards workers' organizations. This might have been due to the policy to industrialize the country and the need for a more docile labour force. Jomo (1994: 141) is critical of both the MTUC and Congress of Unions of Employees in the Public and Civil Services (CUEPACS) for having failed to launch effective action against government measures that seriously weakened labour's position. Many attempts were made to reunite the MTUC and CUEPACS into a single national centre, but these attempts, argues Jomo (1994), were undermined, largely by personal interests and ambitions.

Leadership crisis between factions in unions and in the national labour centre have led to observations that such divisiveness could lead to them being ignored by the government (Fernandez 1993: 18). Some of the MTUC's major weaknesses are the absence of a sound research centre run by professionals, the inability to settle differences (within and outside the organization) and even smug optimism, notes Fernandez (1997). Allegations of misappropriation of funds by union leaders do not put the union movement in a positive light among members and the regulatory authorities (see, for example, *The Sun* 2003; Selvarani and Abas 2004).

Source: Ramasamy and Rowley (2008: 126–129)

Japan has built much of the success of its manufacturing sector on the partnership between management and unions. In Japan one union represents all in the company as an enterprise union. This recognition of a specific trade union could well be preceded by what was called a 'beauty contest' for management to pick its favoured union. One of the most well known examples of the latter, in the UK, was Nissan's recognition of the then AEEU at its new Sunderland factory on a 'greenfield' (newly industrial) site.

A key aspect of such single union deals was often the idea of what came to be labelled 'no strike agreements', along with compulsory and maybe 'pendulum' arbitration (see the points on dispute resolution earlier in this chapter). However, not only are such agreements impossible to enforce, they are better seen as 'strike last agreements'. For instance, how would an employer actually prevent employees from walking away from the workplace or all claiming to be 'sick' at the same time? Ideas of pendulum arbitration have come from the US. Pendulum arbitration was taken as a possible method to prevent the 'chilling' of negotiations that occurred as sides simply waited to go to arbitration, which would then force parties to make realistic demands and offers and reduce extreme cases. These tactics were often used to try to maximise or minimise awards in the all-too-common eventuality that the result was to split competing demands down the middle. In contrast, with pendulum arbitration the most reasonable cases (to attract the pendulum) would be presented by both sides because 'split' awards were not allowed. It was either the whole of one offer or the whole of the other that had to be decided on by arbitration. So, employer and employee positions would now aim to be the most reasonable in order to attract the arbitrator's decision (the pendulum).

However, there are classic problems with these processes. As with other forms of third party intervention, both sides could use this process to opt out of any responsibility for the outcomes. Both sides can lose control over the situation. It means the sides are presented as 'right' or 'wrong'. Yet, negotiations are rarely about a single issue, but are a mixed and tradable set of issues. These issues create tensions and problems for arbitration and single trade unions.

Thus, there are difficult issues. The diversity in this area can also be seen in countries such as Japan, China and India. Japan stresses long-term stability and shared prosperity with low (by Western standards) differences in pay between the top and the bottom of organisations. Theoretical partnerships in Chinese SOEs should mean that all are 'working for the common good' with apparently low differentials in pay (but certainly high differentials in terms of benefits and status) in the expectation of long-term prosperity. Indian politics and economics were, for many years, dominated by socialist ideology so that employers found it difficult to encourage change or greater productivity and tended to hide profits, along with the real level of executive pay and benefits, mainly in the 'black' economy. Trade union officials were often encouraged, discreetly, to take the employer's side, while some officials would pursue their own political ends without seeking to protect their own union members.

We present some Asian examples of employee relations systems in Text Boxes 5.8 to 5.11. These cover China, Vietnam, India and the Philippines.

Text Box 5.8

Employee relations in China

Employee relations involve a variety of activities, particularly industrial relations, employee involvement and participation in decision-making, communication, disciplinary procedures, and legal regulations (CIPD, 2005). Employee relations are important as they are concerned with people's commitment to achieving their organisation's business goals and objectives and ensuring that organisational change is accepted. Employee relations affect the efficiency of deploying labour. According to Cooke and Noble (1998: 581) any 'constraints imposed on management by government regulations and collective bargaining that directly or indirectly reduce the efficient deployment of workforce increase unit labour costs'.

Between 1949 and 1978, workers were claimed to be the 'masters' (*zhu ren*) of SOEs and COEs. Constitutionally, this meant that China's mass of ordinary workers were the 'masters' (i.e. owners) of SOEs and

COEs, which accounted for about 95 per cent of the economy. Therefore, employment relations in China were literally between employees and the State, represented by government under the control of the Chinese Communist Party (CCP). The interests of workers and enterprises were effectively reconciled through political and administrative mechanisms. There was hardly conflict over employment relations among workers, enterprise management and the State due to the unity of interests of the three sides and the system of 'iron rice bowl' (*tie fan wan*), 'iron wage' (*tie gong zi*) and cradle-to-grave welfarism. When labour disputes did occur, they were resolved effectively by the CCP organs within the enterprise or the industry. Trade unions did not need to deal with labour disputes and their main roles were organisation of production campaigns and distribution of enterprise welfare benefits (Ng and Warner, 1998; Shen, 2006; for more about trade unions see Chapter 5). Employee participation in political campaigns and production campaigns was high and conducted via 'mass meetings' (*qing zhong da hui*). To implement the socialist democratic system, workers were involved in making suggestions on how to improve production, business innovation and quality management.

Constitutionally, Chinese workers have the same degree of freedom and rights as those in industrialised economies. The Constitution of the PRC guarantees all people have the right to organise without getting permission beforehand. Citizens of the PRC have freedom of speech, publishing, assembly, and the right to organise themselves, travel and demonstrate (Chapter 2, Article 35). The PRC is a signatory to international agreements, such as the International Convention on Economic, Social and Cultural Rights and the International Convention on Civil Rights and Political Rights, which require the protection of workers against unfair labour practices. These conventions are important reference points for future Chinese legislation aimed at further protecting the right to organise.

The reality is that the right to freedom of expression and association are routinely denied to many groups and individuals in China when the authorities perceive this as a 'threat'. Requests for strikes have never been approved and have normally resulted in numerous negotiations and the intervention (sometimes of a strong-arm nature) of the government. Clarke and Lee (2002: 63) have written, 'There is little doubt that Chinese workers do not enjoy the right of freedom of association and the right to strike'. Chinese experts on labour law have reached a preliminary consensus that the right of Chinese workers to strike should be guaranteed in legislation at an appropriate time (Chang, 2000). The Trade Union Law stipulates that 'workers have the right to participate in and organise labour unions'. In effect, 'labour unions' in the Trade Union Law means affiliates of the All China Federation of Trade Unions (ACFTU) (for more about the movement of organising workers' organisations see Chapter 5). Workers' constitutional rights have not changed nor actually been improved during the transition of the Chinese economy.

The economic reform, however, has resulted in many considerable changes in employee relations in China and these changes are interlocked. The first change is the termination of the obsolete 'iron rice bowl' system through the introduction of a labour contract system and employment relations reforms, which have marketised the labour force. The labour force in China is now employed in a way that has strategic and economic implications for many enterprises and for the workers themselves. Management strategies emphasising profits and competition have ended old harmonious labour relations and created tensions surrounding issues of employment security, wages and other employment relations-related problems that exist between employers and employees.

The second change is that it is clear that workers and employers in China have diverging interests. The economic reform has shifted responsibility for profits and losses to enterprises. On one hand, workers have become employees and are concerned mainly with their incomes and personal development; on the other, enterprise management or enterprise owners have become employers and are concerned mainly with profits and organisational development. As a result, the old 'workers as masters' status has been replaced by increasingly one-sided employer–employee relations. In the words of Taylor (2000: 341), there 'is no doubt that workers have a clear sense of their own distinctive interests, which are often opposed to those of employers and the state'.

The separable interests of workers and employers are the basis from which widespread labour disputes have stemmed. The Chinese people now have more channels for political participation, including lawsuits and complaints that are institutionalised and sanctioned by the government (Cai, 2002; Yu, 2005). However, from the outset, the radical changes in employment relations have not resulted in improved employee involvement in decision-making. In theory, Chinese workers have the right to participate in management and decision-making in enterprises (The 1994 Labour Law, Article 37). In most SOEs, COEs and large-scale POEs, employee assemblies are recognised as the most important participatory scheme in the workplace. However, because the employee assembly still has to comply with the orders of the local Party committee and management within the firm, it does not play an active role in airing workers' views concerning strategic issues and employment relations that affect the interests of their own. Its major role is to pass collective labour contracts that are normally drafted by enterprise management and workers' councils. It is hard for workers' grievances to be heard. Collective leadership is widely used but the participation of workers and lower-level managers in major decisions is superficial and symbolic (Huo and Von Glinow, 1995). Therefore, a real workers' participation mechanism in management decision-making processes is lacking. Business innovation and quality management tend to be more managerial functions and disassociated from ordinary workers.

The third change is the unbalanced state of power in the employment relations between employer and employee. The first stage of employment relations is focused on increasing enterprise efficiency and productivity for the purpose of developing the economy. China has issued a series of labour regulations, such as the 1992 Trade Union Law and the 1994 Labour Law, providing a legal framework for the development of industrial relations at a time of economic restructuring and the transition of many state enterprises to private ownership (Cheng, 2004). The directions of the reform allow enterprises increasingly to recruit, allocate and reward people according to their competence (Benson et al., 2000). These labour regulations have provided employers with almost unlimited power in employment relations. Enterprises normally set wages, working hours, working conditions, as well as other terms of employment relations unilaterally, as long as they conform to statutory minimum labour standards. As a result, employees are disadvantaged and exposed to violation of rights in the workplace. Consequently, tensions between employees and employers have grown and led to spontaneous workers' rights violation and labour disputes. The old harmonious labour relations are history and gone forever.

The fourth change is the emerging roles trade unions play in employment relations. In the course of the economy transition, as organs of the Party-state, unions can no longer claim relevance as 'transmission belts' between the management and workers. Although under no direct pressure to adapt to the changed employment relations situation, China's 1950s trade union model has been challenged. Trade unions have been required by the Party-state to play an active role in maintaining social stability. While the ACFTU and its affiliated unions are still supposed to promote the interests of both employees and employers, their functions start diverging from those of management as indicated in the 2004 Provisions on Collective Contracts. However, how far trade unions can go to in the future in terms of opposing employers is still uncertain.

The fifth change is the enforcement of legal regulations on employment relations. Since the late 1970s, the State has issued more than 20 pieces of legislation, with the 1994 Labour Law and 1992 Trade Union Law as the main decrees responsible for regulating labour relations. At the Eighth Session of the National People's Congress Standing Committee on 5 July 1994, the Labour Law was promulgated and it took effect on 1 January 1995. Standardising the labour standards and practices, this benchmark piece of law integrates a legal framework for all types of enterprise regardless of their ownership and locations in China. The 1994 Labour Law and the supplementary regulations provide legal regulations on employment relations and also increased workers' awareness of their legal rights. The Labour Law and the Regulations for the Handling of Labour Disputes create a three-tier system for handling labour disputes (Chen and Chan, 2004; Clarke, Lee and Li, 2004; Shen, 2006; Zhu and Warner, 2005). While the political and administrative mechanisms are still expected to function, China is relying more on legal channels including labour arbitration and labour litigation.

The sixth and final change, which is the most important in Chinese industrial relations, is the emerging collective bargaining. There is currently no provision for collective bargaining in China. However, there have been collective bargaining-like collective discussions on labour terms in certain areas, particularly in Shanghai (Shen, 2006). These discussions happened mainly between regional unions, which are set up by union councils and cover all enterprises in the region. These regional unions are not part of enterprise management or not funded by enterprises, therefore they are more likely to defend workers' interests. Such collective bargaining-like discussions are enhanced in the 2004 Provisions by authorising workers to initiate discussions on labour terms above statutory minimums, but so far are not yet the norm in China.

Source: Shen (2007: 39–42)

Text Box 5.9

Employee relations in Vietnam

Vietnamese workers are represented by the Vietnamese General Confederation of Labour (VGCL). The role and nature of trade unions do not conform to the Western liberal-democratic model of unionism in which unions are independent representatives of collective employee interests. As in any other communist country, the state is the main employer in Vietnam. The union does not play the role of protecting or furthering the interests of employees, as workers are assumed to have interests similar to those of the government. There is no recognition of the possibility that the interests of the three actors might differ. The main differences between Vietnamese unions in particular, and communist unions in general, and capitalist unions are summarised by Littler and Palmer (1986: 265) as in Table TB5.9.1.

Table TB5.9.1	The nature of communist unions versus capitalist unions	
	Communist unions (classic dualism)	Capitalist unions (classic adversarial model)
1	Unitary view of economic interests: it is axiomatic that no 'industrial conflicts' exist.	Pluralist view of economic interests.
2	The production function is paramount.	Representative function is paramount.
3	Protection of members' rights is secondary.	Production function is either (a) not acknowledged, or (b) secondary.
4	Subordination to the party.	Autonomous organisation.
5	No collective bargaining. Union practices exclude the use of adversarial means.	Adversarial collective bargaining is the typical process of industrial relations.

Prior to *Doi Moi*, at the workplace level, employees were managed by four pillars of power: the Communist Party representative, the management, the trade union representative and the representative of the Youth Union. The party enjoyed the most power. The unions' role was to act as a 'transmission belt' between the party and the 'masses' (Fahey, 1995). Although they claimed to represent and protect the rights of workers, from a perspective of capitalist unionists, they did not execute this fundamental function. Vietnamese trade unions' key aim and objective was to work hand in hand with the management to mobilise workers to fulfil and over-fulfil production quotas set by the command economy. This usually involved launching socialist labour emulation campaigns to encourage workers to increase productivity and to participate in technical innovation activities. They also provided the human touch to bureaucratic institutions by organising social activities and serving as counsellors for employees' work-related and personal problems. The tight integration of trade unions into the management of

SOEs was most evident in their roles in distributing material goods to employees on behalf of the enterprises, such as salary, benefits and bonus, and allocating employees' subsidised housing. Finally, the trade unions were also required to raise an employee's political consciousness, by encouraging them to follow the Party's guidelines and ultimately become a member of the Party.

The economic reform in Vietnam has had an enormous impact on the structure of the Vietnamese economy and consequently on the working condition of employees. With these rapid changes – expansion and diversification of the system – the traditional labour legislation proved increasingly inadequate. Recognising the necessity to adjust to the changing labour situation, the Vietnamese government passed the new Trade Union Law in 1990, the Trade Union Constitution in 1993 and the Labour Law in 1994. These legislations mark the beginning of the transformation of the IR system in Vietnam.

The Vietnamese 1990 Trade Union Law opens by re-stating that the union is an organisation under the leadership of the Communist Party (Article 1.1). However, the substantial details of the law show that the party has taken serious attempts at transforming trade unions by granting them considerably more autonomy and, for the first time, placing them on the opposite side of management. First, a clear-cut division exists between management and labour. The role of the Vietnamese trade unions is no longer limited to assisting management or carrying out managerial functions. Unions are empowered to 'check on' the management (Article 2.2). Secondly, they have the right to get support from foreign organisations. In particular, they can join international trade union organisations (Article 1.3), accept donations from international sources (Article 16.2.a) and keep these as union assets (Article 17). Thirdly, a Vietnamese union official's salary is paid from union funds (Article 15.3). This means that in the workplace, union cadres are expected not to be on the management payroll and to be independent of management.

The Trade Union Constitution of 1993 intended to establish and reinforce occupational trade unions (Article 14). This attempts to reinforce occupational trade unions aiming to voice interests that may be different from those of the state and the local governments. Company-based trade unions are therefore under the control of two hierarchies. The traditional vertical one represents geographical or locally based union structure, while the horizontal one is concerned with the occupational structure. All locally based and occupation-based trade unions, however, are under the same umbrella of the VGCL.

The new Labour Law of 1994 clearly showed that the government accepted a tripartite structure for industrial relations, consisting of labour, employers and the state. The trade unions' role of protecting workers' labour rights is affirmed. Despite persistent objections from other bureaucracies during the heated debate over the drafts, trade unions are to be set up in enterprises of all ownership types, including foreign-invested firms (Article 153.1). Finally, Vietnamese workers were given the right to strike for the first time (Article 173.2), although the exercise of this right was severely limited by law and legislation that govern it.

These laws and constitutions suggest that the Vietnamese Communist Party is willing to relax its hold on the labour unions and that a strong legislative base exists for trade unions to step out of the Party and the state's shadow and reform their organisation to perform the function of workers' representatives in protecting their rights and interests. However, there is an enormous gap between what is written on paper and what is implemented in reality due to the ideological legacies of socialism, organisational inertia and the government's eagerness to maintain labour peace and to attract foreign capital (Nørlund and Chan, 1998).

Prior to *Doi Moi*, at the workplace level, employees were managed by representatives from the four pillars of power: the Communist Party, management, the trade union and the youth union. The party was officially bestowed with most power. The unions' role was to act as a 'transmission belt' between the party and the 'masses' (Fahey, 1995). Although they grandly claimed to protect the rights of workers, they were prevented from having a chance to act out this fundamental function. Their major roles were limited at supporting the management and performing social functions.

The economic reform in Vietnam has had an enormous impact on the working conditions of employees. Recognising the necessity of adjusting to the changing labour situation, the Vietnamese government passed the new Trade Union Law in 1990, the Trade Union Constitution in 1993 and the Labour Law in 1994. These legislations, however, have not led to any fundamental changes in the IR system in Vietnam. Due to organisational inertia, the ideological legacies of socialism, the government's intention to maintain labour peace and limited financial resources, there is an enormous gap between what is written on paper and what is actually implemented (Nørlund & Chan, 1998). It is merely an 'old wine in a new bottle' situation.

After many decades under the shadow of the party, trade union cadres are not equipped with the necessary knowledge to fulfil their roles properly, and their organisation lacks the necessary resources to make use of their newly found autonomy and create their own power. As far as financial resources are concerned, officially the main financial source of unions has been their modest union fees. This amount is clearly insufficient to pay for the union's activities and to finance the salaries of the union cadres. The trade unions' roles and activities in the workplace are limited to organising social activities and providing education to employees regarding labour law and work discipline, and as such have not exceeded the traditional roles and activities defined under the former centrally planned system. While union density is currently high, it is on a decline. Higher union densities are recorded in companies located in the northern area, around Ha Noi, reflecting the concentration of political power (and its indirect influence) and the higher political awareness and interest in the capital and its satellite cities. Meanwhile, a more relaxed and easy-going attitude is evident in the ideology of southerners.

Operating in the peaceful Vietnamese IR environment, in which trade unions are highly co-operative and bear little relation to unions as understood in the West, the studied MNCs are supportive of union activities. They do not see the union as a constraint for their operations and recognise the unions' role in supporting the management to manage employees. The non-adversarial nature of management-labour relations is stressed at length in companies' Collective Labour Agreements. The level of co-operation between the company and the trade union, however, varies significantly, ranging from adopting a minimal approach to the union through to considering the union as an integrated part of the organisation.

Some MNCs have kept contributing 1 per cent of their salary budget to the union after 1997. Unions can use these funds at their will and allocate this money to employee services, such as sports activities, visiting the sick and giving birthday gifts to employees under the joint name of 'the company and union'. The trade union, in this way, becomes an integrated part of the organisation, with the full support of the management to function as an employee services provider for the company. Other MNCs opt for a limited co-operation strategy, which means they do not interfere with trade union activities; however, they do not provide unions with time and/or financial resources. In effect, this significantly decreases the trade unions' roles and activities. Companies use a wide range of HRM techniques to encourage employee direct communication and involvement, such as employee surveys, direct communication channels (speak-out meetings, 'boundary-less' work organisation) and so on. If employees have any complaint, they are encouraged to use either the formal grievance procedure or the direct management-sponsored communication channels by referring their problems directly to the board of directors. In these companies, there is a dual system of employee services: one is the traditional system provided by trade unions and the other is developed by the company. The company makes sure that the HR department, rather than unions, is the main or the only source of welfare and paternalistic generosity.

Source: Vo (2009: 132–134; 157–158; 162–163)

Text Box 5.10

Employee relations in India

This section examines the relevance of the Indian industrial relations system, specifically the existing political/legal framework to the IT/ITES/BPO industries. Unsurprisingly, we come to the conclusion that the national regulatory regime and the global BPO industry mainly exist in different 'worlds'. IT/ITES/BPO is largely regulated by the interaction of global capital flows and local labour market dynamics while existing forms of regulation have been marginalised. We begin by describing what those forms of regulation are. Next, we describe the current HR-employment relations scene in the ITES/BPO sector. These dynamics have important implications for both workers and other organisations in the IR system, such as trade unions. The implications of this are also analysed.

Employment relations in India are regulated by a number of legal instruments, commencing with the Trade Union Act of 1926. This Act, initially provided for the registration of trade unions and, in the process, provided specific immunities from conspiracies in restraint of trade and civil actions for breach of contract (Krishnamurthi, 2002). The legislation still specifies a minimum membership of only seven workers for registration. This, in turn, has given rise to a huge number of registered unions (64,817 in 1999), with a very small average base (786 members) (India Labour Bureau, 2004).

The Trade Union legislation was silent on the question of union recognition by employers and this remained the case until 1958, when the Standing Labour Committee of the Federal Government devised protocols for representation and collective bargaining rights that were agreed to by representatives of industry and labour. These were appended to the Voluntary Code of Discipline, wherein management agreed to recognise the union which had the largest membership constituency for any given establishment or industry. This could be determined by either an examination conducted by the Ministry of Labour of the financial records/membership of the contending unions or, where all parties, including the employer agree, by way of a secret ballot conducted by the Ministry. To trigger recognition, the actual union membership threshold is quite low – minimally 2 per cent of the workforce in question. In exchange for this, unions agreed to subscribe to a code of discipline of their own. This includes such provisions as no strikes without notification, a renunciation of coercion, work to rule tactics and sit-down strikes and a willingness to discipline officials and members who act in disregard of the code (Krishnamurthi, 2002: Ch.6).

With respect to all of these undertakings it is important to keep two essential points in the foreground. First, these protocols represented a *voluntary* undertaking on the part of business and labour leaders. They may or may not be respected in any specific case. Union recognition is not a statutory requirement of Indian employment relations law. As one commentator reminds us, such 'codes are virtually buried for all practical purposes and have become part of industrial relations history' (Ratnam, 2001: 42). In part, inter-union rivalry (see below) has militated against finding agreement on principles for union recognition. Secondly, under the 1926 Act, union membership also remains voluntary. There are no legal provisions for closed or union shop rules, or for the automatic check-off of membership dues. Union recognition is also referred to in the 1947 Industrial Disputes Act. This omnibus bill was designed to foster orderly industrial relations on the sub-continent (Sodhi and Plowman, 2001). Appended to the bill (Schedule Five) is a lengthy list of unfair labour practices, which includes proscriptions against interference in union organising, including discrimination against union members, the use of threats or coercion, including threats to shut down operations, the creation of company or company dominated unions, or the refusal to bargain in good faith with the recognised union. Employers are also forbidden from recruiting replacement workers during legal strikes or employing casual or temporary workers on a long-term basis, although penalties for transgressions of such rules seem to be minimal.

The 1947 Act also establishes rules for the settlement of disputes involving wages, working hours, occupational classifications, layoffs, retrenchments and technological change. Depending upon the issue, a Labour Court may be established to deal with cases of dismissals, the legality of strikes/lockouts, or the withdrawal of existing conditions while an Industrial Tribunal may be created to process disputes over compensation, hours of work, job classification, technological change or reductions in employment. Awards are made by the Labour Courts, Industrial Tribunals or National Tribunals that have been established for that purpose and are binding upon the parties unless vetoed or modified by the relevant state or Federal government. From the available, if dated evidence, it appears as though settlements through adjudication rather than collective bargaining have been the most pervasive form of interest based settlement (Sodhi and Plowman, 2001: 59). Recognised unions are given statutory rights to represent workers in any disputes which come before a conciliation officer, board, labour court or tribunal that is established under the Act.

In addition to specifying a host of unfair labour practices, the Industrial Disputes Act is immediately relevant to two other areas of employment relations. First, it provides detailed rules with respect to employer initiated changes (such as layoffs and retrenchments), which first must receive approval from the appropriate court or tribunal and, second, it criminalises certain categories of industrial action. With respect to the former, in establishments of 100 or more employees who have at least one year of service, workers are entitled to half their normal pay for a period of 45 days in the event of a layoff being approved. One month's notice must be provided for any retrenchments and workers are again entitled to 15 days of their normal pay for each year of service. The same provision also applies to permanent closures, except here the employer is required to provide 60 days' advance notification. Any other changes in the terms or conditions of employment must be preceded by a 21-day notification.

On the union's side, notice of strike action must be provided to employers two weeks before such action is taken, while strikes and lockouts are outlawed during, and seven days after, any conciliation hearings or for the two months following any Labour Court or Tribunal hearings. Additionally, strikes are not permitted during the term of any conciliation award, which may be for a period of up to three years. Existing strikes can also be prohibited once reference has been made to the Act, with fines and jail terms imposed upon transgressors. All provisions in the Act cover establishments and industries that have been declared a public service, but the definition of such, contained in Schedule One of the Act, is very elastic. Governments can rule that just about any activity is temporarily a public service, including manufacturing and financial pursuits in the private sector. Thus, governments may choose to include or to exclude various activities from the provisions of the Disputes Act as they see fit.

The laws regulating strike and lockout activity seem to be 'honoured in the breach'. By no stretch of the imagination has such activity ceased to occur in Indian employment relations. The numbers of recorded strikes has declined dramatically since the early 1980s, falling by more than 80 per cent, although strikes and lockouts have become larger in the sense of involving many more workers. Overall, the number of person days lost on account of disputes has declined somewhat since 1981, but nowhere near as dramatically as the actual number of disputes (India Labour Bureau, 2004). It would be incorrect to attribute any of these trends to statutes that have been on the books for over 50 years. Rather, the foreign exchange crisis of 1990–91, the turn towards the IMF and the subsequent adoption of neo-liberal remedies, as elsewhere, had a chilling effect on employment security, which made its effects known in the number of recorded industrial disputes.

Overall, and given the ambit of the Industrial Disputes Act, it can be seen that it is weighted in terms of the status quo (Chibber, 2003). Proposed changes for shutdowns, labour force reductions, or other significant alterations can quickly be removed from the realm of managerial prerogative and become the subject of an award. The whole tenor of the Indian system is *control through protection*, a logic that is largely at odds with the market rationality of globalisation. And although this is frequently an object of complaint, in truth requirements such as those contained in the Industrial Disputes Act have had little impact on the IT/ITES/BPO sector. There are several reasons for this.

First, existing legislation was mainly intended to apply to and protect low-wage manual workers. Those earning more than 1,600R per month ($US 35) and/or exercising supervisory, administrative or managerial tasks are exempt from the Industrial Disputes legislation. This would include most of the IT/ITES/BPO sector where, for example, average starting salaries in call centres are many times that amount. In other words, salaries in ITES are at a level which exempts workers in the sector from essential features of the system, but still renders them hugely inexpensive by western standards. Second, to date, the main issue for Indian IT/ITES/BPO providers has been recruiting and retaining labour, not shedding it (see next section).

Given this mix of conditions, or what might be best described as a highly unstable 'equilibrium', it is still the case that, despite reports of spontaneous job actions at individual call centres, the IT/ITES/BPO sector remains completely union free. To understand why this is the case, and to appreciate the challenges that union organising in the

IT/ITES/BPO sector face, it is necessary to revert back to the IR context once again.

As part of this legacy, trade unions have been described as a 'frail but enduring part of India's labour relations' (Ratnam, 2001). As we have seen, statutes governing unions have been permissive of the creation of very small entities. As a result, only 2 per cent of registered unions have a membership exceeding 5000, while 40 per cent have less than 100 members (Sodhi and Plowman, 2001: 140-156). Historically, this has gone along with excessive fragmentation. Thus, there are no less than a dozen central labour organizations operating in India, each with its own political affiliations, to which only 20 per cent of registered unions are affiliated (Ratnam, 2001). As a result, specific enterprise unions also proliferate. Multiple plant/office unionism has added immensely to the complexity and divisiveness of the situation. It has resulted in a situation described by one analyst where 'the arduous task of organizing a trade union from scratch has suddenly lost is relevance: the easier path to ascendance as a leader is to take over existing organizations.' (Ramaswamy, 1988). This has gone along with an intense politicization that has left unions beholden to specific political parties, as well as dependent upon state patronage and reliant upon professional outside leaders (Chibber, 2005). None of these traits are favourable to an organising model (Bronfenbrenner, Friedman, Hurd, Oswald and Seeber, 1998) of union growth into information and knowledge based industries. As a result, overall union densities in India are estimated to be about one-third of the organized sector of the economy or about 1 per cent of the total societal labour force (Ratnam, 2001: 32).

On top of the historical legacy and peculiarities of trade unionism in India, more recently, various state governments have announced several special promotional schemes that encompass a comprehensive package of incentives and policies for the IT/ITES/BPO industries and further add to the uniqueness that is encountered in this sector. Most of the states in India have Software Technology Parks (STPs) and Export Processing Zones (EPZs) that offer first world infrastructure within the STP gates. With respect to changes in existing labour codes, a majority of the states have either promulgated a government order or notification permitting all establishments in the respective jurisdictions engaged in IT-enabled services (including call centres) to: work on national holidays; allow women to work through night shifts; and permit offices to function 24 hours a day, all through the year (Nasscom-g, 2005), although such practices have traditionally been banned through urban Shops and Establishment Acts (Confederation of Indian Industry, 2004).

For example, the 2003 IT and ITES Policy (Nasscom-h, 2005) of the state of Maharashtra (of which Mumbai, the commercial hub of the country, is the capital) and which accounts for 20 per cent of the country's exports, aims to 'create hassle-free and industry friendly, 24×7×365 working environment' for the sector by amongst other things:

- Relaxing working hours, work shifts and employment of women under Shops and Establishments Act,
- Applying all relaxations under the Industrial Disputes Act and Contract Labour Act to all IT and ITES units in the state on par with Special Economic Zones,
- Notifying IT & ITES units as continuous process units,
- Issuing special passes to vehicles transporting women workers of IT & ITES units during night times,
- Declaring IT & ITES units as public utility services and essential services (Nasscom-h, 2005).

Similarly, the state of Andhra Pradesh's 'AP Policy on Information Technology Enabled Services' dated 29 January 2002 also commits to providing a supportive environment by amending the AP Shops and Establishments Act to allow ITES companies to:

- Employ women and young persons (between the age group 18–21) during night shifts, subject to provision of adequate security and transport,
- Have 'flex-timing' by asking an employee to work for more than eight hours a day, without exerting an additional financial burden on the companies, in terms of overtime payments, as long as the statutory requirement on the maximum weekly working hours of 48 hours is respected,
- Operate 24 hours a day and 365 days in the year, and
- Reduce the procedure involved in retrenching employees, if certain conditions are satisfied (Nasscom-i, 2005).

Currently, the IT/ITeS sector is devoid of the presence of trade unions. Existing unions appear to be unprepared to enter the new economy, but there is also a growing sense, as one manager put it 'it's not a question of if, but of when' a trade union presence will develop. Considering the massive increase in employment in the ITeS industry and work environments characterised by round the clock work shifts, monotony, burnout and performance based employment, the question of whether trade unions will enter this new age industry raises heated discussion amongst politicians, trade unionists, industry analysts and employers. The employers' view is that there is no need for an external entity to represent employee voice because the IT/ITeS sector needs more people than it can get due to its phenomenal growth rate. This fact is said to promote best practices in people management and according to Bhargava, the former CEO of Progeon, 'there is more that is good here than it has ever been in any single economic sector of India'. Attrition rates in the industry, however, testify to alternative realities. More than likely, should the manager's prognosis cited above come to pass it will be at individual worksites, generated by specific grievances, and will assume the form of enterprise unionism. In the meantime, internal employment relations are largely regulated through HR practices, which are described in the next section.

Source: Thite and Russell (2007: 75–82)

Text Box 5.11

Employee relations in the Philippines

Under the Constitution, the State shall promote full employment and equality of employment, ensure security of tenure and just and humane conditions of work, promote and protect the right to self-organization and collective bargaining, promote workers' participation in decision-making processes directly affecting them, and promote shared responsibility and gain-sharing between employers and workers (Art. XIII, Section 3). The Civil Code recognizes that labor contracts are not just ordinary contracts but are vested with public interest that must yield to the common good. Therefore, these may be regulated through special laws. The Labor Code, first codified in 1974, is the primary enabling law that implements Constitutional objectives. The Code incorporates a number of international standards found in ILO conventions, including the ILO's eight core conventions.

The Code covers a comprehensive range of rights from pre-employment to post-employment. The human resource development policy is a combination of State provision of vocational training, regulation and accreditation of training institutions, and standard setting and skill certification. The employment policy concerns State provision of job facilitation services for local and overseas employment and regulation of recruitment activities. The Code provides minimum standards relating, among other things, to employable age, work hours, wage fixing, leave, occupational health and safety, workmen's compensation and social security. The Code also protects security of tenure, classifies employees, prescribes grounds for termination of employment as well as separation pay where termination is due to economic causes, and provides remedies in case of illegal termination. Throughout the 1990s, legislations were also introduced on emerging policy areas, such as increased penalties against wage violations and gender discrimination, and affirmative measures for the employment of workers with disabilities.

The present regime of labor regulation follows the rights-based approach to regulating employment relations. Statutory rights are formulated as minimum labor standards that cannot be contracted away by the parties. Theoretically, this protects workers from the dangers of market failure, and therefore leads to more predictable and stable employment relations. Nevertheless, there are difficulties in enforcement. There are also perceptions that the statutory standards are too high and too rigid, and consequently limit the flexibility of firms to innovate and expand, especially in a market-driven and rapidly changing business environment. The general debate, heightened by the pressures of globalization, can therefore be framed as a 'State or market' dilemma, or the compatibility of regulation with employment, productivity and income growth.

Minimum wages

By law, the authority to fix minimum wages is exercised by the regional wage boards, under the supervision of the National Wage and Productivity Commission (NWPC), an agency attached to the Department of Labor and Employment. The boards are tripartite in composition. The regional and decentralized structure was conceived to allow differentiated responses to regional differences in terms of levels of development.

The NWPC estimates that there are about 2.6 million workers who are minimum wage earners. These workers are the primary beneficiaries in every wage round. But the wage boards have flexibility to mandate that minimum wage increases be made applicable not only to those actually receiving the minimum wage but also to those receiving beyond the minimum up to a prescribed ceiling. Thus, about 1.5 million more who receive more than the minimum wage but who are within the ceiling also directly benefit from wage increases. Beyond these groups, a wage round may also have upward spillover effects in the wage scale arising from adjustments to correct wage distortions.

As it has evolved, minimum wage setting obviously seeks to satisfy multiple and broader policy objectives other than simply protecting the low-skilled or setting a floor wage. The complex implications of minimum wage setting leaves many unanswered questions, including 1) the effectiveness of minimum wage as an antipoverty measure, 2) the employment and unemployment effects, if any, 3) whether or not minimum wage protects the currently employed but who are on the lower end of the wage scale, or actually undermines their job security, and 4) whether or not it effectively blocks workers, especially the young or new entrants and the low-skilled, from entering the labor market altogether.

Security of tenure and rules of employment termination

The Constitution and the Labor Code guarantee security of tenure to all workers. Employment is classified in the Labor Code as regular employment for a fixed period (also referred to as term or contractual employment), or casual. Notwithstanding any written agreement to the contrary, and regardless of the oral agreement of the parties, employment is deemed regular when the employee has been engaged to perform activities which are necessary or desirable in the business or trade of the employer, except when the employment has been fixed for a specific project or undertaking the completion or termination of which has been determined at the time of the engagement of the employee or when the work or services to be performed is seasonal in nature and the employment is for the duration of the season. Employment is deemed casual if it is not classified as either regular or for a fixed period. However, an employee who has rendered at least one year of service, whether such service is continuous or broken, shall be considered a regular employee with respect to the activity in which he is employed and his employment shall continue while such activity exists.

In the context of the Labor Code, employment is presumed regular. A regular employee may not be dismissed from employment except upon just or authorized cause. Just causes refer to causes attributable to the fault of the employee, while authorized causes refer to those brought about by economic exigencies affecting the employer. Every case of termination from employment may be contested, and the law places the burden of justifying that the termination is for just or authorized cause on the employer.

Termination of employment without just or authorized cause makes the employer liable for back wages, reinstatement of the employee and, in appropriate cases, damages. Termination for just cause exempts the employer from any liability to the employee. Termination for an authorized cause entitles the employee to separation or severance pay, unless the termination is brought about by closure due to proven serious business losses in which case the employer is exempt from liability.

Except when the dismissal is for just cause, termination of employment has costs. With respect to termination for authorized causes, one view is that the legal regime is inflexible and rigid, makes business adjustments difficult and costly, stymies firm-level responses to market forces, encourages litigation, and generally results in a less competitive labor market. The view has also been expressed that these rules protect insiders (the currently employed) at the expense of the outsiders (those who could otherwise compete for available jobs (e.g., Sicat, 2005). The net effect, it has been argued but not empirically proven, is to inhibit hiring, make existing firms choose more technology and less labor, and encourage potential investors to choose other destinations with more flexible industrial relations regimes, thereby depressing demand for jobs.

There is an increasing use, in spite of or arguably because of the provisions of the Labor Code, of non-regular or temporary work particularly in such arrangements as fixed-term or contractual employment, casual employment and subcontracting through agencies. The BITS estimates that the incidence of non-regular or temporary work in establishments employing 20 or more workers is 25 per cent of the total workforce. It is clear from the Labor Code that regular, fixed period or contractual and casual employment are mutually exclusive. However, it appears from the survey that there is no distinction between the work being performed by regular workers and non-regular workers. Firms are motivated to employ non-regular workers to cut costs and to have a buffer to market fluctuations, thus giving them numerical flexibility. At the same time, it enables them to take advantage of labor surpluses in lower-skill categories by allowing them to recycle entry level pay and avoid the carrying costs of employing regular workers, such as seniority pay. It also enables them to avoid paying separation pay which is obligatory in the case of regular employment (Bitonio, 2004). So far, the statistics suggest neither a positive nor negative correlation between increasing an incidence of non-regular work and growth in employment levels.

Industrial relations and unionization

The union and collective bargaining system in the Philippines is divided into public and private sector unionism. Public sector unionism is just starting to develop. Public sector unions are faced with the general limitation that they cannot bargain for terms and conditions of employment that are fixed by law.

Critical issues confront private sector unionism. Though Article 243 of the Labor Code defines the scope of the right to self-organization broadly to include all workers, whether covered by a formal employee-employer relationship or self-employed, this right is effectively available only to wage and salary workers covered by a formal employee-employer relationship. Union organizing and collective bargaining are decentralized and enterprise-based. In 2004, there were over 15 thousand registered unions with about 1.3 million members. Not every union, however, is able to conclude a collective bargaining agreement (CBA). In 2004, there were only 2,798 registered CBAs covering 555 thousand workers, representing roughly 43 per cent of total union membership and 3.3 per cent of wage and salary earners. Union and collective bargaining goals remain focused on traditional issues like wages, additional benefits, work security and job security.

In the past decade, the number of unions, union members and workers covered by CBAs has been declining. Unions typically blame economic liberalization as well as an overly strict implementation of the laws on self-organization for the decline. In reality, government has adopted, through tripartite consultations, major policy and procedural reforms that accommodate atypical work as well as changes in work practices at the firm level, such as simplified requirements for union organizing, recognition of associations for mutual aid and protection, and industry or multi-employer bargaining. In response, many unions have been making adjustments in their organizing and bargaining strategies. Nevertheless, the decline in membership continues. A relatively recent development is the emergence of cooperatives as major players in the economy. The possibility that cooperatives may have a replacement or substitution effect on unions is an emerging issue.

The State advocates free unionism and collective bargaining – and corollarily minimum government intervention in regulating employment relations – on the economic logic that decentralized negotiations will allow workers and employers to agree on the most efficient terms of employment. This logic favors the market mechanism more than the State in adjusting labor-management problems. While this logic remains sound and should be pursued, the statistics clearly indicate that it has not brought about desired outcomes. With profit margins of firms being competed away, unions have a weakened capacity to satisfy members' expectations in the traditional areas of bargaining like wages, additional benefits, work security and job security. As a result, the union strategy is to simultaneously pursue their interests in two fronts, one at the plant level and the other through advocacy for State intervention by way of policy and legislative reforms.

Source: Bitonio (2007: 139–144)

5.9 The future of employee relations

The area of employee relations has evolved, as it has always done, partly driven by business and management, as well as government, concerns. As long as there is a labour process, there will be employee relations and the need to understand its history and traditions and what drives those involved. Long-term predictions of the radical change of employee relations, with the demise of conflict and trade unions, have been unfounded. For example, trade unions and political parties, as in India, have formed close relationships that work well when the particular parties are in power. Political parties, when in government, support their trade union partners but when they are in opposition the favoured trade unions are used against the government – irrespective of the harm this might do to the interests of the trade union members, their employers and the country. As Asia creates more knowledge, and as employees are seen more as human capital rather than just factory 'hands', employee relations will evolve, but with an Asian character.

One of the persistent interests of employee relations, both in terms of a 'cause' and 'cure', is employee involvement – a flexible and heterogeneous term and concept that can cover a wide range of practices, each with radically different implications. This has become an even more 'hot topic', not least driven by practices, ideas and regulations from the US and Europe in Asian suppliers, as was well demonstrated by Litvin (2003) in describing consumer group pressure on Asian work practices.

5.10 Employee involvement

The importance of employee involvement to employee relations, and to HRM more generally, is often made. It is seen as trying to create a sense of belonging and commitment through information about the organisation and its environment. A key management task is to decide if, and how, to share information because important information may be used by employees, such as in negotiations to share with competitors, customers or regulators, among others. Yet, a lack of action by management itself actually amounts to a decision not to share information, demonstrating a lack of trust in their employees. It is primarily a management responsibility to create the conditions and establish the policies and practices to promote effective employee involvement and trust.

Think About/Question 5.5

Why is employee involvement often seen as a cure for problems but is sometimes less favoured in Asia?

In parts of Asia there is a reluctance to share information as this is seen as reducing the power of the source of the information – the owners and managers. Subordinates are expected to provide information, usually positive information, to supervisors, but this is not a mutual exchange, so little reliable information will be passed back. Supervisors are unwilling to share power and authority and expect obedience and loyalty from staff. Staff on their part expect to be told what to do and do not wish to take responsibility for their bosses' tasks, fearing that they would be forced to take the blame when things go wrong. Some Asians often refer to this as upward delegation of decisions.

There has been a whole range of reasons offered for the interest in employee involvement, some of which are shown in Table 5.1.

Table 5.1   Reasons for interest in employee involvement

Factor	Aspects
Efficiency	Improve organisationally
Change	Make more acceptable
Commitment	Enhance
Learning	From employee knowledge and skills
Social	Increased aspirations, reduce alienation
Control	Redefine managerial authority

It is this great diversity of reasons for the interest in employee involvement that partly gives rise to a heterogeneous concept, exacerbated by terms such as 'involvement' and 'participation' used interchangeably, despite the gaps in their implications, including differing levels, power sharing, and so on. Therefore, we need to make some broad distinctions from the start. With this in mind, we can usefully consider the concept of employee involvement within a framework, as demonstrated in Figures 5.5 and 5.6.

Figure 5.5 Employee involvement framework

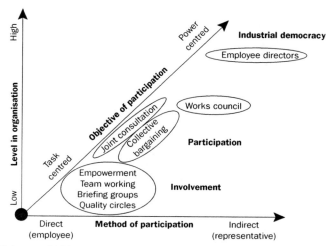

Source: Salamon (2000)

Figure 5.6 Dimensions of employee involvement

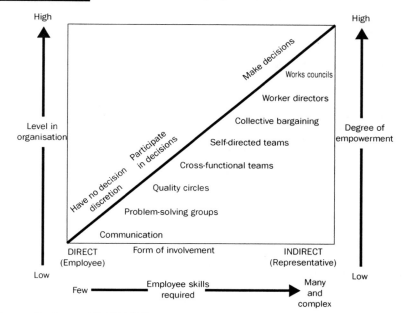

Source: Bratton and Gold (1999)

These types of framework usefully and clearly indicate that there are variations in the area of employee involvement. This is in terms of several dimensions, which include the following.

- Method or extent
- Objective or scope
- Level

These frameworks also usefully display the differences in form and type. As Salaman (2000: 374) put it:

> It is the nature and quality of the process of interaction which determines the extent or depth to which employees (individually, in groups or through their representatives) are allowed and able to contribute to and influence organisational decisions (whether operational or strategic).

He continues:

> This may range from only informing by management through consultation to negotiation and finally co-determination (equal influence in both setting the agenda as well as deciding the outcome or organisational decision making).

Interestingly, he concludes:

> Participation is primarily a philosophy, not a particular institutional form ... Therefore, it can take place at any time and in any organisational framework so long as management is genuinely and unreservedly prepared to share responsibility for the decision-making process with employees and/or their representatives.

Nevertheless, to help understanding, some further details will be illustrative.

5.11 Forms of employee involvement

There is vast range of examples of employee involvement, which have some specific and common advantages and disadvantages.

Think About/Question 5.6

What forms of employee involvement are you aware of?

5.11.1 Communication

Communication is at the basic level of employee involvement. It can be both one-way and two-way.

5.11.1.1 One-way communication

With one-way communication, information is given by one party to another. The HRM objective of one-way communication is to try to ensure that all HR know and understand what they and others in the organisation are doing and why. This is the most common means of communication throughout much of Asia. There is a huge variety of practices here; they are widespread and include notice boards, letters, staff newspapers and magazines, employee reports, in-company videos, performance appraisals and oral presentations. One of the more recently reported systems is 'team briefing'.

Team briefing
This is a system of communication that is often operated by line management. It is based on leaders and their teams getting together in groups on a regular basis. Information is 'cascaded' down through organisational levels and management tiers through supervisors to the lowest levels of the organisation. Part of the team briefing normally contains 'core' information relating to corporate issues. This is supplemented by local news at each stage. Some Asian organisations – for example, in the Kuwait oil sector – use team briefings as a means of communication so that messages can be reported quickly, in a standard format and, hopefully, accurately.

Think About/Question 5.7

What are the likely advantages and disadvantages of team briefings?

Team briefing has its share of both benefits and problems. They include those shown in Table 5.2.

Table 5.2   Benefits of and problems with team briefing

Benefits	Problems
✓ Reinforces management – allows manager to be seen as a leader	✗ Can be irregular
	✗ 'Dispensable' in times of pressure
✓ Informs staff – about what doing/if meeting targets	✗ Variation between HR covered
	✗ Difference between policy and practice
✓ Reduces misunderstandings – weakens 'grapevine' via quick/'clean' information	✗ Top down and information giving
	✗ Feedback, especially on issues not directly related, limited
✓ Acceptance – understanding of why change is necessary, time to adjust	✗ Information utility limited (coverage/ability to use/influence)
	✗ Decisions already made

5.11.1.2 Two-way communication

Unlike simple information giving, two-way communication in HRM attempts to give subordinates some 'voice' and provide feedback to both parties. Again, there is a very wide variety of methods and practices here, which include the following.

'Speak-Out/Up' or feedback programmes
Here people can telephone or write (by email or letter), in confidence, to a company representative to raise concerns. The initiators are usually guaranteed a response within a specified period.

Open-door programmes
This type of programme enables employees to see management who are not their immediate supervisors. Examples are rare in Asia, except for those with influence or connections ('*guanxi*' in China, '*wasta*' in the Arab lands, '*giri*' or '*con*' in Japan, '*inmaek*' in South Korea, '*orang delam*' in Malaysia, '*quan he*' in Vietnam) which can be used to short-cut organisational hierarchies. In theory, bosses in Asia may operate an open-door policy, but those who enter the open door know that they risk drawing attention to themselves and that they probably will upset their immediate supervisor. Mis-steps through the open door can be seriously career limiting, unless the employee has good connections.

'Walking the floor'
Senior executives physically and visibly walk though the shopfloor and offices. This behaviour is to be seen and also to listen. In parts of Asia,

the being seen is far more important than the listening, although this method is regularly used by Asian managers who wish to be seen as part of the organisation's community and who value the opportunity to demonstrate a 'common touch'. It is also used as a means of keeping middle management under pressure in case senior management discover that there are problems that have not been disclosed to them.

Sensing groups

In this system management meet periodically with small random samples of staff. This allows management not only to communicate company policies and goals to the groups, but also to hear employee concerns and suggestions. Trade unions and political or social networks are the more usual form of sensing groups in parts of Asia, but these groups often have agendas other than organisational success and may not necessarily represent the interests of employees.

Task forces

These groups, often of junior managers and employees, can be commissioned on various areas and concerns – for example, to review specific policies or processes or be asked to suggest improvements. Such practices are used with success in Japan, in particular.

Employee attitude surveys

These represent a more systematic means of feedback. This type of survey has spread in use and can be undertaken by specialists or in-house staff. At first sight this method seems more concerned with measuring commitment than involvement. In-house surveys especially are viewed with suspicion in some of Asia as it is doubted whether confidentiality and anonymity will be respected. However, the benefits of surveys are numerous so some Asian organisations favour this method of obtaining information from the workforce – especially as the expectation is that employees will not give negative opinions. The benefits of surveys include the following

- Increased employee involvement
- Ability to check that management's perception of the organisation corresponds with that of employees
- Ability to assess the extent to which HRM policies are having the desired effects
- Simply asking employees for their views may increase morale

Suggestion schemes

Suggestion schemes are often seen as being applicable only to large manufacturing firms and manual workers, but they are also to be found in the service sector and among white collar staff – for example, in banks, airlines and retailing. HR are invited to submit ideas to improve aspects of organisational performance for which they are often rewarded. The reward is usually an award (cash or benefit) of which there can be several types. These can include the following.

- Encouragement – for effort in making suggestions even if they are not implemented
- Valued – for leading to clearly quantified savings (fixed amount or percentage of savings)
- Special – for savings not easily identified (for example, health and safety matters)

Think About/Question 5.8

What are the likely advantages and disadvantages of suggestion schemes?

Suggestion schemes have their own benefits and problems, which can be seen in Table 5.3.

Table 5.3 Benefits of and problems with suggestion schemes

Benefits	Problems
✓ Cost savings	✗ Administration, delays in evaluating/rewarding
✓ Encourage climate of change	✗ Small rewards
✓ Identify those with creative thinking skills	✗ Practical – eligibility (who, what ideas), award type, etc.
✓ Innovations	
✓ Bypass obstructive management in non-confrontational manner without undermining authority	✗ Conflict – is 'constant improvement' a 'normal' part of jobs or something for which extra rewards received?
✓ Practice skills of evaluation and implementation of ideas	✗ Disillusionment if not acted on

5.11.2 Task and work groups

Employee involvement can also occur at a different level and in a different form in the task and work group. These employee involvement occurrences have a long history, deriving from the well known 'Human Relations' experiments in the US in the 1920s. Ideas of job enlargement and enrichment developed from the 1960s, introducing elements of responsibility into tasks. The development in such matters was led by some Scandinavian organisations. Examples of such forms include the following.

Autonomous work groups
In 1972 Saab Scania's factory abolished the classic, Fordist mass production, single assembly line moving at fixed rates past workers. In its place were six separate assembly areas and workers divided work amongst themselves without management direction. Similar experiments occurred at Volvo in its Kalmar and Uddevalla factories.

In Asia, subcontractors are used as autonomous work groups so that firms such as Toyota send specialist work to small firms with whom they have a long-term and close relationship, treating the firms as closely linked to the larger enterprise. Japanese firms are also keen on project-based teams working together with few formal distinctions between the team members, of different seniority levels, or their roles outside the team. However, the levels of employee autonomy, and hence involvement via this route, is debatable. Indeed, autonomous work groups are rare in parts of Asia.

Quality circles (QCs)
Typically these groups are small, with six to twelve members led by a supervisor or team leader in the area; they are 'voluntary', meeting regularly within paid work time (although meetings can be held during 'leisure' time). The QCs identify, select and analyse work-related problems, collect data, present findings and propose solutions intended for approval by management, which are then implemented. After 1945 came the development, in Japan, of this American idea – set out earlier by people such as Deming and Juran. By the late 1980s, Japan had over 10 million workers in QCs. The common requirements for such QCs include the following.

- Management are convinced of the benefits, giving long-term commitment and resources
- Involvement of middle managers
- Facilitator for administration and development of ideas

- Training for leaders and members
- Recognising and publicising activities to maintain interest

> **Think About/Question 5.9**
>
> **What are the advantages and disadvantages of QCs?**

There are several benefits and problems with QCs, as noted in Table 5.4. Total Quality Management (TQM) then emerged, partly as an alternative means of addressing quality issues. TQM is a more integrated approach to quality matters, with 'harder' objectives, which are work-related and performance-led, rather than concerned with employee involvement.

Table 5.4   Benefits of and problems with quality circles

Benefits	Problems
✓ Improve quality/reliability	✗ Sustaining, have short life/high failure
✓ Save costs	✗ Time/expenses in running, training, disruption, etc.
✓ Increase interest/ commitment in job	✗ Challenge notions of authority, criticisms of management
✓ Enhance supervisory authority/leadership skills	✗ Disinterest - middle management allocated responsibility, but denied authority (own agenda; not obliged to follow priorities)

Team working

Team working, in its present guise, has its origins in the UK in practices at organisations such as Japanese companies like Komatsu, Hitachi, Nissan, and especially Toyota. Since the 1990s this form of organising work has become more prevalent in other sectors.

Empowerment

Empowerment became fashionable from the 1980s, although it was linked to earlier movements such as the Quality of Working Life approach in the 1970s. In essence, empowerment is about providing the opportunities and structures (and, of course, the work culture) so that employees can contribute to the organisation. The onus is on management to 'empower' staff. This empowerment is individual and direct involvement in work. A range of benefits flow from this method of organising, including the need for less direct management and supervisory control, with greater employee autonomy, albeit within bounds set by management.

5.11.3 Financial

For some commentators, employees also obtain involvement through particular financial arrangements. This is not, in fact, a new idea (see Chapter 3 on employee rewards). Indeed, there are examples of such financial arrangements from the early nineteenth century in the West and in a few Asian companies, such as Tata in India. Nevertheless, the rise in popularity in the West has occurred since the early 1980s, encouraged by governments through favourable tax legislation, and has been followed by a modest application of the systems in Asian organisations undergoing privatisation, especially in South and South West Asia, and by 'buying out' the jobs of workers in SOEs in China. The types of financial participation include the following.

- Share ownership – employees gain a direct share in the company they work for
- Profit sharing – cash bonus from surplus revenue

5.11.4 Success of employee involvement

Several important elements in the success of employee involvement have been identified, and can be seen in Table 5.5.

Table 5.5   Important elements in the success and failure of employee involvement

Elements	Reasons/Characteristics
<ul><li>Management commitment – more than just initiate</li><li>Support – throughout the management system</li><li>Advance consideration and exposition of objectives</li><li>Training of all involved</li><li>Regular monitoring</li><li>Problems and shortcomings typical</li></ul>	<ul><li>Many schemes costly in time to be properly run</li><li>Middle/lower-level managers pivotal to implementation</li><li>Avoid confusion and conflict between schemes</li><li>Commitment, ensure competence and regularly reviewed</li><li>Measures set against specified objectives</li><li>Should not be unexpected</li></ul>

5.11.5 International variations in employee involvement

There are widespread variations globally in the meaning and practice of employee involvement (see earlier frameworks). This includes the ideas of industrial democracy, workers on the board, co-determination and works councils.

This is also the case across Asia. We provide an example of one form in South Korea in Text Box 5.12.

Text Box 5.12

Labour-Management Councils in South Korea

The Labour-Management Council (LMC) system is one institutionalized channel available to promote communication and cooperation between employees and management, facilitate participation in business administration and improve labour rights and the status of employees. This system was introduced by the Labour-Management Council Act (1980). The act was replaced by the Act on Promotion of Worker Participation and Cooperation (1997). LMCs at workplaces or businesses employing 30 persons or more hold regular (on a quarterly basis) meetings composed of equal numbers (usually three to ten) of representatives from labour and management. When unions represent the majority of employees, union leaders become employee representatives.

Three types of matters are dealt with in LMCs: consultation, resolution and reporting. Employers consult on improvements in productivity, employee welfare and working conditions. Employers and employees together develop the basic plan for training and skills development, establishment and management of welfare facilities and company welfare funds for employees. Employers report on personnel policy and business plans, performance and prospects. However, the LMC system and collective bargaining have different goals in that the former is aimed at pursuing the common benefit of the employer and employee, whereas the latter is fundamentally based on the contradictory positions of the employer and employee.

Source: Rowley and Yoo (2008: 57–58)

5.12 Conclusion

The area of employee relations remains as important, but as changeable, as ever. While the foci of the area have shifted – partly reflective of the practical concerns of business, management and governments – the ideas of a model of a system of actors who have different perspectives remains a useful aid and framework in the understanding of employee relations. The different participants may vary in their relative influence and power, but their interactions and perspectives remain crucial, not only to the functioning of an economy, but also to its competitiveness and the types of production which prosper.

The area of employee involvement is a diverse and elastic concept, seemingly allowing everyone to support it. Involvement also has a range of benefits for organisations and employees. Some of the key ideas and practices are not particularly new, although employee relations fashions do come and go, as witnessed by ideas of 'industrial democracy' in the 1970s versus 'empowerment' more recently. These ideas and practices vary throughout Asia, yet their various forms have radical differences in implications for management and businesses.

End of chapter tasks/questions
Based on the bank and airlines case studies in Appendix 3, using and applying information within this chapter

1. How are employee relations systems likely to vary in each location in which the bank operates to take account of the difference in importance of the individual employee versus collective workers?

2. In Asia it may be considered that harmonious working is the key to economic success. How is harmonious working likely to differ between each airline over the next five years?

3. To what extent might different systems of dispute resolution be applicable in the different locations of the bank and the airlines?

4. What similarities and variations will exist in the system of employee relations in the airlines within each country? Why will these similarities and differences exist?

5. What will be the consequences of trade union activism or lack of activism in each location in which the bank operates?

6. How will the different airlines deal with employee relations in China, India and the GCC? How will the existence or lack of trade unions shape employee relations?

7. In what ways will the illegality of trade union activity in the GCC give long-term competitive advantage or disadvantage to the airline from the GCC when challenging the Indian airline when they operate the same routes?

8. How will the informal network (including the use of *guanxi* and *wasta*) impact on the formal hierarchy and operational effectiveness of each airline?

9. What will cause differences in the acceptability of employee involvement between airlines and banking?

10. Is it acceptable business practice for companies to avoid meeting employment and other legislation by basing staff in a different geographical jurisdiction?

References

ACFTU (2005) 'Chinese trade unions' safeguarding of the legitimate rights and interests of workers and staff members' (2004) Blue Paper, 12 September 2005. Available at http://www.sa8000.org.cn/News Center/1235.html (accessed 23 August 2006).

Alas, R. (ed.) *Implementation of Change in Chinese Organisations*. Oxford: Chandos.

Benson, J., Debroux, P., Yuasa, M. and Zhu, Y. (2000) 'Flexibility and labour management: Chinese manufacturing enterprises in the 1990s', *The International Journal of Human Resource Management*, 11(2): 183–96.

Bishop, D. and Reed, L. (1998) 'Practical guidelines for intervening, selecting and challenging party-appointed arbitrators in international commercial arbitration', *Arbitration International*, 14(4): 395–406.

Bitonio, B.E.R. Jr. (2004) 'Labor flexibility and workers representation in The Philippines'. An initial version of this article was presented at the 5th Asian Regional Congress of the International Industrial Relations Association, Seoul, Korea, in June 2004.

Bitonio, B. (2007) 'The changing nature of work in Asia: The Philippines', in J. Burgess and J. Connell (eds) *Globalisation and Work in Asia*. Oxford: Chandos, 129–150.

Blyton, P. and Turnbull, P. (1998) *The Dynamics of Employee Relations*. Basingstoke: Macmillan.

Bratton, J. and Gold, J. (1999) *Human Resource Management Theory and Practice*. Basingstoke: Macmillan.

Bronfenbrenner, K., Friedman, S., Hurd, R., Oswald, R. and Seeber, R. (1998) *Organizing to Win: New Research on Union Strategies*. Ithaca: Cornell University Press.

Burgess, J. and Connell, J. (eds) *Globalisation and Work in Asia*. Oxford: Chandos.

Cai, Y.S. (2002) 'The resistance of Chinese laid-off workers in the reform period', *China Quarterly*, 170: 327–344.

Chang K. (2000) 'On enacting legislation on unfair labour practices', *Social Sciences in China [Zhongguo Shehui Kexue]*, 2000(5): 71–82.

Chen, D.R. (1995) *Chinese Firms between Hierarchy and Market: The Contract Management Responsibility System in China*. New York: St Martin's Press.

Chen, F. (1995) *Economic Transition and Political Legitimacy in Post-Mao China: Ideology and Reform*. Albany, NY: State University of New York Press.

Chen, F. (2000) 'Subsistence crises, managerial corruption and labour protests in China', *China Journal*, 44: 41–63.

Chen, M.S. and Chan, A. (2004) 'Employee and union inputs into occupational health and safety measures in Chinese factories', *Social Science and Medicine*, 58: 1231–45.

Cheng, Y.Y. (2004) 'The development of labour disputes and the regulation of industrial relations in China', *The International Journal of Comparative Labour Law and Industrial Relations*, 20(2): 277–295.

Chibber, V. (2003) *Locked in Place: State-Building and Late Industrialization in India*. Princeton: Princeton University Press.

Chibber, V. (2005) 'From class compromise to class accommodation: Labor's incorporation into the Indian political economy', in Ray, R. and Katzenstein, M. (eds) *Social Movements in India: Poverty, Power and Politics*. Lanham, MD: Rowman and Littlefield.

China Statistical Yearbook, (various issues), Beijing: China Statistics Press.

China Labour Statistical Yearbooks (various years) Beijing: China Statistics Press.

Choi, Y.J. (2003) 'Managerial styles, workforce composition and labour unrest: East Asian-invested enterprises in China', *Comparative Sociology*, 2(2): 321–354.

CIPD (2005) 'Employee relations'. Available at http://www.cipd.co.uk/mandq/standards/prac/sgpd/emprel.htm (accessed 25 February 2005).

Clarke, S. and Lee, C.H. (2002) 'The significance of tripartite consultation in China', *Asia Pacific Business Review*, 9(2): 61–80.

Clarke, S., Lee, C.H. and Li. Q. (2004) 'Collective consultation and industrial relations in China', *British Journal of Industrial Relations*, 42(2): 235–254.

Confederation of Indian Industry, Northern Region (2004) 'Driving growth through reform: A comparative analysis of labour practices in select northern region states'.

Cooke, W.N. and Noble, D.S. (1998) 'Industrial relations systems and US foreign direct investment abroad', *British Journal of Industrial Relations*, 36(4): 581–609.

Dunlop, J. (1958 and 1959) *Industrial Relations Systems*, New York: Holt.

Fahey, S. (1995) 'Changing labour relations', in B.J.T. Kerkvliet (ed.) *Dilemmas of Development: Vietnam Update 1994*. Canberra: Australia National University Department of Political and Social Change Research School of Pacific and Asian Studies.

Fernandez, L. (1993) 'It's hard to stay together', *Sunday Star*, 7 November: 18.

Fernandez, L. (1997) 'More expected from the MTUC', *The Star*, 25 January.

Flanders, A. (1970) *Management and Unions: Theory and Reform of Industrial Relations*, London: Faber and Faber.

Fox, A. (1966) *Industrial Sociology and Industrial Relations*, Royal Commission Research Paper No.3, London: HMSO.

Fox, J.B., Donohue, J.M. and Wu, J.P. (2005) 'The arbitration of labour disputes in China today: Definition and implications', *Employee Responsibilities and Rights Journal*, 17(1): 19–29.

Hagglund, G. and Provis, C. (2005) 'The conciliation step of the unfair dismissal process in South Australia', *Labour Studies Journal*, 29(4): 65–86.

Harry, W.E. and Nakajima, C. (2007) 'Foreigners' ethnocentric policies in the Asia Pacific region', *Management Revue*, 18, 4.

Hisano, K. (2007) 'Employment in transition: Changes in Japan since the 1980s', in J. Burgess and J. Connell (eds) *Globalisation and Work in Asia*, Oxford: Chandos, 275–294.

Huo, Y.P. and von Glinow, M.A. (1995) 'On transplanting human resource practices to China: A culture-driven approach', *International Journal of Manpower*, 16(9): 3–15.

Hyman, R. (1975) *Industrial Relations: A Marxist Introduction*. London: Macmillan.

India Labour Bureau (2004) *Indian Labour Yearbook*. Delhi: Ministry of Labour, Government of India.

Jomo, K. S. (1994) *U-Turn? Malaysian Economic Development Policy after 1990.* Townsville, QLD: James Cook University.

Kennerly, J.A. (1994) *Arbitration: Cases in Industrial Relations.* Pitman.

Kochan, T., McKersie, R. and Capelli, P. (1984) 'Strategic choice and industrial relations theory', *Industrial Relations,* Winter.

Krishnamurthi, S. (2002) *Commercial's Commentary on Trade Unions Act 1926 as amended by Trade Unions (Amendment) Act 2001.* Delhi: Commercial Law Publishers.

Kuruvilla, S. and Venkataratnam, C.S. (1996) 'Economic development and industrial relations: The case of south and southeast Asia', *Industrial Relations Journal,* 27(1): 9–23.

Labour Law of the Socialist Republic of Vietnam 1994 (Vietnam).

Labourer, The [Ngu.ò.i Lao Dô. ng], 1 January 2002.

Lee, C.K. (2000) 'Pathways of labour insurgency', in E. Perry and M. Selden (eds) *Chinese Society: Change, Conflict and Resistance.* New York: Routledge.

Lee, M.B. (1993) 'Korea' in M. Rothman, D. Briscoe and R. Nacamulli (eds) *Industrial Relations Around the World.* Berlin: de Gruyter, 245–269.

Leong, C.H. (1991) 'Late industrialization along with democratic politics in Malaysia', unpublished doctoral thesis, Harvard University.

Littler, C. and Palmer, G. (1986) 'Communist and capitalist trade unionism: Comparisons and contrasts', in A. Pravda and B.A. Ruble (eds) *Trade Unions in Communist States.* Boston: Allen & Unwin.

Litvin, D. (2003) *Empires of Profit,* New York: Texere.

Maimunah, A. (2003) *Malaysian Industrial Relations and Employment Law* (4th edn). Kuala Lumpur: McGraw-Hill.

Martin, R.M. (1989) *Trade Unionism: Purposes and Forms.* Oxford: Clarendon Press.

McLaren, D.E. (2003) 'Party-appointed vs list-appointed arbitrators: A comparison', *Journal of International Arbitration,* 20(3): 233–245.

McNamara, D. (2002) *Market and Society in Korea: Interest, Institution and the Textile Industry.* London: Routledge.

MHR (2006) 'Statistical Summary of Labour and Human Resource', available at http://www.mohr.gov.my/mohr_key.php (accessed 30 June 2006).

Mo, J. (2000) 'Probing labour arbitration in China', *Journal of International Arbitration,* 17(5): 19–83.

Mok, Ka-ho, Wong, L. and Lee, G.O.M. (2002) 'The challenges of global capitalism: Unemployment and state workers' reactions and responses in post-reform China', *International Journal of Human Resource Management*, 13(3): 399–415.

Morris, J., Sheehan, J. and Hassard, J. (2001) 'From dependency to defiance? Work-unit relationships in China's state enterprise reforms', *Journal of Management Studies*, 38(5): 697–717.

Nasscom-g. (2005) http://www.bpo.nasscom.org/artdisplay.aspx?cat_id=563 (downloaded on 27 November 2005).

Nasscom-h. (2005) http://www.bpo.nasscom.org/download/Maharashtra%20ITeS Policy2003.pdf (downloaded 23 December).

Nasscom-i. (2005) http://www.bpo.nasscom.org/download/AP%20ITES%20Policy.pdf (downloaded on 23 December).

Ng, S.H. and Warner, M. (1998) *China's Trade Unions and Management*. London and New York: Macmillan/St Martin's Press.

NMP (2006) *9th Malaysia Plan 2006–2010*. Putrajaya: Economic Planning Unit, Prime Minister's Department.

Nørlund, I. and Chan, A. (1998) 'Vietnamese and Chinese labour regimes: On the road to divergence', *The China Journal*, 40, 173–197.

NUBE (National Union of Bank Employees) (2006) 'History', available at http://www.nube.org.my/history.asp (accessed 20 October 2006).

Purcell, J. (1987) 'Mapping management styles in employee relations', *Journal of Management Studies*, 24(5): 534–548.

Ramasamy, N. and Rowley, C. (2008) 'Trade unions in Malaysia: Complexity of a state-employer system', in J. Benson and Y. Zhu (eds) *Trade Unions in Asia*. London: Routledge, 121–139.

Ramaswamy, E.A. (1988) *Worker Consciousness and Trade Union Response*. New Delhi: Oxford University Press.

Ratnam, V. (2001) *Globalization and Labour-Management Relations: Dynamics of Change*. New Delhi: Sage.

Rowley, C. (2001a) 'Alan Fox', in M. Witzel (ed.) *Biographical Dictionary of Management*. Bristol: Thoemmes Press, 325–327.

Rowley, C. (2001b) 'Hugh Clegg', in M. Witzel (ed.) *Biographical Dictionary of Management*. Bristol: Thoemmes Press, 168–170.

Rowley, C. (2002a) 'Conciliation', in T. Redman and A. Wilkinson (eds) *The Informed Student Guide to HRM*. London: Thomson Learning, 39.

Rowley, C. (2002b) 'Mediation', in T. Redman and A. Wilkinson (eds) *The Informed Student Guide to HRM*. London: Thomson Learning, 157.

Rowley, C. (2002c) 'Allan Flanders', in M. Warner (ed.) *The International Encyclopaedia of Business and Management*. London: Thomson Learning, 2036–41.

Rowley, C. (2009) 'Do we need processes of dispute settlement in managing today?', *Effective Executive Magazine*, XII(4), April.

Rowley, C. and Bhopal, M. (2006) 'The ethnic factor in state-labour relations: The case of Malaysia', *Capital and Class*, 88: 87–116.

Rowley, C. and Poon, I. (2008) 'HRM best practices and transfer to the Asia Pacific region', in C. Wankel (ed.) *21st Century Management.* US: Sage, 209–220.

Rowley, C. and Yoo, K.S. (2008) 'Trade unions in South Korea: Transition towards corporatism', in J. Benson and Y. Zhu (eds) *Trade Unions in Asia*. London: Routledge, 43–62.

Salamon, M. (2000) *Industrial Relations: Theory and Practice.* Harlow: Pearson Education.

Selvarani, P. and Abas, M. (2004) 'Airline's union officials under probe', *Malay Mail*, 31 January.

Sheehan, J. (1998) *Chinese Workers: A New History.* London and New York: Routledge.

Shen, J. (2006) 'Analysis of changing industrial relations in China', *The International Journal of Comparative Labour Law and Industrial Relations*, 26(3): 347–368.

Shen, J. (2007) *Labour Disputes and their Resolution in China.* Oxford: Chandos.

SHMTUC (Shanghai Municipal Trade Union Council) (2002) *Lao Dong Guang Xi Diao Cha* (Labour Relations Survey). Shanghai: Shanghai Municipal Trade Union Council (in Chinese).

Sicat, G.P. (2005) 'What it will take to reform RP's labor market?' Paper presented at the National Tripartite Policy Conference on Wages and Productivity, Manila.

Sodhi, J.S. and Plowman, D. (2001) *Economic Change and Industrial Relations: India and Australia.* Nedlands, WA: Scholastic Press Australia.

Song, L.B., Zhao, J. and Li, H. (2003) 'Approaches to the revision of the 1994 Arbitration Act of the People's Republic of China', *Journal of International Arbitration*, 20(2): 169–189.

Sun, The (2003) 'NUBE may face legal action, says Fong', 12 August.

Taylor, B. (2000) 'Trade unions and social capital in transitional communist states: The case of China', *Policy Sciences*, 33: 341–54.

Thireau, I. and Hua, L.S. (2003) 'The moral universe of aggrieved Chinese workers: Workers' appeals to arbitration committees and letters and visits offices', *The China Journal*, 50: 83–103.

Thite, M. and Russell, B. (2007) 'India and business process outsourcing', in J. Burgess and J. Connell (eds) *Globalisation and Work in Asia.* Oxford: Chandos, 67–92.

Todd, P. and Peetz, D. (2001) 'Malaysian industrial relations at century's turn: Vision 2020 or a spectre of the past?' *International Journal of Human Resource Management*, 12(8): 1365–82.

Vo, A. (2009) *The Transformation of HRM and IR in Vietnam*. Oxford: Chandos.

Walder, A.G. (1986) *Communist Neo-traditionalism: An Introductory Essay*. Berkeley, CA: University of Chicago Press.

Wu, M.A. (2006) *Industrial Relations Law of Malaysia* (3rd edn). Kuala Lumpur: Longman.

Yu, X.M. (2005) 'State-intervened legal activism: Case studies of labor unrest at foreign-invested enterprises in South China', Hong Kong University, University Service Center for Chinese Studies. Available at http://www.usc.cuhk.edu.hk/wk_wzdetails.asp?id=3299 (accessed 12 May 2005).

Zhu, Y. and Warner, M. (2005) 'Changing Chinese employment relations since WTO accession', *Personnel Review*, 34(3): 354–69.

Conclusion

6.1 Introduction

Over the course of this book we have looked at the terrain and the main contours of the key areas of HRM from the perspective of the common tensions inherent within it (see Chapter 1, Figure 1.1). These differences have implications for perspectives in HRM (see Table 6.1).

Table 6.1 Tensions in perspectives in HRM

Tension	Perspective
Universal versus contingent	Implication for best practice
Short versus long	Time frames
Specialist versus line	Delivery
Espoused versus actual	Reality

This includes the tension between the common desire to seek universal, simple answers to perennial HRM issues versus the contingent and complex reality of working life and the management of people.

There is then the implicit and inherent long-term timeframe of HRM versus the common short termism of many businesses (especially those in an Anglo-American context), some of which have been adopted by some organisations in parts of Asia. For instance, think of the 'payback' from sophisticated recruitment and selection, training and involvement.

Furthermore, there is the tension between HRM's use by specialist practitioners or line managers. This has an impact on areas such as training and time as well as consistency and strategy.

There is a further tension in HRM – between espoused versus actual policies and practices. These tensions can be found both within and between organisations, such as those with a head office in the West and operations in Asia. Thus, the rhetoric of much management is about the value and importance of people as 'our greatest asset'. Yet, this is combined with a continuance of working systems that do not seem to indicate support in practice of this platitude of valuing people. Again, this can be seen both in the West and in the context of some Asian employers who may constantly look for sources of 'cheaper' labour.

Therefore, with these considerations in mind, over the course of this book we have examined the key areas of HRM, along with their issues, theories and practices. This was undertaken in terms of the following broad areas.

- Employee resourcing – with particular attention to HRP, recruitment and selection
- Employee rewards – specifically, remuneration and performance-related pay
- Employee development – principally, training and performance appraisal
- Employee relations – with the employee relations system and employee involvement

6.2 Key points

This examination of HRM theory and practice has resulted in a set of key points and conclusions. These include the following.

6.2.1 How is HRM different?

The management of people has a long history, which we broadly traced. It can also be acknowledged that there are Asian views of effective people management systems dating back over millennia. HRM can be seen as either simply the latest twist in this, or a turn that has produced a radically different concept.

Think About/Question 6.1

What, if anything, is different between HRM and earlier people management systems? To what extent is HRM simply the latest incarnation of people management?

There are supporters of both 'yes' and 'no' camps here. There is the idea of 'old wine in new bottles' for some commentators. In contrast, for others, HRM is actually a distinctive approach '... which seeks to achieve competitive advantage through the strategic deployment of a highly committed and capable workforce, using an integrated array of cultural, structural and personnel techniques' (Storey, 1995: 5). If we take some credence from the latter camp, how is HRM different? We can attempt to make distinctions in terms of the following three aspects of HRM.

- Integration
- Strategy
- Responsibility

Yet, what is the evidence and likelihood that HRM, conceptualised in this form, is actually in existence or developing? The answer to this, it seems, is 'not a lot'. For instance, research shows that the take-up of HRM-type initiatives and a strategic quality is not always new or proved. This is for several reasons, which include the following.

6.2.1.1 Conflicts

There are conflicting tendencies and tensions within HRM, some of which may be mutually exclusive and so actually make the adoption of the 'whole package' of HRM somewhat difficult. This is so within some Asian organisations undergoing rapid change, which make the tensions even more challenging. To what extent, for instance, can management expect both high commitment and large investment in employee development consistent with high numerical flexibility from the same workforce?

6.2.1.2 Opportunities and constraints

There are HRM-type changes, policies and practices in people management. Yet, these can actually reflect pragmatic responses (as has commonly been the case in the areas of people management) to opportunities and constraints in the socio-economic and political environment (see Legge, 1995).

6.2.1.3 Reasons

The reasons for this failure to develop an HRM approach, as in some parts of Asia, is as a result of a set of factors related to the strategic role of people in organisations and the value that employers place on their effective management. However, it '... is not just a question of will or conviction, but of deep-seated features' (Storey and Sisson, 1991: 174).

Think About/Question 6.2

What might be some of the factors that could help to explain the limited role of HRM in business strategy?

There are several possible reasons, including those noted in Table 6.2. These reasons constitute a group of impediments that are mutually reinforcing. Therefore, '[h]opes that HRM would lead to a more strategic approach to the management of human resources have been largely frustrated' (Sisson, 1995: 105).

Table 6.2 Constraints on the development of HRM

Factor	Characteristics
Management composition	■ Dominance of financial function ■ Weakness of HRM at senior levels
Ownership patterns	■ Role of institutional investors ■ Not tied to long-term development
Organisational structures	■ Importance of diversification ■ Multi-divisional pattern

6.2.2 Dynamism

The emergence and development of HRM indicates the inherent dynamism and changeable nature of the area of work and employment and its management. We examined the management of people in Asia, as well as in the West, and considered some of the main practices, methods and implications and the issues and problems that may arise here. This examination indicated the need for a questioning approach as dynamic change continues to impact on organisations. A PEST (political, economic, social, technology factors) analysis shows important influences and impacts on this. Thus, management need to be aware of, and keep up with, changes that impact on HRM. Some of the main types of change in our broad HRM areas include the following.

- Employee resourcing – changes in workforce composition and flexibility

- Employee rewards – levels of performance pay, internal disparities and equal pay

- Employee development – measurement and the need for long-term perspectives

- Employee relations – partnerships and participation

6.2.3 Universal recipes or specific ingredients?

One reason why this dynamic change is important is that it affects ideas of 'best practice' in this field of management (Rowley and Poon, 2008). Yet, for one group of commentators the question remains – if we look hard enough, are there universal solutions to some of the key issues and practices in people management? This argument involves the commonality or peculiarity of HRM, the transferability or specificity of its practices to/from/within countries, including those in Asia. While these are not new issues, they have taken on powerful resonance in some rapidly changing Asian economies and societies. Part of this has been due to areas such as developments in the European Union and ideas of 'common' employment rights or a 'level playing field', and the exporting of such ideas as part of globalisation in business and management ideas. This area has been looked at in two ways.

6.2.3.1 Universalism

For this camp HRM is universal and this can be over time, industry sector and location. It is only a question of learning what these HRM techniques are (for example, the 'best practices'), and then transfer them and apply them for maximum impact and benefit. Even if these techniques may have varied before, in an increasingly globalised and swiftly changing world they will vary less and less.

6.2.3.2 Contingency

In contrast to this first approach, some view management, especially HRM, as more specific and unique to its location and context. This is neatly indicated in the following quote: 'Many aspects of management work can be developed into a science: successful personnel management is an art' (Torrington and Hall, 1998: 696). What underpins this 'art' of people management? The factors include both culture (norms, values) and institutions (the state, organisation, trade unions), which retain salience and influence on the HRM system.

We can see the ideas and issues in these areas in the following two text boxes. Text Box 6.1 provides an analysis of 'best practices' in Asia in terms of definitions, application and types. Text Box 6.2 covers HRM transfers and business systems.

Text Box 6.1

HRM best practices in Asia?

Approaching the second decade of the 21st century provides a fresh opportunity to think about kinds of possible management. In this regard, the area of human resource management (HRM) has become even more important to business, policymaking and nations, including in the economically dynamic Asia-Pacific region. Most of the Asian economies had rapid growth rates for the past two to three decades, although uneven from year to year, and were then hit by the 1997 Asian Financial Crisis. Interestingly, now the very same HRM practices formerly seen as paragons (and taken as "best practices" by some), partly responsible for such success and emulated and exported around the world (e.g., via "Japanization"), have become seen by some as problematic. In such a milieu, some Asian companies began looking to other countries for exemplars of HRM to import. Such issues raise important questions: Are there any HRM best practices? Can they be transferred? The search for best practice in comparative management research relates to the debate on convergence toward common practices that apply to all countries versus continuing or even growing divergence practices.

Many Asian economies do share common features, for example, fast economic growth, social development, surge in foreign direct investment (FDI), multinational companies (MNCs), and so forth. These factors can provide a strong momentum to practice transference to Asia. Despite common features across the region, however, their specific institutional forms vary from one country to another (Hamilton, 1995) and act as serious constraints on transfer and, hence, convergence and promote continuing distinctiveness or even increasing divergence. Besides, since the transfer of practices occurs in a multifaceted context (between headquarters and overseas subsidiaries: Briscoe, 1995; Dowling, Schuler, & Welch, 1994) and at different stages (from pre-institutionalization to full implementation: Tolbert & Zucker, 1996), the issue of transferability becomes more about "degree," less about "all or nothing," and more about "what" practices (Pudelko, 2005) and to what extent.

The aim of this chapter is to examine if there are best practices in HRM that can be transferable to Asia and whether this indicates convergence in HRM. Key HRM practices and policies of employment, rewards, and development will be used to examine these issues.

Theory

Classical management thought and more recent variants assume that a set of "best" management practices, as in HRM, can be valid in all circumstances and help organizations perform better and obtain sustainable competitive advantage (Becker & Gerhart, 1996; Huselid, 1995; Lado & Wilson, 1994).

What are 'best practices'?

This idea can be traced back for some considerable time. For instance, Taylor's (1911) earlier "scientific management" implied that there was "one best way" of managing. We can recall, as do Boxall and Purcell (2003), that studies of individual best practices within the major HR categories of selection, training, and appraisal have a very long tradition, such as when much effort was put into improving selection practices for officers and training for production workers during both World Wars. In the 1960s, best practice would have been taken as those associated with an American model (Kerr, Dunlop, Harbison, & Meyers, 1962) and in the 1980s, a Japanese one (Oliver & Wilkinson, 1992). Such universalistic views continued to appear and returned in various forms, as belief held that practices could be applicable across countries. Thus, "in best practice thinking, a universal prescription is preferred" (Boxall & Purcell, 2003, p. 61).

One strand in the area is the development of lists of best practices. Among the most famous are those of Pfeffer (1994, 1998), whose list of 16 (of relevance here included employment security, selectivity in selection, promotion from within, high pay, incentive pay, wage compression, and training and skill development), later narrowed to seven (of relevance here were employment security, selective and sophisticated hiring, high compensation contingent on performance, extensive training and development, reduction of status differentials, and sharing information self-managed teams/teamworking; see overviews of other lists in Boxall & Purcell, 2003; Redman & Wilkinson, 2006). Some take a broad definition that best practices are those that can add value to the business. Others are more specific and pinpoint certain practices in particular situations. For others, they are those present in successful and/or high-profile companies. Indeed, research on best practices including collective issues of work organization and employee voice is rare (Boxall & Purcell, 2003).

Some unresolved issues and questions muddy what at first sight seems simple and clear. The whole notion of best practices raises several questions (Bae & Rowley, 2001; Thang, Rowley, Troung & Warner, 2007). There may be quite agreement on what "bad practices" are (Boxall & Purcell, 2003), but there is no consensus on what "best practices" are. Their conceptualization, interpretation, and measurement remain subjective and variable among people, countries, and time. Therefore, while some commonalities exist across various lists, there is less of a consensus, and lists vary over time, location, and researcher. The varied use of terms and concepts such as "work systems" for high "performance," "commitment," "involvement," and so on create more uncertainty and opaqueness. Thus, we could quickly agree on and coalesce around sensible HR practices, but "things tend to get out of hand, however, when writers aggregate their favourite practices—and their implicit assumptions—into more ambitious lists and offer them to the world at large. Such models generally overlook the way that context affects the shape of the HR practices that emerge in a firm over time" (Boxall & Purcell, 2003, p. 68).

In addition to the identification and definition are the following issues. First, we can question the extent to which all organizations might wish, or be able, to implement best practices due to costs and/or sectors in business strategy and location. Thus, "lower value-added approaches may prove highly profitable in specific industries and locales" (Redman & Wilkinson, 2006, p. 266), and consideration of cost-effectiveness is important (Boxall & Purcell, 2003). Second, we need to ask, for whom is this best practice: organizations, shareholders, senior executives, managers, or employees? Much literature fudges this (Boxall & Purcell, 2003) or assumes "for all" (Redman & Wilkinson, 2006). Yet, such unitary perspectives are not common throughout the world (Rowley & Warner, 2007), and organizations are composed of a plural and divergent range of interests. Third, to whom are these practices applied, and is a minimum coverage needed of such groups and the organization's total HR? Fourth, are all best practices equally important, and are single practices or "bundles" of practices needed? If such groups are needed, what about the conflictual tendencies and contradictions best practices can generate? Thus, there may be incompatibility between practices. One example is Pfeffer's (1994) list which had incentive pay, high wages, and wage compression as three best practices in the rewards area. Are these practices actually likely to occur together? The furor in the media over excessive chief executive rewards and the vast gap in comparison to the pay of other employees, especially in American companies, shows that this is unlikely. Fifth, there has been only limited actual (as opposed to prescriptive or normative) diffusion and take-up, both at individual practice or HRM system level (see Boxall & Purcell, 2003).

An important issue is about global transference of such practices. The theory of take-up of Western practices derives in part from assumptions that they are somehow superior (Bae & Rowley, 2001). Economic dominance has led to diffusion of theory and organizational practice from the United States. While some researchers (see, e.g., Pudelko, 2005) believe that managerial practices in other countries are deviations from the American model, others (see, e.g., González & Tacorate, 2004) argue that competition between dominant countries means that no single "best" model persists. Rather, countries use their unique cultural and institutional frameworks to create distinct national competitive advantage, potentially militating against the diffusion of best practices. Cultural theorists concur that if practices and cultural values are compatible, it will be easier for employees to understand and internalize practices (Rowley & Benson, 2002, 2004). Historical contexts, unique cultural values, and institutional variations all retain their influence over organizations and local workforces in Asian economies and may foster the development of a unique Asian management model (Rowley, Benson, & Warner, 2004).

In summary, there is debate about best practices in terms of precisely what they are and what their universal application is. "Beyond a certain level of obviously sensible practices, managers start to think about their unique context. This naturally engenders diversity rather than uniformity in HRM" (Boxall & Purcell, 2003, p. 63).

Application

Questions arise as to whether theories and frameworks developed in the West apply in different contexts. To apply the HRM concept in other countries it is important to understand its meanings. Legge (1989) and others explain the term HRM by encapsulating its various differences from personnel management (PM): (a) whereas HRM concentrates on the management of teams, PM focuses on the control of subordinates; (b) line managers play a key role in HRM in coordinating resources, but they do not do so under PM; (c) the management of organizational culture is an important aspect of HRM but not PM; and (d) HRM is a more strategic task than PM.

Furthermore, HRM cannot be divorced from its institutional context. HRM (and best practices) are criticized as Anglo-American concepts and culturally bound (Easterby-Smith, Malina, & Lu, 1995). Whether they can, or even should, be replicated in the Asian context is a matter of opinion. Warner (1995) has cast doubt on applying the term *HRM* in Asia given the cultural differences that exist with the West. He used China as an example to argue that Western notions of HRM were not present in enterprises. The roles of PM were far from the concept of HRM as understood in Western theory. HRM with "Chinese characteristics" (Warner, 1995, p. 145) may be a more appropriate term to use.

Attempts to compare changes of HRM practices in different Asian economies often raise the question of what to include. The literature provides no clear list or model of HRM practices, and different researchers have their own lists. For instance, Rowley et al. (2004) used the common practice categories of recruitment and selection, training and development, and rewards and employment relations to compare HRM across three Asian countries (Korea, Japan, and China). Björkman and Xiucheng (2002) used rigorous recruitment and selection processes, extensive training, and performance contingent compensation systems.

Even if an agreement could be reached upon what to cover in the Asian context, it is difficult to encompass all HRM elements in a single, short chapter. Therefore, key areas where potential developments and changes can be reflected over time must be chosen. The approach taken here is to search for HRM areas where changes have occurred and where it is possible to observe transfer and adoption of best practices.

Huselid (1995) grouped HRM practices into dimensions that augment people skills, motivate employees, and organize workforces. Therefore, the best HRM practices are those that concern employment, rewards, and development. Some studies (see, e.g., Lado & Wilson, 1994; Pfeffer, 1994) show that companies utilizing their human capital as their unique advantage over others place top priority on people recruitment, reward, and development. Accordingly, three HRM practices are identified as best practices: employment flexibility, performance-based rewards, and employee development investment. These commonly appear on various best practice lists (see earlier discussion). These HRM practices will be discussed using examples and evidence from a range of Asian economies including economic superpowers, both existing (Japan) and emerging (China), "little dragons" (Hong Kong, Korea, Singapore, and Taiwan), and developing nations (Malaysia, Thailand, Philippines, Indonesia, and Vietnam). While not totally comprehensive of the Asia-Pacific region, these countries do encompass the major economic and population centers.

HRM best practices

Employment flexibility

Ideas of sophisticated recruitment and selection (Pfeffer, 1994) slightly metamorphosed into selective and sophisticated hiring (Pfeffer, 1998). Also, Pfeffer (1994) earlier had put forth promotion from within.

Seen as a Western HRM prescription, employment flexibility allowed for easier matching of labor to demand than was possible with former Asian lifetime employment models. Employment flexibility has various dimensions to it—not only numerical (dealt with below) but also financial and functional. The numerical flexibility in employment arrangements, for instance use of nonregular employees (i.e., part-time workers, casual workers, temporary employees, etc.), allows the organization to increase or decrease employment quickly in line with fluctuations in business demand without the costly overheads associated with full-time, permanent employees.

Contradiction and tension, however, exist between security and flexibility (numerical). For people like Pfeffer (1998), employment security was fundamental and underpinned other best practices. This is because HR outputs such as increased performance and motivation require some expectation of employment stability and concern for future careers and links to notions of the "psychological contract," "mutuality," "reciprocity," "partnership," and so on. This presents a dichotomy in the treatment of HR as critical assets for the long-term success of organizations and not as variable costs (Marchington & Wilkinson, 2005).

Performance-based rewards

Expectancy theory suggests that individuals are motivated to perform if they know that their extra performance is recognized and rewarded (Vroom, 1964). Consequently, companies using performance-based pay can expect improvements. Performance-based pay can link rewards to the amount of products employees produced. As such, attraction, retention, productivity, quality, participation, and morale may improve. Yet, for best practice gurus such as Pfeffer (1998), rewards had twin elements and needed to be not only performance-related but also higher than average.

Employee development investment

Extensive and quality (with focus and delivery) development is one of the most widely quoted aspects of best practice HRM (Marchington & Wilkinson, 2005). For several authors, training and development play a crucial role in international competitiveness (see, e.g., Finegold & Soskice, 1988). Investment in employee development is valuable to meet the needs of economies and organizations with increasing demands for higher levels of skills. Besides, training is often regarded as a benefit offered by organizations to reinforce employee dependence on the organization. Completion of training can lead to promotion. As such, training plays an important role in social mobility and acceptance. Thus, substantial and continuous investment in employee development can be seen as a best practice.

What type of development should companies invest in? And, for whom in the companies should it be offered? Does it need to be job specific or general?

These three best practices are very different from traditional practices predominately used in Asia (i.e., lifetime employment, seniority-based pay, and organizational specific/technical skills training) (see Table TB6.1.1).

Table TB6.1.1   Comparison between Asia traditional practices and West best practices

HRM practices	Asia (traditional practice)	West (best practice)
Employment	Recruitment at fixed times to low level entry from trusted sources Strong internal labour market Lifetime employment Emphasis on technical skills, education, credentials or relationships Seniority (age and tenure) Promotion	Recruitment on demand at all levels from open market Rigour in recruitment and selection techniques Emphasis on ability
Rewards	Seniority (age and tenure) Group based Egalitarian distribution of income	Performance-based (ability and competency) Use of performance appraisals
Development	Extensive socialization and on-the-job training Technical and vocational Often organizational-specific	Continuous learning General skills Sophisticated needs analysis and assessment Encourage team building

Comparison

A discussion of the three HRM best practices using examples of Asia-Pacific economies follows.

Employment flexibility

Companies in different countries have taken different approaches to fit in with their institutional context. Some argue that national cultures affect hiring practices in various countries (Yuen & Kee, 1993). The restructuring of Asian economies due to globalization and industrialization, however, has led to a number of consequences including factory relocations, cutbacks and lay-offs, unemployment and subsequent retraining, and so forth (Warner, 2003) because businesses are looking for changes and adjustments in workplace HRM practices. After the Asian Crisis, companies realized that seniority-based systems and lifetime employment were costly; they needed flexibility in headcount adjustments to enable quicker responses to market fluctuation and competition.

Classic lifetime employment was found is Japan. In recent years, however, a new group of workers known as "job-hoppers" has evolved. Opposed to seeking out a reliable company after graduating from university and staying until retirement, some younger Japanese have chosen to change jobs every few years (Benson & Debroux, 1997). According to a survey in Japan Statistics (2002), 18% of high-school graduates left their first job within a year. In addition, large companies employ flexible employment policies that relied on nonregular workers. This indicates change in traditional Japanese employment practice.

Lifetime employment is also changing in Korea. In 1999, the terms of the post-1997 Crisis International Monetary Fund (IMF) bailout forced the government to legalize layoffs, weakening this traditional concept. The general direction has moved away from lifetime employment toward easier employment adjustments. Consequently, permanent, full-time workers markedly declined and were replaced by part-time or nonregular employees (Rowley & Bae, 2004).

Nevertheless, the type of organization remains important. For example, public sector organizations, SOEs in countries like China and Vietnam, and government-linked firms in countries like Malaysia all retain greater lifetime employment.

Performance-based rewards

Some Asian managers believe that performance-based rewards of various forms (commissions, bonuses, profit-sharing, share options, etc.) are

Western best practices because they tie rewards to job performance as opposed to traditional Asian "seniorityism" of compensation based on age and/or tenure. Companies offering such plans try to be more attractive than their competitors in recruiting and retaining the best talent. The earlier Asian Crisis and global competition, however, have made companies more conservative in making increases to all employees and more likely to take the form of performance-based incentives. The spread of Western compensation systems and performance appraisals through FIEs in China has been significant since the 1990s (Björkman & Xiucheng, 2002). Variable compensation in the form of stock options, employee shareholding, and the like have also seemingly spread and exerted influence over Asian compensation schemes.

We can, however, question the spread of such schemes across both sectoral types and with organizational hierarchies. Also, instilling a performance-based culture, a shift in HRM system architecture, demands consistent policy mixes and practices. Indeed, some companies are reverting to seniority-based systems as companies struggle to effectively assess work and productivity. According to one report, over 75% of Japanese companies that had introduced performance-based pay systems experienced difficulties in managing them (Japan Institute of Labor Policy and Training [JILPT] 2004). The major difficulties were (a) lack of a performance rating system to assess performance, (b) insufficient training for managers to make them commit to the system, and (c) feelings of a lack of job security and company loyalty. It seems that the transfer of a practice is one thing, but making it effective is another. If the transfer is not followed by a deeper level of internalization, both managers and employees will have difficulty in commitment and ownership of the practice (Kostova, 1999; Rowley & Benson, 2002).

Employee development investment

A well-trained and educated labor force is considered a major contributor to the economic performance records of Asia (Cooke, 2005). The need for skilled professions and high-quality executive training have created a boom for managerial training courses, MBA programs, and higher education opportunities in Asia. While an attractive choice for larger corporations, not every company has the resources to establish in-house training schools. Therefore, some large companies may send employees abroad to foreign universities for training. Small-and-medium-sized enterprises (SMEs) need to rely more on governments. China and Vietnam have only recently joined the WTO (2001 and 2007, respectively), strengthening international educational exchange and helping distribution and application of new knowledge.

Nevertheless, not all Asian countries employ a Western approach to development, but blend practices with Asian characteristics and institutional needs. The focus of management training in Korea, especially in large companies, is somewhat different than in the West. In Korea, emphasis was placed on team spirit and commitment to the company and coworkers (Drost, Frayne, Lowe, & Geringer, 2002). Companies took a more holistic approach to incorporate company value and business practices in people development.

Again, however, the sectoral and hierarchical coverage and spread of such practices can be questioned. It is a common finding that the most senior HR in organizations receive the most development expenditure.

In sum, our overview of these three HRM practices shows that it seems that HRM change involves gradual experimentation, and best practices cannot simply be adopted. As with most experimentation, the final outcomes may be difficult to predict and, hence, pose challenges in management research in such area.

Source: Rowley and Poon (2008: 209; 210–212; 214–215; 216–217

Text Box 6.2

Transferring HRM policies and practices

This chapter aims to examine the interaction between 'country-of-origin' and 'country-of-operation' effects in determining human resource management (HRM) policies and practices in multinationals (MNCs) in the context of globalisation. As national institutional patterns can penetrate a firm's internal operations, this study investigates the transmission and adaptation of the home country's HRM policies and practices within the MNC subsidiaries in the developing host country. Based on an investigation of the reward systems and performance management practices of a sample of US and Japanese companies based in Vietnam, this chapter argues that while 'low power' environments pose little in the way of formal constraint mechanisms, they can facilitate the penetration of novel HRM practices. Findings also suggested a complex and challenging situation exists for MNC operations, requiring a very high level of adaptation and flexibility on the part of the host country firm.

Introduction

Recent trends concerning regional integration, the removal of trade barriers, deregulation, the opening of previously closed national markets to international competition, the rise of Asian countries and the integration of Central and Eastern Europe and China into the world economy have inevitably provoked speculation in relation to a globalised world. This has led to a renewal of the debate on the identity of firms and the convergence/divergence of their behaviour patterns. Despite the strength of the globalisation phenomenon which supports the theory of a 'borderless world', stateless firms (Ohmae, 1990) and the homogeneity of firms' structure and behaviour (Bartlett and Ghoshal, 1989), many authors argue that the nation state continues to be a key element in the understanding of MNCs' management practices across borders (Porter, 1990; Whitley, 1992; Lane, 1995).

Globalisation is not a homogeneous process. Instead, it increases inequality across countries, especially between developed and developing countries (Guillén, 2001). It emphasises the dependency of peripheral developing countries on investment from centre economies. In this context, the features of capitalist development are not simply expressed in a uniform fashion across borders. They are, in many respects, refracted in a distinctive fashion within specific national states. For example, even though developing economies have become increasingly internationalised and integrated into the global system, their firms are, like those in East Asia, in a weaker position in the 'global commodity chains' (Gereffi, 1996). Japanese transplants in Malaysia, for instance, produce mature goods which compete in world markets mainly on price, engage in relatively low value activities, particularly mass assembly, undertake limited product design work, and engage only in highly limited ways in process innovation (Wilkinson, Gamble, Humphrey, Morris and Anthony, 2001). The globalisation processes of uneven development, interdependence between equals and those who are less equal alongside interactions of conflicting and common interests, within which national state institutions are embedded, do not simply sustain a single and homogenous pattern of firm behaviours.

The relationship between national features and firm distinctiveness has been highlighted by the institutionalist school of thought. Institutionalists argue that firm activities bear the imprint of specific national institutional arrangements (Orrù, Biggart and Hamilton, 1997; Hollingsworth and Boyer, 1997; Lane, 1995; Whitley, 1999), as they 'gravitate towards the mode of coordination for which there is institutional support' (Hall and

Soskice, 2001: 9). Firms are also likely to reflect their national origins with regard to behaviour in their foreign operations (Ferner, 2000). This is because, to varying degrees, the particular features of the home country become an ingrained part of an MNC corporate identity influencing their international orientation as the general approach. Furthermore, in some cases, the particular configuration of the home system can give MNCs an advantage when competing outside their home countries (Taylor, Beechler and Napier, 1996).

Many authors have attempted to answer the research question: how far do national states influence the international transfer of MNCs' management practices? The literature on MNCs and the transfer of HRM practices across countries suffers from a lack of research on the application of these issues in developing countries. One key question is centred on the formation and implementation of HRM systems in subsidiaries within weak host countries. This chapter addresses the transfer of HRM practices in relation to how institutional differences (distance) operate to mediate the transfer of such practices. It aims to investigate the transmission and adaptation of the home country's HRM policies and practices at MNCs' subsidiaries in a low-power host country.

In exploring the question of the effect of nationality on multinationals' behaviour, the literature reviews an analysis of the transfer of HRM policies and practices between different national business systems. The empirical study is based on eight main case studies of US and Japanese MNCs operating in Vietnam in automotive and fast-moving consumer goods (FMCG) industries. The chapter discusses two different yet related HR issues – the reward system and performance management practices of the sample firms. It argues that developing and transitional economies, such as Vietnam, may facilitate the penetration of novel forms of economic organisation. Then again, they suggest a complex situation for MNC operations and require from them a very high level of flexibility, and in some cases compromise, when forming and implementing transferred managerial practices.

The transfer of HRM policies and practices between different national business systems

Comparative institutionalism theory has been widely used to study the diffusion of organisational practices across countries. Operating in more than one country, MNCs confront a multitude of different and possibly conflicting institutional pressures (Ferner and Quintanilla, 1998; Westney, 1993). Since it is vital for MNCs to establish and maintain organisational legality in all their host environments, they need to conform to the legal environment, particularly on labour issues as well as be responsive to the cultural environment. Furthermore, as argued by Birkinshaw and Hood (1998), subsidiaries possess their own capabilities and resources such as consumption market, resources, and efficiency, which are desirable to the parent company. MNCs therefore are under pressure to adopt local practices in the host countries (Kostova and Zaheer, 1999; Ghoshal and Barlett, 1988; Taylor et al., 1996). At the same time, an important source of competitive advantage for the MNC is the utilisation of organisational capabilities worldwide (Ghoshal and Barlett, 1988; Nohria and Ghoshal, 1997). Hereby lies the central question in the literature on MNCs: the extent to which their various foreign subsidiaries act and behave as local firms (local adaptation) versus the extent to which their practices resemble those of the parent firm (global integration). This is the core research question addressed in this chapter.

There is some evidence that the home country exerts a distinctive influence on the way labour is managed in MNCs. Ferner (1997, 2000) argues that the parent company is embedded in an institutional environment located in the home country. To varying degrees, the particular features of the home country become an ingrained part of each MNC's corporate identity and shape its international orientation as the general philosophy or approach taken by the parent company in the design of the HRM systems used in its overseas subsidiaries. Thus, "ethnocentricity' and 'polycentrism' have been seen as traits characteristic of multinationals of different national origins: thus Japanese and American companies tend to be more ethnocentric than their European counterparts, other things such as sector of operation being equal' (Ferner, 1994: 88; see also Bartlett and Ghoshal, 1989; Johansson and Yip, 1994; Kopp, 1994; Dicken, 1998; Berggren, 1999).

Taylor et al. (1996) assert that business system differences, including cultural distance and institutional distance, are the most important constraints on the 'context generalisability' of HRM practices. Kostova and Zaheer (1999) argue that each subsidiary of the MNC is faced with the task of establishing and maintaining both external legitimacy in its host environment and internal legitimacy within the MNC. As suggested by institutional theorists, organisations may achieve legitimacy by becoming 'isomorphic' with the institutional environment (DiMaggio and Powell, 1991). However, they do not necessarily adapt to the local environments, but, rather, manage their legitimacy through negotiation processes with their multiple environments (Kostova and Zaheer, 1999; Doz and Prahalad, 1984). Adaptation and hybridisation result from these processes. 'Hybridisation' refers to the mixing of two or more different practices. For example, if a Vietnamese subsidiary (a joint venture between a Japanese partner and a Vietnamese partner) has a salary policy which is based on that of the Japanese parent company (the *nenko* system) while their benefit policy is the same as that of the Vietnamese parent company, their reward system would be considered a 'hybridisation'.

Almost all empirical studies that look at the cross-border transfer of HRM come to the conclusion that a certain amount of change is always necessary to successfully implement a HRM system that has been developed in the home business system. Ferner and his colleagues, for instance, have observed that, in recent years, elements of Anglo-American business practices are being incorporated into the German business system. The authors term this process 'Anglo-Saxonisation', but argue that it occurs 'in the German manner' (Ferner and Quintanilla, 1998; Ferner and Varul, 2000).

The transfer of HRM/IR policies and practices between two economies needs to be seen as part of the global economy. Smith and Meiksins (1995) argue that 'countries can be slotted into [global] commodity chains relative to societal endowments, and have their comparative superiority and inferiority reinforced'. The 'dominance' (Elger and Smith, 1994) or inferiority of a business system strongly determines what and how the HRM system is transferred from one business system to another. From the home country perspective, Elger and Smith (1994) argue that the dominance, largely in economic terms, of a home system itself is one mechanism of diffusion. Dominant states are more able to exert or invite dissemination and adoption of their version of capitalism in other national systems. 'Firms from strongly integrated and successful economies may carry over national character to subsidiaries when locating abroad, and transfer home country practices rather than adopt the practices encountered in the host country' (Smith and Meiksins, 1995: 262). For example, the post-war era witnessed American economic and political dominance of the international political economy. This period saw a dissemination of American managerial and production techniques in the world; while the1980s witnessed the transitory dominance of Japanese companies and the 'Japanisation' of production and management systems in the US and other parts of the world.

From the host country perspective, the superiority/inferiority of the host system determines its relative openness or receptiveness to dominant 'best practice' (Whitley, 1992). In a permissive/open host country environment which poses fewer constraints on firms, the introduction of country of origin practices is easer (Whitley, 1992). In contrast, MNCs may be prevented from transferring country-of-origin practices into a constraining/closed host country environment which is highly regulated and distinctive (Whitley, 1992). Moreover, the subsidiaries can utilise their resources (expertise about local environment and market, specialist knowledge, culture and so on) to block diffusion (Edwards, Ferner and Sisson, 1993).

The literature on MNCs and the transfer of HRM practices has concentrated overwhelmingly on the Triad of the European Union, America and Japan and the interactions amongst firms which are of those nationalities and located within these locations (Bartlett and Ghoshal, 1989; Guest and Hoque, 1996; Tempel, 2001; Evans, Lank & Farquhar, 1989; Quintanilla, Ferner & Varul, 2001; Edwards, Chris and Coller, 1999; Schmitt and Sadowski, 2003, to name but a few). This reflects the heavy concentration of FDI amongst the Triad (Hirst and Thompson, 1999). Meanwhile, little is known about the same phenomenon in developing economies, which are located in weak and disadvantageous positions in the global commodity chains. There are a series of related analytical questions to be answered in this niche: What are the possible constraints and opportunities placed by a low power host country on the operation of MNCs coming from dominant economies? Are MNCs from dominant countries less likely to adopt local practices in weaker host countries and more likely to transfer their own practices? Or are many aspects of their progressive systems lost when firms work in permissive environments? What mechanisms do MNCs develop to cope and adapt to constraints and take advantage of opportunities? These are the research questions that this chapter attempts to answer.

Conclusion

The aim of this research study was to examine the transmission and adaptation of the host country's HRM policies and practices within MNC's subsidiaries in a developing host country, in this case Vietnam. Overall some important conclusions were reached.

Primarily this research confirms that the globalisation process does not simply sustain a single and homogenous pattern of firm behaviour and that greater economic efficiency in work systems within a country does not automatically lead to the dispersal of these practices to other countries. Even if it can be demonstrated that a particular set of HRM practices contributes significantly to superior performance in home country operations, a MNC has to determine whether it wishes to transfer these practices. This research argues that MNCs may consider that the transfer of HRM policies and practices is not necessary for successful operation within a Vietnamese context. In the case of JP FMCG, they basically decided to stop the transfer of their home practices to the Vietnamese subsidiaries. Instead, there was a high degree of localisation of managerial practices (even though the same conclusion cannot be drawn for transferring production technology). The first few attempts to copy home practices (the *nenko* system) quickly disappeared in the Vietnamese environment. The argument is strengthened when some attempts to compare their practices with regard to other subsidiaries are made. Elsewhere, JP FMCG is described as a 'classic global company' where international operations are largely formulated and controlled by headquarters. Their global strategy seeks to build competitive advantage by treating the world as a single, largely undifferentiated market. Instead of home-grown methods, the company seeks to use fairly universalistic forms of 'common sense' management, experimenting, learning and copying pieces from other firms in a haphazard and eclectic manner. Thus, the low degree of transfer might be attributed to the perceived lack of necessity and assumptions concerning the importance of particular management practices.

It is argued that a developing country poses a minimal *formal mechanism of constraint* to the design and implementation of MNCs' remuneration and PM practices. The Vietnamese government has been conscious of the necessity to keep the base level of salary in foreign invested companies at a minimum level and to reduce personal income tax rates. In this context MNCs are allowed to design and/or implement suitable rewards and performance management systems. That said, companies are faced with an *informal mechanism of constraint* in the form of a default labour market and job-hopping practices. This encourages the implementation of attractive and effective reward systems. The combination of these factors might explain the transfer of well-developed and standardised reward and PM systems in the sample firms.

The home country effects were also evident in this study. For example, MNCs kept tight control of the reward systems in the Vietnamese subsidiaries. A well-defined salary position, permitted salary ranges, and the practice of variable pay which strongly emphasises individual performance were exercised. There were also instances of adaptation to local situations as seen in fixed bonuses, allowances and benefits practices. These practices were very similar in the studied firms and resemble those found in Vietnamese SOEs. Gaps in legislation and weak law enforcement mechanisms have seen companies develop practical tactics to reduce labour costs, such as the '70/30' salary package.

The distinctiveness of the US and Japanese traditions of rewarding and appraising employees was also evident in their Vietnamese subsidiaries with some minor adaptations. In the US firms, the PM process was closely linked with financial measurements and individual performance. The companies also applied a wide range of advanced PM tools and techniques, including the use of 360-degree feedback and forced distributions of performance. Conversely, the Japanese *nenko* system was transferred to Vietnam in the form of an age-linked payment. Some adaptations of the *nenko* system were apparent, such as a greater weight being given to individual merit and a higher starting salary.

Finally, although it was not a focus of this research, this chapter acknowledges certain cultural influences with regard to the practices of PM. However, the successful implementation of the US 360-degree feedback and forced distribution system and the limitations of the Japanese top-down appraisal process illustrate the transience and indeterminacy of national cultural traits. In opposition to Hofstede (1980) and other culturalists who see some unchanging national differentiation with regard to culture, this chapter illustrates that cultural values can actually evolve in some situations. The transitional period in Vietnam, which witnessed the fall of the centrally planned system and its promises, is receptive to new and seemingly contrasting practices. It remains to be seen how these develop over time.

Source: Vo (2007: 197–202; 216–218)

6.3 Comparisons

These points were discussed and highlighted when we looked at HRM comparatively and internationally. There are many differences in the use of HRM internationally between different countries as we have seen (and can be seen in, for example, Rowley, 1998; Rowley and Benson, 2000 and 2004; Rowley et al., 2004; Zhu et al., 2007).

Think About/Question 6.3

For management, what might be some of the uses of knowledge of HRM practices in other locations?

Comparative views are useful for a range of reasons. These include those noted in Table 6.3.

Table 6.3   Usefulness of comparative views

Element		Result
Ethnocentrism	→	Reduced, ground views
Own system	→	Put in perspective
Public policy	→	Examples provided
Research/views	→	Ground/test results
Overseas operations	→	Understand more

Think About/Question 6.4

How would you explain variations in HRM practices between countries?

These differences may result from several factors. These can be explained by the reasons noted in Table 6.4.

Think About/Question 6.5

How would you go about examining HRM practices in different countries?

Several options are available to look at HRM internationally. These can be seen in Table 6.5.

Table 6.4 Reasons for differences in HRM

Approach	Characteristics	Issues	Problems
Convergence	◆ Process of industrialisation and use of technology move all towards similar political and economic systems ◆ Are universal truths applicable everywhere	⋏ Some countries remain at different stages ⋏ Even with same technology, implementation of practices varies	❖ Fail to understand way in which practices interpreted and implementation differs between countries
Contingency	◆ Recognise practices affected by factors ◆ Common variables of organisational size, technology, environment	⋏ Contingent factors still impose rational logic of administration and organisation ⋏ So still 'best way' given contingencies	
Culture	◆ Collective programming of mind of group ◆ Reflected in particular assumptions, beliefs and norms ◆ Much made of differences	⋏ All differences may not be explained in terms of people's attitudes ⋏ Emphasis on history and individuals' perceptions, but little account of how values change over time ⋏ Values on their own not enough; need to be rooted in social and economic structure of society	❖ Fail to recognise that divergent and contradictory range of practices may exist within a society and static views
Institutional	◆ Understand social and economic institutions supporting values and practices ◆ Cannot examine separate aspects of system without locating in specific societal context	⋏ Static view of national industrial order ⋏ Little attention to role of the state	

Table 6.5	Discovering HRM in other countries

Method	Characteristics	Issues
Large-scale data sets secondary analysis	◆ Nationally representative ◆ Establish changes and trends over time ◆ Cheap if already generated ◆ 'Representative'	❖ Cannot give reasons why or causality ❖ Definitional difficulties ❖ Inadequate data problems ❖ Data 'filtered' and generated for other purposes
Questionnaires	◆ Popular in employment research ◆ Generate standardised data ◆ Relative cheapness ◆ Provides some breadth	❖ Obtain superficial evidence ❖ Questions pre-determined ❖ Unexpected findings difficult to integrate ❖ Susceptible to ethnocentrism
Case studies	◆ In-depth interviews, observational methods, do the work itself ◆ Realities of how work organised at closer level ◆ Pick up unforeseen issues ◆ Examine why practices used	❖ Time-consuming ❖ Knowledge of society/language ❖ Difficult to generalise ❖ Lose objectivity/ independence – 'go native'

6.4 The future of HRM

Several organisational trends will have impacts on the development of HRM. These include the following.

6.4.1 HRM as a subject

HRM as a subject faces a healthy future in terms of academia, teaching and research – partly driven by the increasing popularity of business and management qualifications at different levels. Within these qualification courses, the study of people management is covered in a variety of ways and from various aspects. Much research in the area is durable and is continuing, although the exact focus of this continues to change and develop. Thus, there is less work on 'conflict' and more on the contributions by HRM to the performance of businesses and economies, for instance.

6.4.2 HRM as a function

As a function, HRM faces a different set of issues. For some commentators, it may lead to a decline, although others see some greater continuity functionally. A range of developments will have different impacts on the HRM function.

> Think About/Question 6.6
>
> What might be some of the impacts on the decline or continuity of HRM as a function?

The impacts are numerous and varied, as can be seen in Tables 6.6 and 6.7. While the management of people will remain, it seems that who does it, and where, may change. One of the more recent trends in countries such as the US and UK is to outsource either the whole of the HRM function or certain aspects of it, such as recruitment, to specialists. Yet, what is the likely impact of such outsourcing for ideas of HRM and consistent universal frameworks?

Table 6.6   Impacts on HRM as a function

Developments	Impacts	Results
Business decentralisation	➤ Centre involved in strategy ➤ Divisions involved in operational issues	❖ Inconsistency/ variability in policy and practice within/ across organisations ❖ Strategic role, input and integration of HR issues impacted on
Decentralising HR specialists	➤ From corporate to business unit ➤ Within business unit to departmental level	
Devolving HR activities to line managers	➤ Use of non-specialists ➤ Line management variability	
Outsourcing	➤ Dedicated call centres ➤ Use of external consultants	

Source: Adapted from Sisson (1995); Hall and Torrington (1998)

Table 6.7	Decline and continuity of HRM

Decline	Continuity
In recession, fewer people resourced, rewarded, developed	In recession, still deal with redundancies, retaining even recruiting
Trade unions more docile, less 'trouble-shooting'	Trade unions remain, alternative sanctions (i.e. overtime bans, PR campaigns)
Routine administration reduced with automation (i.e. pay, records)	Increasingly heterogeneous workforce requiring managing diversity
Subcontracting out aspects (i.e. resourcing, rewards, development)	In economic boom, attract/retain sufficient quality key HR
'Macho management' reasserting managers 'right to manage'	Myriad laws require consideration (i.e. need to consult over changes)

6.5 Conclusion

The area of people management is not new and we have seen that directions for managing people have existed, even in Asia, for thousands of years. In the modern era, management of people has evolved and been labelled and relabelled in several ways. However, for some people HRM is different and marks a break with this past as HRM contains some elements that 'old' PM simply did not possess, or even claim that PM was interested in such topics. This sort of hard distinction is less proven in some parts of Asia where PM is currently stronger than HRM. Nevertheless, that should not distract businesses and managers from the fact that HRM remains critically important.

Furthermore, while HRM is important, the introduction and use of 'text book' practices varies between Asian organisations. We have examined this through a prism of context that has shown variability, and we have explored some of the many reasons (country, culture and sector) why this may be so. This variability in HRM needs to be remembered when faced with the often naïve nostrums and platitudes of many proponents of the latest 'fashion' to solve the HRM problems and issues of all organisations in Asia and elsewhere. If only managing people was simple, organisations would have solved their HR issues already! The management of people needs to be put in context and viewed through this lens.

End of chapter tasks/questions
Based on the bank and airlines case studies in Appendix 3,
using and applying information within this chapter

1. What are likely to be the major obstacles to using US and UK methods of managing HR in Asia?

2. Analyse why there might be tension between line and HR managers.

3. Why are there differences between head offices in the West and operating units in Asia when it comes to valuing people?

4. To improve business practices what can Asian ways of managing people teach those in the West?

5. The twenty-first century will belong to Asia – discuss why some commentators think this will be true.

References

Bae, J. and Rowley, C. (2001) 'The impact of globalization on HRM: The case of South Korea', *Journal of World Business,* 36(4): 402–428.

Bartlett, C.A. and Ghoshal, S. (1989) *Managing Across Borders: The Transnational Solution.* Chatham, UK: Mackays.

Becker, B.E. and Gerhart, B. (1996) 'The impact of HRM on organizational performance: Progress and prospects', *Academy of Management Journal,* 39(4): 779–802.

Benson, J. and Debroux, P. (1997) 'HRM in Japanese enterprises: Trends and challenges', *Asia Pacific Business Review,* 3(4): 62–81.

Berggren, C. (1999) 'Introduction: Between globalisation and multi-domestic variation' in J. Belanger, C. Berggren, T. Bjorkman and C. Kohler (eds) *Being Local Worldwide: ABB and the Challenge of Global Management.* New York: Cornell University Press.

Birkinshaw, J. and Hood, N. (1998) 'Multinational subsidiary evolution: Capability and charter change in foreign-owned subsidiary companies', *Academy of Management Review,* 1998, 23(4): 773–795.

Björkman, I. and Xiucheng, F. (2002) 'HRM and the performance of Western firms in China', *International Journal of HRM,* 13(6): 853–864.

Boxall, P. and Purcell, J. (2003) *Strategy and Human Resource Management*. London: Palgrave.

Briscoe, D.R. (1995) *International Human Resource Management*. Englewood Cliffs, NJ: Prentice Hall.

Cooke, F.L. (2005) 'Vocational and enterprise training in China: Policy, practice and prospect', *Journal of the AP Economy*, 10(1): 26–55.

Dicken, P. (1998) *Global Shift: Transforming the World Economy* (3rd edn). London: Paul Chapman Publishing Ltd.

DiMaggio, P.J. and Powell, W.W. (1991) 'The iron cage revisited: Institutional isomorphism and collective rationality in organization fields' in W.W. Power and P.J. DiMaggio (eds), *The New Institutionalism in Organizational Analysis*. Chicago and London: The University of Chicago Press, 41–63.

Dowling, P.J., Schuler, R.S. and Welch, D.E. (1994) *International Dimensions of HRM*. Belmont, CA: Wadsworth Publishing.

Doz, Y.L. and Prahalad, C.K. (1984) 'Patterns of strategic control within multinational corporations', *Journal of International Business Studies*, 15(2): 55–72.

Drost, E.A., Frayne, A., Lowe, B. and Geringer, J.M. (2002) 'Benchmarking training and development practices: A multi-country comparative analysis', *Human Resource Management*, 41(1): 67–88.

Easterby-Smith, M., Malina, D. and Lu, Y. (1995) 'How culture sensitive is HRM? A comparative analysis of practice in Chinese and UK companies', *International Journal of Human Resource Management*, 6(1): 31–59.

Edwards, P., Ferner, A. and Sisson, K. (1993) *People and the Process of Management in the Multinational Company: A Review and Some Illustrations*, Warwick Papers in Industrial Relations. Coventry: IRRU.

Edwards, T., Rees, C. and Coller, X. (1999) 'Structure, politics and the diffusion of employment practices in multinationals', *European Journal of Industrial Relations*, 5(3): 286–306.

Elger, T. and Smith, C. (1994) 'Global Japanization? Convergence and competition in the organisation of the labour process' in T. Elger and C. Smith (eds) *Global Japanization? The Transformation of the Labour Process*. London: Routledge.

Evans, P., Lank, E. and Farquhar, A. (1989) 'Managing human resources in the international firm: Lessons from practice' in P. Evans, Y. Doz and A. Laurent (eds) *Human Resource Management in International Firms*. London: Macmillan.

Ferner, A. (1994) 'Multinational companies and human resource management: An overview of research issues', *Human Resource Management Journal*, 4(3): 79–102.

Ferner, A. (1997) 'Country of origin effects and HRM in multinational companies', *Human Resource Management Journal*, 7(1): 19–37.

Ferner, A. (2000), *The Embeddedness of US Multinational Companies in the US Business System: Implications for HR/IR*, Occasional Paper No. 61. Leicester: De Montfort University Business School.

Ferner, A. and Quintanilla, J. (1998) 'Multinationals, national identity, and the management of HRM: "Anglo-Saxonisation" and its limits', *International Journal of Human Resource Management*, 9(4): 710–731.

Ferner, A. and Varul, M.Z. (2000) '"Vanguard" subsidiaries and the diffusion of new practices: A case study of German multinationals', *British Journal of Industrial Relations*, 38(1): 115–140.

Finegold, D. and Soskice, D. (1988) 'The failure of training in Britain: Analysis and prescription', *Oxford Review of Economic Policy*, 4(1): 21–53.

Gereffi, G. (1996) 'Commodity chains and regional divisions of labor in East Asia', *Journal of Asian Business*, 12: 75–112.

Ghoshal, S. and Bartlett, C. (1988) 'Creation, adoption, and diffusion of innovations by subsidiaries of multinational corporations', *Journal of International Business Studies*, Fall: 365–388.

González, S.M. and Tacorate, D.V. (2004) 'A new approach to the best practices debate: Are best practices applied to all employees in the same way?', *International Journal of Human Resource Management*, 15(1): 56–75.

Guest, D. and Hoque, K. (1996) 'National ownership and HR practices in UK greenfield sites', *Human Resource Management Journal*, 6(4): 50–74.

Guillén, M. (2001) 'Is globalization civilizing, destructive or feeble? A critique of five key debates in the social science literature', *Annual Review of Sociology*, 27: 235–260.

Hall, L. and Torrington, D. (1998) *The HR Function: The Dynamics of Change and Development*. London: Financial Times/Pitman.

Hall, P. and Soskice, D. (2001) 'An introduction to varieties of capitalism' in P. Hall and D. Soskice (eds) *Varieties of Capitalism: The Institutional Foundations of Comparative Advantage*. Oxford: Oxford University Press.

Hamilton, G. (1995) 'Overseas Chinese capitalism' in W. Tu (ed.), *The Confucian Dimensions of Industrial East Asia*. Cambridge, MA: Harvard University Press, 112–125.

Hirst, P. and Thompson, G. (1999) *Globalization in Question* (2nd edition). Malden, MA: Polity Press.

Hollingsworth, R.J. and Boyer, R. (1997) 'Coordination of economic actors and social systems of production' in R.J. Hollingsworth and R. Boyer (eds) *Contemporary Capitalism: The Embeddedness of Institutions*. Cambridge: Cambridge University Press.

Huselid, M.A. (1995) 'The impact of HRM practices on turnover, productivity, and corporate financial performance', *Academy of Management Journal*, 38(3): 635–670.

Japan Institute of Labour Policy and Training (2004) Report published by the Japan Institute of Labour Policy and Training. Retrieved 17 August 2007 from *http://www.stat.go.jp/english/index.htm*

Johansson, J. and Yip, G. (1994) 'Exploiting globalisation potential: US and Japanese strategies', *Strategic Management Journal*, 15(4): 579–601.

Kerr, C., Dunlop, J.T., Harbison, F.H. and Meyers, C.A. (1962) *Industrialism and Industrial Man*. London: Heinemann.

Kopp, R. (1994) 'International human resource policies and practices in Japanese, European, and United States multinationals', *Human Resource Management Journal*, 33(4): 581–599.

Kostova, T. (1999) 'Transnational transfer of strategic organizational practices: A contextual perspective', *Academy of Management Review*, 24(2): 403–428.

Kostova, T. and Zaheer, S. (1999) 'Organisational legitimacy under conditions of complexity: The case of the multinational enterprise', *Academy of Management Review*, 24(1): 64–81.

Lado, A.A. and Wilson, M.C. (1994) 'HR systems and sustained competitive advantage: A competency-based perspective', *Academy of Management Review*, 19(4): 699–727.

Lane, C. (1995) *Industry and Society in Europe. Stability and Change in Britain, Germany and France*. Aldershot: Edward Elgar.

Legge, K. (1989) 'HRM: A critical analysis' in J. Storey (ed.), *New Perspectives on Human Resource Management*. London: Routledge.

Legge, K. (1995) 'HRM: Rhetoric, reality and hidden agendas' in J. Storey (ed.) *HRM: A Critical Text*. London: Routledge, 33–59.

Marchington, M. and Wilkinson, A. (2005) *Human Resource Management at Work*. London: CIPD.

Nohria, N. and Ghoshal, S. (1997) *The Differentiated Network. Organizing Multinational Corporations for Value Creation*. San Francisco: Jossey-Bass Publishers.

Ohmae, K. (1990) *The Borderless Word*. London: HarperCollins.

Oliver, N. and Wilkinson, B. (1992) *The Japanization of British Industry: New Developments in the 1990s*. London: Heinemann.

Orrù, M., Biggart, N.W. and Hamilton, G.G. (1997) 'Organisational isomorphism in East Asian' in W.W. Powell and P.J. DiMaggio (eds)

The New Institutionalism in Organizational Analysis. Chicago: University of Chicago Press.

Pfeffer, J. (1994) *Competitive Advantage through People.* Boston: Harvard Business School Press.

Pfeffer, J. (1998) *The Human Equation: Building Profits by Putting People First.* Boston: Harvard Business School Press.

Porter, M. (1990) *The Competitive Advantage of Nations.* London/Basingstoke: MacMillan.

Pudelko, M. (2005) 'Cross-national learning from best practice and the convergence–divergence debate in HRM', *International Journal of Human Resource Management,* 16(11): 2045–2074.

Quintanilla, J., Ferner, A. and Varul, M. (2001) 'Country-of-origin effects, host country effects and the management of HR in multinationals: German companies in Britain and Spain', *Journal of World Business,* 36(1): 107–128.

Redman, T. and Wilkinson, A. (2006) *Contemporary Human Resource Management.* London: FT/Prentice Hall.

Rosenzweig, P. (2007) *The Halo Effect and the Eight Other Business Delusions that Deceive Managers.* New York: Free Press.

Rowley, C. (1998) *HRM in the Asia Pacific Region: Convergence Questioned.* London: Frank Cass.

Rowley, C. and Bae, J. (2004) 'HRM in South Korea after the Asian financial crisis', *International Studies of Management and Organization,* 34(1): 52–82.

Rowley, C. and Benson, J. (2000) *Globalization and Labour in the Asia Pacific Region.* London: Frank Cass.

Rowley, C. and Benson, J. (2002) 'Convergence and divergence in Asian HRM', *California Management Review,* 44(2): 90–109.

Rowley, C. and Benson, J. (2004) *The Management of HR in the Asia Pacific Region: Convergence Reconsidered.* London: Frank Cass.

Rowley, C. and Poon, F.H. (2008) 'HRM best practices and transfer to the Asia-Pacific region' in C. Wankel (ed.) *21st Century Management.* US: Los Angeles: Sage, 209–220.

Rowley, C. and Warner, M. (2007) 'Globalizing international HRM?', *International Journal of Human Resource Management,* 18(5): 703–716.

Rowley, C. and Warner, M. (2008) *Globalizing International HRM,* London: Routledge.

Rowley, C., Benson, J. and Warner, M. (2004) 'Towards an Asian model of HRM: A comparative analysis of China, Japan and Korea', *International Journal of Human Resource Management,* 15(4/5): 917–933.

Rowley, C., Zhu, Y. and Warner, M. (2007) 'HRM with Asian characteristics', *International Journal of Human Resource Management*, 18(5): 745–768.

Schmitt, M. and Sadowski, D. (2003) 'A rationalistic cost-minimization approach to the international transfer of HRM/IR practices: Anglo-Saxon multinationals in the Federal Republic of Germany', *International Journal of Human Resource Management*, 14(3): 409–430.

Sisson, K. (1995) 'HRM and the personnel function' in J. Storey (ed.) *HRM: A Critical Text*. London: Routledge, 87–109.

Smith, C. and Meiksins, P. (1995) 'System, society and dominance effects in cross-national organisational analysis', *Work, Employment and Society*, 9(2): 241–267.

Storey, J. (1995) *Human Resource Management: A Critical Text*. London: Routledge.

Storey, J. and Sisson, K. (1991) 'Looking to the future' in J. Storey (ed.) *New Perspectives on HRM*. London: Routledge, 167–183.

Taylor, F. (1911) *Scientific Management*. New York: Harper and Row.

Taylor, S., Beechler, S. and Napier, N. (1996) 'Toward an integrative model of strategic international human resource management', *Academy of Management Review*, 21(4): 959–985.

Tempel, A. (2001) *The Interaction of Country-of-Origin and Host Country Effects on Human Resource Management Practices in German and British Multinational Companies*, Paper for Conference on Multinational Companies and Human Resource Management: Between Globalisation and National Business System Conference, De Montfort University, Leicester.

Thang, L.C., Rowley, C., Troung, Q. and Warner, M. (2007) 'To what extent can management practices be transferred between countries? A comparative analysis of China, Japan and South Korea', *Journal of World HRM*, 42(1): 113–127.

Tolbert, P. and Zucker, L. (1996) 'The institutionalization of institutional theory' in S. Clegg, C. Hardy and W. Nord (eds) *Handbook of Organization Studies*. Thousand Oaks, CA: Sage, 175–190.

Torrington, D. and Hall, L. (1998) *Human Resource Management*. London: Prentice Hall.

Vo, A. (2007) 'An investigation into the transfer of HRM policies and practices of US and Japanese companies based in Vietnam' in J. Burgess and J. Connell (eds) *Globalisation and Work in Asia*. Oxford: Chandos.

Vroom, V.H. (1964) *Work and Motivation*. San Francisco: Jossey-Bass.

Warner, M. (1995) *The Management of HR in Chinese Industry*. London: Macmillan.

Warner, M. (2003) 'China's HRM revisited: A step-wise path to convergence?', *Asia Pacific Business Review*, 19(4): 15–31.

Westney, D.E. (1993) 'Institutionalization theory and the multinational corporation' in S. Ghoshal and D.E. Westney (eds) *Organization Theory and the Multinational Corporation*. Basingstoke: St. Martin Press.

Whitley, R. (1992) 'Societies, firms and markets: The social structuring of business systems' in Whitley, R. (ed.) *European Business Systems: Firms and Markets in their National Contexts*. London: Sage Publications.

Whitley, R. (1999) *How and Why are International Firms Different? The Consequences of Cross-border Managerial Coordination for Firm Characteristics and Behaviour*, Presented to Sub theme 3 'Business Systems in their International Context' of the 15th EGOS Colloquium held at the University of Warwick, 4–6 July 1999.

Wilkinson, B., Gamble, J., Humphrey, J., Morris, J. and Anthony, D. (2001) 'The new international division of labour in Asian electronics: Work organisation and human resources in Japan and Malaysia', *Journal of Management Studies*, 38(5), July: 675–695.

Yuen, E.C. and Kee, H.T. (1993) 'Headquarters, host-culture and organizational influences on HRM policies and practices', *Management International Review*, 33(4): 361–383.

Zhu, Y., Warner, M. and Rowley, C. (2007) 'HRM with Asian characteristics: A hybrid people management system in East Asia', *International Journal of Human Resource Management*, 18(5): 745–768.

Appendix 1
Contemporary developments

To assist in keeping up with the rapid changes in HRM, the quality journals and newspapers should be consulted. Particularly good are *The Economist, The Financial Times, Far East Economic Review* and *International Herald Tribune*, all of which provide contemporary international and comparative insights.

There is also a range of journals, from the more academic to practitioner type that provide HRM-related information. These include those listed below, and cover specialist, general management and geographically focused journals.

British Journal of Industrial Relations
British Journal of Management
California Management Review
Employee Relations
Employment Gazette
Employment Relations Record
European Industrial Relations Review
European Journal of Industrial Relations
Human Relations
Human Resource Management
Human Resource Management Journal
Incomes Data Services
Industrial Relations
Industrial Relations Journal
Industrial Relations Services (10 journals)
International Employment Relations Review
International Journal of HRM
Journal of General Management
Journal of Industrial Relations
Journal of International Business Studies
Journal of Management Studies

Journal of World Business
Labour
Management Revue
New Technology, Work and Employment
People Management
Personnel Review
Personnel Today (5 magazines)
Work, Employment and Society

Asia Pacific Business Review
Asia Pacific Journal of Business Administration
Asia Pacific Journal of Human Resource Management
Business Management Review
China Quarterly
Korean Journal of Management

Appendix 2
Managing people – as seen in art and culture

The importance of work, employment and the management of people can readily be seen in popular culture in a variety of art and music as well as documentaries, television series and programmes, 'docu-soaps', 'docu-dramas', films and books. These forms indicate the historical and contemporary importance of employment issues, in various fashions, guises and ways. Those with a particular Asian aspect are highlighted with an asterisk (*).

Art

This includes the post-1930s paintings of the Soviet Union's Socialist Realism era, with its art depicting themes of hard work and productivity. These include works such as *In The Fields, Aeroplanes Overhead* (1954) by Sergie and Aleksei Tkachev; several by Viktor Popv, such as *Electricians* (1958), *Building Bratsk Hydroelectric Power Station* (1960–61), *Midday* (1961); Nikolai Bashakov, such as *The Metro Builders* (1967); and Feodo Baranovsky, who painted workers in agriculture and construction.

Music

Employment, work and related issues appear in popular music. This can be heard in songs from artists ranging from folk musicians, Woody Guthrie and Pete Seeger, to Merle Haggard, Steve Earle, Billy Bragg and Bruce Springsteen, amongst very many others.

Documentaries

The Money Programme (from 1966, BBC2)

The Family (1974)

The Life and Times of Rosie the Riveter (1981) Documentary on women working in American industry during the Second World War.

Final Offer (1984, Toronto) UAW twists and turns to negotiate with both UAW International and GM.

Collision Course (mid-1980s, USA) The rescue and ultimate collapse of Eastern Airlines following deregulation, unitarism and workers' participation.

*Manufacturing Miracles (late 1980s) Post-war story of Japan's Mazda, women workers, company unions, quality circles, pay.

Roger and Me (1989, with Michael Moore) The life and times of GM in Flint, Michigan; political documentary, insightful and funny.

Trouble at the Top (1990s)

Blood on the Carpet (1990s)

Working Lunch (1994)

The Factory (1995, C4) Work and life in Robinson Willey, a Liverpool gas fire factory.

People's Century (1995, BBC), episode 'On the Line (1924)' The development and impacts of the assembly line and mass production (cars, radios, biscuits) and countries (US, UK, France, Italy, Germany).

The House (1996, BBC) Covent Garden, especially with regard to negotiations on agreements.

Red Base One Four (1996, C4) Attempts by the London Ambulance Service to introduce new technology and change working practices.

The Ship (1996, C4) Management, work and employment relations at Swan Hunter shipyard in the North East of England.

When Rover Met BMW (1996, BBC) The area of recruitment and induction is especially interesting.

Hotel (1997, BBC1) The Adelphi Hotel in Liverpool, employment and management.

Airport (1999, BBC1) Behind the scenes at Heathrow airport.

Airline (1999, ITV) The workings of the easyJet airline at Luton.

Back to the Floor (1999–2001, BBC2) A series of job swaps within different sectors (e.g. rail, Gardner Merchant, Sainsbury's, Wedgwood, hotels).

Troubleshooter (2000, BBC2) Sir John Harvey-Jones returns to earlier businesses.

*Bubble Trouble (2000, BBC2) Episode on Japanese management and changes in Japan, US and the UK (e.g. Toshiba, Matsushita, Nissan).

Behind the Label: Garment Workers on US Saipan (2001) Demonstrates the exploitation of workers producing top-brand goods.

Startup.Com (2001) Charting the rise and fall of an online firm and workforce.

The Secret Life of the Office (2002, BBC2) Work at the Holiday Autos call centre under the close direction of the boss.

Boss Swap (2004, C4) The manager of a carrier-bag business switches with the boss of an advertising agency.

Strike: When Britain Went to War (2004, C4) The social and economic climate of the UK in the early 1980s, the lead up to and the strike itself.

The Miner's Strike (2004, BBC2) Partly dramatised account focusing on the experiences of those living near Hatfield Main Colliery, Yorkshire.

I'll Show Them Who's Boss (2005, BBC2) Gerry Robinson gives advice to family firms.

China Blue (2006) Made in secret on the reality of clothing production in China.

Brits Get Rich in China (2007, Ch4) Follows three British entrepreneurs as they open businesses in China despite the financial risks involved.

Phone Rage (2008, C4) Tensions in call centres and practices at First Direct, Leeds.

What Britain Earns (2008, C4) A look at earnings and whether they reflect the job's real worth to society.

Gerry's Big Decision (2009, BBC2) Three-part series with Gerry Robinson helping struggling businesses during the economic crisis (e.g. micro breweries, a chair manufacturer, a pie and pastry firm, hotel and department store chains).

Undercover Boss (2009 and 2010, C4) Executives go undercover in a range of jobs to see what needs fixing, e.g. comparing Park Resorts caravan holiday company sites, Clugson construction and maintenance, Best Western Hotels, Harry Ramsden's fish shop chain, the Jockey Club, Tower Hamlets council, Vividor recycling and waste management, the Crown Worldwide Group international relocation company, and their labour issues, including minimum wages, working conditions and redundancies.

I'm Running Sainsbury's (2009, C4) Four-part series on employee suggestions and ideas, 'The Big Pitch', offering new fast-track management training scheme for shopfloor workers.

The Trouble with Working Women (2009, BBC2) Two-part series exploring attitudes to women in the workplace, especially towards success and rewards.

Can Gerry Robinson Fix Dementia Care Homes (2009, BBC2) Two-part series on attempts to turn around privately-run care homes with problems of culture, specialist training and staff.

Dispatches (2009, C4) 'Britain's Bankers' episode; looks at complex rewards for failure.

Capitalism: A Love Story (2009) with Michael Moore. Explores the history of corporate America and impacts on lives.

Inside John Lewis (2010, BBC2) Three-part series on the Partnership, covering performance, sales and control.

The September Issue (2010, C4) Behind the scenes following US Vogue editor, meetings and conflicts.

Rhod Gilbert's Work Experience (2010, BBC2) Four-part series as the comedian tries different jobs, including refuse collector, hairdresser and soldier.

'Reality' shows

The Apprentice (from 2004, BBC2) US-derived version dishing out advice.

In Good Company (2005, ITV) Business figures sent to help smaller companies.

Risking it All (2005, C4) The struggles of a family who give up their jobs to run a guesthouse.

Dragon's Den (from 2007, ITV) Japanese-derived show involving aspiring entrepreneurs.

Tycoon (2007, ITV)

*Blood, Sweat and Tears (2009, BBC3) Young Britons learn about world fast-food production (e.g. from a tuna factory in Manos) and Indonesian labour conditions.

There are also several restaurant-themed shows that have work-related issues.

Comedies

The Fall and Rise of Reginald Perrin; The Return of Reginald Perrin, The Better World of Reginald Perrin (1976–79) Parody of office life.

The Office (2001 and 2002, BBC2) Mock 'fly-on-the-wall' documentary at a paper materials company, US and French version.

The Richard Taylor Interviews (2003, C4) Spoof recruitment for jobs, including consultants, security, bar managers, cabin crew and event organisers.

The Armstrongs (2004 and 2006, BBC2) Full of management speak; set in U-Fit, Coventry's third largest double-glazing firm.

*Mumbai Calling (2007 and 2009, ITV) Sitcom with a British Indian accountant sent to turn around his boss's newly acquired Mumbai call centre.

HR: An Appraisal (2007, BBC4) Assessment in advance of appraisal and listening to recorded client conversations.

Television dramas

The Lump (1967, BBC) Building industry working conditions; the sacking of a whistle blower on a unionised site.

Leeds United (1974, BBC) 1970 Leeds clothing workers strike, union issues and attacks on employers and union leadership that sold out.

Days of Hope (1975, BBC) Mini-series using labour history (First World War to the General Strike) to reflect on contemporary government.

Bill Brand (1976, Thames TV) New Labour MP interested in workers' control, nationalisation and power to the people at the lower level.

Play for Today 'The Spongers' (1978, BBC) How welfare cuts affected daily lives.

Boys from the Blackstuff (1982, BBC) Backdrop of work and increasing unemployment in Thatcher's Britain.

Our Friends in the North (1996, BBC) Covers the period 1964–94 and includes corruption in the Labour movement.

The Scar (1997) (with Charlie Hardwick) Drama of working-class life in the decimated Durham mining community in England.

Dockers (1999) Jimmy McGovern. Co-written by 14 of the participants in the Liverpool docks dispute.

The Navigators (2001) Ken Loach. The effects of rail privatisation on group of track workers; management and contractors in 1995.

The Battle of Orgreave (2002) Mike Figgis. A re-creation, with many veterans, of a pivotal coking plant conflict during the 1984 miners' strike.

Hearts of Gold (2000, BBC1) Based on Catrin Collier's novel, set in 1930s Wales; includes politics, feminism, unions, strike breaking.

Trouble at the Top (2003, BBC2) Latest run in the series of a range of sectors and industries.

Clocking Off (2003, BBC1) Latest run in the series set in a factory.

North and South (2004, BBC1) Based on Elizabeth Gaskell's book, in several parts; includes working life and conditions and strikes.

*Still Life (2006) Dramatisation of the social tragedy caused by the Three Gorges dam project in China.

*Wu Yung (2007) Culture and consumerism in the Chinese clothing industry.

Sex, The City and Me (2007, BBC2) Real-life experiences used to show a high-flying investment banker sidelined following maternity leave.

**Japan, A Story of Love and Hate* (2008, C4) Middle-aged, down on luck, part-time worker scraping by; showing a rigid work discipline.

The Last Days of Lehman Brothers (2009, BBC2) Inspired by the events of 2008 when one of the US's largest investment banks failed.

Monday, Monday (2009, ITV) Drama series following employees, especially in HR, at the head office of a recently relocated supermarket chain.

Films

Labour's Reward (1925)

The Passaic Textile Strike (1925)

Metropolis (1927) with Birgitte Helm
1920s vision of city and work conditions in 2000.

A Nous La Liberte (*Give Us Our Liberty*) (1932)
Satire of the assembly line in a gramophone factory: tyrannical managers, timid workers.

Black Fury (1936) with Paul Muni (originally banned in several US States)
Pennsylvanian miner forms a breakaway union, taking on owners and strikebreakers.

Modern Times (1936) with Charlie Chaplin
Classic; light-hearted view of Taylorism.

Stand-In (1937) with Leslie Howard
Efficiency expert and accountant sent to assess failing Hollywood studio.

The Stars Look Down (1939) with Michael Redgrave
Working-class life; the son of a Welsh coalminer uses his education to fight dangerous working conditions.

How Green Was My Valley (1941) with Walter Pidgeon
Welsh mining family, community and work at the turn of the nineteenth century; labour dispute and challenge owners.

The Devil and Miss Jones (1941) with Jean Arthur, Charles Coburn
  Store owner, sensing union unrest, goes undercover on the shopfloor
  to uncover union activists.
Millions Like Us (1943) with Patricia Roc
**The Most Beautiful* (1944) directed by Akira Kurosawa
  A group of women in a wartime factory producing lenses for Japanese
  planes.
Fame is the Spur (1947) with Michael Redgrave (adapted from the novel,
  inspired by Labour Prime Minister, Ramsay Macdonald)
  Labour politician's story; socialist values eroded by seductive powers
  of establishment from the 1870s to the 1930s, with strikes, hunger
  marches, depression.
Cheaper by the Dozen (1950) with Clifton Webb, Myrna Loy
  Efficiency expert tries to run his house along time-and-motion
  principles
Chance of a Lifetime (1950) with Basil Radford, Kenneth More
  Workers in agricultural machinery factory set up a co-operative, until
  a currency crisis destroys credit.
The Man in the White Suit (1951) with Alec Guinness
  Connivance of management and unions to perpetuate inefficiencies
  and halt technology.
On the Waterfront (1954) with Marlon Brando
  Union corruption on New York's docks in the 1940s with 'D&D' (deaf
  and dumb) code of longshoremen.
Hell Drivers (1957) with Stanley Baker
  Driver rebels against employer practices and dangerous schedules in
  the world of trucking.
**Windom's Way* (1957)* with Peter Finch (written by Jill Craigie)
  Dispute between workers and plantation owners in Malaysia in the
  context of political conflicts between villages, government and
  communist rebels.
*Cairo Station (1958) with Youssef Chahine
  Lives of labourers and achieving unionisation during change in Egypt.
**The Hidden Fortress* (1958) directed by Akira Kurosawa.
  A son's efforts to destroy the corporation that drove his father to suicide.
I'm All Right Jack (1959) with Peter Sellers
  Classic satire on unions, the closed shop and management practice in
  post-war British employment.
The Angry Silence (1960) with Richard Attenborough
  A worker defies a strike call in a Midlands factory, becoming a
  'blackleg' and 'sent to Coventry'.

The Apartment (1960) with Jack Lemmon
New York insurance clerk's ('Desk Number 861') relations with bosses; ideas of the Orwellian workplace.

The Battle of the Sexes (1960) with Peter Sellers
A long-serving accountant in an Edinburgh tweed-making firm clashes with US consultant/efficiency expert.

Saturday Night and Sunday Morning (1961) with Albert Finney
Nottingham engineering factory worker; alienation and pay systems (piecework).

Flame in the Streets (1961) with John Mills, Sylvia Sims
An early attempt at dealing with racism and the aspirations of immigrants in Britain via standing as a trade union shop steward.

Memories of Underdevelopment (1968)
Critique of Castro's Cuba.

The Molly Maguires (1970) with Sean Connery
Factual; Catholic miners fight Protestant employers over working conditions in nineteenth century Pennsylvania.

Company Limited (1971)
A satire on Western capitalism's effects on India as a sales manager saves the factory by creating a labour dispute.

Manthan (1976) with Naseerudin Shah
Sharp political satire of Gujurati dairy co-op workers' clash with middlemen exploiting villagers.

Harlan County, USA (1976)
Industrial conflict

Blue Collar (1978) with Richard Pryor, Harvey Keitel
Oppressive US factory jobs; car workers exploited by their own union.

Norma Rae (1979) with Sally Field
US textile worker turns union activist.

Used Cars (1980) with Kurt Russell
A satire on the US way of doing business with a car salesman drawn into an all-out trade war with a rival.

All Night Long (1981) with Gene Hackman
The frustration of demotion from the company's HQ to night manager at a 24-hour drugstore in the US.

Kentucky Woman (1983) with Cheryl Ladd
Discrimination; the role of laws in the US as a woman fights to be accepted as a coal miner.

Silkwood (1983) with Meryl Streep
The true story of a worker campaigning against a US nuclear plant; includes trade unions and union decertification.

*Congratulatory Speech (Shukuji) (mid-1980s) with R. Saotome
   A satirical film of a 'salaryman's' supreme dedication when asked to
   give a speech at the wedding of the VP's son.
The Killing Floor (1984) with Damien Leake
   Narrative of struggle of trade unionism birth in slaughter and packing
   houses in First World War Chicago.
Brazil (1985) with Jonathan Pryce
   Satirical and blackly comic look at bureaucracy.
Door to Door (1985) with Arliss Howard and Ron Leibman
   Vacuum cleaner salesmen (honest and con man) team up to hustle
   people out of money.
Wall Street (1986) with Michael Douglas and Charlie Sheen
   Ruthless mergers and acquisitions.
*Gung Ho (1986) with Michael Keaton
   Classic; xenophobic view of work and employee relations in a
   Japanese car plant in a US town.
Matewan (1987) with Chris Cooper
   Labour, ethnic and racial troubles; violent clashes with striking miners
   in 1920s Virginia.
The Secret of My Success (1987) with Michael J. Fox
   Mailroom worker in large US corporation establishes second identity
   as a wheeler-dealer company executive.
Tin Men (1987) with Richard Dreyfuss and Danny De Vito
   Classic; rivalry between unscrupulous aluminum siding salesmen in
   Baltimore in 1963.
Tucker – The Man and his Dream (1988) with Jeff Bridges
   A car designer battles to manufacture his revolutionary new
   automobile in post-war America.
Big Business (1988) with Bette Midler and Lily Tomlin
   Set of twins mismatched at birth meet again later on opposing sides of
   a property development battle.
Prejudice (1989) with Grace Parr
   Discrimination; impact of legislation in Australia; gender in
   newspapers; ethnicity in health care.
The Big Man (1990) with Liam Neeson
   Set in post-miners' strike Scottish town ravaged by unemployment, with
   an out-of-work miner forced to turn to illegal bare-knuckle boxing.
Spotswood (1991) with Anthony Hopkins
   Efficiency expert examines work practices in a Melbourne shoe factory.
Hoffa (1992) with Jack Nicolson
   History of (in)famous leader of the US Teamsters union.

Glengarry Glen Ross (1992) with Al Pacino and Jack Lemmon
Classic; view of work, teams and motivation via a day in the life of US real-estate salesmen.

Teamster Boss: The Jackie Presser Story (1992) with Brian Dennehy
One of US's political power brokers using bribery, blackmail and murder to achieve ambitions.

Of Mice and Men (1992) with John Malkovich
Steinbeck's tale of itinerant labour working the fields of California during the Depression.

Barbarians at the Gate (1993) with James Gardner
Power struggles in takeover bid against American conglomerate, Nabisco, in 1983.

Germinal (1993) with Gerard Depardieu
Help for oppressed miners, depicting a hellish coalmine at the centre of this tale of industrial exploitation.

Philadelphia (1993) with Tom Hanks
An organisation dealing with AIDS in the workplace.

*Rising Sun (1993) with Sean Connery and Wesley Snipes
The investigation of a death and nuances of Japanese etiquette at a conglomerate in the US.

*Patent Pending (1994) directed by Meera Dewan
A study of the exploitation of small farmers in India by an MNC.

Disclosure (1994) with Michael Douglas and Demi Moore
Office politics and sexual harassment in the workplace, set in a hi-tech Seattle company.

The Scar (1996) with Charlie Hardwick and Bill Speed
A former miners' union activist forms an unlikely relationship with the manager of a Durham coalmine.

Brassed Off (1996) with Tara Fitzgerald
Local communities set against the backdrop of the UK miners' conflict and pit closures.

Daens (1996) with Jan Decleir
A priest tries to improve working conditions in a nineteenth century Belgian textiles industry.

Hostile Advance: The Kerry Ellison Story (1996) with Rene Sofer
True story of sexual harassment in the US workplace and a court case to stop the advances of a fellow employee.

Mother Trucker – The Diana Kilmury Story (1996) with Barbara Williams
Truck-driver pursuing long-term disability benefits after an accident discovers that the union is in the hands of the mafia in the US.

The Full Monty (1997) with Robert Carlyle
Changes in workforce gender composition and unemployment in the Sheffield steel industry.

Ivory Tower (1997) with Patrick Van Horn and Kari Wuhrer
Big-business politics as corporate marketing director has integrity tested on joining a hi-tech computer firm.

Among Giants (1998) with Pete Postlethwaite
Camaraderie among a gang of Northern England cash-in-hand workers painting electricity pylons.

Office Space (1999) with Ron Livingstone
The tedium of corporate office life and the tedious routines of work, with redundancies in a computing company.

Pushing Tin (1999) with John Cusack
Rivalry and a new recruit unsettle a close-knit team of New York air-traffic controllers.

The Insider (1999) with Russell Crowe and Al Pacino
A whistle-blower in a tobacco company exposes scandalous practices.

Ressources Humaines (Human Resource) (2000) with mainly non-professional cast, real workers and bosses
Management trainee scheme at a French factory where the father was a worker; protest over firings, 35-hour working week.

Billy Elliot (2000) with Julie Walters and Jamie Bell
Set against the backdrop of the 1984 miners' strike.

Bread and Roses (2000) with Pilar Padilla
Illegal immigrant office cleaners, some from Mexico, in Los Angeles take collective action to secure benefits, better pay and the right to join a union.

Boiler Room (2000) with Giovanni Ribisi
The dreams of easy money of US salesmen (brokers selling worthless stock) are just as deluded as the people they fleece.

Antitrust (2001) with Ryan Phillippe
Set in Silicon Valley as software designer discovers a sinister secret behind the employer's ambition.

The Closet (2001) with Daniel Auteuil and Gerard Depardieu
Office politics and PC pieties when accountant whose job is under threat pretends to be gay in the hope that the boss will not want to appear to be discriminatory.

L'Emploi du Temps (Time Out) (2001) with Aurelien Recoing and Karin Viard
A French consultant does not tell his family he has lost his job; covers work and the vacancy it fills in people's lives.

Dirty Pretty Things (2002) with Chiwetel Ejiofor and Audrey Tautou
Behind the scenes of a smart London hotel and migrant workers who prop up the economic structure.

Night Shift (2002) with Gerald Laroche and Marc Barbe
Tensions in the workplace in a French provincial bottle factory and the atmosphere of modern factory routines.

The First $20 Million is Always the Hardest (2002) with Adam Garcia
Satirical and light-hearted take on the US dotcom boom as a top marketing man quits his job and teams up with software geeks to create a revolutionary new PC.

The Battle of Mary Kay (2002) with Shirley MacLaine
US cosmetic make-up company rivals with different views on worker motivation.

Blind Shaft (2003)
Unregulated working practices flourishing in modern China via a tale of a scam at an independent coal mine.

Life and Debt (2003) by Stephanie Black
An account of the costs of globalisation, IMF and 'free' trade using the example of the Jamaican economy.

Bartleby (2004) (modern dramatisation of Herman Melville's story)
An enigmatic clerk achieves existential autonomy by doing only the work he feels like doing in a grim office.

The Corporation (2004)
History of the US corporation, obsessed by profit, devoid of social responsibility, and exploiting.

Lost in Translation (2004) with Bill Murray and Scarlett Johansson
Colliding cultures when a US movie actor shoots a whisky commercial in Tokyo.

Mondays in the Sun (2005) with Javier Bardem
Shipbuilding job losses and the demoralising effects of unemployment (i.e. hiding true age from interview panels).

The Take (2005)
An account of how Argentinean workers responded to the 1990s economic crisis by forming co-operatives.

In Good Company (2005) with Dennis Quaid
Modern corporate capitalism; concerns a middle-aged head of sales at a US magazine that has been taken over by a large corporation with a new, young whiz kid who comes to downsize, cut jobs and boost profits.

Blind Mountain (2005)
Shows the abandonment of free health care and education in China.

On a Clear Day (2005) with Peter Mullen
Shows a bleak future after being laid off after three decades in a Glasgow shipyard.

The Aviator (2005) with Leonardo de Caprio
Presents Howard Hughes as an old-style businessman who is fanatically reluctant to delegate.

Wal-Mart: The High Price of Low Cost (2006)
The company's rise and its practices, such as pay that is so low that full-time employees are on welfare, hours of unpaid overtime demanded, illegal workers locked in every night.

Enron: The Smartest Guys in the Room (2006)

North Country (2006) with Charlize Theron
A true story of a female iron miner fighting harassment in the workplace in a pioneering lawsuit – the first ever class action for sexual harassment.

True North (2006) with Peter Mullen
Tension among Scottish trawler crew smuggling Chinese immigrants into the UK from Belgium.

The Armstrongs: The Movie (2006)
A compilation of the best of the documentary following the trials and tribulations of husband-and-wife double-glazing entrepreneurs.

7 Islands and a Metro (2006)
Life in Mumbai and tensions between different communities.

Employee of the Month (2006) with Dane Cook
Comedy about rivalry for the monthly award given to conscientious workers at a Wal-Mart-type store.

Fast Food Nation (2006) with Greg Kinnear
Working conditions in fast food suppliers and outlets; Mexican illegal workers in the US.

Ghosts (2007) acted by non-professionals
The drowning of 23 illegal Chinese cockle-pickers in Morecambe Bay in 2004, with examples of other low-paid jobs such as meat-packing, onion and fruit-picking, and gang masters.

The Pursuit of Happiness (2007) with Will Smith
The story of a homeless and almost penniless salesman whose ambition was a job on the trading floor of Dean Witter, the stockbroking firm, open to a 20-strong group of unpaid interns, only one of whom wins a trading job.

A Comedy of Power (2007) with Isabelle Huppert
An investigation of business corruption based on a disguised version of the Elf Aquitaine 1990s scandal in France.

The Heartbeat Detector (2008) with Mathieu Amalric
A corporate psychiatrist is hired to spy on the boss by a rival; the idea of 'human resources' and department treating humans as economic units.

*Tokyo Sonata (2008) with Teruyuki Kagawa
A salaryman loses his job but keeps his unemployment from his family.

Novels

Mary Barton, Elizabeth Gaskell (1848)
An account of the starving 'wage slaves' in 1840s Manchester.

North and South, Elizabeth Gaskell (1854)
An industrial novel that includes the reciprocal responsibilities of employers and employees.

The Jungle, Upton Sinclair (1906, Penguin)
An exposure of working conditions in the Chicago meat-packing industry, and the low-skilled and disadvantaged workers. It made such an impact that new legislation was introduced to reform food production.

The Financier, Theodore Dreiser (1912)
Set in the late nineteenth century, it recounts how power and wealth were achieved.

The Brass Check, Upton Sinclair (1919)
First use of the phrase 'white collar worker', describing the 'petty underlings of the business world, ... the poor office clerks ... who, because they are allowed to wear a white collar, regard themselves as members of the capitalist class'. The author understood the appeal of the office to people whose boiler-suited fathers had known nothing other than dirty factory work.

Babbitt, Sinclair Lewis (1922)
A satirical portrait of 'efficiency' and business in a medium-sized city.

Brave New World, Aldous Huxley (1932, Penguin)
The portrayal of a brutal, standardised, emotionless society dominated by mass production.

The Big Money, John Dos Passos (1937)
> The pursuit of the 'American Dream'; the dehumanising effects on workers in the age of mechanisation, 'efficiency', mass production and assembly lines.

Point Of No Return, John P. Marquand (1949)
> The turbulent inner life of a banker searching for identity in his chosen profession.

The Ragged Trousered Philanthropists, Robert Tressell (1955, Lawrence and Wishart)
> Classic novel of working conditions in the nineteenth century; important to the labour movement.

The Man in the Gray Flannel Suit, Sloan Wilson (1955)
> Executives ready to bury emotions and values in the name of corporate uniformity.

Last Exit To Brooklyn, Hubert Selby, Jnr. (1957, Paladin)
> Highlights the often brutal nature of early post-war US labour relations.

Office Politics, Wilfred Sheed (1968)
> A novel about inter-personal conflicts in a publishing house.

Smallcreep's Day, Peter Currell-Brown (1977, Picador)
> Alienation and frustration on the shopfloor.

The Fall and Rise of Reginald Perrin, David Nobbs (1977, Penguin)
> Includes a portrayal of the tedium of organisational life and parody of the self-important boss.

Survivors of Steel City: A Portrait of Sheffield, Geoffrey Beattie (1986, Chatto & Windus)
> An anthropological account of people in Sheffield after the decline of the steel industry.

Nice Work, David Lodge (1989, Penguin)
> Compares industrial and academic worlds.

Something Happened, Joseph Heller (1989, Dell)
> Black comedy about corporate culture and executives in an office.

Rivethead: Tales From The Assembly Line, Ben Hamper (1986–1992, Fourth Estate)
> A fascinating record of working life by an assembly worker in a GM plant.

The Road to Nab End (formerly *Billy Boy*), William Woodruff (1993, Ryburn Press/Little, Brown)
> Childhood in the Lancashire cotton town of Blackburn in the 1920s.

Human Resources: A Business Novel, Floyd Kemske (1996, Nicholas Brealey Publishers)
HR manager and 'strange' turn-around specialist; differences on company reorganisation.

Fictions of Business: Insights on Management from Great Literature, Robert A. Brawer (1998, Wiley)
Insights into the various human problems of management indicated in novels and plays.

You Look Nice Today, Stanley Bing (2003, Bloomsbury)
HR manager in a multinational conglomerate in Chicago involves a clinically insane temporary secretary who brings a sexual harassment claim. It illustrates how the office provides comfort, laughter, reassurance, and even drinks and food, and how unsettling it is to be sacked by a blue-chip employer.

Vodka, Boris Starling (2004, HarperCollins)
Set against the backdrop of the hasty and symbolic privatisation of a fictional Moscow vodka factory after the collapse of the Soviet Union. Depicts the way in which factory bosses reared in the planned economy turned into ruthless market-minded owner-managers and what their colleagues and workers thought. Also involves organised crime, which turns out to have been running the factory for years with the tacit consent of the authorities; the overlap between business, government and gangsterdom in Russia's move to capitalism.

Bonjour Paresse (Hello Laziness: The Art and Importance of Doing the Least Possible in the Workplace) Corinne Maier (2004, Editions Michalon)
French corporate life and how to work less hard, by a part-time economist and manager at state-owned Electricité de France. This challenges managers with a damning portrayal of the futility of work and the absurdity of organisational life.

Martin Lukes: Who Moved my Blackberry?, Lucy Kellaway (2005, Viking)
A satirical take on corporate culture born from the author's FT column documenting the travails of Chief Personal Ethics Champion at a-b global (UK) – self-aggrandising, cliché-sprouting Martin Lukes.

*Death of a Salaryman, Fiona Campbell (2007, Chatto & Windus)
Centres on a salaryman at a Japanese TV network whose life is thrown into disarray when he is fired on his 40th birthday.

London and the South East, David Szalay (2007, Jonathan Cape)
The failure of a telesales person working for a London publisher selling advertising space in publications who ends up stacking shelves at a supermarket.

Then We Came to the End, Joshua Ferris (2007)
A study of boredom and disaffection in an advertising agency.
The Imperfectionists, Tom Rachman (2010)
A group of journalists plug away pointlessly on a doomed newspaper.

Books

Shifts, A. Lively (2000, Cape)
A collection of stories on a range of occupations/work, geographical and historical locations.
Nickel and Dimmed: On (Not) Getting by in America, Barbara Ehrenreich (2001, Granta)
A look at low-wage work in the US; the author assumed a new identity working as a waitress, a shelf stacker at Wal-Mart and a housekeeper.
The No-Nonsense Guide to Fair Trade, David Ransom (2001, Verso).
Working Class Hollywood, Steven J. Ross (2002, Princeton)
A trawl through films depicting labour-capital conflicts.
Fast Food Nation, Eric Schlosser (2002)
Exposing the fast-food industry around the world; includes low-wage immigrant labour and workplace injury.
IBM and the Holocaust, Edwin Black (2002, Time/Warner)
Demonstration of technology coupled with effective bureaucratic organisation and a strategic alliance with the Nazis using Hollerith tabulating machines to conduct a census later used for other purposes.
Hard Work: Life in Low-Pay Britain, Polly Toynbee (2003, Bloomsbury)
A journalist working in, and living on, low-paid work (e.g. hospital porter).
TAXI: Cabs and Capitalism in New York City, Biju Mather (2005, The New Press)
The labour struggles of taxi drivers and the grim economics of driving yellow cabs, where most of the money goes to cab company owners and where even minor problems, such as a few tickets or a short illness, can spell disaster. It notes the former mayor's staunch opposition to organised labour. The plight of individual drivers is described, mainly recent immigrants, facing an enormous bureaucracy and strong business interests.
Bait and Stitch: The (Futile) Pursuit of the American Dream, Barbara Ehrenreich (2005)
This takes the same approach as her book above (*Nickel and Dimmed*) but this time focuses on the white-collar world – the middle managers

and account executives who toil at the corporate coalface, 'who did everything right' (e.g. earned degrees, postponed child-bearing and dedicated themselves to climbing career ladders) but who are now in trouble. The author set out to find a job as a PR director or speech-writer and found a white-collar 'netherworld' full of people who were downsized or outsourced or were still employed but heard 'the drumbeats of layoffs'; or had survived cuts but were burning out doing the jobs of two people.

Wall Street Noir, Peter Spiegelman (2007, Akashic Books)
A collection of short stories recounting the human side and wide spread of the financial world on Wall Street, tackling issues such as working conditions in a Honduras factory.

Factory Girls, Leslie T. Chang (2008, Spiegel and Grua)
Exposes the poor conditions and pay and long hours in China's factories and Dongguan's assembly lines through the workers' eyes – for example, the Yue Yuen factory employs 70,000 to make Nike and Adidas shoes – and the role of migrant labour and hence the remittance economy.

Biographies, memoirs and company histories

Aneurin Bevan, Michael Foot (1962, Paladin)
Working conditions in mining.

Twenty One Dog Years – Doing Time at Amazon.Com, Mike Daisey (2002, Fourth Estate)
Organisational socialisation and culture; the author's experience of being recruited and inducted.

Other People's Money: The Corporate Mugging of America, Nomi Prins (2004, New Press)
The tale of a Goldman Sachs insider of how Wall Street went off the rails during the 1990s stock market bubble and the pernicious effects of failure to manage conflicts of interest at the heart of the financial system.

The King of Sunlight: How William Lever Cleaned up the World, Adam Macqueen (2004, Bantam)
The story of one of Britain's greatest brand makers.

Mr China: A Wall Street Banker, an Englishman, an ex-Red Guard and $418,000,000 Disappearing Day By Day, Tim Clissold (2004, Constable & Robinson)

A shocking, funny and culturally sympathetic tale of the perils of doing business in Asia's 'wild west'. A first-hand account of one of the most expensive forays.

House of Lies, Martin Kihn (2005, Warner Business Books)

A management consultant exposes the consulting firm he worked for.

Rip-Off: The Scandalous Inside Story of the Management Consulting Money Machine, David Craig (2005, The Original Book Company)

The author (whose real name is Neil Glass) exposes his former work in consultancy and the tricks used, such as creating 'client dependency'; includes the example of the UK's NHS.

The Accidental Investment Banker: Inside the Decade that Transformed Wall Street, Jonathan Knee (2006, Oxford University Press)

An entertainingly indiscreet memoir of the author's years with large investment banks as corporate financiers lost their influence and independence to financial trading.

The Last Tycoon: The Secret History of Lazard Freres & Co., William D. Cohan (2007, Doubleday)

A tale of investment banking and Wall Street; it confirms the worst fears.

*The Romance of Tata Steel, R.M. Lala (2008, Penguin)

The rise of the symbol of India's transformation.

Appendix 3

Case studies

(A) HRM in the Asian banking and airline industries

These case studies are based on an amalgamation of employers and organisations operating in Asia. They illustrate real issues facing local and foreign firms. The first is an international bank with branches in India, China and the Gulf Co-operation Council states (GCC). The second case study is based on typical airlines operating in the same locations, but again they are not specific companies. The cases were constructed before the full impact of the post-2008 global credit crunch was felt. That event in itself can usefully be applied to the case studies, for example, in terms of the impact it will have on growth predictions, and how might organisations respond to those changes.

When answering questions or undertaking tasks, consider also the material provided in the relevant chapters of the book, as well as material in the case study itself.

Case Study A3.1

Occidental Bank of the Orient

Background

While many beneficial systems and technologies were developed in Asia long before those in Europe, there was no indigenous banking system before Western commerce arrived in the region, along with its attendant traders and colonial power structures. While banking as a structured business activity developed in Renaissance Italy, Asia relied for investment on money lenders and the pooling of family

---

resources. The South Indian *Chettiars* dominated money lending in South and South East Asia, as well as in the coastal centres of China. Overseas Chinese (predominantly Fujianese) were competitors for the Indians in South East Asia.

Banking in Asia was often in the hands of Scots, who, as a result of their education, had knowledge of financial products such as life assurance, which had been initiated in the eighteenth century by Scottish church ministers. Religion in Asia, especially Islam, reduced the scope for banking in which capital and customers' deposits were used as the basis for lending money to others. The first Islamic bank was not established until the 1970s in Dubai. So, until very recently, Western-owned banks and Western-trained bankers dominated this sector.

The case study

The Occidental Bank of the Orient (OBO) is over 100 years old. While it started business in Asia, OBO now also operates widely in Europe and North America. The bank has been in India since before independence in 1947, in China since before the People's Republic of China was established in 1949, and in the GCC since the 1950s. Further basic data about OBO concerning organisational, financial and HRM matters can be seen in Table A3.1.

Table A3.1   Occidental Bank of the Orient basic data

Type	Item	Average for year	India	China	GCC
Financial statistics	Turnover US$000s	1993 – 1997	100,000	10,000	200,000
		1998 – 2002	150,000	15,000	150,000
		2003 – 2007	250,000	50,000	400,000
	Profit US$000s	1993 – 1997	10,000	–3,000	30,000
		1998 – 2002	10,000	–3,000	10,000
		2003 – 2007	20,000	5,000	50,000
	Annual training budget (US$000s)	1993 – 1997	100	10	200
		1998 – 2002	100	15	50
		2003 – 2007	1,000	1,000	1,000

Table A3.1 Occidental Bank of the Orient basic data (*Cont'd*)

Type	Item	Average for year	India	China	GCC
Human resource management	Staff (number)	1993 – 1997	3,000	200	1,500
		1998 – 2002	4,000	300	1,200
		2003 – 2007	5,000	400	2,000
	Service (average number of years)	1993 – 1997	20	25 (but 150 staff with more than 30 years' service)	5
		1998 – 2002	22	15 (but 150 staff with more than 25 years' service)	7
		2003 – 2007	15	15 (but 200 staff with more than 20 years' service, and 150 have less than 2 years' service)	3
	Graduate trainees – length of service (years)	1993 – 1997	25	25	5 (for GCC nationals)
		1998 – 2002	25	10	7 (for GCC nationals)
		2003 – 2007	5	2	3
	Average annual pay increase (%)	1993 – 1997	1	2	2 (decrease)
		1998 – 2002	3	10	5 (decrease)
		2003 – 2007	10	15	8
	Strikes (number)	1993 – 1997	0	0	0
		1998 – 2002	1 (lasting 15 days)	0	0
		2003 – 2007	0	0	0
	Average annual sick leave per employee (days)	1993 – 1997	10	20	3
		1998 – 2002	20	5	12
		2003 – 2007	5	2	5

Note: Currency is in US$ at relevant exchange rate for the year.

India

In India the government and state-owned banks do not compete for the same type of customer (mainly industrialists and those providing high added-value services) as OBO; nor are they particularly interested in the skills and behaviour of OBO's staff, or willing to pay the salaries and benefits expected by staff in international banks. In India OBO has more than 50 branches in the main commercial centres, such as Mumbai and Bangalore, as well as in each state capital, giving wide coverage of the whole country. The typical OBO branch has a staff size of about 30, although the largest branches employ over 150 staff. Each branch offers a full range of banking services; the OBO branches in New Delhi, Mumbai, Bangalore and Hyderabad also offer investment banking and personal banking services. Even during the time of Indian nationalism (from the 1950s until the early 1990s), OBO was able to operate with few restrictions. OBO has been profitable for almost the whole time it has been operating in India.

Staff at OBO tended to join as graduates, especially those from prestigious universities such as the Institutes of Technology, and from elite social groups such as successful industrialists and politicians. A few staff joined from the feudal landowner (*zaminder*) class – especially in the non-industrialised states, such as Bihar – as trainee managers and as marketing officers where they can generate accounts through their family networks. The recruits from elite backgrounds are expected to be able to help OBO make use of their 'connections' for business development. There are well-organised training and career development plans and, until 2000, staff rarely left before retirement. The main competition for existing OBO staff used to be other international banks, especially those operating abroad and able to offer higher salaries than were then available in India. Now, however, rivals include very active privately owned Indian banks and recently arrived international companies attracted by well-trained staff, capable of providing high quality customer service and knowledge of financial matters.

Until the 1990s a typical OBO branch manager would be paid about IR10,000 per month (about US$250 at 2008 exchange rates), which was many times higher than a typical managerial post in industry or government. Additionally, OBO would have paid for a prestigious house, car, club membership and servants, as well as providing a generous expense account. Since 2000 it has been necessary for OBO to pay more than IR50,000 a month plus generous loan facilities, as well as greater benefits than those previously given, which include up to two months' bonus per year. Despite these improvements in its reward packages, OBO still finds it difficult to attract and retain staff. Although Indian nationals have reached high levels within OBO outside India itself, within the country it is expatriates who hold the top three positions (Chief Executive, Head of Retail Banking and Head of Corporate Banking). Young expatriates, who are deemed to be highly talented, are posted from other locations (especially from Europe) to India on two-year assignments to learn the practicalities of operational bank management.

Trade unions, especially the All India Trade Union Congress (AITUC), All India Bank Officers Confederation and in-house unions, such as the State Bank of India Officers Association, are powerful in the Indian banking industry. For example, in 2008 unions planned a banking sector-wide series of strikes and *hartals* (mass protests during which businesses are forced to close) against 'anti-labour' policies, which are generally seen to be those policies which are profit-driven ways of working.

Also, although not strong in OBO itself for a long time, some trade unions did have impacts. For example, trade unions prevented the use of technology such as computers, the implementation of individual incentive plans (which only came into being in 2005) and the replacement of old systems of job evaluation – a points rating system fitting jobs into narrow grades that had existed since the 1960s – with systems more suitable for modern banking, such as those based on contribution and 'broad banding' of grades.

Additionally, under trade union pressure, public sector banks were constrained to allow promotions only after between five and seven years' service at a particular level. This practice was seen to encourage 'time-serving' rather than performance in promotion. The trade unions and political parties are often linked in philosophy and many politicians (as well as HR managers) spent part of their early career as trade union activists and officials. Owners and senior managers of banks, and other organisations, believe that former trade unionists can use their experience and contacts to keep workers in order. Thus, the AITUC is linked to the Communist Party of India and would have liked to introduce similar promotion and recruitment policies within OBO as it had imposed in state-owned banks. Management had little control over who was appointed in state-owned banks because the political parties, unions and powerful local interests (such as prominent business people and landowning families) would impose quotas or lists of candidates to be recruited to enable them to direct the resources of the business in the ways they wished, as well as to be a reward (for example, to favour particular customers) to those who were loyal followers by giving them jobs.

China

OBO has not made a profit in China since the 1940s. The People's Bank of China still restricts many of the activities of OBO and places limits on the charges it can make to customers. Although OBO does not make a profit, its top management believes that the size and importance of the Chinese market is such that the bank must have a presence and remain in the country.

OBO in China has been restricted to only a few independent branches as part of the strategy to limit foreigners competing with the Chinese domestic banks. However, OBO does have a 10 per cent investment in a recently 'commercialised' (profit motivated) bank which was previously state-owned, but which has placed some of its shares on the Hong Kong and Shanghai stock-markets.

For almost 30 years OBO was forced to keep three expatriates within the country, and they could not leave without a replacement being found first. Consequently, those staff were *de facto* 'hostages', kept within China to enable the government to maintain pressure on the foreign owners of the bank to behave in the way the authorities wished them to. OBO is now under pressure to minimise the number of expatriate staff. Particularly in the 1960s and 1970s, it was often difficult to recruit and retain staff in China. Chinese nationals working for foreigners were viewed as highly suspect by their own government and could not show loyalty to foreign banks. In turn, non-Chinese banks rarely trusted their local Chinese staff. Recruitment and selection was undertaken by the national or provincial governments and thus OBO was told who it could employ.

Pay for local staff was low and special taxes (on wages, on expatriate management and other staffing costs) were levied by the government to reduce the possibilities of foreigners profiting at the expense of the Chinese. This situation pushed up the cost of employment. Pay and tax was very high for expatriates who did not wish to live under the severe restrictions on their life in China – such as needing a replacement expatriate to arrive before they could leave the country. Training was rudimentary and the use of technology was neglected until the 1990s.

In the post-1990s rush by foreign companies to enter the Chinese market came improved business opportunities, but simultaneously it became even more difficult to find and retain capable staff. The provincial government agencies and individuals with good connections recommend recruits, most of whom OBO is compelled to employ if it does not want to have problems with bank regulators, police and immigration departments. Yet, few of these imposed candidates have the necessary skills and attitudes to be good employees.

There were almost no well qualified and capable staff above the age of 35 because of the disruption in the education system resulting from the Cultural Revolution, as well as inertia in the curriculum until the 1980s. The relatively few Chinese nationals who had gained foreign qualifications sought to recoup the costs of their studies and so sought very high salaries (usually higher than those of expatriates), along with the full range of generous benefits. Even with these high rewards, senior staff still usually leave within two to five years to seek even higher paid posts with other employers based on their potential connections and skills. Junior staff seek pay increases at least twice a year because of high increases in the cost of living (resulting from high inflation rates in China) and competition for capable staff in the labour market. Those people with experience of working for foreign banks are now very attractive to other employers. OBO struggles to keep up-to-date with the external and internal labour markets, which are both rapidly changing, and so managing internal relativities occupies much of the time of local and regional HR managers.

Trade unions are not powerful locally at OBO. However, local Communist Party officials are keen to become involved whenever there is even a hint of employee relations strife as a means of increasing their power and status and as opportunities to gain employment for their friends and relations.

GCC

During the time in which OBO has been present in the Gulf region in several of the states of the GCC – Bahrain, Kuwait, Oman, Qatar, Saudi Arabia and the United Arab Emirates (UAE) – many bank branches were taken over by governments or merchant families as a consequence of nationalisation or restrictions placed on foreign banks. However, there are still strong links between OBO and its former branches within the region, and in states such as Saudi Arabia management contracts are held by the bank to provide banking expertise to locally owned banks which lead to the bank seconding staff to the GCC banks.

In the early part of OBO's involvement in the region, all its staff were foreigners – mainly a few Western expatriates with the majority being Arabs from Egypt and Palestine, along with Indians and Pakistanis. Since the 1980s the pressure to 'localise' – to replace expatriates with host country nationals (HCNs) – has been growing. At times of high oil prices the pressure for such localisation was at its lowest as governments could create public sector jobs for their citizens while the banks made high profits. When oil prices are low there is pressure to speed up localisation while profits have been lower.

OBO has never made a loss in the Gulf region since the late 1960s. One important factor in OBO's profitability has been the low cost of expatriate labour, especially those from other Arab lands and South Asia, who more than offset the cost of expensive Western expatriates. As there have been so few well experienced bankers among the HCN population, and as governments have imposed HCN employment quotas on the banking sector, those people with experience and expertise have been able to demand salaries much higher than those of expatriates at all organisational levels within OBO.

The expatriates recruited by OBO are all well trained and developed for the jobs for which they are recruited. Consequently, OBO has spent almost nothing on training and development, except to deal with specific technology, product or operational changes. If there are expatriates who are not capable of meeting OBO's needs then other, ready trained, expatriates from other foreign banks in the GCC or from India, Sri Lanka or Europe, are recruited and employed. Those people no longer capable of working at the required level are dismissed. Recruitment is mainly through headhunters, advertisement or word of mouth for senior expatriate staff, and employment agents or existing staff for middle and lower level expatriate staff. The traditional recruitment methods of the 'classic trio' – examination of application forms, references and interviews – are used to select all levels of staff.

For HCN recruitment, recommendation (from directors, major customers and existing staff) is the main way of selecting staff. In countries with a large number of potential HCN recruits (Bahrain, Oman and Saudi Arabia) OBO does not advertise as it knows through experience that there would be many thousands of applicants, a scenario that would overwhelm the HR recruitment function. Furthermore, where there are few potential HCN candidates, in countries such as the UAE, local candidates are unwilling to go through what they consider the demeaning process of applying and possibly being rejected by the expatriate staff of the bank.

As few HCNs have the necessary banking expertise, large amounts of money are spent on training these recruits and potential candidates for promotion. Indeed, many HCNs consider that they are entitled to attend courses or familiarisation events in attractive locations as part of their overall reward package. HCNs consider their connections to be of much greater use to their career development than their training and ability.

Rates of pay at OBO depend on the nationality of the staff. HCNs are paid more than all expatriates at comparable levels. Western passport holders are paid more than other expatriates, with North Americans paid the most. Indians are paid more than Pakistanis. Arabs are paid less than Asians. Although OBO Head Office imposes a standard performance management and assessment (PMA) across the organisation, the actual methods of rating staff vary depending on the location and nationality of the staff. In addition, no senior manager and no HCN is willing to be rated as other than 'outstanding'. The lower level expatriate staff tend to be rated as 'above average' and those who are rated 'average' know that they will soon be replaced. Indeed, in one state, OBO's country manager insists that a minimum of 10 per cent of expatriate staff be dismissed at the end of each PMA cycle.

In terms of employee relations, at least formally, trade unions are banned in most GCC states. Even where union activity is allowed, expatriates and many HCNs would be dismissed if they took part in any action which the bank considered harmful to its interests. Consequently, bullying is rife. The other actors in the employee relations system, the state and employers, are important and more powerful.

Case tasks/Questions

1. Discuss the ways in which HRM can make contributions to business success in each separate location.

2. What are the advantages and disadvantages of the bank using the same system of performance management and assessment in each location?

3. If pay is linked to profit, what implications will this have for recruitment and retention in each location?

4. What systems of recruiting and training staff should the bank use in each location?

Case Study A3.2

Asian airlines

Background

The aviation sector, especially in Asia, has undergone rapid changes in both 'demand' and 'supply' factors since 2000. Set out below are the developments and trends on the demand side.

With the increasing deregulation of aviation, many new airlines were set up, offering more services and making Asia the world's fastest growing aviation market. However, partly as a result of this expansion and growth, the sector faces the particular problem of a shortage of pilots. For example, in India more than 6,000 pilots will be required to meet the anticipated doubling of passenger traffic between 2007 and 2017. China's General Administration of Civil Aviation warned that in 2007 it had the capacity to train only 7,000 of the 9,000 pilots who will be required by the country's airline industry by 2010. In 2007 the no-frills Spice Jet had 15 aircraft, with 50 more on order. Alteon Training stated that India had fewer than 3,000 pilots, but would need over 12,000 by 2025, while China needs to find over 2,200 new pilots per year (which equals 40,000 pilots by 2025) just to keep up with the growth in air travel. At the same time as this growing demand the big international airlines were still training only a few hundred pilots per year.

Despite Air India (the government-owned carrier) having 800 pilots (117 of whom were foreigners), it too faces shortages, especially for Boeing 777s; this has led to the suspension of a service to London and has threatened other routes. The crisis began when the three-year contracts with 20 pilots expired in May 2008, coinciding with the retirement of another 10 pilots, who mostly flew 777s. The airline responded by implementing its own training (turning out three pilots per month) and sending young pilots for training overseas (to the US). However, this response did little to address the immediate need for experienced pilots, which the airline sought abroad. Indeed, India's dozen or so carriers have scoured the globe in search of qualified captains and struggled to train Indian pilots. Spice Jet, for example, has turned to recruiting foreign pilots, with 42 (30 of whom were American), and it expected to add 30 more in 2007.

At the same time as these demand developments, there have been changes and trends on the supply side. Demand rose just as the pool of available pilots dwindled owing to decisions by many Asian countries to reduce their air forces – a traditional training ground for commercial aviation. The profession has also become less financially attractive as airlines such as Cathay Pacific became embroiled in high-profile disputes to try to cut staff costs.

In the face of those trends, Asian airlines have taken to poaching pilots, often from each other. Philippines Airlines lost 75 pilots to overseas airlines between 2005 and 2008. Despite the unwritten 'no-poaching' pact among Indian airlines, it still occurred. As many as 31 Boeing 737 pilots left the Jet Airways low-cost arm, Jetlite (the former Air Sahara), between March and April 2008 and joined Kingfisher Airlines. It was maintained that these pilots could fly Boeing 777s after just four simulator sessions.

An obvious response to labour shortages is to increase the supply of commensurate training. Thus, the multi-crew pilot licence (MPL) was approved in 2006 by the International Civil Aviation Organisation, the sector's regulatory body, to help address the dearth of pilots, particularly in Asia. The MPL was pioneered at three aviation schools (in the Philippines, Denmark and Australia). The Philippines operation was established in partnership with Alpha Aviation, a private British group, sponsoring 59 of the 104 students. Alpha was also talking to several Asian airlines about replicating its joint venture model and expects 10 more aviation schools in the region over the next five years. As the flight operations manager at the Philippines school argued, their model is clearly very attractive to Asian and Middle Eastern airlines that are facing the same need to find more pilots.

The MPL cost US$ 80,000 in 2007; it lasts 12 months and is composed of a minimum of 70 hours' flying, including 30 hours' solo, as well as at least 180 hours spent on simulators, although the bulk is spent in class with much of the learning coming from computer-based homework. The MPL reduces schooling time by tailoring training to specific types of aircraft and using flight simulators more than aircraft. The creation of the MPL illustrates how companies facing a recruitment crunch can use a combination of technology and smart training to fill the gap.

Case studies

The organisational, financial and HRM trends and developments at the three airlines can be seen in Table A3.2.

Table A3.2 Asian Airlines basic data

Type	Item	Average for year	South Asian Airways (India)	Chunghua Airways (China)	Arabian Peninsula Airways (GCC)
Financial statistics	Turnover (US$000s)	1993 – 1997	Not yet in operation		6,000
		1998 – 2002	10,000	15,000	20,000
		2003 – 2007	50,000	25,000	40,000
	Profit (US$000s)	1993 – 1997	Not yet in operation		−2,000
		1998 – 2002	2,000	2,000	5,000
		2003 – 2007	4,000	3,000	1,000
	Annual training budget (US$000s)	1993 – 1997	Not yet in operation		1,000
		1998 – 2002	1,000	100	2,000
		2003 – 2007	4,000	2,000	3,000
Human Resource Management	Staff (number)	1993 – 1997	Not yet in operation		1,200
		1998 – 2002	1,000	1,000	1,700
		2003 – 2007	2,000	1,500	2,500
	Service (average number of years)	1993 – 1997	Not yet in operation		2
		1998 – 2002	2	3	4
		2003 – 2007	1.5	2.5	5
	Average length of pilot service (years)	1993 – 1997	Not yet in operation		2
		1998 – 2002	1.5	5	4
		2003 – 2007	3	7	4
	Average annual pay increase (%)	1993 – 1997	Not yet in operation		2
		1998 – 2002	5	7	5
		2003 – 2007	10	10	10
	Strikes (number)	1993 – 1997	Not yet in operation		0
		1998 – 2002	1 (lasting 15 days)	0	0
		2003 – 2007	0	0	0
	Average annual sick leave per employee (days)	1993 – 1997	Not yet in operation		5
		1998 – 2002	10	15	5
		2003 – 2007	15	5	5

Note: Currency is in US$ at relevant exchange rate for the year.

South Asian Airways (SAA)

SAA was created in the 1990s when India withdrew the monopoly position previously enjoyed by the government-owned Indian Airlines for domestic services within the country. The airline charges higher fares than Indian Airlines, but offers a higher quality of service and has more modern aircraft.

In terms of employee resourcing, the new airline, SAA, was not able to recruit pilots from Indian Airlines, although it was able to recruit pilots who had served in the Indian Air Force as well as from the international labour market – mainly foreigners with experience on modern aircraft types or who had reached mandatory retirement ages in their home countries. For example, British Airways pilots currently may retire at 55 (although this is gradually being increased) while the US Federal Aviation Authority has pilots forced to retire at 60. Such pilots could still fly in India where the retirement age for pilots was 62. The cabin crew at SAA are all Indian nationals who are mainly young females, many of whom are graduates seeking well-paid work with a measure of social and financial independence, which had been rare for females in India to achieve.

The number of privately owned airlines in India had rapidly expanded and there was now greater competition for pilots from the Indian, and also the international, labour markets with the expansion of low-cost airlines across many markets and countries in Asia. Even the supply of cabin crew became more limited as graduates turned away from the aviation industry and many preferred careers in financial services or information and communications technology.

There was rapid change in employee rewards. As for employee relations, the three groups of actors in the system – employees, employers and state – varied in importance.

Chunghua Airways (CA)

This Chinese airline had earlier been part of CAAC (formerly the Chinese national airline). It is now a large regional airline based in a Chinese province, flying domestic and international routes.

In respect of employee resourcing, all CA staff employed in China are Chinese. The pilots are all former military personnel and all are male. CA cabin crew have mainly been young females recruited from the military or those with good *guanxi* with the management of the airline or provincial government. With the increase in the number of regional airlines in China there is greater competition for pilots and there are no longer enough pilots coming out of the military to meet the demands of the aviation industry as a whole.

CA placed a large order for new aircraft and knows that it will not be able to recruit enough Chinese pilots. It is therefore considering recruiting non-Chinese flight deck crew. However, there are grave concerns about security (as there are many sensitive areas over which the government does not wish foreign pilots to fly), as well as the cultural and employment consequences of employing foreigners at CA. For example, foreigners will want higher salaries and benefits such as housing, which the Chinese are rarely granted at present. At the same time cabin crew recruitment has become more difficult as more young females, especially those with the desired language and social skills, now prefer to work for international employers in the major cities of the province. Other Asian airlines have recruited cabin crew from poorer countries, such as Thailand and the Philippines, where well-educated young females are willing to work for low wages in the service industries. However, while there are many potential recruits with English language skills, few have fluency in Chinese languages.

Employee rewards were rapidly changing, while employee development was in the context of tight labour markets.

In the area of employee relations, we can note the following. In terms of management style, top management and pilots expect their commands to be obeyed without question, even in areas outside their responsibility or competence. Employees may belong to a trade union, but the union must be part of the All China Federation of Trade Unions. This is a government-controlled organisation and will not support employees against management. Within CA itself employee relations have apparently been good, but the high rates of staff turnover (more than 20 per cent a year for pilots and management, above 25 per cent a year for cabin crew and office staff, and over 30 per cent of licensed engineers leave every year) suggest that there are hidden problems. Indeed, in early 2008 several airlines experienced disputes with pilots over contracts, recruitment and training bonds which would prevent pilots from moving within 99 years of joining.

Arabian Peninsula Airways (APA)

APA was established in the late 1990s by the country's government to reduce dependence on the airlines of neighbouring states and the international airlines based in the West.

With regard to employee resourcing, recruitment at APA has been based on employing expatriate pilots and cabin crew from Western airlines. The pilots had been laid off by airlines during economic downturns in their home countries or were faced with many years of 'sitting in the right hand seat' as first officers while waiting for a captain vacancy to occur. Opportunities for promotion within airlines depend on serving time as a first officer (in the right hand seat of the flight deck) before being considered for training and proving capability as a captain in the left hand seat.

Cabin crew at APA were usually young females who were attracted to the lifestyle available in the tax-free and exciting social environment. The airline specified age, physical looks, marital status and nationality in its cabin crew recruitment and selection policies. Very few local citizens were employed as pilots at APA and even fewer as cabin crew. Indeed, no local females sought employment at APA. Fewer than 10 per cent of the APA cabin crew are male and over 90 per cent of the crew are from European countries. When female staff reach 30 years of age they are dismissed unless they have reached senior cabin crew ranks. The most junior level of cabin crew must remain unmarried – only those in cabin crew supervision may be married. When the airline started flying to the US it decided not to recruit North American cabin crew as it would have had to radically change recruitment policies to comply with equal opportunity and anti-discrimination legislation. Even within the European Union (EU) APA recruitment policies would be against many laws, but as the employment is outside the EU the airline has been able to continue its local practices. Nevertheless, under pressure from EU airlines, claiming unfair competition (younger, single employees tend to be cheaper to employ than older, married staff), the EU started to pressurise APA for these discriminatory recruitment and selection practices to be addressed. Meanwhile, the twin pressures of competition from other Asian airlines for pilots and fewer lay-offs in Western airlines has reduced the supply of potential flight deck crew.

Regarding employee rewards, although salaries are still tax free, expatriate employees have to be housed within the country and the cost of accommodation is now very high and costs the airline 30 per cent of its wage bill. Typically, international full service airlines have one third of operating expenses accounted for by staff costs, but being 'typical' means one less competitive advantage to the APA.

Employee development is in the context of the tight labour market, and is especially for key staff in the sector.

Employee relations take place within the national context. The three groups of actors – employees, employers, state – vary in importance and power given the changes in the national and local political, economic, social and technological context in which they operate.

Source: Minder (2007); Pepper (2007); *Professional Pilot News* (2006); Economist.com (2008).

Case tasks/Questions

1. What are the similarities and differences in likely recruitment policies for pilots in each airline?

2. Why has each airline appeared to seek young females as recruits for cabin crew jobs?

3. Airlines always have to train pilots in their company operating procedures and often have to train on the specific airline type used but none of these Asian airlines undertake basic pilot training. Why is basic training not undertaken?

4. Is it fair business practice for companies to avoid meeting employment and other legislation by basing staff off-shore?

(B) HRM practices and changes in Asia

Case Study A3.3

Employee resourcing – Wong Yu Pharmaceutical and Textile

The problems

Staff turnover is increasing in many Chinese organizations due to the high demand for skilled labour due to the expanding economy. This goes against the traditional Chinese concept of *guanxi*. As a result, many companies are having to rely on expatriate labour, which is, in many instances, not accepted by the existing skilled workforce. This case examines an organization that hired a number of expatriate staff to overcome its shortages due to the increased demand for its products, the dissatisfaction of staff as a result of the expatriates being employed, and the turnover that resulted from this employment decision. The strategies adopted, resulting in a move to staff development and localization to reduce this turnover, are discussed.

Wong Yu Pharmaceutical and Textile is a major manufacturer of prescription and non-prescription Western and traditional medicines, as well as chemical-based textiles, and is located in Southern China. It commenced operation as a small, family-run business in the early 1970s, providing traditional remedies to local people, and has prospered as the economy in China has expanded and become more market-driven. Today, it employs in excess of 110 staff, many of them with appropriate qualifications in chemistry and research. Management of the organization at the different levels has been through promotion of suitably qualified staff, who were encouraged to obtain external management qualifications to allow them to take management roles within the organization.

Many of the employees have been with the company for a number of years and are extremely loyal to the organization. Conditions under which the employees work are excellent, with staff being paid above average wages, with end-of-year bonuses. All staff are made to feel as if they are part of an extended family and respect the management and, in turn, their autonomy to undertake research with new drugs and textiles is also acknowledged. This has provided Wong Yu Pharmaceutical and Textile with an entrepreneurial spirit and initiative, allowing them to compete more on innovation and quality products, as compared to organizations who produce carbon copies of overseas products, or are franchised to produce products at a cheaper unit price, due to the cheap labour cost in China.

Wong Yu Pharmaceuticals and Textile had experienced a major growth in business in the last 12 months, due to the expanding economy and increased interest by a number of countries in purchasing comparatively cheap but high quality and innovative products from the Chinese market. As part of this expansion it was necessary to increase the staff numbers and restructure the organization to achieve efficiencies in scale and to ensure that all divisions were achieving their new targets. However, due to the shortage of appropriately qualified and skilled management and other staff, and the need to put on more staff urgently, the organization used a recruitment firm to source staff from areas outside China. As a result of this, a number of expatriates, both chemical and management professionals, were hired to take certain positions of responsibility in the company. The mix of these people came from various parts of the world, with two from Singapore, two from Europe, one from the USA, and one from Australia.

Unfortunately, as the owner/manager filled the new positions in the organization, he found that many of the older and more experienced staff were giving in their resignations. As there was no shortage of positions in the industry, many were taken up by competitors almost immediately. This left a large gap in the key management and research staffing areas.

After discussing the problem with the line managers, many of whom had been working with the company for in excess of five years, to try to stop the flow of talent from the company, he was no further advanced as to the reason for the exodus of staff. He then found, through various communication channels, that a number of those managers interviewed were also considering other job offers. However, they would not give a reason as to why they wished to depart, despite the good communication that was thought to be present in the company.

In an attempt to solve the problem, he approached the HR manager, who had been a relatively recent appointment, and asked her to:

1. Determine the reasons for this sudden rash of departures, and

2. Develop strategies to halt, or at least reduce, the numbers of staff from all levels and departments leaving.

Despite the apparent commitment of staff, and pressure put on them to give reasons for their loss of commitment and dedication to a company that had taken care of them as if they were a family unit, turnover was still occurring. If it continued for too long a time, the creativity and initiative that was present would gradually dissipate, leaving the organization as just a production factory. Retention was then considered to be the priority issue, followed by methods to ensure the skills were maintained and further developed.

The HR manager had previously worked in a major manufacturing company, and had appropriate qualifications in HR and psychology. She had not, however, had much experience in dealing practically with retention issues. She did realize, though, that HR issues were becoming a high priority in Chinese organizations, with staff recruitment coming from a diminishing pool of skilled and qualified labour, and it was becoming increasingly difficult to retain staff who were being poached by competitors providing increased pay and better conditions of employment.

Having had experience in research, the first task that the HR manager performed was to revise her understanding of the literature on turnover and retention, and to discuss the issues with HR management staff in other industries. Many of them were having similar problems. She found that substantial work and research had gone into this area of management, in both China and western countries. She also realized that due to the increasing liberalization of the Chinese economy, many employees were becoming familiar with western styles of organizational structure and western attitudes. This was particularly the case with the staff who had studied for higher qualifications. The conclusion that was drawn was that the *guanxi* concept of loyalty and commitment to management was declining.

She then undertook a confidential survey of staff to see if there were any major areas of discontent. The survey revealed that there was some resentment with the company's decision to hire expatriate labor into the organization, and place them in senior roles over many of the staff who had been there a number of years. The lack of internal development of staff was also a cause of dissatisfaction, and it was found that many of the company's competitors were providing substantial training and career development opportunities for their employees.

Additionally, the conditions to which the expatriates were entitled were causing dissatisfaction among the staff. These conditions included higher remuneration, assistance with accommodation as well as assistance for those with family, such as subsidization of educational expenses. The feeling within the long-term employees was that preference was given to the foreign talent, and they could see no long-term role for themselves.

These additional benefits, coupled with the higher positions given to the expatriates and the feeling of discontent, caused the internal labor market to consider that there was an inequity in treatment. Thus the staff considered that their positions would gradually be controlled by people who they considered to be outsiders, resulting in a loss of status to their roles in the organization and the wider community.

A number of random interviews were then held with select staff to determine if there were any deeper reasons for the resignations. These interviews revealed another aspect of the changes, which was that the organizations did not have in place a development strategy to provide staff with suitable training, allowing them to increase their position and status in the company. It was considered that internal recruitment was declining.

Following the research undertaken by the HR manager, a number of suggestions were proposed. Here external research had found that many multi-nationals were adopting a policy of localization of staff, by using expatriate labour as mentors to the local staff in management and through the introduction of new methods of research.

Additionally, the conditions and benefits being paid to expatriates were gradually shrinking. Localization was a factor in this, as was the increasing expatriate immigration into China. This increased immigration allowed organizations to offer rates of pay more in line with local workers.

The solutions

The HR manager wrote a position paper to Mr Wong, the owner of the company, with the following recommendations:

1. An examination of the pull-and-push factors be undertaken to determine the reason for the departure of staff. This examination was to include a regular staff survey as well as an external review of competition from other companies.

2. Use the expatriate staff as mentors, to train the local staff with the skills being brought into the organization from other countries. As the expatriate staff were on contract, after their term was completed, local staff would be trained to take over their roles.

3. If expatriate staff wished to remain within the organization after their initial term had completed, they were to be offered a contract more in line with the pay and conditions of local staff.

4. An internal staff development strategy was to be introduced, with any relevant training subsidised by the organization. In return for this training, staff were obliged to remain within the company for a particular period of time, to repay their training debt.

5. To ensure that the learnt skills were not wasted, trained staff were to be placed in positions that utilized the learnt skills.

6. Introduction of a training scheme to ensure that staff were multi-discipline within the various departments.

7. A restructure of the organization take place, in which three distinct areas were to be formed: technical career paths, management career paths, and administrative career paths. This would allow distinct areas for development, and better options for internal staff and as an attractor of staff to the company.

Next

Following the presentation of the position paper giving the above recommendations, the following initiatives were introduced.

1. A staff satisfaction survey was brought in to determine what was pushing staff away from the organization or pulling staff to look for other jobs. The initial survey found that money was not the major factor. It was more the perceived inequity of new staff being put in positions of greater authority than staff who had been working with the organization for many years. The pull factor was the chance of greater career path development in another company. Examination of the competition revealed that many companies had adopted a strong localization policy, only bringing in expatriate staff as a short-term solution, when specific expertise was required. This ensured that a part of the *guanxi* concept was acknowledged and recognized as a major factor in staff retention.

2. Expatriate staff were advised that their positions would not be renewed on the current conditions after the cessation of their current contracts. They would, however, be able to apply for positions if they were available, but conditions of employment would be comparable with those of the current workforce. The long-term result of this was that a number of the expatriate staff did return home, but a small number decided to stay within the company.

3. In recognition of recommendations 4 and 7, a number of training programs relevant to the company were investigated, and a training provider contacted to do an analysis of staff training needs. This analysis determined a number of suitable training programs that would improve the skills of employees in the areas of technical, management, and administrative fields. After some discussion, it was decided that the opportunities would be open to all staff, with the provision mentioned in recommendation 4 which stated that employees would need to give their loyalty to the organization for a particular period of time following completion of their training. If they left before this time, partial payment was to be given to the company for the training received.

4. Research by the HR manager, through discussion with staff, found that a number of staff were under-utilized. To ensure that staff with specific skills were given the opportunity to use those skills, a program was introduced to allow staff to work on special projects, when available, thus ensuring that those skills were relevant and useful to both the employee and the employer.

   Additionally, special project teams were set up to acknowledge staff who had undertaken training, thus reinforcing the recognition of training programs. This had the added benefit of ensuring that employees were given recognition as part of the family, reinforcing their loyalty to the firm, and assisting in building high organizational commitment. Although not guaranteeing that newly-trained staff would be placed in positions that fully used their skills, the value of this learning was enforced through the intrinsic reward factor of recognition and status.

5. The restructure of the company was more complicated. A partial solution was adopted in which staff were allocated into particular streams, with the requirement that they be prepared to work across departments if needed. This had the advantage of ensuring that employees, over time, became multi-disciplined and of more value to the company.

Management decided to adopt the plans suggested by the HR manager, with the exception of the complete adoption of recommendation 5. Their view was that there were not sufficient roles within the company to ensure that all people could be placed in jobs which fully utilized their new skills. However, partial recognition through the project teams and adequate acknowledgement of the training received through internal rewards was considered to be at least a partial commitment by the company to increase the status of the employees. Also, as mentioned, a multi-disciplinary team gradually began to take place over time, increasing the value of the human resources within the company.

As a result of the initiatives, staff turnover did reduce, although it was still above average for the industry. Generally, however, conditions were more settled, with the trend of turnover decreasing.

Lessons learnt from this study are that employees do appreciate the value that the organization places on them. In the Chinese culture, the concept of *guanxi*, as recognized by the intrinsic rewards and promotion, along with the special projects as reward for skills development, resulted in reduced turnover, as the employees felt that their loyalty was now being rewarded by equivalent loyalty by the company. Thus the increased job satisfaction and employee involvement through skills recognition increased commitment and reduced the number of staff looking for job alternatives.

Source: Davies and Xinyan (2009)

Case Study A3.4

Employee rewards – Guangzhou Enterprise

This case entails a joint venture company which is located in the province of Guangdong. This JV was formed by a Chinese partner (its core business being in the metals industry and was established in 1958) and foreign partners from Europe. The core business of the European partners is in the chemical industry. This JV was formed in the year 1994 and after two years of promising performance, the investments were substantially increased with the Chinese side contributing assets and the foreign parties injecting cash in 1996. For ease of reference, let this JV be called the Guangzhou Enterprise. The JV agreement stipulated that management would be the purview of the foreign partner and the chairmanship of the Board would be a nominee of the Chinese side. There was a mix of nominations from both sides for the various departmental head positions.

The case study

In 2003, the foreign partner decided that a change in management was needed to bring the Guangzhou Enterprise onto a higher growth path and profitability level. From the SWOT analysis done, it was felt that the way by which the management team performance was appraised and rewarded needed an overhaul. The then prevailing practice was that the JV board would decide the quantum to be set aside from the annual net profits of the JV to be distributed to the employees. This quantum would be arithmetically divided by the headcount who had served the complete calendar year of service. The end result is that everyone would be receiving the same absolute quantum regardless of any other factor, including seniority of position or performance. This was considered to be counter-motivational to the senior level staff as their actions/decisions would have the biggest impact on the company's profits or business and yet, in terms of rewards, they are receiving the same absolute quantum as everyone else.

Given the circumstances of the case, the question that arose was why was there no feedback from the management level staff since this directly affected them? The answer lay in the Chinese way of doing things when it was under the planned economy days and, considering the collectivist culture of the Chinese, no one would want to be seen to be rocking the boat. Neither would anyone wish to be seen as being self-centred.

Management decision – change

The decision taken and supported by the China corporate management team was to change the way employees of the Guangzhou Enterprise were rewarded. The principle that was considered was 'rewards by performance and position'. This was clearly a significant departure from the old way of doing things. The old way of granting everyone the same absolute quantum was a legacy which was brought forward from the state-owned days where the concept of fair treatment was equated with equal treatment, regardless of personal background or individual capability or responsibility weightage or contribution. This thinking is very much aligned to post imperial China's era of Communist ideology, which emphasizes collectivist values and systems.

Is change an inevitability?

In this particular instance, this change can be described as a major one. The old way was being totally discarded and a conceptually new one put in its place. The largest impact is that the change would be seen as one which brings benefit to a minority and, at the same time, perceived as being at the expense of the majority. If one were to look at any commercial organization, it will invariably be the case where general staff (both office and operatives) will far outnumber the managerial and senior level staff. As long as the total pie is not enlarged, and when one changes the distribution rules from an equal to an unequal sum game, it will certainly be seen as robbing Peter to pay Paul. However, if the aim was to reward only a smaller percentage of the population proportionately more, then it would look like robbing Peter, James, and John to pay Paul more handsomely.

On the surface, this will appear like a 'no-can-go' situation as it would create a huge uproar from the shop-floor. However, on a closer and deeper examination of the matter, the merits of the case for change and the attendant benefits to be gained from its successful implementation were greater than the setbacks that could arise.

Factors favoring proposed change

In planning for the change, it was found that there were certain factors that worked to its advantage. Firstly, this proposed change effectively amounts to two forms of differentiating rewards payment. One is that the better contributors would proportionately be better rewarded and next, the more senior staff would be given weighted consideration. The rationale for this was straightforward: that decisions made by senior position holders would cause a greater impact on the profitability and growth of the company. Even assuming that the strategic direction of the company had been determined and thus taken as given, the management team of the company still needs to undertake the planning, organizing, co-ordination, and implementation activities before success could be achieved. In this way, the management team and senior staff would be motivated to attain the given key performance indicators.

Secondly, it is aligned to the reward practices of the foreign partner's global compensation philosophy, which essentially relates rewards directly to contribution. Thirdly, besides aligning rewards to individual contribution, the financial performance of this JV business unit also influences the quantum of bonus to be distributed. Fourthly, since this was viewed as a major change, its successful implementation could lead to the opening of doors for other changes to be made in the future. In this instance, the resistance factor is a mental barrier rather than one arising from technology or lack in knowledge.

Lastly, rewards can be easily measured as performance is largely driven by financials and thus nothing would be guaranteed. The only way to achieve an increase in annualized earnings is to ensure that the agreed financials are correspondingly enhanced.

Hurdles to clear

On the other hand, there were also other factors that tend to work against the grain of the proposed scheme. In the first instance, the scheme could be seen to benefit the senior staff at the expense of the more junior staff. This could lead to organized resistance and the worst case scenario would be a demonstration being organized and staged at government offices or at the parent company premises of the Chinese partner. For this to happen would be unthinkable and the Chinese partner would not accept this even as a remote possibility, let alone having to give it any consideration. This makes this particular hurdle an even higher one to clear.

Secondly, since bonuses are under the purview of the board, there is a possibility that the board members appointed by the Chinese side might not be adequately convinced of its merits to agree to the change.

Placing the hurdles under close examination, it was clear that both the costs and risks of failure were high. It thus became even more pressing that the solution plan addressed these areas in great detail, leaving no stone unturned. In change management parlance, for this particular issue identifying change agents and creating a change imperative takes on added emphasis. We were thus acutely aware that not only did we need a solution to be of superior quality but, more critically, the implementation needed meticulous attention and a watchful monitoring.

Creating an imperative

From various literature on change management, the foreign partner knew that an imperative would only exist when the cost of staying at the current state could be shown to be greater than the costs of making the change. This was the challenge that the writer faced when dealing with this case: could a convincing case be made out that staying at the status quo would be more painful in the longer term. In preparing the case, certain underlying conditions needed to be satisfied to ensure a smoother implementation subsequently.

1. Since all employees were eligible for a bonus payment and this affected livelihood, it also means that everyone must be made aware of the change and convinced as to why the change would make things better for at least most of the people, if not all. If an environment of dissatisfaction with the prevailing state could be created and a promise of a brighter future state could be envisioned, then acceptance would be virtually assured.

2. It was also clear that if the bonus pie were to remain the same as previous years, then to redistribute it such that a small class got the larger slice could only lead to doom from the word go. So a financial analysis of the likely business growth in the following three years was necessary to gauge whether the timing of implementation was going to be effective.

3. The immediate resistance hurdles were identified to be the union and the Chinese nominees on the board. Without these two parties being convinced of the greater advantage of this proposed change, nothing else would matter. Following this, other parties or agencies that needed informing and to be won over were the management team, Labour Bureau (to pre-empt any potential dispute which might be brought for mediation), and the general employee body (in that order).

4. As a test case, it was thought that talking to the HR and finance heads would provide an indicator of things to come. The reason

for selecting these two individuals was that the HR head was also the Union Chairman and the Party Secretary concurrently. For readers of this case study who are used to Western management concepts, this would certainly appear confusing or even incomprehensible as there was definitely a conflict of interests. But this is a Chinese corporate situation with Chinese characteristics; so one needs to be mindful of this fact. So let us just put the conflict of interest angle aside and focus on the case. The inclusion of the finance head as a target change agent is that he knows the business plan and the budget, both annual and three-year planning. If conditions were to be considered favorable, resistance from the shop-floor staff would be considerably lessened. As for the HR head, his Union-hatted role would provide an alternative channel for communications.

5. Looking at the case from up close, it was apparent that the success of this entire change project hinged on only one consideration, i.e., the question of fair play. In so far as the board was concerned, the change should not cause unhappiness and disruption to business; as far as the union and government were concerned, there should be no widespread grievances and, as far as the employees were concerned, they should not be getting a smaller bonus quantum relative to previous years. For all four parties (board, government, union and employees) the pie should be adequately larger so that employees would not view it as being robbed in order to reward the more senior ones.

Planning for success

From an industry standpoint, we were aware that in any change situation, its success was very much dependent upon the quality of its implementation. However, where the quality of solution is just as high, then the chances for success will be greatly enhanced.

In order to create the sense of urgency and resolve for people to take the plunge, we had first to create a selling line, i.e., a story that could turn itself into the tipping point. At the onset, effort was concentrated on poring through the HR statistics, payroll figures, job grading and salary system, performance appraisal system, and employee dispute records to secure a thorough understanding of the situation and avoid potential pitfalls.

In the midst of it all, the writer then found that the concept of equality could be looked at from different perspectives. At that point in time, in so far as the employees, managers, union and board of the Guangzhou Enterprise were used to, equality meant the 'same absolute amount of dollars or RMB' that counted. However, there was also the alternative of looking at equality being the same denomination of months of salary, e.g., every employee would get one month salary as bonus, and this meant looking at the same thing from a different angle. Be it a conceptual Quality of Solutions, Quality of Implementation, Success, or arithmetic or logic standpoint that one used to look at this matter, it would certainly appear that this was one equitable way of determining things. And this certainly looked like a solid selling platform upon which our story line would stand. However, there was still no assurance that the concerned parties would be swung in favor of this argument. They possibly could steadfastly hold on to the view that the absolute amounts had varied and this was a departure from the status quo and was thus not acceptable. Thus, a fall back argument was needed.

After further searching, an effective solution was found. This lay in the concept of 'pay for job' and this was not a revolutionary idea in so far as the Chinese industry landscape went. In fact, before the 1978 reform policy was enunciated by China's then paramount leader, Deng Xiao Ping, a discrepancy already existed between the salaries of a General Manager versus that of a shop-floor operative staff, albeit the difference was not pronounced. When foreign enterprises made their foray into China, this discrepancy widened. This meant that there was already general acceptance that a position with higher responsibilities would command a higher salary. So the argument to be used to back this proposed change would be predicated upon this concept and the argument was that for the same contribution, the bonus should be corresponding to salary level rather than absolute quantum. As a matter of fact, using the absolute quantum method to reward all employees was not only archaic but unfair to those holding more senior level appointments. The degree of unfairness was accentuated the higher one went up the corporate ladder. The strength of the argument therefore lay in the unfairness to the other group of senior employees. On the basis of this back-up argument, the proposed changed now appeared even stronger.

The next step was to test this out with the HR and finance heads concurrently. Not unexpectedly, when this idea was put forth to the two of them, it was the HR head who raised objections as he persisted in holding onto the view that the resulting amounts would create issues as this was a departure from prevailing practice of doing things. What is interesting about this objection from the HR head is that he would certainly be a potential beneficiary of the proposed change once this was implemented.

Despite this, he raised his objection. This would be certainly baffling to the Western mind. The explanation of this queer incident lies in knowing his background. For decades, he had been a party cadre and steeply ingrained with the Chinese society value system, which placed the emphasis on the group (which can be the country, society, or organization) ahead of the individual. Being prepared for such an outcome, the writer then clarified with him if all employees were paid the same salary. The answer was clearly a 'no' and he was requested to explain the rationale for this salary disparity. He explained that it was owing to the differences in responsibility of the different positions in the company. It was, however, pointed out to him that the salary disparity was to recognize not just the responsibility weightage factor, but also that decisions made by more senior level employees would have a greater impact on the company's profitability and growth. Bringing the point a step further, decisions did not just have an immediate impact on business operations, but more critically, on future profits as certain decisions are of a long-term strategic nature. This point was emphatically put across as it was felt that the general employee body would not see this and they needed to be aware of this.

As for the finance head, he confirmed the business growth projections. The general economic conditions prevailing at that point in time were such that the country as a whole was on an accelerated path of infrastructural expansion. Arising from this, the JV stood to gain as their production was used to support the metals industry. The financial projections showed that the bonus pie would enlarge substantially and that employees as a whole would be able to enjoy a higher quantum all round. The more senior ones would certainly end up getting substantially more than previously. This first step forward could thus be said to be resoundingly well received as both the HR and finance heads went away with the conviction that the change was for the better overall.

Since these two managers were both appointees from the Chinese side, they therefore were made the change champions to undertake the initial dialogue with the board chairman. In a subsequent formal meeting with board members and the union leadership, there was not even the slightest of resistance or objection. It is believed that the talk with the two managers was the tipping point.

With the union and the board standing behind the Guangzhou Enterprise management, the follow-on communications process to the Labour Bureau and employees was a mere formality. However, the case did not end here. As could be seen from here, the breakthrough was that the company had gained acceptance from all parties concerned that the new bonus system was salary-based and not quantum-based. This was a major psychological breakthrough in the sense that, from a quantum perspective, there was a disparity although from a salary denomination perspective it looked the same. On this basis of doing things, in the following year another departure was made. The second year's bonus payout (i.e., using the new system) was singularly based upon absolute quantum without any reference to salary denomination. The reason for the avoidance of a reference to salary denomination is to preclude any dispute that the company used individual salary as a determinant in the grant of a bonus award. It could now be seen that there could be occasions that an effective solution might require a two-step approach instead of a singular step.

Conclusion

This case brought forth one most important lesson: i.e., the Chinese mind-set can be changed if one could find a different perspective of looking at things and this could prove to be a viable alternative to what they had. In order to achieve this, one needs to adopt a painstaking attitude in understanding their way of doing things, the historical precedent and cultural heritage, and the measurement standards used. Coupled with this is also the need to know the path of resistance, who are the likely sources of resistance. As can be seen from this case study, the entire proposal rested on building the chain of arguments around one initial concept, i.e., pay for position. This can be likened to an advertising campaign which is built upon one commercial theme and all the print and tele-media then revolve around it. The rest will be dependent upon identifying the target audience that mattered and gaining their confidence, understanding, and acceptance.

Source: Chin Seng Koh (2009)

Case Study A3.5

Employee resourcing and employee development – Z-Park Industrial Zone

In 2006, Zhongguancun Science Park, also known as Z-Park, was the largest and oldest among the 53 hi-tech industrial zones in China. By the end of that year, Z-Park generated close to $86 billion in revenues while exports accounted for almost $13 billion (Beale, 2007). These results propelled Z-Park to the status as the most important center for further economic growth of Beijing. By 2007, more than 18,000 companies were operating in the park, including about 1,550 foreign clients (Beale, 2007), making China's Silicon Valley the biggest concentration area of intellectual capital and information resources in the country. Graduates of Beijing and Qinghua University, as well as research institutions including the Chinese Academy of Sciences and the Chinese Academy of Engineering, were well represented in Z-Park. In fact, as many as 37% of the academicians coming from these two academies worked and lived in the science park (Administrative Committee of Zhongguancun Science Park, 2002f).

However, despite attracting the most sophisticated intellectual talent in the world, human capital might prove to be Z-Park's weak link in the long run. Though highly trained and educated, many workers at Z-Park showed little loyalty toward their employers and switched to competitors with a vision of a higher paycheck. With the workforce becoming more mobile, ambitious, and independent, employers at Z-Park were having a tough time getting the employees commit to the company. While job hopping is generally regarded as negative for the economy, some believe that employee mobility may actually encourage productive innovation in certain types of industries. The question remains whether the increased employee turnover in Zhongguancun is going to make or break the park's success.

Background

Z-Park was first founded in 1980, when a researcher at the Chinese Academy of Science, Chen Chuxian, returned from a trip to Silicon Valley in California. Inspired by one of the most productive hi-tech zones in the United States, Chuxian opened the Advanced Technology Service Association, the first Chinese scientific and technological consulting firm run by a civilian and sponsored through private funds. Intrigued and attracted by the support of the Chinese Academy of Science as well as the central government, many talented scientists started to flow to the Haidan District, facilitating the growth of new ventures. In 1988, the municipal government in Beijing officially recognized the area known as Zhongguancun Electronic Street in the Haidan District as the 'Beijing Experimental Zone for the Development of New Technology Industries', a national innovation base with great potential (Beale, 2007). In 1991, Beijing Shangdi Information Industry Base, the first incubator in Zhongguancun Science Park, was set up. However, it was not until June 1999 that the State Council of China officially approved the 'Note of request to expedite the building of Zhongguancun Science Park for the purpose of implementing the strategy of rejuvenating the country through science and education'. The council also instructed the municipal government and the Ministry of Science and Technology to speed up the construction process of Zhongguancun Science Park (Administrative Committee of Zhongguancun Science Park, 2002f) and to build it into the first state-level hi-tech innovation zone.

In 1999, three important clients, Beijing Science Park Bidding Co. Ltd., Beijing Science Park Construction Co. Ltd., and Beijing Science Park Guarantee Co. Ltd., were brought in to expedite the construction of Zhongguancun Science Park. By the end of the millennium, there were approximately 1,100 wholly foreign-owned companies as well as joint and cooperative ventures in Zhongguancun Science Park, accounting for close to 20% of the total enterprises (Wang, 2003). The investment by foreign-funded business had reached almost $3.5 billion USD, and the foreign exchange earned by export accumulated to $820 million (Administrative Committee of Zhongguancun Science Park, 2002b). The IT industry in China was dominated by foreign-invested enterprises, particularly in the computer manufacturing and software sectors. Even though the US firms used to control the software market, with the growing technology, capital, and managerial experience, the competitiveness of Chinese enterprising in Z-Park was expanding (Wang, 2003). With economic growth averaging at over 30% per year, Zhongguancun Science Park's share contributing to the economic growth in Beijing increased to more than 50% of this amount (Administrative Committee of Zhongguancun Science Park, 2002b).

On January 1, 2001, the municipal government in Beijing promulgated 'Regulations of the Zhongguancun Science Park', which provided the legal basis and guidelines for Z-Park's future expansion. In order to encourage further development of hi-tech enterprises in the

Chinese Silicon Valley, the central government decided to set new tax policies. First, the income tax rate for foreign-funded hi-tech enterprises was cut to 15%. Moreover, if the export output reached over 40% of the gross output, the income tax would then be 10% (Administrative Committee of Zhongguancun Science Park, 2002b). The preferential policies induced new growth and lured in many globally recognized corporations, including Microsoft, IBM, Nokia, Sun, and Microsoft, which all set up their R&D centers in Z-Park. P&G and other non-tech companies were also drawn to the park, and homegrown firms like Founder, Lenovo, and UFSoft all originated in Z-Park (Beale, 2007). In 2001, Z-Park's income generated from the trade, industry, and technology represented almost 20% of the total income of the 53 industrial hi-tech zones in China (Administrative Committee of Zhongguancun Science Park, 2002f). Many significant engineering centers and state-level laboratories were also located in Z-Park, allowing thousands of experiments and research discoveries to emerge in this developmental zone and spread nationally throughout China.

As of 2007, Z-Park was nationally the biggest and most sophisticated software development and production center with approximately 6,690 hi-tech enterprises located within the park's area (Administrative Committee of Zhongguancun Science Park, 2002f). Among them, one enterprise's gross revenue reached more than 10 billion RMB, while 20 others accumulated revenues of over 100 million RMB (Administrative Committee of Zhongguancun Science Park, 2002b).

Z-Park structure

Zhongguancun Science Park is located in Dongbeiwang of the Haidian district, an area that is the cross junction of Beijing's ecological zone, hi-tech industry, and academia zone, making the park a hot breeding ground for new talents and strategic business ventures. Z-Park comprises two main zones – an R&D zone and a public service zone. While the R&D zone is circled around the park's central green and lake, the public service zone is located at the south-east corner of the park. The zone itself is composed of a software plaza, an international software building center, an information center, an incubation center, a recreation center, and other parts. Many incubators in the Z-Park have become the starting points for the commercialization of scientific achievement, innovation, and development of sophisticated hi-tech ventures. Zhongguancun Science Park comprises three important development centers: the Fengtai

Innovation Center, Qinghua Innovation Center, and the Haidian Innovation Center for Overseas Chinese Scholars (Administrative Committee of Zhongguancun Science Park, 2002b).

Z-Park is further divided into five science zones, covering an area of about 340 acres with 700,000-square meters of office space at the northwest edge of Beijing. The park is located close to internationally recognized educational institutions, including the University of Beijing, Tsinghua University, as well as the CAS (Beale, 2007). The five main sub-parks of Zhongguancun Science Park include Haidian Zone, Fengtai Zone, Electronic Zone, Changping Zone, and Yizhuang Zone. Haidian Zone, located in the Haidian district, comprised the Shangdi Information Industrial Base and the Yongfeng Experimental Base. Haidan Zone is a concentrated area of many scientific and engineering talents, and is also known as the leading incubator of hi-tech enterprises in the park.

Fengtai Zone is in the Fengtai district, which is located in the southern suburb, while the Changping Zone occupies the northern suburb called the Changping district. Each of the two zones covers an area of about eight square kilometers (Administrative Committee of Zhongguancun Science Park, 2002b). The Fengtai Park is the center for over 3,000 hi-tech ventures involving electronic information, bio-engineering and pharmaceutics, advanced manufacture, as well as new materials and new technology. In the year 2005, Fengtai Park contributed 306 million yuan to Fengtai District, which accounted for approximately 17% of the total revenue of the district. The Yizhuang Zone of the Zhongguancun Science Park is near the starting point of the Beijing-Tianjin-Ganggu expressway.

Yizhuang Science & Technology Zone is located in the Beijing Development Area that provides a complete service network including a foreign investors' service center, insurance companies, banks, commercial and industrial departments, import and export companies, customs service units, commodities inspection departments, and bounded warehouses. Electronics City is located in the Jiuxianqiao District of Beijing and stretches over one half square kilometer. The five zones of Zhongguancun Science Park form a strong hi-tech developmental zone along the Fourth Ring Road of Beijing (Administrative Committee of Zhongguancun Science Park, 2002b).

Workforce at Z-Park

Zhongguancun is a zone with a high concentration of intellectual talent, first-rate technological resources, and scientific accomplishments. With the total enrolment of 300,000 students, Beijing University and Qinghua University are without a doubt the two most influential among the 68 institutions of higher learning represented at Z-Park. The great number of scientific and educational institutions, including the largest national library in Asia, provides the Z-Park with a great competitive edge and potential to become the leader in the development of a knowledge-based economy (Administrative Committee of Zhongguancun Science Park, 2002c). The park represents a continuous national effort to bring a talented and creative workforce to China from all over the world, while waiting for the new generation of educated youth to mature. In fact, attractive benefits, including affordable rent, competitive salaries, and easier start-up conditions, have even drawn many Chinese expatriates away from foreign industrial zones (Beale, 2007).

Zhongguancun Science Park represents an important job market for Beijing. In 2005, total staff reached 700,000 employees, and in 2004 alone, Z-Park created 68,000 new job opportunities. The regulations set by Beijing People's Municipal Government in 2001 aimed at maintaining the most sophisticated intellectual talent at Z-Park. According to the principles governing the construction of regulations at Z-Park, 'the number of employees having received college education shall account for over 30 percent of all the employees; and the number of scientific and technological personnel having received college education of those enterprises producing high- and new-technology products or labor-intensive new-technology enterprises that offer high- and new-technology services shall account for over 20 percent of the total employees' (Administrative Committee of Zhongguancun Science Park, 2002a).

The census conducted by the Zhongguancun IT Industry human resources department in 2001 revealed that approximately 73% of all the employees had previous work experience and were recruited in the job market while 27% of employees came directly from the schools. The census showed that about half of the employees at Zhongguancun Science Park were younger than 29 years old and only 7.6% were older than 50 (Administrative Committee of Zhongguancun Science Park, 2002e). The continual accumulation of quality personnel has not only optimized the crowd structure but also accelerated culture transformation in Zhongguancun. Building an innovative culture at the park includes encouraging risk-taking among the employees, tolerating failure, and supplying the talent with more opportunities to fully realize their potential.

However, the combination of young and sophisticated workforce in the new and dynamic environment has produced a major side effect – serial job hopping.

Job hopping and industry performance

According to the results of the Zhongguancun IT Enterprises HR Census, average employee inflow among Zhongguancun IT companies reached about 11% of total staff number while outflow accounted for almost 7% in the first half of year 2001. The human resources flow featured three major trends. First, a large part of employee outflow represented moving to regions such as Shanghai, with more developed economies and flexible policies. A second trend was moving abroad; and a third, to different enterprises. The major reasons for job hopping at Z-Park included career development and wages. Out of the total number of employees leaving in 2001, about 17% chose companies with better development prospects, approximately 16% headed for more attractive salaries and benefits, and another 16% went for an opportunity of position advancement (Administrative Committee of Zhongguancun Science Park, 2002d).

Increased job turnover, however, was not a phenomenon exclusive to Zhongguancun Science Park. The overall turnover rate in China accelerated to a record 14% in 2005 from 8% in 2000 (not including workers who were terminated), according to a survey by consulting firm Hewitt Associates. In comparison, the 2005 employee turnover rate in the United States was approximately 3% (Lee, 2006), including terminated workers. In bustling zones including Guangdong province or Shanghai, many employers lose as many as one out of three employees every year.

A survey conducted by the Shanghai municipal government revealed that approximately 24% of young workers in the nation's leading industrial and commercial center had switched employers at least once in 2003. Attitudes about employment in China have certainly changed since the 1970s mainly due to the new market-oriented reforms (Xinhua News Agency, 2003, http://www.xinhuanet.com). A land once known as the socialist 'iron rice bowl', or a haven for lifetime employment, has become a revolving-door society leading to a job hopping crisis. Under the planned economy, China was a country where loyal workers served their state-owned employers until death. The employers used to cover all the housing and medical expenses for their staff, and if the employees decided to leave, they would lose everything, making them think twice about their decision.

With the new reforms in place, however, the Chinese labor market has experienced significant changes. Among many others, medical care or housing expenses are no longer covered by the employers (Xinhua News Agency, 2003). Moreover, restrictions on labor mobility have been lowered, allowing the ambitious and talented employees to switch jobs, disciplines, and firms more freely to broaden their experience. Unlike their parents who were influenced by the Cultural Revolution – greatly valuing social status and loyalty – young Chinese workers of 2007 consider themselves free agents with endless opportunities. Rapid economic growth and an erosion of traditional values in China enable workers to live a more entrepreneurial lifestyle and find jobs that better balance their work and life (Xinhua News Agency, 2003). The top reasons for job hopping in China include better compensation and benefits, career development prospects and job dissatisfaction.

While increased job mobility undoubtedly provides workers with exciting opportunities, the fast pace at which workers are changing employers has taken its toll on many companies. Company managers fear the time around the Chinese New Year, when many employees take their annual bonus and promptly say goodbye. While the amount of bonus can reach up to several times their monthly wages, some employees will leave if they are dissatisfied with their '13th month pay' (Lee, 2006). Those who plan to leave anyway for a different reason will wait just long enough to take their bonus and never come back. Increased employee mobility is generally regarded as having a negative impact on industry's performance. Job hopping tends to drive up training and recruiting costs for employers, disrupt business, and contribute to salary increases.

Losing employees to competitors is particularly harmful for a firm because the resources possessed by these workers can be used against the former employer, thereby eroding its competitive advantage in the marketplace. When trying to solve the issue of employee retention, Chinese employers are being forced to come up with new strategies and re-evaluate how they measure up against their competitors. To recruit and keep a quality workforce in today's cut-throat labor market, employers are now required to provide new employees with personal attention, offer better training programs, and demonstrate room for advancement. For many Chinese firms, retaining high caliber workers also involves attracting employees with compensation packages that include competitive salaries and flexible benefits (Zuehlke, 2001). For higher-skilled jobs, Chinese enterprises have started offering some of the same incentives as in Europe or the United States: retention bonuses, stock options, and housing allowances (Lee, 2006). However, not all industries follow the traditional path and, instead of hampered production, show gains from the increased employee turnover.

California's Silicon Valley is one of the business environments contradicting the popular notion that job hopping negatively affects industry performance. Located in Northern California, Silicon Valley is the top hi-tech hub in the United States, with the largest group of engineers and venture capitalists. An innovative and decentralized system such as the one at the Silicon Valley involves a lot of technical uncertainty that requires spending lots of resources on experiments, including the ones that will not be successful. Therefore, in environments with high technical uncertainty, particularly the IT industry, the quickest way to arrive at the best solution is to conduct many independent experiments, and therefore high employee turnover might actually encourage productive innovation (Postrel, 2005). When workers switch from one employer to another, they take their knowledge, skills, and talent with them. The job hopping rate of those in the IT industry is higher than in other industries, as employees move at a fast pace and seek companies that come up with the most sophisticated technology.

According to the 2002 survey by the Federal Reserve Board economists, 'computer industry employees are more likely to move than employees in other industries', and the mobility rates of Silicon Valley workers are on average 40% higher than those of other employees in the IT industry (Postrel, 2005). According to Anna Lee Saxenian, an economic development scholar at the University of California, Berkeley, 'the system's decentralization at Silicon Valley encourages the pursuit of multiple technical opportunities through spontaneous regroupings of skill, technology and capital' (Postrel, 2005).

Z-future

Thanks to its intellectual talent and advanced technology, Z-Park has facilitated the technological transformation and structural readjustment of traditional industries (Wang, 2003). Some of the future goals for the Zhongguancun Science Park include further rejuvenating the nation through science and technology, as well as building the park into a national development base, a training base for breeding high-quality talent, an incubating zone for new scientific accomplishments, and finally, creating the leading science park in the world (Administrative Committee of Zhongguancun Science Park, 2002b). However, due to deepening of Chinese reforms, erosion of traditional values, increasing demand for skilled workers, and greater availability of information, job hopping has become a common practice at Z-Park, causing many economists and investors to question its future prospects. With high technical uncertainty, large experimental zones, and a focus on innovation, the business environment, and its future goals, Zhongguancun Science Park closely resembles the Californian Silicon Valley. Although many fear that the rapid employee turnover at Z-Park may deteriorate its success, just as at the Silicon Valley in California, these forces could possibly increase the productive innovation of Zhongguancun Science Park and thus contradict economists' common assumption that job hopping negatively affects industry performance.

Source: Vojtkova et al. (2009)

Case Study A3.6

Employee rewards, employee development and employee relations – Zheng Chang Cereal and Feed Machinery Company

Using both quantitative and qualitative approaches, this case study investigates the changes in employment relations and employees' responses at Zheng Chang Cereal and Feed Machinery Co. Ltd. (ZC), a Chinese privately-owned manufacturing enterprise. It emerges that while the levels of employees' satisfaction with performance appraisals, staffing, and pay were between high and moderate, the levels of satisfaction with training and development were low. Employees' responses to employment relations varied according to personal characteristics including gender, age, education, position, working years, and registration status. The practical implications are discussed.

The case study – introduction

Zheng Chang Cereal and Feed Machinery Co. Ltd. (hereafter referred to as ZC) was founded in 1918 in Liyan City, Jiangsu Province, and the factory's name since then has changed five times. It was China's largest food machinery manufacturer and designer. ZC had 24 branches in China and more than 30 sales offices all over the world at the time this study was conducted. It was the first and only company that had the honor of using China's well-known trademark and obtained a quality system certificate of ISO 9001. ZC's high-tech pellet processing machinery and complete project equipment were widely used in the fields of food and aqua-food production, pasture processing, fertilizer production, and the petrochemical industry. ZC pellet mills and turnkey projects for food processing operated in most of China's food mills, special aqua-food mills, and additive mills. While it had 75% share of the domestic market the company had built up long-term relationships with worldwide customers; its products had been exported to many Asian, African, European, and North and South American countries.

Due to its outstanding achievements and remarkable contributions to the Chinese cereal and food industry, the Chinese government awarded ZC many special awards, such as 'Jiangsu Provincial Award for Quality Supervision', 'A Civilized and Advanced Enterprise of Jiangsu Province', 'Jiangsu Provincial Enterprise with High Credit in Respecting Contract', 'One of the Top Hundred Enterprise with Patents in China', and 'One of the Key High-Tech Enterprises of China'. President Hao Bo had been granted the Roosevelt Business Achievements Award by the US-China Entrepreneurs Federation of the USA. ZC's products have been honored with the title of the famous brand of Jiangsu Province for the past 10 years. The company's details are shown in Table 1 [Table A3.3]. At the

Table A3.3   Profile of the company

Total assets	US$ 42.14 billion
Sales	51.8 in 2001, 54.8 in 2002, 63 in 2003 (US$ million)
Ownership change	1918–1949 POE; 1950 COE; 2001 POE
Number of employees	3,500
Gender of employees	85% male; 15% female
Age of employees	20–30 35%; 31–40 43%; 41–50 12%; 51–60 7%; 61–65 3%
Education of employees	Pre-high school 46% High school graduates 19% Diploma degree 34% University degree 1%

Note: All information unless specified was collected in June 2004.

time when this study was conducted, there were 3,500 employees, of which around 85% of employees were males.

The employment relations reform at the national level

During the planned economy China developed socialist employment relations systems, such as the 'iron rice-bowl' (*tie fan wan*) and 'iron wage' (*tie gong zi*), which ensured 'jobs for life' and 'cradle to grave' welfares policy (Shen, 2007; Warner, 2004). Chinese workers were thus born into, educated by, spent all their working lives in, and then enjoyed their retirement in *danwei* (work unit). Decisions about human resources and services were planned ahead of time by the State. Consequently, enterprises could not use their workforce in order to obtain a strategic or competitive advantage (Child, 1994; Chen, 1995; Shen, 2007; Warner, 2004). This approach to human resource management often resulted in a mismatch of skills and human resources with enterprise needs.

The economic reforms, particularly that of *san xian gai ge* (three reforms), has necessitated significant changes in employment relations in China. Since the late 1990s a significant number of pieces of legislation, including the 1994 Labour Law, 2001 Trade Union Law, and 2007 new Labour Law, affecting employment relations have been introduced. The directions of the reform have allowed enterprises increasingly to recruit, allocate, and reward people according to their competence and the state of the market (Benson et al., 2000). The most important features of the Chinese employment relations reform include the shift of state responsibility for and political control on human resources to enterprise management, the abolition of the 'iron rice-bowl' (*tie fan wan*) policy of lifetime employment, 'cradle-to-grave' welfares and egalitarianism in pay and benefits (Benson and Zhu, 1999; Shen, 2006; Warner, 2004). The most significant steps in the employment relations reform are the introduction of the labour contract system, which became compulsory in 1994, and individual compensation schemes, recognizing differences in educational background, skills, training, performance, and work experience (Shen, 2007).

According to Shen and Darby (2006) and Zhu (2005), since the old apprenticeship system was abolished Chinese industry organizations have not provided adequate training to their employees. Training in organizational values and cultures, business or organizational procedures, understanding of business and behavioral training techniques such as teambuilding and interpersonal skills, is rare (Chow, 2004). Although promotion opportunities in theory are open to everyone, the promotion process and associated criteria often are not objective due to the fact that *guanxi* (a combination of interpersonal relationships and social networks) plays an important role in management development (Shen and Darby, 2006). In general, *De* (political and moral attitudes), *neng* (ability and educational background), *qing* (working attitudes), and *ji* (performance and achievement) have remained the criteria for promotion and performance appraisals (Shen, 2004; Shen and Darby, 2006).

Shen (2007) and Zhu and Warner (2005) argued that while the employment relations reform has greatly improved productivity and competitiveness of Chinese enterprises, it has also caused massive and often unfair dismissal, non-payment of wages, social and unemployment insurance, a lack of production protection and training, and inadequate social welfare. Workers have been disadvantaged due to the fact that employers or enterprise management have been given almost unlimited power over workers in employment relations (Cooke, 2005; Shen, 2006, 2007; Zhu and Warner, 2005). Privatization is a key process of the economic reform that has exerted considerable impact on employment relations.

Researchers have suggested that industrial relations are more acrimonious and labour disputes increase much faster in privately-owned enterprises (POEs) than in SOEs (Li and Rozelle, 2000; Shen and Leggett, 2004; Shen, 2007; Zhu and Warner, 2005). Together with an undeveloped labour market and inadequate social security system, many Chinese workers, especially those who are laid-off, have been losing their basic livelihoods. Therefore, the unequal employment relations and employees' disadvantaged status have become the major causes of widespread labour confrontation in China.

Changes in employment relations at ZC

Employment relations under the planned economy

ZC was founded as a family business in 1918 and was confiscated and transformed into a COE by the CCP in 1949. Between 1949 and 1979 workers were allocated by the Liyan Labour Bureau and party cadres were dispatched by Liyang Personnel Bureau to ZC. All employees enjoyed 'iron rice bowl' (*tie fan wan*) permanent employment status but also had no freedom to choose a job or transfer to other organizations.

The major benefit of having such an employment system was virtually no unemployment. It was usually compulsory for workers to take on-the-job apprenticeships with experienced workers. Cadres who were regarded as potential leaders were selected by the Liyan Personnel Bureau to attend training at the School of Liyan Communist Party. Training programs mainly involved political studies. Workers could advance their grades in work skills but could not become cadres. Cadres' promotion to senior positions was mainly based on their attitudes toward the Communist Party, seniority, behavior in the workplace, and interpersonal relations. Performance appraisals were rarely conducted for workers; rather, they were often conducted for cadres who were considered for promotion. ZC adopted the national grade wage scales, which were associated with skill levels and cardres' positions.

Performance-based pay did not exist and differences in wages between grades were negligible. However, wages were only a part of the so called 'cradle-to-grave welfare,' which also included medical treatment, housing benefits, and fringe benefits. It is worth noting that these mentioned employment relations policies and practices were not unique to ZC, but were universally implemented in all Chinese industrial organizations in the pre-reform era.

Employment relations under the transitional economy

In the early 1980s ZC began to address the number of employees it needed and recruit and select new workers to meet its business needs. This was despite the fact that China's labour authorities still maintained a strong presence in ZC's employment relations. The main recruitment channels ZC used included individual recommendations (word of mouth), job fairs organized by Liyang Labour Bureau or Liyang Personnel Bureau, media advertising, recruitment agencies, and university-based employment services. Selection criteria had shifted from a focus purely on political ideology and seniority to *De* (moral attitudes, personality), *Neng* (ability, age, knowledge, working experience, health and education level), *Qian* (working attitudes, willingness to learn), *Ji* (performance and achievement), with a heavy focus on *Neng* and *Ji*. The 'soft' aspects, i.e. political ideology, which used to be the main selection criterion, became less relevant. The Deputy General Manager explained:

> We are looking for someone who can do the job rather than someone who is the member of the CCP. It is no good if the criteria are too abstract. It is also inappropriate if the criteria are

too detailed and fixed. They should be flexible enough to meet the needs of different positions.

ZC was not strict on education qualifications in order to employ adequate workers; in fact, it was cautious about recruiting over-qualified applicants because these people would not stay long. As the HR manager stated:

> We do not recruit over-qualified candidates, such as Master and PhD degree holders as it is hard to retain them. We would rather be realistic.

Job interviews were conducted for all new positions, and candidates applying for technical and administration positions were required to take additional written tests on literacy and specific knowledge.

Managers commented that freedom to fire or hire had contributed to ZC's control of the quantity and quality of the labour force. Some employees had been forced to retire (so called 'internal retirement,' *nei tui*) before they reached the legal retirement age so that ZC could control the size of its workforce. Such early retirement practices stopped when ZC began to sign labour contracts with new employees in 1988. At the beginning only new employees were asked to sign labour contracts, usually for five years. This new contract system caused employment uncertainty and anxiety for the contracted employees. Since 1996, two years after the promulgation of the 1994 Labour Law, signing a labour contract became compulsory in ZC. From 1994 to 2000, ZC allowed employees to take jobs outside the company for a certain period, but retained their employment status without receiving salaries. Such an employment practice is called *ting xing liu zhi*, which was then widely implemented by Chinese businesses. Employees who were on *ting xing liu zhi* needed to pay fees to ZC to retain employment status. The practice of *ting xing liu zhi* practice was phased out in 2000 when China implemented a drastic reform on enterprise welfare, including housing, medical treatment, and pensions. ZC was privatized in 2000 and since then it has had no permanent employee working for it.

Although the Labour Law requires the compulsory signing of labour contracts, ZC had not complied fully with this law. In ZC, all new recruits were put on 3–6 months probation. Employment contracts were signed only after the probation period and were renewed yearly. Employment contracts for blue collar workers were set for three years and for middle managers five years. About 30% of employees had not signed contracts; most of them were migrants who did not want to pay the employee contribution to social insurance. ZC did not need to pay employer contributions to social insurance for employees either if a labour contract had not been signed. Managers argued that some employees did not sign contracts because they wanted the freedom to change jobs when the opportunity arose. Also, according to the managers, not signing a contract did not affect pay and working conditions for employees as the contract contained only basic labour terms anyway. One month's notice was required if employees wished to quit. Some workers had only oral agreements on labour terms including employment durations and pay. Those workers who did not sign formal employment contracts could be sacked at any time, but normally were not allowed to leave before they had finished the agreed working time. Employees were required to pay for breaching labour contracts if they left the company before their contracts were completed.

ZC provided induction training for new employees and a short on-the-job training. Training for new recruits normally took 2–3 days in the form of in-house training, focusing on the company's regulations on appraisal, pay and work safety. On-the-job training mainly took the form of analyzing good or bad examples of on-site operations for the purpose of improving product quality or when clients had special product requirements. All units were required to submit a report outlining training needs at the beginning of each year. There was no management development scheme identifying and fostering potential managers so when managerial vacancies arose, new managers were usually promoted from the existing employees. The major criteria for management promotion were performance record, management skills, and organizational loyalty (willingness to work for the company for a long period). The final decision regarding promotion was made by the General Manager. Self-recommendation was encouraged for managerial or technical positions even if there was no vacancy.

ZC adopted a product unit-based appraisal system for production workers. The major appraisal criteria were quantity and quality of products and compliance with discipline, e.g., working hours. Production satisfaction rate needed to reach above 98%. Sales people were simply assessed by the number of sales they made. Office workers and managers compared their actual performance with their goals set at the beginning of each month. The major appraisal criteria were the proportion of tasks completed, workers' comments on non-production employees, and compliance with the firm's regulations. Appraisals were conducted between the appraisee and the direct manager, and no feedback was provided to appraisees as giving feedback was not regarded as necessary.

ZC adopted the individual performance-based pay system. Production workers were paid according to the quantity, quality, and overtime they worked and sales people were paid based on sales. Salaries included basic salaries and bonuses. For sales people and production workers basic salaries accounted for less than 20% of their pay. For managers and office workers basic salaries accounted for 80% of their pay. Bonuses were based on appraisal results: the production managers' bonuses related to the production outcome of the entire department during a certain period; the bonuses of other line managers and office workers were decided by their individual performance. ZC stopped providing company houses to employees in 1985, but housing subsidies were provided. Employees had to pay between about 70% of their own medical costs. Fringe benefits were very limited and consisted mainly of time off and free food to celebrate festivals and free uniforms. Salaries would be deducted if workers had damaged products or equipment. ZC paid superannuation only to those workers who signed employment contracts.

Employees' responses to the employment relations reform

This section presents the findings on employees' responses to the employment relations reform.

[P]erformance appraisal was regarded as being of little help for personal development. As Shen (2007) has pointed out, performance appraisals in Chinese industries are concerned mainly with short-term goals and used to determine pay. With means greater than four, five items including equitable pay, satisfaction with dismissal policy, equal job opportunity, fair selection process, and criteria and competitive pay were well received. The data show that performance-based equitable pay became the norm, indicating the ideology of Socialist egalitarianism had effectively become a thing of the past during the era of economic reform. A number of employees commented: 'We feel it is fair compared to our colleagues, and our performance.'

Employees were reasonably satisfied with diverse recruitment channels and merit-based selection, indicating a 'two-way selection' process. In other words, free selection of occupation and employees had become normal and the abolition of the 'iron rice bowl' employment system was regarded as beneficial not only to employers but also to employees. This finding supports the argument made in Shen (2007) that for many marketable workers, changing jobs was no longer impossible and had become an opportunity for career development. As 45% of employees in ZC were specialized technicians, their skills made it possible for them to find jobs in other companies. However, the terms of labour contracts were not well received. This was explained by Shen (2007) that Chinese workers are at a disadvantage in determining labour terms in terms of employment duration, working hours and working conditions. Employees had medium to low levels of satisfaction (means between 3.58 and 2.63) regarding promotion criteria, welfare and benefits, promotion opportunity, training and its link to personal development, and organizational support for individual education and development.

Overall, employees had a high to medium level of satisfaction with performance management, medium level of satisfaction with staffing and pay, and low level of satisfaction with training and development.

Differences in responses between groups

The differences in employees' responses between males and females that did reach statistical significance were staffing and performance management. An inspection of mean scores indicated that male employees were more satisfied with staffing and performance management. The differences between urban citizens and off-farm migrants on all four variables appeared to be significant. Mean scores indicated that compared to urban citizens, migrants were less satisfied with staffing, training and development, and performance management, but more satisfied with pay.

Significant differences were found between workers and managers only in regard to their responses concerning training and development. Mean scores indicated that managers were more satisfied with training and development and performance management. Significant differences were found between married (including those with children) and unmarried employees regarding their responses to all four variables. An inspection of mean scores revealed that single employees were more satisfied with staffing, and performance management, but less satisfied with pay.

Employees of varying ages and working years and different education levels had significant different responses to all four variables. An inspection of mean scores indicated that employees aged between 50 and 60 were most satisfied with all variables. The levels of satisfaction decreased when ages decrease from 50 and increase from 60, with one exception that those aged 30–40 had a higher satisfaction level than those at 40–50 in regard to staffing and performance management. Mean scores indicated that employees who had completed higher education tended to demonstrate higher levels of satisfaction with all four variables.

Employees who had worked for 10–20 years had the highest level and employees who had worked for over 20 years had the lowest level of satisfaction with all four variables.

Discussion and conclusions

The economic reform has resulted in drastic changes in employment relations in ZC. Since the late 1970s, like other Chinese industries and businesses, ZC had become responsible for the use and management of its own human resources, and gradually abolished the old 'iron rice bowl' employment relations system. Privatization in 2001 had further pushed forward its employment relations reform. The key features of its employment relations included market and profit-orientation, pragmatism, and the focus on equity in performance appraisal and pay. There was a lack of organizational commitment to training and developing employees into a long-term competent workforce. While ZC had adopted the labour contract system it did not fully comply with the Labour Law, leaving a large number of workers not protected by any social security provisions.

The new employment relations had greatly increased the productivity and efficiency of the company. Employees were relatively more satisfied with performance management, particularly objective performance appraisal criteria and appraisal execution, than other employment relations policies and practices. Performance-based pay and the two-way selection process were highly regarded by employees because these two aspects of employment relations gave employees the freedom to choose jobs and employers, and to obtain equal and fair financial rewards. Workers have become accustomed to the idea that the 'iron rice bowl' of job security and enterprise-provided welfare is a thing of the past. Employees, however, were very unsatisfied with limited or non-existent training and management development opportunities, and organizational support for personal development.

Employees' responses to the employment relations reform varied significantly according to their own personal characteristics and experiences. A general conclusion can be drawn that employees who were males, managers, aged between 40 and 50, had higher education and urban citizens, scored the highest on satisfaction with employment relations. It can be explained those people who were more satisfied with employment relations were treated better than others at this particular enterprise. The finding of this study indicates that different economic groups in China interpret the employment relations reform in different ways. It is worth noting that Chinese employees sometimes do not realize that they are disadvantaged in employment relations. Furthermore the situation is unfair to them as all firms do the same, particularly with regard to migrants from rural areas. In this study empirical evidence shows that migrants were more satisfied than urban citizens with pay even though they were often underpaid.

The changes in China's employment relations are actually many of the direct causes of labour confrontation. Adopting effective and equitable employment relations policies and practices would greatly help prevent labour disputes from occurring. Hence, the findings of this case study have significant implications for practitioners with regard to what precautions should be taken with employment relations. Currently, like many other organizations, ZC had not signed labour contracts with all employees. As a result, a significant number of Chinese employees are not protected by the social security system. An organization should regard signing labour contracts and entitling workers to social security as an important social responsibility, especially when fringe benefits are currently diminishing. Moreover, Chinese enterprises need to pay more attention to training and development in order to cultivate talented and potential managers. Currently, 'buying' skilled workers and capable managers is regarded by enterprise managers as the most economical way of employing people. Such a policy is actually costly as it de-motivates employees and causes long-term strategic concerns and a lack of sustainability and personal biases. Furthermore, some economic groups, such as migrants, women, and old workers, are currently disadvantaged in employment relations. Therefore, equity in employment relations has become an urgent issue facing Chinese enterprises managers. Due to different employees having different demands and needs, enterprise managers should develop employee-tailored employment relations policies and practices, such as more work-life balance concerns for female employees with children.

Source: Shen (2009)

References

Administrative Committee of Zhongguancun Science Park. (2002a). 'The Regulations of Beijing Municipality on the confirming of the new technology'. Available at http://www.zgc.gov.cn/english/Lawsand Regulations/Laws&RegulationsRegardingSettingup/24561.htm (retrieved 17 December 2007).

Administrative Committee of Zhongguancun Science Park. (2002b). 'Principles governing the construction of the Science Park'. Available at http://www.zgc.gov.cn/english/AboutZhongguancunSciencePark/ Z-ParkProfile/27965.htm (retrieved 19 December 2007).

Administrative Committee of Zhongguancun Science Park. (2002c). 'Director of the leading group for the construction of Zhongguancun Science Park'. Available at http://www.zgc.gov.cn/english/About ZhongguancunSciencePark/Z-ParkProfile/27968.htm (retrieved 17 December 2007).

Administrative Committee of Zhongguancun Science Park. (2002d). 'HR flow in Zhongguancun features three trends'. Available at http://www.zgc.gov.cn/english/NewsandEvents/20942.htm (retrieved December 18, 2007).

Administrative Committee of Zhongguancun Science Park. (2002e). 'Zhongguancun IT industry HR census result released.' Available at http://www.zgc.gov.cn/english/NewsandEvents/20952.htm (retrieved 18 December 2007).

Administrative Committee of Zhongguancun Science Park. (2002f). 'The general picture of Zhongguancun Science Park'. Available at http://www.zgc.gov.cn/english/AboutZhongguancunSciencePark/ Z-ParkProfile/27964.htm (retrieved 18 December 2007).

Beale, C.-J. (2007) 'Z-Park: China's Silicon Valley', *Business Week Online*, 5 June, Innovation section.

Benson, J., Debroux, P., Yuasa, M. and Zhu, Y. (2000) 'Flexibility and labour management: Chinese manufacturing enterprises in the 1990s', *International Journal of Human Resource Management*, 11(2): 183–196.

Benson, J. and Zhu, Y. (1999) 'Markets, firms and workers in Chinese state-owned enterprises', *Human Resource Management Journal*, 9(4): 58–74.

Chen, F. (1995) *Economic Transition and Political Legitimacy in Post-Mao China: Ideology and Reform*. Albany, NY: State University of New York Press.

Child, J. (1994) *Management in China During the Age of Reform*. Cambridge: Cambridge University Press.

Chow, I. Hau-Siu (2004) 'Human resource management in China's township and village enterprises: Change and development during the economic reform era', *Asia Pacific Journal of Human Resource Management*, 42(3): 318–35.

Cooke, F. L. (2005) *HRM, Work and Employment in China*. London: Routledge.

Davies, D. and Zhang Xinyan (2009) 'Case 6 – Retention and turnover in Wong Yu Pharmaceutical and Textile' in R. Alas (ed.) *Implementation of Changes in Chinese Organizations*. Oxford: Chandos, 149–156.

Economist.com (2008) 'Asia's skills shortage'. Available at http://www.economist.com/displaystory.cfm?story_id=9645045

Koh, Chin Seng (2009) 'Case 7 – Change in bonus payment system' in R. Alas (ed.) *Implementation of Changes in Chinese Organizations*. Oxford: Chandos, 156–164.

Lee, Don. (2006) 'Job hopping is rampant as China's economy chases skilled workers', *Los Angeles Times*, 21 February, C1.

Li, H.B. and Rozelle, S. (2000) Saving or stripping rural industry: An analysis of privatization and efficiency in China, *Agricultural Economics*, 23(3): 241–252.

Minder, R. (2007) 'Asia's airlines call for reinforcement in the cockpit', *Financial Times*, 8 October.

Pepper, J. (2007) 'India's cockpit crisis', *Fortune Magazine*, 30 October.

Postrel, Virginia. (2005) 'In Silicon Valley, job hopping contributes to innovation', *The New York Times*, 1 December, Economic Scene section.

Professional Pilot News (2006) 'Pilot shortage in India', 11 May.

Shen, J. (2006) 'An analysis of changing industrial relations in China', *International Journal of Comparative Labour Law and Industrial Relations*, 26(3): 347–68.

Shen, J. (2007) *Labour Disputes and Their Management in China*. Oxford: Chandos Publishing (Oxford) Ltd.

Shen, J. (2009) 'Case 2 – The implementation of a new employment relations system and employees' responses in a Chinese manufacturing enterprise' in R. Alas (ed.) *Implementation of Changes in Chinese Organizations*. Oxford: Chandos, 109–123.

Shen, J. and Darby, R. (2006) 'International training and management development in Chinese multinational enterprises', *Employee Relations,* 28(4): 342–62.

Shen, J. and Leggett, C. (2004) 'Signs of industrial relations transformations in China: Precursors in Shanghai'. ANZIBA Conference Proceedings, CD Rom, 5–6 November, Canberra.

Vojtkova, L., Eisner, A. and Korn, H. (2009) 'Case 5 – Job hopping in Z-Park' in R. Alas (ed.) *Implementation of Changes in Chinese Organizations.* Oxford: Chandos, 141–149.

Wang, Z.M. (2003) 'Managerial competency modelling and the development of organizational psychology: A Chinese approach', *International Journal of Psychology,* 38(5): 323–334.

Warner, M. (2004) 'Human resource management in China revisited: Introduction', *International Journal of Human Resource Management,* 15(4/5): 617–34.

Xinhua News Agency (2003) 'China's young seek to better themselves by job-hopping'. Available at http://english.eastday.com/epublish/gb/paper1/994/class000100006/hwz154380.htm (retrieved 20 December 2007).

Zhu, C.J. (2005) *Human Resource Management in China: Past, Current, and Future HR Practices in the Industrial Sector.* London and New York: Routledge.

Zhu, Y. and Warner, M. (2005) 'Changing Chinese employment relations since WTO accession', *Personnel Review,* 34(3): 354–369.

Zuehlke, L. (2001) 'Job hopping: The favorite pastime of today's work force?' Available at http://maysbusiness.tamu.edu/old/2001/01/jobcmt.html (retrieved 21 December 2007).

Index

LaVergne, TN USA
30 March 2011
222147LV00006B/1/P